SIMP CHOLOGY

SIMPLY PSYCHOLOGY

MICHAEL W. EYSENCK
Royal Holloway University of London

Psychology Press

An imprint of Erlbaum (UK) Taylor & Francis

Copyright © 1996 by Psychology Press, an imprint of Erlbaum (UK)
Taylor & Francis Ltd.

Psychology Press, Publishers
27 Church Road
Hove
East Sussex, BN3 2FA
UK

British Library Cataloguing in Publication Data

A catalogue record for this book is available from the British Library

ISBN 0-86377-435-0 (hbk)
    0-86377-436-9 (pbk)

Subject index compiled by Christine Boylan
Cover design by Peter Richards
Printed and bound by Biddles Ltd., Guildford and King's Lynn

To Maria with love

A man should keep his little brain attic stocked with all the furniture that he is likely to use, and the rest he can put away in the lumber-room of his library, where he can get it if he wants it.

Sir Arthur Conan Doyle

Contents

Preface

There has been a dramatic increase in the number of students of psychology in recent years. This increase has happened at all levels, and includes GCSE, A-level, and university degree courses. In addition , there are many more students of nursing, education, business studies, and so on, who study psychology as part of their courses. It is my hope that this book will be of use to all students who are starting to study psychology. However, it may be particularly useful to those studying GCSE psychology. the content of the book takes full account of the current syllabuses for GCSE psychology for the Northern Examinations and Assessment Board, the Midland Examining Group, and the Southern Examining Group.

There are two main approaches to writing a simple introduction to psychology. One is to leave out everything that is difficult or challenging in psychology; this is what might be called the "filleted" approach. The other is to present a more rounded and accurate account of modern psychology in a simple and easy-to-understand fashion. I have done my best to follow the second approach. Whether or not I have succeeded is for the readers of this book to decide.

The book has involved other members of my family. My wife, Christine, and my elder daughter, Fleur, kindly combined forces to produce the last chapter, on study skills.

Acknowledgements

Sample questions from the Multidimensional Coping Inventory ©1990 Multi-Health Systems Inc., 908 Niagara Falls Boulevard, North Tonawanda, NY, 14120-2060, (800) 456-3003. Reproduced by permission. Featured on page 64.

Sample questions from Eysenck Personality Questionnaire published by EdITS San Diego, CA 92107. Eysenck Personality Questionnaire Revised, Copyright 1993 by H.J. & S.B.G. Eysenck. Reproduced by permission. Featured on page 333.

Introduction 1

What is psychology?

A useful starting point for this book is to consider what is meant by *psychology*. Most people have some idea what psychology is about, but they are often confused by the distinction between psychology and psychiatry. It is easier to define psychiatry than psychology: *psychiatry* is concerned with the study and treatment of mental disorders, and psychiatrists have medical degrees.

Psychology is concerned with the attempt to understand humans and other species. How can we achieve this understanding? Until about 100 years ago, the most popular answer to that question was as follows: ask people to report on their thoughts and feelings. This approach is known as *introspection*. It may sound like a good way of understanding other people, but there are some problems with it:

Charles Darwin:
Mary Evans
Picture Library.

1. In the middle of the nineteenth century, Charles Darwin put forward the theory of evolution. According to this theory, the human species has evolved or developed from other species. That suggests that other species (e.g. apes) are similar to our own, and so deserve to be studied. The problem for introspection is that we cannot expect the members of other species to tell us what they are thinking and feeling!

2. In the early years of the twentieth century, the *behaviourists* in the United States argued that psychologists should study behaviour rather than introspection. Introspection cannot be used with other species, but it is easy to study the behaviour of every species. Behaviour can be observed and measured, whereas mental processes cannot.

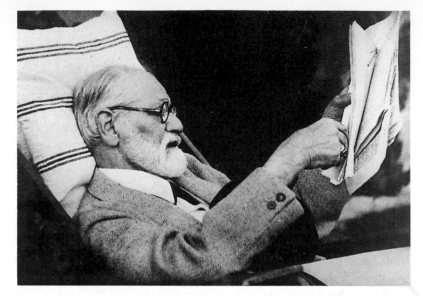

3. At the end of the nineteenth century, Sigmund Freud argued that we are only consciously aware of a small fraction of our mental processes. Other psychologists also favour what may be called the "iceberg" theory of the mind. According to this theory, the conscious mind is like the visible tip of an iceberg. It follows from this theory that people are simply unable to tell us much about their mental processes.

The current view of most (but not all) psychologists is that psychology is the science of human and animal behaviour. However, psychologists are interested not so much in behaviour itself, but in the internal processes producing that behaviour. For example, psychologists studying aggression in adolescents do not only focus on their aggressive behaviour; rather, they want to know *why* adolescents behave in this anti-social fashion. Thus, modern psychology can be regarded as a scientific discipline which is designed to understand why humans and other species behave as they do.

"Psychology is just common sense"

One of the unusual features of psychology is the way everyone is to some extent a psychologist. We all observe the behaviour of other people and of ourselves, and everyone has access to their own conscious thoughts and feelings.

This "everyman" factor is relevant. One of the tasks of psychologists is to predict behaviour, and the prediction of behaviour is important in everyday life. The better we are able to anticipate how people will react in any given situation, the more contented and rewarding our social interactions are likely to be.

The fact that everyone is a psychologist has led many people to under-estimate the achievements of scientific psychology. If the findings of scientific psychology are in line with common sense, it can be argued that they tell us nothing we didn't know already. On the other hand, if the findings do not accord with common sense, a common reaction is, "I don't believe it!"

There are various problems with the view that psychology is no better than common sense. It is misleading to assume that common sense forms a coherent set of assertions about behaviour. This can readily be seen if we regard proverbs as providers of common-sense views. A girl parted from her lover may be saddened if she thinks of the proverb "Out of sight, out of mind", but she will be cheered up if she tells herself that "Absence makes the heart grow fonder." There are several other pairs of proverbs which express opposite meanings—"Look before you leap" can be contrasted with "He who hesitates is lost", and "Many hands make light work" is the opposite of "Too many cooks spoil the broth". As common sense involves such inconsistent views of human behaviour, it can't be used as the basis for explaining that behaviour.

The notion that psychology is just common sense can also be disproved by considering psychological studies in which the results were very different from those most people would have predicted. A famous example is the work of Stanley Milgram (1974; see Chapter 15). An experimenter divided his participants into pairs to play the roles of teacher and pupil in a simple learning test. The "teacher" was asked to give electric shocks to the "pupil" every time the wrong answer was given, and to increase the shock intensity each time. At 180 volts, the "pupil" yelled "I can't stand the pain", and by 270 volts the response had become an agonised scream. If the "teacher" showed a reluctance to give the shocks, the experimenter (a professor of psychology) urged him or her to continue.

Do you think you would be willing to give the maximum (and potentially deadly) 450-volt shock in this experiment? What percentage of other people do you think would be willing to do it? Milgram found that everyone denied that they personally would do any such thing. Psychiatrists at a leading medical school predicted that only one person in a thousand would go on to the 450-volt stage. In fact, about 50% of Milgram's subjects gave the maximum shock—which is 500 times as many

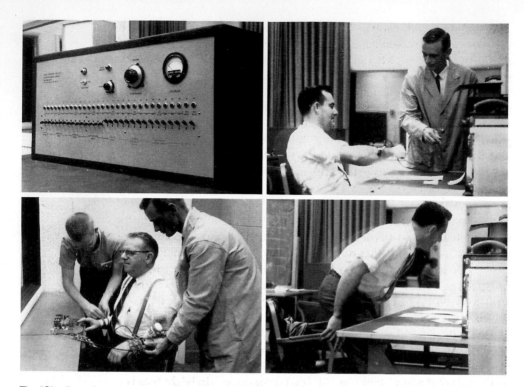

The "Obedience" experiment (Milgram, 1974). Top left: the "shock box"; Top right: the experimenter demonstrating the shock box to the "teacher"; Bottom left: wiring the "pupil" up to the apparatus; Bottom right: one of the "teachers" refusing to continue with the experiment. Photos courtesy Mrs A. Milgram.

people as the expert psychiatrists had predicted! In other words, people are much more conformist and obedient to authority than they realise. There is a strong tendency to go along with the decisions of someone (such as a professor of psychology) who appears to be a competent authority figure. (In case you are wondering about the fate of the unfortunate "pupil" in this situation, he didn't actually receive any shocks at all.)

In sum, we can see that common sense isn't much use in understanding and predicting human behaviour. According to most psychologists, the best way of achieving these goals is by means of the experimental and other methods available to the psychological researcher. These methods are discussed in Chapter 2.

Hindsight bias

We have seen that it is wrong to assume that the findings in psychology merely confirm common sense. Why is it, then, that so many people claim that most psychological findings are not surprising, and fail to tell them anything new? In other words, why do they argue, "I knew it all along"? An important part of the answer was discovered by Baruch Fischhoff and his colleagues in some research to which we now turn.

In one study (Fischhoff & Beyth, 1975), American students were asked to estimate the probability of various possible outcomes on the eve of President Nixon's trips to China and Russia. After the trips were over, the students were asked to do the same task, but without taking into account their knowledge of what had actually happened. In spite of these instructions, participants with the benefit of hindsight gave events that had actually happened a much higher probability than did the same participants before the events had occurred. It seemed as if the participants had added their knowledge of what had happened to what they already knew in such a way that they could not remember how uncertain things had looked before the trips. This tendency to be wise after the event is known as *hindsight bias*.

Slovic and Fischhoff (1977) carried out a similar study involving predictions about the results of a series of scientific experiments. Some of the participants were told what had happened in the first experiment of the series, but were told not to use this information when making their predictions. However, participants thought a given outcome was much more likely in future experiments if it had been obtained already. This is another example of hindsight bias.

Hindsight bias seems to be very powerful, and it is hard to eliminate. In another study, Fischhoff (1977) told his participants about hindsight bias, and encouraged them to avoid it. However, this had little or no effect on the size of the hindsight bias. As you can imagine, hindsight bias is a problem for teachers of psychology, because it produces students who are unimpressed by almost everything in psychology!

Psychology and the world

Cross-cultural differences

Anyone who has travelled abroad will have observed at first-hand what are known as *cross-cultural differences* in attitudes and behaviour. In other words, what is true of one culture is often not true of another culture. A clear example of this was reported by Sidney Jourard (1966). He watched pairs of people talking in cafes, noting down the number of times one person touched another during a period of one hour. In San Juan, the capital of Puerto Rico, the total number of touches was 180. In contrast, the total in Paris was 110, and in London it was 0.

It might be imagined that psychologists would devote much effort to the study of cross-cultural differences. In fact, that is not the case, even though some psychologists have devoted themselves to such research. More psychological studies in general have been carried out in the United States than in the rest of the world put together. The United States is followed by Europe, with relatively little psychological research in general having been carried out in Africa, Asia, or South America. A common complaint in Asia is that most of the studies in that part of the world are done by American psychologists with American funding. As a result, the topics of research tend to be determined by American rather than Asian cultural values.

This neglect of most of the world's cultures restricts our understanding of human behaviour. Some psychologists have gone further. Bempah and Howitt (1994) argued that Western psychologists often regard Western cultures as superior to non-Western cultures. As they pointed out, American textbooks sometimes refer to non-Western cultures as "undeveloped", "under-developed", or "primitive". According to Bempah and Howitt, it would be more accurate to say that all cultures are highly developed in some ways but not in others: "[there is] a materially advanced but spiritually bankrupt culture in the West; a spiritually developed and relatively socially stagnant culture in the East; and a developed social consciousness, but relatively undeveloped material culture in Africa."

Unrepresentative groups

So far, we have focused on the narrowness of psychology in terms of its focus on the United States and Europe. However, at least until fairly recently, studies in psychology were narrow in a different sense. An analysis of published research in American journals some years ago showed that those taking part in almost 80% of the studies were university students, although students account for only 3% of the adult population. Very similar findings emerged from a survey of articles in two British journals. Students were used in 76.4% of non-clinical studies of adults.

If we want to argue that what is true of university students is also true of the entire adult population, then we must assume that students are representative or typical members of society. However, students tend on average to be younger, more intelligent, and more middle-class than the adult population in general, and so they are clearly unrepresentative in some ways. This matters more in some experiments than others. For example, students will generally perform better than the general population on intellectually demanding tasks, but they may well experience visual illusions in the same way as everyone else.

In recent years, psychologists have carried out fewer experiments on students and more on various special groups within society. For example, brain-damaged patients are being studied to understand human language, children of different ages are being studied to chart developmental processes, and anxious and depressed patients are being investigated to understand the processes leading to mood disorders. So it is becoming less true every year that our knowledge of human behaviour is based almost entirely on the study of students.

What is needed is for the experience and behaviour of all groups within society to be studied by psychologists. This is starting to happen. However, it will be several years before the rich diversity existing within society is fully reflected in the work of psychologists.

Why is psychology interesting?

Psychology has some unique advantages over most other academic subjects. Most people are very interested in other people. They want to be able to understand them better, and to develop deeper and more fulfilling relationships with them. They also want to develop a fuller understanding of themselves, in the hope that this will allow them to become happier and to cope better with their lives.

Another major reason why psychology is interesting is because it has numerous applications to everyday life. Perhaps the most important of such applications is clinical psychology. Back in the nineteenth century, Sigmund Freud argued that most people who were then regarded as "mad" or severely disturbed were really suffering from mental disorders of one kind or another. He claimed that psychological forms of treatment (such as psychoanalysis) could allow such people to lead fuller and happier lives. Clinical psychology has developed enormously since then, and psychoanalysis is no longer considered one of the most effective forms of treatment. However, there is now conclusive proof that clinical psychology is of great value in treating mental disorders.

Psychology has been applied in numerous other areas, but we will mention only two more at this point. Educational psychologists make use of knowledge about human nature, and about the processes involved in learning, to help children who are experiencing learning difficulties. Some occupational psychologists focus on stress at work. Stress-related illnesses cost British industry billions of pounds a year in lost production and human misery, and so work stress is clearly a major issue. Occupational psychologists are increasingly successful at devising programmes of stress management which allow workers to function more effectively and with less stress.

Many readers of this book probably enjoy watching detective series on television. There are a number of reasons for this. It is interesting to make use of the clues that become available to try to work out the identity of the murderer. In similar fashion, psychology is interesting because psychologists are like detectives trying to make sense of various clues about human behaviour. This detective-like quality of psychology is often not apparent in psychology textbooks. They provide an up-to-date viewpoint, but do not indicate how views have changed as more and more evidence has been gathered.

Consider, for example, the memory of brain-damaged patients suffering from amnesia. These patients have very poor memory, and often fail to recognise people they have met several times before. It used to be thought that the whole of the long-term memory system in amnesic patients was damaged, and that was why they had such poor memory. However, it has become increasingly clear that these patients have good memory for many things including motor skills such as riding a bicycle or playing the piano. This led psychologists to change their minds. It is now assumed that the long-term memory system is more complex than was previously thought, and that only the part of it concerned with general knowledge and personal experiences is damaged in amnesic patients.

Organisation of the book

We saw earlier that psychology is the study of human and animal behaviour. That means it is very broad in scope. There are several approaches that have been taken to the study of human behaviour. For example, social psychologists focus on our interactions with other people; psychophysiologists focus on the ways in which the physiological system relates to behaviour; and developmental psychologists consider the behaviour of children and the way their behaviour develops and changes over time. The organisation of this book is based on some of the major approaches to psychology. There are six main sections, as follows: biological approach; behaviourist approach; developmental approach; social approach; individual differences approach; cognitive approach. Finally, there is a rather different section called effective learning. This provides a practical account of what you can do to improve your study skills and ensure that you derive the greatest possible benefit from this book.

Personal viewpoint

Near the start of most chapters in this book, you will find a box labelled "Personal viewpoint". Within each box are some questions relating to the subject matter of the chapter. You are invited to think about them on the basis of your personal experience and knowledge.

One key reason for having these boxes relates to some of the material on study skills contained in Chapter 23. You are more likely to learn and remember the information you read if you focus on major questions and issues while you are reading. The personal viewpoint boxes are designed to achieve precisely that.

There is another key reason for having the personal viewpoint boxes. As we saw earlier, many people claim the results of psychological research are obvious because they are influenced by hindsight bias. You might find it of value to use the questions in the personal viewpoint box of each chapter to write down your personal account of each area of psychology. When you have finished reading each chapter, you can compare your account with the one given in the book. Hopefully, you will be surprised at the differences between the two!

Three additional features of this book are designed to make it as useful as possible. First, psychologists often use words in ways that differ from the ways in which they are used in everyday language, and this can be confusing for students. Accordingly, at the end of each chapter is a list of key terms with their definitions. Second, there are structured essay questions at the end of nearly every chapter to focus your mind on important issues. Third, there are self-assessment questions at the end of nearly every chapter, so that you can test yourself and find out how much (or how little!) you have learned.

Further reading

Colman, A.M. (1988). *What is psychology?* London: Hutchinson. A very readable introduction to psychology for those with little background knowledge of the subject.

References

Jourard, S.M. (1966). An exploratory study of body-accessibility. *British Journal of Social and Clinical Psychology, 5,* 221–231.

Slovic, P., & Fischhoff, B. (1977). On the psychology of experimental surprises. *Journal of Experimental Psychology: Human Perception and Performance, 3,* 544–551.

Summary

- Psychology used to be based mainly on introspection, but is now based largely on the study of behaviour.
- Psychology is not just common sense: common sense does not form a coherent set of assumptions about human behaviour, and many psychological findings differ substantially from what most people would have predicted.
- We are often surprised by events, but looking back at them with the benefit of hindsight we no longer find them surprising; this is known as hindsight bias.
- There are large cross-cultural differences; cultures differ in their emphasis on money, on spiritual values, and on social values.
- Psychologists used to study mainly students, but a wider range of people have been studied in recent experiments.
- Psychology is increasingly applied to everyday life; some of the main applications are to be found in clinical, educational, and occupational settings.

Key terms

Behaviourists: psychologists (especially in the United States) who argued that psychologists should study behaviour and ignore **introspection**.

Cross-cultural differences: psychological differences between different cultures.

Hindsight bias: the tendency to be wise after the event, using the benefit of hindsight.

Introspection: study of the human mind based on people's reports of their thoughts and feelings.

Psychology: a scientific discipline designed to understand the behaviour of humans and other species.

Structured essay questions

1. What are some of the strengths of modern psychology? What are some of its weaknesses?

2. Is there a common-sense view of human behaviour? Does psychology differ from common sense?

Self-assessment questions

1. Most psychologists nowadays argue that psychology is:
   a) the science of human and animal behaviour
   b) the science of human behaviour only
   c) the science of introspection
   d) none of the above

2. It is important to study cross-cultural differences because:
   a) all cultures are similar in many ways
   b) what is true of one culture is often not true of other cultures
   c) they show the superiority of Western culture
   d) they allow Western psychologists to look at what happens elsewhere in the world

3. It is not a good strategy to study mainly students in experiments because:
   a) they tend not to be co-operative
   b) they know too much about psychology
   c) they are likely to guess what the experiments is about
   d) they are not representative or typical members of society

4. Hindsight bias is involved when people:
   a) see the future accurately
   b) have poor memories for the past
   c) are wise after the event
   d) remember the past as better than it actually was

Methods of investigation 2

In common with other sciences, psychology is concerned with theories and with data. A *theory* provides a general explanation or account of certain findings or *data*. It also generates a number of *hypotheses*, which are predictions or expectations about behaviour based on the theory. For example, someone might put forward a theory in which it is argued that some people are consistently more sociable or friendly than other people. This theory could be used to produce various hypotheses or predictions, such as the following: sociable people will smile more at other people; sociable people will talk more than unsociable people; sociable people will agree more than unsociable people with the views of others.

Psychologists spend a lot of their time collecting data in the form of measures of behaviour. Data are collected in order to test various hypotheses. Most people assume that this data collection involves proper experiments carried out under laboratory conditions, and it is true that literally millions of laboratory experiments have been carried out in psychology. However, as we will see, psychologists make use of several methods of investigation, each of which has provided useful information about human behaviour.

As you read through the various methods of investigation, it is natural to wonder which methods are the best and the worst. In fact, it may be more useful to compare the methods used by psychologists to the golf clubs used by the golf professional. The driver is not a better or worse club than the putter, it is simply used for a different purpose. In similar fashion, each method of investigation used by psychologists is very useful for testing some hypotheses, but is of little or no use for testing other hypotheses.

Experimental method

The experimental method is the method of investigation most often used by psychologists. It can be used either for laboratory experiments in controlled conditions or for field experiments carried out under more natural conditions. We will first consider the use of the experimental

---

Personal viewpoint

Suppose that you wanted to carry out some studies to increase your understanding of human behaviour. For example, you might be interested in the issue of whether watching violence on television tends to make people more aggressive. How do you think you might go about studying that issue? How many different methods could you use to shed light on the effects of television violence? Which of these methods do you think would be most useful? Why do you think that?

method in laboratory studies, and then consider its use in field experiments and other forms of field studies.

Laboratory studies

Most experimental research starts with someone thinking of an *experimental hypothesis*, which is simply a prediction or expectation of what will happen in a given situation. For example, you might think of the experimental hypothesis that loud noise will have a disruptive effect on people's ability to carry out a task such as learning the information in a chapter of an introductory psychology book.

As with most experimental hypotheses, the one just mentioned predicts that some aspect of the situation (in this case, the presence of loud noise) will have an effect on the participants' behaviour (in this case, their learning of the information in the chapter). In more technical language, the hypothesis refers to an *independent variable*, which is usually some aspect of the experimental situation that is manipulated by the experimenter. In our example, the presence versus absence of loud noise is the independent variable. The hypothesis also refers to a *dependent variable*, which is some aspect of the participants' behaviour. In our example, some measure of learning would be used to assess the dependent variable. In a nutshell, then, most experimental hypotheses predict that a given independent variable will have some specified effect on a particular dependent variable.

The experimental hypothesis consists of the predicted effect of the independent variable on the dependent variable. This can be contrasted with the *null hypothesis*. The null hypothesis simply states that the independent variable will have no effect on the dependent variable. In a sense, the purpose of most laboratory studies is to decide between the merits of the experimental hypothesis and those of the null hypothesis.

It might seem easy to do a study to test the experimental hypothesis that loud noise disrupts learning. However, there are various pitfalls that need to be avoided. The first issue that needs to be considered is how to manipulate the independent variable. In our example, we want to compare loud noise with no noise, so we have to decide exactly how loud we want the noise to be. If it is very loud, then it might damage the hearing of our participants, and so would be totally unacceptable. If it is relatively soft, then it is unlikely to have any effect on our participants. It is also likely to make a difference whether the noise is meaningful (e.g. music or speech on the radio) or meaningless (e.g. the noise of a road drill).

The second issue to consider is how to measure the dependent variable or aspect of the participants' behaviour. We could ask our participants various questions to measure their understanding of the material in the book. However, selecting the questions so that they are not too easy or too difficult requires careful thought.

Confounding variables.   Another issue to consider is whether or not our experiment contains any *confounding variables*. These are variables that are mistakenly manipulated along with the independent variable. Suppose that one group of participants receives no noise and reads the chapter at midday, whereas the other group of participants receives loud noise and reads the chapter at midnight. If the latter group learns less well than the former group, we would not know whether this was because of the loud noise or because they did their learning late in the evening when they were very tired. In this example, time of day is a confounding variable.

Controlled variables.   How do we avoid having any confounding variables? One good approach is to turn them into *controlled variables*. Suppose that we want to study the effects of noise on learning, and we are concerned that time of day may have an effect. We could make time of day into a controlled variable by testing all our participants at a particular time of day, such as late morning or early evening. If we did that, then we would know that time of day cannot distort our findings.

Selecting participants.   Experiments in psychology rarely use more than about 100 participants, but the experimenter generally wants his or her findings to apply to a much larger group. In technical terms, the participants used in an experiment consist of one or more *samples* drawn from some larger *population*. If we want the findings from a sample to be true of a population, then those included in the sample must be *representative* of the population.

In terms of our example, we might study the effects of loud noise on learning in students preparing for their GCSE in psychology. The best way to obtain a representative sample from that population would be to make use of *random sampling*. We could obtain lists of names from the various Examination Boards of all students due to sit their GCSE in psychology in a given year. Participants would then be selected at random from these lists. This could be done by picking names out of a hat or by sticking a pin repeatedly into the lists. However, it is likely that many of those asked to take part would refuse.

Another way of obtaining a representative sample is by using what is known as *quota sampling*. Suppose that we know that 70% of GCSE psychology students are female, and that 40% of all GCSE psychology students live in the north of England. We could then make sure that the participants used in our experiment were selected so that 70% of them were female, and 40% of them lived in the north of England. If we include enough criteria, then quota sampling can be an effective way of finding a representative sample.

Random sampling and quota sampling are often expensive and time-consuming. Accordingly, many studies in psychology simply make use of what is known as *opportunity sampling*. With opportunity sampling, participants are selected on the basis of their availability rather than by any other method. This is the easiest way to proceed, but it has the severe disadvantage that the participants may be nothing like a representative sample.

Standardised procedures. In order to carry out an experiment successfully, it is very important that every participant in a given condition is treated in the same way. In other words, it is necessary to use *standardised procedures*. For example, consider the instructions that are given to the participants. In order to ensure that all the participants get precisely the same instructions, the experimenter should write them down. He or she should then either read them to the participants, or ask the participants to read them themselves.

In similar fashion, standardised procedures need to be used for the collection of data. Suppose we want to assess the effects of loud noise on learning from a book chapter. We might ask the participants to write down everything they could remember about the chapter. However, it would be very hard to compare the recalls of different participants with any precision. A standardised procedure would be to ask all the participants the same set of, say, 20 questions relating to the chapter. Each participant then obtains a score between 0 and 20 as a measure of what he or she has learned.

Is it easy to make sure that standardised procedures are being used? No, it is not. Most experiments can be thought of as social encounters between the experimenter and the participant, and it is natural to behave differently with different people. Robert Rosenthal (1967) studied some of the ways in which experimenters fall short of standardised procedures. For example, he found that male experimenters were more pleasant, friendly, honest, encouraging, and relaxed when their participants were female than when they were male. This led him to conclude: "Male and female subjects [participants] may, psychologically, simply not be in the same experiment at all".

Experimental designs. If we wish to compare two groups with respect to a given independent variable, it is essential to make sure that the two groups do not differ in any other important way. This general rule is important when it comes to selecting participants to take part in an experiment. Suppose all the least able participants received the loud noise, and all the most able participants received no noise. We would not then know whether it was the loud noise or the ability level of the participants causing poor performance.

How can we select our participants so as to avoid this problem? There are three main types of experimental design:

- *Independent design:* each participant is selected for only one group.
- *Matched subjects design:* each participant is selected for only one group, but the participants in one group are matched with those in the other group in terms of some relevant factor (e.g. ability; sex; age).
- *Repeated measures design:* each participant appears in both groups, so that there are exactly the same participants in each group.

With the independent design, the most common way of deciding which participants go into which group is by means of *randomisation*. In our example, this could involve using a random process such as coin tossing to decide whether each participant is exposed to loud noise or to no noise. It is possible with randomisation for all the most able participants to be selected for the same group. However, what happens nearly all the time is that the participants in the two groups are similar in ability, age, and so on.

With the matched subjects design, we make use of information about the participants to decide the group into which each participant should be put. In our example, we might have information about the participants' ability levels. We could then use this information to make sure that the two groups are matched in terms of range of ability.

With the repeated measures design, every participant is in both groups. In our example, that would mean that each participant learns the chapter in loud noise and they also learn the chapter in no noise. The repeated measures design means that we do not need to worry about the participants in one group being cleverer than those in the other group—because the same participants appear in both groups, the ability level is identical in the two groups!

The main problem with the repeated measures design is that there may well be order effects. Their experiences during the experiment may change the participants in various ways. For example, they may perform better when they appear in the second group because they have gained useful knowledge about the experiment or about the task. On the other hand, they may perform less well on the second occasion because of tiredness or boredom. It would be difficult to use a repeated measures design in our example: participants are almost certain to show better learning of the chapter the second time they read it, regardless of whether or not they are exposed to loud noise.

Suppose we used a repeated measures design in which all the participants first learn the chapter in loud noise and then learn it in no noise. We would expect the participants to show better learning in no noise simply because of order effects. A better procedure would be to have half the participants learn the chapter first in loud noise and then in no noise, while the other half learn the chapter first in no noise and then in loud noise. In that way, any order effects would be balanced out. This approach is known as *counterbalancing*, and it is the best way of preventing order effects from disrupting the findings from an experiment.

Replication

When psychologists design and carry out experiments, they are very concerned that other psychologists should be able to obtain similar findings to them. This is known as *replication*, meaning that the experimental procedures and findings can be repeated by others. Careful selection of participants, the avoidance of confounding variables, and the use of standardised procedures are all of value in allowing findings to be replicated or repeated.

Field experiments

Field experiments involve using the experimental method in real-life situations. As an example of a field experiment, consider a study by Lance Shotland and Margaret Straw (discussed in more detail by Eysenck & Eysenck, 1989). It was designed to look at some of the factors influencing whether onlookers will intervene in a violent quarrel. They arranged for a man and a woman to stage a fight close to a number of onlookers. In one condition, the woman screamed, "I don't know you". In a second condition, she screamed, "I don't know why I ever married you". When the onlookers thought the fight involved strangers, 65% of them intervened, against only 19% when they thought it involved a married couple. In other words, people are less likely to lend a helping hand if they think it is a "lovers' quarrel".

Field observations

For some purposes, it is possible to make use of *field observations* rather than field experiments. The distinction between the two is that field experiments involve at least partial control over the situation, whereas field observations merely involve the experimenter observing the behaviour of people as they go about their everyday lives.

Photo courtesy TRIP, photographer H. Rogers.

Seeing the ways in which children interact in a playground is an example of an observational study. It might be predicted that girls would tend to interact in a more co-operative way than boys, whereas boys would tend to interact more aggressively than girls. Two or more observers could spend some time recording the number of co-operative and aggressive actions by boys and girls in order to test these hypotheses. It could be very demanding to try to do this non-stop for an hour or so. Accordingly, researchers often use time-sampling, in which they only observe for part of the time. For example, they might observe the children's behaviour for ten minutes, have a five-minute break, observe for ten more minutes, and so on.

There are two related problems that can arise in observational studies. First, the observers may have different ideas about the meaning of the different cate-

gories of behaviour that they are looking for. For example, one observer may regard a gentle tap as aggressive behaviour, whereas another observer may not. It is, therefore, highly desirable to have very clear definitions of the behaviour that is to be measured.

Second, the existence of clear definitions of the various categories of behaviour to be recorded is a great advantage, but it may not sort out all the problems. For example, some observers may fail to spot pieces of behaviour through a lack of attention. It is possible to see whether or not two observers produce similar judgements. This is done by working out what is known as inter-observer reliability: the higher this reliability, the closer the agreement between the observers.

Cross-sectional and longitudinal studies

Suppose that we were interested in exploring the effects of age on learning and memory. The most frequently used approach is the *cross-sectional method*, in which different age groups are tested at the same point in time. When this method is used, it is generally found that older people perform less well than younger ones (Schaie, 1970). However, it is not clear from such evidence whether the difference is really due to age as such. Older people have often had poorer educational opportunities than younger people, and so their lower level of learning and memory may be due to their relative lack of education rather than to age.

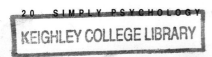

A superior way of assessing the effects of age on learning and memory is to carry out a *longitudinal study*. In such a study, the same group of individuals is studied at several points in time. Because the same people are studied at different ages, any effects of age on performance are likely to be genuine. It turns out that many of the negative effects of age on learning and memory which emerge from cross-sectional studies disappear when longitudinal studies are carried out (Schaie, 1970). It thus appears that differences from one generation to the next in educational opportunities are more important than age in affecting learning and memory.

In view of the fact that longitudinal studies are superior to cross-sectional studies, you might wonder why there are far more cross-sectional studies. The main reason is that such studies are much easier and less time-consuming to carry out. Indeed, a longitudinal study looking at people as they change over a period of several decades might well have to be brought to a premature halt because of the deaths of the experimenter or experimenters who started the study!

Correlational studies

Suppose that we were interested in the hypothesis that watching violence on television leads to aggressive behaviour. One way of testing this hypothesis would be to obtain two kind of information from a large number of people: (1) the amount of violent television they watched; (2) the extent to which they behaved aggressively in various situations. If the hypothesis is correct, then we would expect that those who have seen the most violence on television would tend to be the most aggressive.

In technical terms, this study would be looking for a *correlation*, or association, between watching violent programmes and being aggressive. Thus, the closer the link between them, the greater would be the correlation or association.

The main problem with correlational studies is that it is very difficult to interpret the findings. In our example, an association or correlation between the amount of television violence watched and aggressive behaviour would certainly be in line with the hypothesis that watching violent programmes can cause aggressive behaviour. However, it might be that aggressive individuals choose to watch more violent programmes than those who are less aggressive. Finally, there may be some other variable which accounts for the findings. People in disadvantaged families may watch more television programmes of all kinds than those in non-disadvantaged families, and their deprived circumstances may also make them behave aggressively. If that were the case, then the number of violent television programmes watched might have no effect at all on aggressive behaviour.

Why do experimenters carry out correlational studies? First, many hypotheses cannot be examined directly by means of experimental studies. For example, the hypothesis that smoking causes a number of physical diseases cannot be tested by forcing some people to smoke and forcing others not to smoke! All that can be done is to examine associations or correlations between the number of cigarettes smoked and the probability of suffering from various diseases.

Second, it is often possible to obtain large amounts of data on several variables in a correlational study much more rapidly than would be possible with experimental designs. For example, use of questionnaires would permit an experimenter to study the associations or correlations between aggressive behaviour and a wide range of activities (such as watching violent films in the cinema; reading violent books; being frustrated at work or at home).

Case studies

Most studies in psychology have involved the use of experimental or correlational methods on groups of participants. However, there are sometimes good reasons why it is not possible to use large numbers of participants in a study. A busy clinician or therapist may find the behaviour of a patient to be very revealing, but he or she may have no possibility of collecting information from other patients with the same problem. In such circumstances, it can be very useful to carry out what is known as a *case study*, in which one or two individuals are studied in detail.

One of the best-known case studies was carried out by Watson and Rayner (1920) on a young child called Albert. Every time that Albert played with his pet rat, the experimenters would present a loud noise. This produced, through classical conditioning (see Chapter 7), an association between the rat and the noise. As a result, Albert became frightened of his rat and of other similar creatures such as white rabbits. According to Watson and Rayner (1920), this case study showed how phobias (strong, uncontrollable fears) develop. Some people suffer from spider phobia and others from snake phobia, and these phobias may develop through classical conditioning.

The greatest advantage of case studies is that they can provide far more information about a specific individual than is usually obtained from experimental studies. Their greatest disadvantage is that what is true of a given individual may not be true of other people. That means that it is somewhat dangerous to draw general conclusions from the study of a single person. It is possible that Albert was an unusually nervous child, and that most other children would not have become as frightened of their pets as he did.

Survey studies

Survey studies involve collecting opinions from large numbers of people. They generally make use of questionnaires or interviews which are given to all the groups of interest. These questionnaires or interviews often measure attitudes. However, they can also assess personality, patterns of behaviour, and so on. A characteristic of many survey studies is that they require hundreds (or even thousands) of participants. As a result, the questionnaires or interviews are generally designed to be completed quickly and easily.

As an example of a survey study, there was a study by Lowenthal et al. in the 1970s. They studied four groups of people: students in their last two years at school; young newly-weds; middle-aged parents, aged about 50; and those preparing for retirement. Questionnaires were used to assess happiness and well-being, and to decide whether individuals were high or low in their positive and negative experiences. The four groups differed little in their overall levels of happiness. However, the two younger groups were much more emotionally changeable than the older groups, and experienced more emotional highs and lows.

Survey methods are often used in cross-cultural studies, in which two or more different cultures are compared. For example, cross-cultural studies of happiness levels have been conducted using various questionnaires. Not surprisingly, people living in Western societies tend to be happier than those living in very poor Third World countries, but the differences tend to be smaller than might have been imagined (Eysenck, 1990).

Evaluation.   The interviews and questionnaires used in surveys tend to have different strengths and weaknesses. Interviews possess a certain amount of flexibility, and during them it is possible for misunderstandings to be resolved. However, they have the disadvantage that the data obtained may reveal more about the social interaction processes between the interviewer and the person being interviewed (the interviewee) than about the interviewee's thought processes and attitudes. To make interviews as useful as possible, they should be structured, in the sense that most (or all) of the questions to be asked are worked out beforehand by the interviewer. It is also important for the interviewer to take detailed notes. It has been found (Smith, 1988) that interviewers often forget half of the information given by the interviewee by the time the interview is over.

Questionnaires provide a consistent and structured assessment of an individual's personality and attitudes, without any influence from an interviewer or other person on the findings. However, a weakness is that all participants are asked the same questions, regardless of the suitability or relevance of particular questions to particular individuals.

A problem common to the data obtained from both interviews and questionnaires is social desirability bias. Most people want to present themselves in a good light, so there is a danger they will provide socially desirable rather than honest answers to questions about themselves. This problem can be handled in the interview situation by a sensitive interviewer asking additional questions to establish the truth. In questionnaires, the problem is addressed by including a lie scale. Lie scales contain questions to which the socially desirable answer is likely to differ from the honest answer (e.g. "Do you ever talk about other people's private lives?"). Anyone who consistently answers such questions in the socially desirable direction is assumed to be lying, and their questionnaire data are discarded.

Archive studies

Governments, polling organisations, political parties, and other groups collect large amounts of information about different sections of society. This information, which is sometimes available in the form of archives (collections of records), can be of use to social psychologists.

An example of the use of archive material is a study by Hovland and Sears (1940; see also Chapter 6). They wanted to test the frustration–aggression hypothesis, according to which frustration produces aggression. Drops in cotton prices in the United States were assumed to cause frustration, and the number of lynchings was taken as a measure of aggression. As predicted, when archive material was studied, those years in which the cotton prices were the lowest tended to be the ones with the most lynchings.

Archive studies have the advantage that trends over long periods can be studied easily, without the experimenter having to spend years collecting his or her own data. The most obvious disadvantage is that the archive material was usually collected for a purpose that differs from that of the psychologist who later uses it. As a result, data that would be of particular value to the psychologist may not be available. Another disadvantage is that it is often difficult to interpret the data. For example, although Hovland and Sears found an association or correlation between cotton prices and the number of lynchings, it is not possible to be confident that the number of lynchings was actually influenced by the frustrations associated with low cotton prices.

Data presentation and interpretation

When the data from a study have been collected, the experimenter then needs to make sense of them. The starting point is to summarise the "raw" data in such a way as to make clear exactly how the participants in the various conditions or groups differed in their performance. After that, it is necessary to carry out one or more statistical tests in order to decide whether there are genuine differences among the conditions. Finally, the experimenter has to decide how to interpret his or her findings. We will deal with some of the issues here, but will omit any consideration of the various statistical tests that can be used.

Data presentation

Suppose that we have carried out an experiment on the effects of noise on learning with three groups of nine participants. One group was exposed to very loud noise, another group to moderately loud noise, and the third group was not exposed to noise at all. What they had learned from a book chapter was assessed by giving them a set of questions, producing a score between 0 and 20.

What is to be done with the raw scores? The first step is to work out the *mean* in each group or condition. This is done by adding up all of the scores in a given condition, and then dividing by the number of participants in that condition. Suppose that there are nine participants in the no noise condition, and their scores are as follows: 1 2 4 5 7 9 9 9 17. The mean is given by the total, which is 63, divided by the number of participants, which is 9. Thus, the mean is 7. Two other ways of describing the general level of performance in each condition are known as the *median* and the *mode*. The median is the middle score, having an equal number of scores higher and lower than it. In the example, the median is 7. The mode is the most frequently occurring score; in the example, this is 9.

It is also useful to work out the *range* for each condition. This is easy to do, because it is simply the difference between the highest and the lowest score in any condition. In the case of the no noise group, the range is 17− 1 = 16. The range gives some idea as to whether the participants in a condition tended to behave in similar or dissimilar ways.

Information, especially information about group means, can be presented in several ways. The simplest way is in the form of a table.

Examples of data presentation. Right: a table of data: the first nine rows show each participant's individual score. The bottom three rows show the mean, median and mode scores calculated for each group. Bottom left: a line graph, showing how the participants' ability to answer questions declined when the noise was loudest. Bottom right: a bar chart or histogram illustrating the same results.

Participant number	No noise	Moderate noise	Very loud noise
1	1	2	0
2	2	2	0
3	4	4	1
4	5	5	1
5	7	6	1
6	9	6	2
7	9	6	3
8	9	11	4
9	17	12	6
Mean	7	6	2
Median	7	6	1
Mode	9	6	1

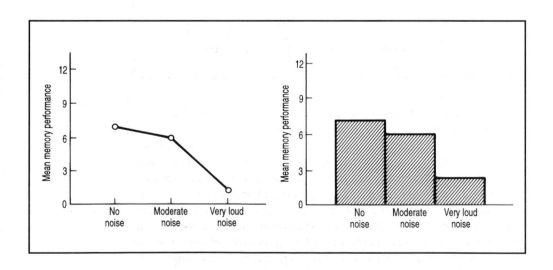

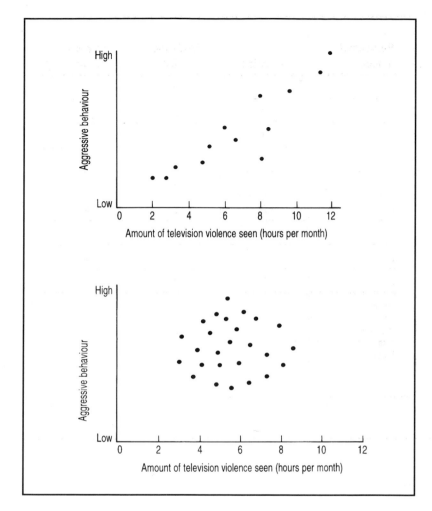

Examples of scattergrams. Top: positive relationship between watching violent television and aggressive behaviour. Bottom: no relationship between watching violence and aggression.

However, it is somewhat easier to grasp the findings of a study if they are portrayed in the form of a graph or a histogram.

In the case of correlational studies, the data are in the form of two measures of behaviour from a single group of participants. What is often done is to present the data in the form of a scattergram. Suppose that we have carried out a study on the relationship between the amount of television violence seen and the amount of aggressive behaviour displayed. We could have a scale of the amount of television seen on the horizontal axis, and a scale of the amount of aggressive behaviour on the vertical axis. We could then put a dot for each participant indicating where he or she falls on these two dimensions. If there is a positive relationship between watching violence and aggression, then the dots should tend to form a pattern going from the bottom left of the scattergram to the top right. If there is no relationship between the two variables, then the dots should be distributed in a fairly random way within the scattergram.

Drawing conclusions

You may remember that experimenters start by putting forward an experimental hypothesis (what they predict will happen) and a null hypothesis (the assumption that there are no genuine effects). The purpose of a statistical test is to decide whether there is enough evidence in the data to reject the null hypothesis in favour of the experimental hypothesis. In the case of the study on the effects of noise on learning discussed earlier, we might be able to conclude that noise has an adverse effect on learning.

Close inspection of the data on noise and learning suggests that it may be wrong to argue simply that loud noise impairs learning. It looks as if it is only very loud noise that has much of an effect, because there is little difference in performance between those exposed to moderately loud noise and those exposed to no noise at all. In other words, it may be that there is a kind of threshold effect: people can cope with a fair amount of noise without letting it affect their ability to learn, but they cannot cope with intense noise.

Ethical issues

It is probably true to say there are more major ethical issues associated with research in psychology than in any other scientific discipline. There are various reasons for this. First, all psychological experiments involve the study of living creatures (whether human or the members of some other species), and their right to be treated in a caring way can be infringed by an unprincipled or careless experimenter.

Second, the findings of psychological research may reveal what appear to be unpleasant or unacceptable facts about human nature, or about certain groups within society. No matter how morally upright the experimenter may be, there is always the danger that extreme political organisations will use the findings to further their aims.

Third, psychological research may lead to the discovery of powerful techniques that can be used for purposes of social control. It would obviously be dangerous if such techniques were to be exploited by dictators or others seeking to exert undue influence on society.

Psychologists have become increasingly concerned about ethical issues in recent years. In the United Kingdom in 1990, the British Psychological Society issued its *Ethical principles for conducting research with human participants*. These principles should be followed by everyone, including students who carry out experiments as part of their course.

General principles

The key to conducting research in an ethical fashion is expressed in the following way in the *Principles*: "The essential principle is that the investigation should be considered from the standpoint of all participants; foreseeable threats to their psychological well-being, health, values, and dignity should be eliminated". In other words, every effort should be made to make sure that participants do not experience pain, stress, or distress.

Most ethical problems in human research stem from the participant being typically in a much less powerful position than the experimenter. One way of dealing with this is to make sure that the participant is told precisely what will happen in the experiment, before requesting that he or she give *voluntary informed consent* to take part. In the case of young children, their parents or guardians can provide the necessary consent.

Voluntary informed consent is very desirable, and it is important to try to avoid deception. However, there are many experiments in which it is not posssible either to obtain consent or to avoid deception. For example, consider the study by Shotland and Straw discussed earlier, in which they studied the willingness of onlookers to intervene in a violent quarrel. If they had told the onlookers that it wasn't a real quarrel, but was merely being staged for their benefit, the whole purpose of the study would have been ruined.

When is deception justified? There are various factors that need to be considered. First, deception is more acceptable if the effects of the deception are not damaging. Second, it is easier to justify the use of deception in studies that are important in scientific terms than in those that are trivial. Third, deception is more justifiable when there are no other, deception-free, ways of studying an issue.

It is very important that participants have the right to withdraw from an experiment at any time. They should not have to say why they are withdrawing from the experiment if they choose not to. In addition, they can also insist that the data they have provided during the experiment should be destroyed.

Although the right to withdraw is now standard practice, this was not the case in the past. Consider, for example, the research by Milgram (1974) on obedience to authority (see Chapter 15). When any of his participants said that they wanted to leave the experiment or to stop giving electric shocks, they were told they had to continue with the experiment.

At the end of the experiment, the experimenter should provide what is known as a *debriefing*. There are two aspects to debriefing: (1) provision of information about the experiment; and (2) attempts to reduce any distress that may have been caused by the experiment. Milgram's (1974) research on obedience to authority is an example of good debriefing. All the participants were reassured that they had not actually given any electric shocks. They then had a long chat with the experimenter and with the person who had apparently received the shocks. Those participants who had been willing to give severe shocks were told that their behaviour was normal. Finally, all the participants were given a detailed report on the study.

Another important aspect of ethical research is confidentiality, which means that information about individual participants should not be revealed. It is usual in psychology for published accounts of research to refer to group means, but not to give information about the names and performance of individual participants. If the experimenter cannot guarantee confidentiality, then this should be made clear to participants before the start of the experiment.

Further reading

Eysenck, M.W. (1994). *Perspectives on psychology*. Hove, UK: Lawrence Erlbaum Associates Ltd. In Chapters 5 and 6, several different methods of investigation are discussed in more detail than has been possible here.

References

British Psychological Society. (1990). Ethical principles for conducting research with human participants. *The Psychologist, 3*, 270–272

Coolican, H. (1990). *Research methods and statistics in psychology*. Sevenoaks, UK: Hodder & Stoughton.

Rosenthal, R. (1966). *Experimenter effects in behavioural research*. New York: Appleton-Century-Crofts.

Schaie, K.W. (1970). A re-interpretation of age-related changes in cognitive structure and functioning. In L.R. Goulet & P.B. Baltes (Eds.), *Life-span developmental psychology: Research and theory*. London: Academic Press.

Summary

- An experimental hypothesis is a prediction of what will happen in a given situation; it refers to the predicted effect of an independent variable on a dependent variable.
- Confounding variables must be avoided when using the experimental method; this can be done by making sure as many variables as possible are controlled.
- Participants should form a representative sample from some population; this can be done by random sampling or quota sampling, but sometimes only opportunity sampling is possible.
- Within the experimental method, there are independent designs, repeated measures designs, and matched subjects designs.
- Repeated measures designs can produce unwanted order effects; this can be handled by counterbalancing.
- Field experiments use the experimental method in real-life situations; they have the advantage that observations can be made without the participant's knowledge, but there are problems of control and of informed consent.
- Observational studies require the use of carefully designed categories of behaviour and high levels of inter-observer reliability.
- Cross-sectional studies involve a number of groups studied at a single point in time, whereas longitudinal studies involve one group studied several times; the data from longitudinal studies are easier to interpret, but such studies are expensive and time-consuming.
- Correlational studies involve comparing two measures of behaviour from the same participants; the findings are hard to interpret.
- Case studies involve studying one or two individuals in detail.
- Survey studies usually involve interviews or questionnaires; both kinds of measures are liable to social desirability bias.
- Average performance within a group can be summarised by a mean, median, or mode, and variability within a group can be indicated by the range.
- The findings of a study can be presented in the forms of tables, graphs, or histograms; the findings of correlational studies can be presented in scattergrams.
- Ethical research requires the use of voluntary informed consent, trying to avoid deception, providing the right to withdraw, adequate debriefing, and confidentiality.

Key terms

Archive studies: studies based on the use of archives or collections of records.

Case study: the intensive study of one or two individuals rather than the study of larger numbers of individuals or groups.

Confounding variable: a variable, not of interest to the experimenter, which is manipulated along with the **independent variable**.

Controlled variable: a variable, not of interest to the experimenter, which is held constant or controlled.

Correlation: an association that is found between two **dependent variables**.

Counterbalancing: this is used with the **repeated measures design**; each condition is equally likely to be used first or second with the participants.

Cross-sectional method: this uses different age groups who are studied at the same time; see **longitudinal method**.

Debriefing: providing participants at the end of an experiment with information about it and reducing any distress.

Dependent variable: some aspect of the participants' behaviour which is measured in an experiment.

Ecological validity: the extent to which the findings of a study can be applied to the real world.

Experimental hypothesis: prediction as to what will happen in a given situation, often based on a **theory**; see **null hypothesis**.

Experimental method: a method involving a generally high level of control over the experimental situation, and especially of the **independent variable**.

Field experiments: experiments carried out in real-world situations using the **experimental method**.

Field observations: observations of behaviour in real-world situations without use of the **experimental method**.

Independent design: each participant is included in only one group or condition; see **repeated measures design**.

Independent variable: some aspect of the situation which is manipulated by the experimenter; see **repeated measures design**.

Longitudinal method: the study of the same group of individuals over a relatively long period of time; see **cross-sectional method**.

Matched subjects design: this is a form of **independent design** in which the participants in two or more groups are matched in terms of some relevant factor or factors, such as intelligence or age.

Mean: an average worked out by dividing the total of all participants' scores by the number of participants; see **median** and **mode**.

Key terms (continued)

Median: the middle score out of all participants' scores in a given condition; see **mean** and **mode**.

Mode: the most frequently occurring score among the participants in a given condition; see **mean** and **median**.

Null hypothesis: the prediction that the **independent variable** will have no effect on the **dependent variable**.

Opportunity sample: a **sample** selected from a **population** simply on the basis of availability.

Population: a large collection of people from whom the **sample** used in a study is drawn.

Quota sample: a **sample** that is chosen from a **population** so that the sample is similar to the population in certain ways (e.g. proportion of females; proportion of university graduates).

Random sample: a **sample** that is chosen from a **population** in a random fashion (e.g. coin tossing).

Randomisation: placing participants into groups on some random basis (e.g. coin tossing).

Range: a measure of the spread of scores within a condition, given by working out the difference between the highest and lowest scores.

Repeated measures design: each participant in an experiment appears in both groups; see **independent design**.

Replication: repeating the findings of a study by using the same design and procedures.

Representative sample: a **sample** that is chosen to be typical of the **population** from which it is drawn.

Sample: the participants actually used in a study, drawn from some larger **population**.

Standardised procedures: carrying out an experiment in the same way for all the participants in any given condition or group; this includes instructions and data collection.

Survey studies: studies involving the use of questionnaires and / or interviews to assess the opinions of large groups of people.

Theory: a general explanation of a set of findings; it is used to produce experimental hypotheses.

Voluntary informed consent: an ethical requirement involving making sure that the participants in a study agree to take part knowing exactly what they will be asked to do.

Structured essay questions

1. What are the main methods of investigation available to psychologists? What are the advantages of these methods? What are the disadvantages of these methods?
2. What is the experimental method? Why has it been used so often in psychological research?
3. What are the main features of ethical experimentation? Why is it important for experiments to be ethical?

Self-assessment questions

1. An experimental hypothesis usually refers to:
   a) two independent variables
   b) two dependent variables
   c) one independent and one dependent variable
   d) one independent and one confounding variable

2. When selecting participants for an experimental study, we should:
   a) make sure that the samples are representative of some larger population
   b) choose those individuals who are most willing to take part
   c) simply ask for volunteers
   d) ask our friends to suggest names of those who might take part

3. An experiment in which each participant is selected for only one group is known as:
   a) a matched subjects design
   b) a repeated measures design
   c) a randomised design
   d) an independent design

4. Field experiments are experiments in which:
   a) the experimental method is used in real-life situations
   b) observations are made in real-life situations
   c) there is no attempt to manipulate an independent variable
   d) there are very few participants

5. Longitudinal studies are studies in which:
   a) different age groups are tested at the same point in time
   b) the same group of individuals are studied at several points in time
   c) different groups of individuals are studied at several points in time
   d) children are investigated

6. The main problem with correlational studies is that:
   a) they are difficult to carry out
   b) they are expensive to carry out
   c) only limited numbers of participants can be studied
   d) it is very difficult to interpret the findings

7. Adding up all the scores in a given condition, and dividing by the number of participants, gives us:
   a) the median of that condition
   b) the mode of that condition
   c) the mean of that condition
   d) none of the above

8. For ethical experimentation, it is necessary to make sure that participants:
   a) give voluntary informed consent only
   b) have the right to withdraw from the experiment only
   c) are debriefed
   d) give voluntary informed consent, have the right to withdraw from the experiment, and are debriefed

Biological approach

part
1

Biological bases of behaviour 3

Psychology is linked to other sciences such as physiology, sociology, and biochemistry. Of particular importance are the links between psychology and biology. However, it was only after the publication of the book *The origin of species* by Charles Darwin (1807–1882) that the relevance of biology to psychology became accepted. Before its publication in 1859, people had assumed that only human beings have minds, thus making us radically different from other species. The notion that human beings have evolved from other species meant that this inflated view of the importance of the human species had to be reassessed. Many people found it very hard to come to terms with the idea that humans should be regarded simply as members of the animal kingdom.

Darwin was a biologist rather than a psychologist. However, his theory of evolution has had at least four major effects on psychology. First, psychologists began to develop theories of human psychology from the biological perspective. The most famous psychologist to do so was Sigmund Freud, whose emphasis on the sex drive in humans would have been almost unthinkable in the days before Darwin.

Second, one of the lessons of the theory of evolution was that the study of animals could be of great value in trying to understand human behaviour. This led to the development of animal or comparative psychology.

Third, Darwin argued that heredity is important in the development of a species, and that offspring tend to be like their parents. These ideas led psychologists to explore the role of heredity in influencing human behaviour.

Fourth, Darwin focused on variation among the members of a species. According to his notion of survival of the fittest, evolution favours those members of a species who are best equipped to live in a given environment. These ideas led to an interest in individual differences, and to the study of intelligence and personality.

Whole books have been written about the biological bases of behaviour. However, it will only be possible to deal with a few selected topics in this chapter. Our main focus will be on the brain, which is far more

---

Personal viewpoint

A long time ago there were people called phrenologists, who claimed that it was possible to understand how the brain works by feeling the bumps in the skull. That approach did not work very well. What kinds of measuring instruments do you think could be used to shed light on the mysteries of how the brain works? The phrenologists assumed that each part of the brain had its own special function. Do you think they were right to make this assumption? How could we decide?

important than any other biological structure in influencing behaviour. However, we begin with the issue of the impact of heredity on behaviour.

Inborn characteristics

Human beings differ from each other in endless ways. Some are tall and thin, whereas others are short and fat; some are intelligent and hard-working, whereas others are unintelligent and poorly motivated; and so on. At the most general level, there are only two possible reasons for individual differences: heredity, or nature; and environment, or nurture. In other words, people may differ either because of differences in what they have inherited, or because of differences in the environment or experiences they have had. In fact, it is very probable that heredity and environment both play an important role in producing individual differences in behaviour.

The issue of the relative importance of heredity and environment is often known as the *nature/nurture controversy*. This controversy is dealt with in various places in this book, in connection with the development of language (Chapter 9), individual differences in intelligence (Chapter 17), and individual differences in personality (Chapter 18). The focus of this chapter is on the biological bases of behaviour, and so we will consider here some of the evidence suggesting that nature or heredity is important.

A key point is that species vary a lot in terms of how much their behaviour is determined by heredity. In general terms, the behaviour of lower species (such as ants and bees) is much more influenced by heredity than is the behaviour of higher species such as apes and humans. For example, von Frisch (1954) found that honey bees naturally perform a rather complex "wagging" dance in a figure-of-eight pattern. This dance provides information to other bees about the direction and distance away of a food supply. In contrast, humans have to learn most of the skills they possess in a lengthy and effortful way.

Is it better to be born equipped to behave in complex ways or to have to learn how to behave skilfully? Being born with the ability to produce many fixed patterns of behaviour saves effort, and can be very useful if the environment remains much the same from generation to generation. However, if there is a major change in the environment, then being born with fixed behaviour patterns can be a problem. In such circumstances, the human ability to learn ways of behaving that are suitable for the given situation gives a very valuable flexibility.

Ethology

During the 1930s and 1940s, a number of scientists including Lorenz and Tinbergen developed an approach to animal psychology known as *ethology* (see Chapter 6). The basic idea behind the ethological approach was that it is very important to study other species in their natural surroundings. The ethologists argued that the behaviourist approach of studying other species in the laboratory was very limited, and told us very little about how they behaved in the wild.

The ethologists found that several other species seemed to show *instinctive behaviour*, that is, behaviour which does not depend on learning at all. They used the term *fixed action pattern* to refer to instinctive behaviour, and claimed that each fixed action pattern was produced in response to a given stimulus (known as a *sign stimulus* or a *releasing stimulus*). An example was given by Tinbergen (1951). When a female stickleback moves close to the territory of a male stickleback with a bright red stomach, the male responds by swimming in a zig-zag fashion. The female reacts to this by lifting her head and her tail, and by having her stomach sticking out as she swims. After that, the male swims to the nest, and points the top of his head in the direction of the entrance. The female then lays her eggs in the nest, and then leaves it. Finally, the male stickleback enters the nest and fertilises the eggs. Here we have several fixed action patterns with each one acting as the trigger for the next one.

The zig-zig swimming pattern of the male stickleback.

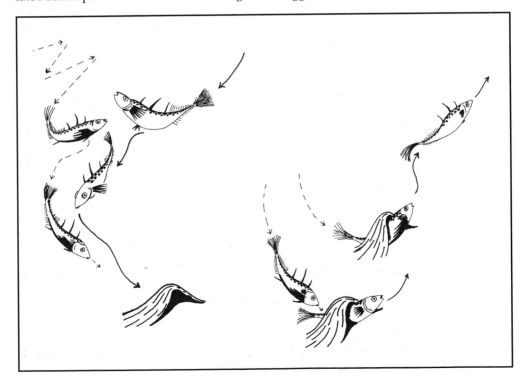

Fixed action patterns may look as if they involve no learning, but that is not usually the case. For example, Lorenz (1958) looked at a greylag goose that was incubating a nest of eggs. When an egg needed to be rolled back to the nest, the goose showed the fixed action pattern of stretching out its neck, putting the bottom of its beak on the far side of the egg, and pulling the egg. This fixed action pattern was not simply produced in exactly the same way regardless of the situation. If the egg started slipping away from the intended direction, the goose made sideways movements with its beak to sort out the problem.

Human species

We have seen that there is some evidence for instinctive behaviour in other species. What about the human species? Very little of human behaviour is instinctive, but there are a few exceptions. For example, consider *reflexes*, which are rapid, unlearned responses to stimuli. Newborn babies show the stepping reflex. If they are held by the armpits and gentle pressure is applied to the soles of their feet, they seem to step. Another reflex shown by newborn infants is the Moro reflex, in which the infant stretches its arms wide and then brings them together very rapidly when its head drops suddenly. These reflexes die out after a few days. It is not very clear what function these reflexes serve, but they seem to point ahead to later stages of development in which infants learn to walk and to protect themselves.

An important notion from the biological viewpoint is that of *maturation*. Maturation is involved when some aspect of children's development occurs with little or no influence of learning or experience. Some of the strongest evidence for maturation in humans was obtained by Gesell (1954). He studied the motor development of children during the first few years of their lives. They were observed at frequent intervals in standard conditions, and very precise measures of their behaviour were taken. What Gesell found was that the pattern of motor development was very similar in all young children. In general terms, the more developed and precise forms of motor behaviour occur first in the area around the head and only later in the lower parts of the body.

Nearly all other aspects of psychological development in humans depend mainly on learning rather than maturation. It has been argued that maturation plays an important part in the development of language. However, that argument remains controversial and unproved (see Chapter 9).

In sum, instinctive behaviour and maturation are less important to the human species than to other species. Most of the behaviour of adult humans depends mainly on learning and experience, but it is important not to ignore biological factors.

The nervous system

The brain forms a key part of the *nervous system*. The nervous system contains all of the nerve cells in the body. It is divided into two main subsystems:

- *Central nervous system:* this consists of the brain and the spinal cord, and is protected by bone and by fluid circulating around it.
- *Peripheral nervous system:* this consists of all the other nerve cells in the body; it is divided into the somatic nervous system, which is concerned with voluntary movements of skeletal muscles (those attached to our bones), and the autonomic nervous system, which is concerned with involuntary movements of non-skeletal muscles (e.g. those of the heart).

Central nervous system

As there is detailed coverage of the brain later in the chapter, we will focus here on the spinal cord part of the central nervous system. The *spinal cord* consists of a large collection of nerves running from the brain to the lower part of the back. This collection of nerves is protected by the vertebrae of the backbone.

The spinal cord has two major functions. One function is to pass sensory information on from the peripheral nervous system to the brain, with receptor nerves being used to do this. The other main function is to transmit motor information from the brain to peripheral nerves, with effector nerves being used for this purpose. The spinal cord and the brain usually work in a co-ordinated fashion. With reflexes, however, information goes directly from receptor nerves to effector nerves without involving the brain. An example of a reflex is your leg jerking forward when someone taps you on part of your knee. The knee-jerk reflex works very rapidly, and much faster than making a conscious decision to move your leg. Reflexes have the advantage of speed, but they have the disadvantage of working in a rather rigid and inflexible way.

Receptor nerves transmit information to the brain via the spinal cord. Instructions from the brain are sent via the effector nerves.

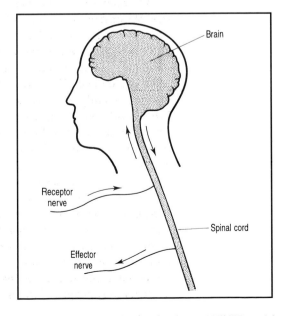

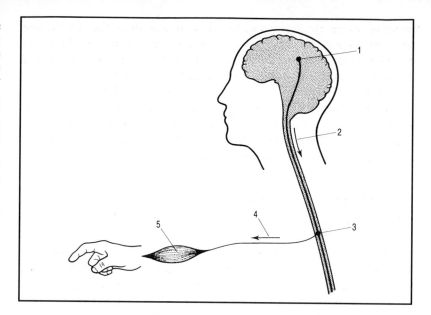

The somatic nervous system: What happens when you decide to move your fingers. 1) the decision arises in the brain; 2) is transmitted via the spinal cord; 3) transfers to another nerve (or series of nerves); 4) the instruction is transmitted to the skeletal muscles; 5) the muscles contract or relax, moving the fingers.

Peripheral nervous system

The peripheral nervous system is used to transmit information between the central nervous system and the receptors and effectors outside the central nervous system. The peripheral nervous system is linked up with receptors in external sensory organs such as the eyes and ears, and with receptors in internal structures such as the stomach.

As was mentioned earlier, the somatic nervous system controls the voluntary movements of our skeletal muscles. These skeletal muscles are also known as striated muscles, because they have striations or stripes. Nearly all of our movements, except those controlled by reflexes, involve the somatic nervous system.

The autonomic nervous system controls the movement of our non-skeletal muscles. The organs within the control of the autonomic nervous system include the heart, lungs, eyes, stomach, and the blood vessels of internal organs. The autonomic nervous system itself is divided into the *sympathetic nervous system* and the *parasympathetic nervous system*. The sympathetic nervous system is called into play in situations needing arousal and energy. It produces increased heart-rate, reduced activity within the stomach, pupil dilation or expansion, and relaxation of the bronchi of the lungs. These changes make people ready for fight or flight.

The parasympathetic nervous system is involved when the body is trying to save energy. The effects of activity in the parasympathetic nervous system are the opposite of those of activity in the sympathetic nervous system. The parasympathetic nervous system produces decreased heart-rate, increased activity within the stomach, pupil contraction, and constriction of the bronchi of the lungs.

The sympathetic nervous system and the parasympathetic nervous system are both important. For example, consider the case of someone having excessive activity of the sympathetic nervous system, but very little activity of the parasympathetic nervous system. He or she would almost certainly be a highly stressed person who found life very demanding.

Structure and function of the brain

The first point that needs to be made about the brain is its complexity. Thousands of psychologists and other scientists have studied the human brain, and yet there is still much about it that is unknown. In order to understand the brain, we need to learn about its structure and about the functions of its different parts. It has proved rather easier to study structure than function. If scientists open up the skull or cut sections of the brain and put them under slides, then they can obtain some idea of the ways in which the brain is structured or organised. However, it is much harder to know what is going on inside the living brain. It is only recently that technological advances have allowed us to see the functions of the brain by watching it in action.

At the most general level, the brain can be divided into three main regions: *forebrain*; *midbrain*; and *hindbrain*. It is important to note that these terms refer to their locations in an embryo's nervous system, and they do not indicate clearly the relative positions of the different brain regions in an adult. We will consider each of the main regions of the brain in turn. Because the forebrain is in many ways the most important part of the brain, we will start with it.

Forebrain

The forebrain is located towards the top and the front of the brain. It consists of four parts:

- *Cerebrum:* this contains 70% of all the neurons (nerve cells) in the central nervous system, and it plays a crucial role in thinking, use of language, and other cognitive skills.
- *Limbic system:* one main part of this system (the amygdala) is involved in anger and aggression; another main part (the hippo-

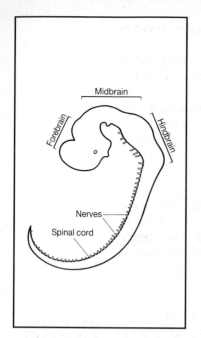

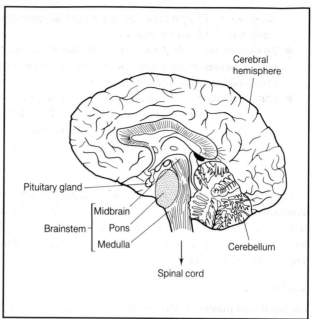

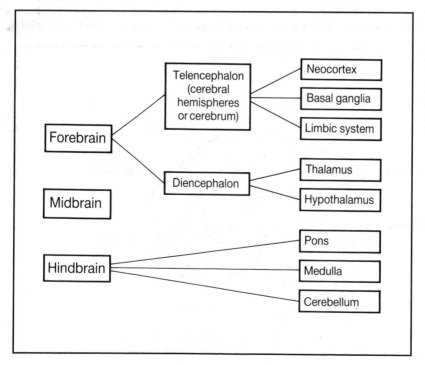

Top left: the nervous system of a 30-day-old embryo.
Top right: the mature brain.
Bottom left: the main subdivisions of the brain.

campus) is of importance in learning and memory; the septum is concerned with anger and fear.

- *Thalamus:* the main function of the thalamus is as a relay station which passes information on to higher brain centres; it is also involved in wakefulness and sleep.
- *Hypothalamus:* this structure serves a number of purposes, including the control of several autonomic functions such as body temperature, hunger, and thirst; it is also involved in the control of sexual behaviour and the endocrine (hormonal) system, and in reactions to stress.

It is in terms of the forebrain that the human species differs most clearly from other species. In particular, the development of the cerebrum and its outer layer (the cerebral cortex) distinguishes us from all other species. Indeed, the cerebral cortex is so important that it is dealt with at some length later in this chapter.

Midbrain

The midbrain plays a much less central role in human behaviour than the forebrain. However, it has various important functions. First, parts of the midbrain are involved in vision and in hearing, although most perceptual processes occur in the forebrain. Second, some parts of the midbrain are

Cross section of the human brain. The front of the brain is on the left.

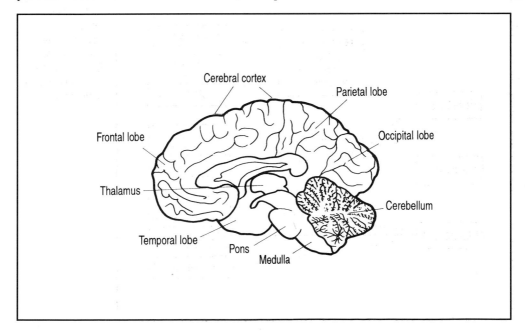

used in the control of movement. Third, the midbrain contains the *reticular activating system*, although parts of that system also extend into the hindbrain. The reticular activating system is an important structure in the control of consciousness. This covers the regulation of sleep, arousal, and wakefulness, in part through the influence of the reticular activating system on heart-rate and breathing-rate.

Hindbrain

In evolutionary terms, the hindbrain is a very old part of the brain. Its brain structures are like those of reptiles, leading the hindbrain to be called the "reptilian brain". It consists of three parts, each of which serves one or more important functions:

- *Medulla oblongata:* this is part of the reticular activating system, and is involved in the control of breathing, digestion, and swallowing, so damage to it can cause death; it is also the part of the hindbrain in which nerves from one side of the body cross to the other side of the brain.
- *Pons:* this is also part of the reticular activating system, being involved in the control of consciousness; it acts as a relay station passing messages between different parts of the brain; finally, cells associated with vision have been found in the pons, and it is very active during vivid dreams.
- *Cerebellum:* its main functions are the fine control of balance and bodily co-ordination generally; information about "over-learned" skills such as riding a bicycle or typing is stored in the cerebellum.

Cerebral cortex

The cerebral cortex is the outer layer of the cerebrum in the forebrain. It is only two millimetres deep, but has great importance for our ability to perceive, think, and use language. Those who have tried to understand which parts of the cerebral cortex are responsible for particular functions have divided it up in two ways. First, the cerebral cortex can be divided into four lobes or areas known as the frontal, parietal, temporal, and occipital. The lobes are anatomical regions named for the bones of the skull lying closest to them. The frontal lobe is at the front of the brain, and the occipital lobe is at the back of the brain. The other two lobes are in the middle of the brain, with the parietal lobe at the top of the brain and the temporal lobe below it. Second, the entire brain is divided into two hemispheres, and this has led psychologists to distinguish the left and right cerebral hemispheres.

Lobes of the cerebral cortex

The four lobes of the cerebral cortex differ somewhat in terms of what they do. Robert Sternberg (1995, p.93) provided a good summary of their functions: "higher thought processes, such as abstract reasoning and motor processing, occur in the frontal lobe, somatosensory processing (sensations in the skin and muscles of the body) in the parietal lobe, auditory processing in the temporal lobe, and visual processing in the occipital lobe".

The *frontal lobe* contains the primary motor cortex. This is involved in the planning and control of movements. Far more of the primary motor cortex is devoted to parts of the body that make very precise movements (e.g. the fingers) than to those that do not (e.g. the toes). In addition, the frontal lobe is involved in thinking and reasoning.

The *parietal lobe* contains the primary somatosensory cortex. This area receives information from various senses about temperature, pain, and pressure. Those parts of the body most represented in the primary motor cortex also tend to be well represented in the primary somatosensory cortex.

The *temporal lobe* is involved in auditory processing. The most important form of this processing is speech perception. Within the temporal

Side view of the brain showing the lobes of the hemispheres and the primary sensory motor areas.

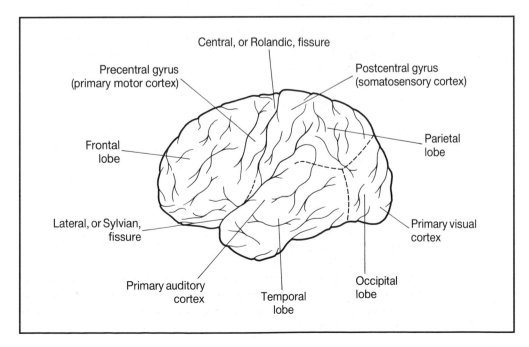

lobe, some parts respond most to certain kinds of sound (e.g. those high or low in pitch).

The *occipital lobe* is mainly concerned with visual processing. Nerve fibres from the right side of each eye go to the left occipital lobe, whereas those from the left side of each eye go to the right occipital lobe. If you are struck on the back of the head close to the occipital area, you will see "stars". The occipital lobe plays a key role in vision, but the temporal and parietal lobes are also involved. Indeed, it has been estimated that as much as 50% of the entire cerebral cortex is devoted to visual processing.

It is important to note that none of the four lobes is devoted exclusively to the processes described so far. Large areas within each lobe are *association areas*, which link sensory and motor processing. Association areas integrate or organise different kinds of sensory information to produce appropriate behaviour. The frontal association area in the frontal lobes is of great importance. It is centrally involved in complex planning and problem solving.

Hemispheric specialisation

So far we have discussed the cerebral cortex as if its two hemispheres or halves were very similar in their functioning. However, this is by no means the case. There is much *hemispheric specialisation*, meaning that the two hemispheres differ in their functions. This produces numerous situations in which there is *cerebral dominance*, with one hemisphere being mainly responsible for processing information in that situation.

Some of the earliest evidence about hemispheric specialisation was obtained by Paul Broca in the 1860s. He studied patients suffering from expressive aphasia, in which there is partial or total loss of the ability to

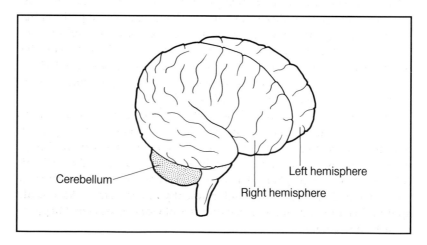

Cerebellum

Left hemisphere

Right hemisphere

The hemispheres of the brain.

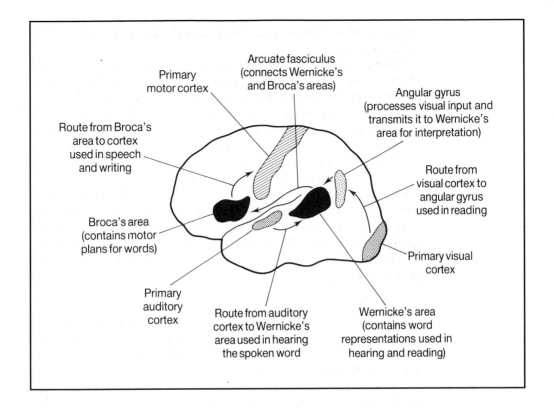

Primary motor cortex

Arcuate fasciculus (connects Wernicke's and Broca's areas)

Primary motor cortex

Angular gyrus (processes visual input and transmits it to Wernicke's area for interpretation)

Route from Broca's area to cortex used in speech and writing

Route from visual cortex to angular gyrus used in reading

Broca's area (contains motor plans for words)

Primary visual cortex

Primary auditory cortex

Route from auditory cortex to Wernicke's area used in hearing the spoken word

Wernicke's area (contains word representations used in hearing and reading)

speak. He found that these patients had brain damage in a part of the left cerebral hemisphere of the brain now known as *Broca's area*. A few years later, Carl Wernicke studied other patients who were able to speak, but who had very poor ability to understand language. These patients had suffered damage to another part of the left cerebral hemisphere later called *Wernicke's area*. The findings of Broca and Wernicke suggested that the left hemisphere is specialised for language. This is so for about 85% of adults. The other 15% either have language in the right hemisphere or language processing occurs in both hemispheres.

Much of our knowledge of hemispheric specialisation and cerebral dominance comes from the study of *split-brain patients*. These patients had suffered from severe epilepsy. They had the *corpus callosum* or bridge between the two hemispheres surgically cut to contain the epileptic seizures to one hemisphere. The two hemispheres of the brain in these patients function more or less independently of each other. As a result, split-brain patients provide an exciting way of working out what happens in each hemisphere.

The left hemisphere language system.

There is evidence that language is centred in the left hemisphere, whereas most visual and spatial processing takes place in the right hemisphere. Relevant research has been carried out in the United States by Roger Sperry, Michael Gazzaniga, and their colleagues. Consider, for example, the following study by Levy et al. (1972). Split-brain patients were shown faces, in which the left half of one person's face was presented next to the right half of another person's face. These faces were presented very briefly to prevent the eyes moving during presentation. This made sure that information about the right half of the picture went to the left hemisphere, and information about the left half of the picture went to the right hemisphere. The patients were asked to say what they had seen. They generally reported seeing the right half of the picture. However, when they were asked to use their fingers to point to what they saw, most of the patients pointed to the left half of the picture. These findings suggest that language is mainly (or exclusively) based in the left hemisphere, whereas the spatial processing involved in pointing to something depends far more on the right hemisphere.

Sperry and his colleagues have carried out other research which leads to the same conclusion. In one study, a picture of an object was presented briefly to the right hemisphere. Split-brain patients were usually unable to say the name of the object, presumably because the right hemisphere possesses very poor language abilities. After that, the patients were asked to put their left hands behind a screen and try to decide which of the objects hidden there corresponded to the picture. Most of the patients were able to do this because of the good ability of the right hemisphere to process spatial information.

You can test some of these ideas by doing a simple experiment which was originally devised by Kinsbourne in the 1960s. You balance a rod on either the right or the left index finger for as long as possible. If right-handed people do this while remaining silent, they can balance the rod longer on the right index finger than on the left. However, if they talk while they try to balance the rod, then the opposite result is obtained: they can now balance the rod longer on the left index finger than on the right. It is as if speaking knocks the rod off the right index finger.

What is happening here? Speech and the right hand are both controlled by the left hemisphere, and so interfere with each other. In contrast, speech and the left hand are controlled by different hemispheres, and so hardly interfere with each other.

Some theorists have used findings from split-brain patients to argue that the two hemispheres are very different from each other. According to Levy (1974), the right hemisphere usually processes information in a holistic fashion (as a whole), whereas the left hemisphere processes information in an analytic fashion (bit by bit).

The findings from split-brain patients are dramatic. However, we must be careful not to fall into the trap of assuming that the two hemispheres of normal individuals are independent of each other. For those having an intact corpus callosum, information is transferred from one hemisphere to the other in a few milliseconds. As a result, our two hemispheres normally function together in a co-operative fashion. Indeed, even split-brain patients function very well unless special experiments are set up to show their limitations. Remember that most of the studies on split-brain patients we have discussed involved presenting visual information so rapidly that no eye movements were made during presentation. When split-brain patients look at a visual stimulus long enough for eye movements to be made, then the visual information goes into both hemispheres. As a result, they are able to say what has been presented, and to point to the right object.

Brain organisation

Theorists have used our growing knowledge of the workings of the brain (and especially the cerebral cortex) to put forward accounts of brain organisation. For example, Volkow and Tancredi (1991) argued that brain functioning is based on three basic principles, each of which will be considered in turn.

The first principle is that the brain is *interconnected*. It is assumed that there are numerous modules (relatively independent groupings of cells) handling different parts of a task. The outputs of these modules are then combined and integrated, because the modules are interconnected. Evidence for the existence of modules comes from brain-damaged patients who have very specific problems. For example, patients suffering from prosopagnosia cannot recognise familiar faces even though their visual perception otherwise is almost normal. Perhaps a small number of modules relevant to face recognition have been damaged.

The second principle is that the brain organisation is *hierarchical*. The basic idea is that processing exists at a number of levels, starting with limited processing of specific kinds of information and moving on to more general and integrated processing. In the case of vision, early processing modules respond to information about the edges of lines and to line orientation, with later processing modules integrating this information to work out what object or objects are present.

The third principle is that of *functional differentation*, which means that any given brain area tends to be responsible for specific functions. For example, the temporal lobes are mainly involved in hearing, whereas the occipital lobes are mainly involved with vision. The principle of functional differentiation is also supported by the evidence for hemispheric specialisation.

Ways of studying the brain

So far we have focused mainly on the structure of the brain rather than on the ways in which it functions. As was mentioned earlier, it is easier to study structure than function. However, much progress has been made in recent years in understanding how the brain works. This progress is due to exciting technological advances. Before turning to recently developed methods, we will consider two methods invented several decades ago.

Electroencephalogram (EEG)

The electroencephalogram (EEG) is based on electrical recordings taken from the scalp. It was first used by Hans Berger over 65 years ago. Very small changes in electrical activity within the brain are picked up by electrodes placed on the scalp. These changes are shown on the screen of a cathode-ray tube by means of an instrument known as an oscilloscope. The pattern of changes is sometimes referred to as "brain waves".

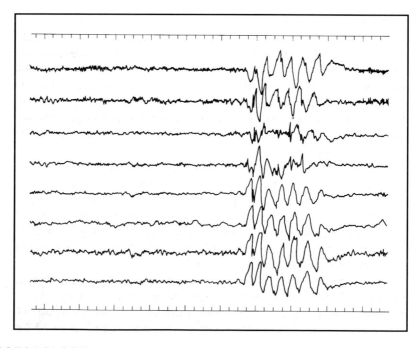

An EEG trace. Each line is drawn by a pen connected to an electrode placed on a specific point on the scalp. The left-hand side of the trace shows the signals from a resting brain. The jagged "peaks" on the right are in response to an epileptic seizure.

The EEG has proved useful in many ways. For example, it has been found that there are five stages of sleep, varying in terms of the depth of sleep and the presence or absence of dream activity. These stages differ in terms of the EEG record, and EEG research was of great importance in identifying these stages. Dreaming occurs during rapid eye movement or REM sleep, in which the EEG is irregular and there are numerous rapid eye movements.

The EEG has also been of value in identifying the functions of the two hemispheres of the brain. There is more activity in the left hemisphere than in the right hemisphere when someone is carrying out a language-based task, but the opposite is the case during a spatial task (Kosslyn, 1988). These findings confirm those from other lines of research, such as that on brain-damaged patients.

In spite of these successes, the EEG is no longer used very much in research. Why is this? The EEG is a rather blunt instrument in two ways. First, it measures electrical activity in several different areas of the brain at once, and so it is hard to work out which parts of the brain are more and less active. Second, it is an indirect measure of brain activity, because the recording electrodes are on the scalp rather than in the brain itself. This has led to the EEG being compared to trying to hear what people are saying in the next room by putting your ear to the wall.

Evoked potentials

Some years after the invention of the EEG, it was found that much could be learned about cognitive processes by using a related method known as *evoked potentials*. A stimulus is presented several times, and the EEG recordings obtained from each presentation are then averaged. Why is this done? There is so much EEG activity going on all the time in the brain that it can be hard to detect the effects of stimulus processing on brain-wave activity. Several trials are needed to distinguish genuine effects of stimulation from background brain activity.

One of the many ways in which evoked potentials have been of use, is in studying selective attention. Some psychologists argue that unattended stimuli are processed as thoroughly as attended stimuli, whereas others claim that unattended stimuli are hardly processed at all. Who is right? The evidence indicates that unattended stimuli are not processed as thoroughly as attended ones, because the evoked potentials to unattended stimuli are much smaller (Loveless, 1983).

The method of evoked potentials has the great advantage that it provides a detailed moment-by-moment record of brain activity when a stimulus is being processed. However, there are two major limitations. First, it is not possible to identify with any precision which parts of the

Summary

- Darwin's theory of evolution led psychologists to develop theories of psychology from the biological perspective.
- The behaviour of lower species such as ants and bees is less influenced by learning than is the behaviour of higher species such as apes and humans.
- Some species (e.g. geese) produce instinctive behaviour in the form of fixed action patterns to sign stimuli or releasing stimuli.
- The nervous system consists of the central nervous system and the peripheral nervous system; the latter is divided into the somatic nervous system and the autonomic nervous system.
- The spinal cord passes on information in both directions between the brain and the peripheral nervous system.
- The autonomic nervous system controls the heart, lungs, eyes, stomach, and the blood vessels of internal organs; it is divided into the sympathetic nervous system and the parasympathetic nervous system.
- The brain can be divided into three main regions: forebrain; midbrain; and hindbrain.
- The forebrain consists of the cerebrum (used in thinking), the limbic system (involved in aggression, fear, learning, and memory), the thalamus (a relay station), and the hypothalamus (used in the control of several autonomic functions).
- The midbrain is used in the control of movement; it contains much of the reticular activating system, which controls sleep, arousal, and wakefulness.
- The hindbrain or "reptilian brain" consists of the medulla oblongata (used in the control of breathing, digestion, and swallowing), the pons (used as a relay station), and the cerebellum (used in the control of balance).
- The cerebral cortex is the outer layer of the cerebrum; it consists of the frontal lobe (front of the brain), the occipital lobe (back of the brain), the parietal lobe (top of the brain), and the temporal lobe (in the lower part of the brain).
- Higher thought processes occur in the frontal lobe, sensations from the skin and muscles are processed in the parietal lobe, visual processing occurs in the occipital lobe, and auditory processing in the temporal lobe.
- The cerebral cortex exhibits hemispheric specialisation, with the two hemispheres differing in their functions; language is usually centred in the left hemisphere, whereas most visual and spatial processing occurs in the right hemisphere.

Summary (continued)

- Some of the evidence for hemispheric specialisation comes from split-brain patients, in whom the corpus callosum or bridge between the two hemispheres has been cut to reduce severe epilepsy.
- The brain seems to operate according to three principles: interconnectedness; hierarchical structure; and functional differentiation.
- The EEG is based on the detection of very small changes in electrical activity within the brain by scalp electrodes; it has been used to identify the various stages of sleep and to study the functions of the two hemispheres of the brain.
- Evoked potentials are based on averaging the EEG recordings from several presentations of the same stimulus; they provide a moment-by-moment record of brain activity.
- Computerised axial tomography or CAT scans and magnetic-resonance imaging or MRI scans provide detailed information about brain structures.
- Positron-emission tomography or PET scans provide a motion picture of the activity levels of different parts of the brain, and so tell us about brain functions; however, they do not provide moment-by-moment information.

Key terms

Association areas: areas within the **cerebral cortex** in which sensory and motor processes are linked.

Broca's area: a part of the **cerebral cortex** in the left hemisphere of the brain involved in speech production.

Central nervous system: the brain and spinal cord; it is protected by bone and by cerebrospinal fluid.

Cerebral cortex: the outer layer of the **cerebrum**; it is involved in perception, thinking, and language, and consists of the **frontal lobe**, the **occipital lobe**, the **parietal lobe**, and the **temporal lobe**.

Cerebral dominance: the notion that many perceptual, thought, and language processes within the **cerebral cortex** occur mainly in one **hemisphere.**

Computerised axial tomography (CAT scan): three-dimensional pictures of a cross-section of the brain produced with the use of X-rays.

Corpus callosum: the bridge between the two hemispheres of the brain.

Electroencephalogram (EEG): a record of changes in electrical activity within the brain, also known as "brain waves".

Ethology: an approach to animal psychology that involves studying animals in their natural surroundings.

Evoked potentials: a record of changes in electrical activity within the brain, based on averaging the brain's response to repeated presentations of a stimulus; see **electroencephalogram**.

Fixed action pattern: a term used within ethology to refer to a fixed pattern of behaviour which does not depend on learning; see **instinctive behaviour**.

Forebrain: an area towards the top and the front of the brain, consisting of the cerebrum, limbic system, thalamus, and hypothalamus.

Frontal lobe: a part of the **cerebral cortex** concerned with the planning and control of movements and with higher thought processes.

Hemispheric specialisation: each hemisphere or half of the brain carries out its own specific functions to some extent.

Hindbrain: the "reptilian brain", concerned with breathing, digestion, swallowing, the fine control of balance, and the control of consciousness.

Instinctive behaviour: behavour that is produced in the absence of any learning.

Magnetic-resonance imaging (MRI scans): three-dimensional pictures of the brain based on the detection of magnetic changes; see **computerised axial tomography**.

Maturation: aspects of development in children owing little to learning or experience.

Midbrain: the middle part of the brain; it is involved in vision, hearing, and the control of movement. It also contains most of the **reticular activating system**.

Nature/nurture controversy: the issue of the relative importance of nature (or heredity) and nurture (or environment) in determining behaviour.

Nervous system: the system containing all the nerve cells in the body; it consists of the **central nervous system** and the **peripheral nervous system**.

Key terms (continued)

Occipital lobe: a part of the **cerebral cortex** concerned with visual processing.

Parasympathetic nervous system: the part of the autonomic nervous system reducing arousal and energy use; its effects are the opposite of those of the **sympathetic nervous system**.

Parietal lobe: a part of the **cerebral cortex** concerned with information about temperature, pain, and pressure.

Peripheral nervous system: this consists of the somatic nervous system (concerned with voluntary movements of skeletal muscles) and the autonomic nervous system (concerned with involuntary movements of non-skeletal muscles).

Positron-emission tomography (PET scans): pictures of brain activity based on radioactive glucose levels within the brain.

Reflexes: Rapid, unlearned responses to stimuli; reflexes do not involve the brain.

Reticular activating system: a system mainly in the **midbrain**; it controls consciousness, and regulates sleep, arousal, and wakefulness.

Sign stimulus: within **ethology**, the stimulus that triggers a **fixed action pattern**.

Spinal cord: a large collection of nerves going between the brain and the lower part of the back; part of the **central nervous system**.

Split-brain patients: patients who have had the **corpus callosum** cut in order to reduce severe epileptic seizures; in these patients, the two hemispheres of the brain work separately to some extent.

Sympathetic nervous system: the part of the autonomic nervous system producing arousal and energy; it prepares for fight or flight, and its effects are the opposite of those of the **parasympathetic nervous system**.

Temporal lobe: a part of the cerebral cortex concerned with auditory processing.

Wernicke's area: a part of the **cerebral cortex** in the left hemisphere of the brain concerned with language understanding.

Structured essay questions

1. What is the nervous system? What is it used for?
2. What are the main areas of the cerebral cortex? What is the function of each area?
3. What are the main functions of each hemisphere of the brain? What evidence is there for cerebral dominance and hemispheric specialisation?
4. What methods have been developed for studying the brain? What are the advantages and disadvantages of these methods?

Self-assessment questions

1. Which of the following is true:
   a) instinctive behaviour is more common in other species than in humans
   b) instinctive behaviour is more common in humans than in other species
   c) instinctive behaviour is equally common in humans and other species
   d) instinctive behaviour is rare in all species

2. The nervous system:
   a) is a single system
   b) is divided into the central nervous system and the peripheral nervous system
   c) is divided into several smaller systems
   d) none of the above

3. The autonomic nervous system:
   a) is another term for the nervous system
   b) consists only of the sympathetic nervous system
   c) consists of the sympathetic nervous system and the parasympathetic nervous system
   d) consists only of the parasympathetic nervous system

4. The brain can be divided into:
   a) front and back regions
   b) four quarters
   c) outer and inner regions
   d) forebrain, midbrain, and hindbrain

5. The lobes of the cerebral cortex are known as:
   a) frontal, temporal, and occipital
   b) parietal, temporal, and occipital
   c) frontal, parietal, temporal, and occipital
   d) frontal, parietal, and occipital

6. Hemispheric specialisation means that:
   a) the two hemispheres differ in their functioning
   b) the two hemispheres do not differ in their functioning
   c) the left hemisphere is larger than the right hemisphere
   d) the right hemisphere is larger than the left hemisphere

7. Split-brain patients:
   a) have massive brain damage
   b) have had the corpus callosum surgically cut
   b) are born with unusual brains
   c) have more fragile brains than other people

8. Brain functioning is based on the following principles:
   a) it is interconnected, has hierarchical organisation, and has functional differentiation
   b) it is interconnected, lacks hierarchical organisation, and lacks functional differentiation
   c) it is not interconnected, has hierarchical organisation, and has functional differentiation
   d) none of the above

9. Of the various different kinds of brain scanners:
   a) CAT scans tell us more about the brain in action than do MRI or PET scans
   b) MRI scans tell us more about the brain in action than do CAT or PET scans
   c) PET scans tell us more about the brain in action than do CAT or MRI scans
   d) none of the above

Stress 4

In the last chapter, there was some discussion of the sympathetic nervous system. This is the part of the autonomic system that is involved in producing arousal and energy. In our everyday lives, high levels of activity within the sympathetic nervous system are often found when we are feeling stressed and are finding it hard to cope. It is because stress has this important biological aspect to it that it is dealt with in the section on the biological approach to psychology. However, there are several kinds of changes that occur inside someone when he or she is stressed. Many psychologists have argued that there are four major kinds of effects associated with the stressed state: emotional; physiological; cognitive; and behavioural. Here are some specific examples of what stress looks like:

1. *Emotional effects*
   - Feelings of anxiety and depression
   - Increased physical tension
   - Increased psychological tension
2. *Physiological effects*
   - Release of adrenaline and noradrenaline
   - Shut-down of digestive system
   - Expansion of air passages in lungs
   - Increased heart-rate
   - Constriction of blood vessels
3. *Cognitive effects*
   - Poor concentration
   - Increased distractibility
   - Reduced short-term memory capacity
4. *Behavioural effects*
   - Increased absenteeism
   - Disrupted sleep patterns
   - Reduced work performance

What causes stress? One answer is provided by the engineering model (Cox, 1978). According to this approach, stress is something that happens

---

Personal viewpoint

We all know the feeling of being stressed; indeed, some people have argued that most of us are more stressed than ever. However, the term "stress" is often used in a rather vague way. What do you think are some of the main signs of stress? In your everyday life, what are the main factors that cause you stress? How do you try to cope with the stress that you experience? How successful are these attempts to cope with stress?

to us when we are exposed to a stressor (e.g. a forthcoming examination; intense noise). This approach might work well if we all responded in the same way to any given situation. However, we do not. Someone taking their first driving lesson finds driving very stressful, whereas an experienced driver generally does not.

The transactional model (Cox, 1978) is better able than the engineering model to account for individual differences in the stress produced by a given situation. According to the transactional model, stress depends on the interaction between an individual and his or her environment. More specifically, stress occurs when the perceived demands of a situation exceed the individual's perceived ability to handle those demands. Driving is stressful to a learner driver because he or she has limited ability to meet the demands of handling a car in traffic. It is not stressful to experienced drivers because they are confident that their driving ability will allow them to cope with most driving situations.

Those individuals who believe they have control over a stressful situation feel less stress than those who believe they have no control. For example, there is much greater tolerance of shock among those who think they can control it than among those who do not (Bowers, 1968).

Lazarus (1982) put forward an influential approach resembling the transactional model. According to him, cognitive appraisal plays a key role in emotional experience (see Chapter 5). Cognitive appraisal consists of two main forms of appraisal:

- *Primary appraisal:* the situation is regarded as being positive, stressful, or irrelevant to well-being.
- *Secondary appraisal:* account is taken of the resources that the individual has available to cope with the situation.

Within this framework, stress is experienced when primary appraisal indicates that the situation is stressful, and secondary appraisal indicates that there are inadequate resources available to cope with it.

Physiology of stress

As we have already seen, people in a stressful situation show a variety of physiological effects. Most of these effects prepare the body to face up to the challenge of the situation or to escape from the situation. In other words, the body prepares itself for fight or flight.

Some of the most influential work on the physiological effects of stress was carried out by Hans Selye (1950). He studied hospital patients with various injuries and illnesses, and noticed that they all seemed to show a similar pattern of bodily response. Selye called this pattern the *general adaptation syndrome*. He argued that it consists of three stages:

1. *The alarm reaction stage:* there is activation of the sympathetic branch of the autonomic nervous system, leading to greater arousal. The *sympathetic nervous system* triggers the release of hormones from the adrenal glands; these hormones include adrenaline, noradrenaline, and corticosteroids. These hormones have several effects: heart and respiration rate are increased; activity in the digestive system is slowed down or stopped; more blood is made available to other organs; muscle tension is created; there is increased energy consumption, producing heat; there is increased perspiration, which cools the body; and there is increased release of clotting factors into the bloodsteam to reduce blood loss in case of injury.
2. *The resistance stage:* the physiological efforts to deal with stress that started in the alarm reaction stage are at full capacity; however, as this stage proceeds, the *parasympathetic nervous system* (which is involved in energy-storing processes) calls for more careful use of the body's resources. There is also much use of coping strategies (e.g. denying that the situation is stressful).
3. *The exhaustion stage:* eventually the physiological systems used in the alarm reaction and resistance stages become ineffective, and stress-related disease (e.g. high blood pressure; asthma; heart disease) becomes more likely. In extreme cases, there is enlargement of the adrenal cortex, shrinkage of parts of the body's immune system (e.g. the spleen and thymus), and bleeding stomach ulcers.

Psychology of stress

We have seen that there are several physiological processes which enable individuals to cope with stressful situations. There are also various psychological processes or *coping strategies* which can be used to reduce stress. These coping strategies have often been assessed by means of self-report measures such as the Multidimensional Coping Inventory (Endler & Parker, 1990). This inventory measures the use of three major coping strategies:

- *Task-oriented strategy:* this involves obtaining information about the stressful situation and about alternative courses of action and

---

Sample Items from the Multidimensional Coping Inventory

Task-oriented coping
1. Outline my priorities
2. Work to understand the problem
3. Think about the event and learn from my mistakes

Emotion-oriented coping
1. Become very tense
2. Blame myself for being too emotional about the situation
3. Fantasise about how things might turn out

Avoidance-oriented coping
1. Treat myself to a favourite food or snack
2. Visit a friend
3. Take time off and get away from the situation

---

their probable outcome; it also involves deciding priorities and acting so as to deal directly with the stressful situation.

- *Emotion-oriented strategy:* this can involve efforts to maintain hope and to control one's emotions; it can also involve venting feelings of anger and frustration, or deciding that nothing can be done to change things.
- *Avoidance-oriented strategy:* this involves denying or minimising the seriousness of the situation; it also involves conscious suppression of stressful thoughts and their replacement by self-protective thoughts.

There are considerable individual differences in usage of these coping strategies. Those who are high in *trait anxiety*, and thus experience much stress and anxiety, tend to use the emotion-oriented and avoidance-oriented strategies rather than the task-oriented strategy (Endler & Parker, 1990). The situation is very different in those with the *Type A Behaviour Pattern*. Such individuals are competitive, have a chronic sense of time urgency, and express hostility towards others. They have a strong tendency to use the task-oriented strategy, even when it is not appropriate (Eysenck, 1994).

Which kind of coping strategy is most effective in reducing stress? There is no simple answer to this question, because the effectiveness of any coping strategy depends on the nature of the stressful situation. In general terms, task-oriented coping tends to be most effective when the

Time pressure
Always working against the clock
Doing two or more things at once
Irritation with slow-moving traffic or queues
Impatience with others
Agitation when forced to do nothing

Competitiveness
Always playing games to win
Very self-critical
Measuring success as material productivity

Anger and hostility
Feelings of anger, both towards the outside world and sometimes towards oneself

individual has the resources to sort out the stressful situation. On the other hand, emotion-oriented coping or avoidance-oriented coping is preferable when the individual cannot resolve the situation.

Ways of measuring stress

Numerous ways of measuring stress have been used by psychologists. However, nearly all of the measures belong to one of the four following groups: self-report; physiological; biochemical; and performance. This section is organised according to this framework.

Self-report measures

The most common way of assessing stress is by means of self-report questionnaires, in which individuals answer a series of questions about their mental and/or physical state. For example, use is often made of mood adjective checklists such as the Multiple Affect Adjective Check List (Zuckerman & Lubin, 1965) and the Profile of Mood States (McNair, Lorr, & Droppelman, 1971). These checklists provide an overall score for mood disturbance, plus scores for specific stress-related moods such as anxiety, depression, and guilt.

An example of a self-report questionnaire measuring the anxiety component of stress is Zung's (1978) Self-rating Anxiety Scale. This contains questions designed to find out the extent to which the individual experiences various symptoms, including the following: nervousness and anxiety; shaking and trembling; headaches; weakness and tiredness;

stomach aches and indigestion; blushing; feelings of panic; nightmares; feeling afraid for no good reason.

More severe signs of stress, including some psychiatric symptoms, can also be assessed by self-report questionnaires. One of the most used of such questionnaires is the General Health Questionnaire (Goldberg, 1972). It assesses the symptoms of depression, anxiety, behavioural disturbances, and hypochondriasis (excessive anxiety about one's health).

How useful are self-report measures? On the positive side, it seems reasonable to find out how stressed someone is by asking them. Self-report measures also have the advantage of being quick and easy to use. On the negative side, such measures are open to bias. Individuals who are experiencing stress may exaggerate and distort their symptoms. On the other hand, some individuals may minimise how stressed they are.

Physiological measures

There are several physiological measures that provide indications of the level of sympathetic nervous system arousal. These measures include heart-rate, blood pressure, skin temperature, as well as changes in EEG patterns (brain-wave activity), respiration rate, and muscle tension. Until fairly recently, these physiological measures were mainly obtained under laboratory conditions. The reason why they were rarely obtained in field research was because of the bulky equipment that was needed. However, as a result of technological advances, it is now possible to use small portable recording devices to record heart-rate, skin conductance, and other measures.

How useful are physiological measures? There is no doubt that high levels of stress have effects on all the measures that have been mentioned. However, there are various problems with these measures:

- They provide an *indirect* rather than a direct assessment of the functioning of the sympathetic nervous system.
- The measures are not only affected by stress; excitement and concentration both affect several physiological measures.
- The different measures do not usually show much agreement with each other; this makes it hard to estimate the underlying level of sympathetic nervous system arousal.

Biochemical measures

General sympathetic arousal can be assessed by taking a variety of biochemical measures. Among the most used biochemical measures are those involving the following hormones: *adrenaline, noradrenaline,* and *cortisol.* The levels of these hormones can be assessed either in the bloodstream or in urine. The main problems with assessing hormone levels from blood samples are the complexity of the procedures and the need for medical supervision. The main problem with using urine samples is that they provide an indication of the level of stress over a period of several hours. As a result, it is not possible to pinpoint the time at which stress was experienced.

Adrenaline, noradrenaline, and cortisol are all very useful measures of stress. However, high levels of these hormones can occur in the absence of stress. If someone is running or trying hard to solve a problem, then hormone levels will rise.

Performance measures

High levels of stress are often associated with poor levels of performance. Patrick (1934) gave his subjects the task of discovering which of four doors was locked. As the same door was never unlocked on two successive trials, the best strategy was to try each of the other three doors in turn. When the conditions were non-stressful, the best strategy was followed 60% of the time. This figure dropped to 20% when the subjects were stressed by having cold water streams directed at them, or had their ears blasted by a car horn, or were given continuous electric shocks.

The finding that performance becomes worse at high levels of stress is consistent with what is known as the *Yerkes-Dodson law* (Yerkes & Dodson, 1908). According to this law, performance is best when the level of arousal or stress is intermediate, and it becomes worse as stress increases or decreases from that level. Much of the evidence supports this law.

Yerkes and Dodson also argued that the level of stress leading to the best performance is lower for hard tasks than for easy ones. Thus, a high level of stress should have worse effects on hard tasks than on easy ones. Mayer (1977) found that stressed individuals did well with easy arithmetical problems, but did worse than non-stressed individuals when faced with complex problems.

The main problem with performance measures of stress is that stress has somewhat variable effects on performance. Stressed individuals sometimes maintain their level of performance by trying harder (Eysenck & Calvo, 1992). In addition, there are various reasons why someone might perform a task poorly. Stress is one reason, but lack of motivation or lack of relevant knowledge are others.

Conclusions

Self-report, physiological, biochemical, and behavioural measures of stress have all now been considered. Each type of measure has its own advantages and disadvantages. This means that we cannot really say that one type of measure is better than any of the others. In the light of the available evidence, the most appropriate conclusion is probably the following: "self-report, performance, psychophysiological, and biochemical measures of stress are not necessarily highly intercorrelated [in good agreement]. Each approach provides unique kinds of information, and a combination of all of them is likely to offer an optimal understanding of stress outcomes" (Martin, 1989).

Causes of stress

There are very many different causes of stress, and it would be impossible to discuss them all here. However, various categories of factors causing stress can be identified. One category is stressful life events, which occur mainly as a result of our relationships with other people. Another major category is that of environmental stressors such as noise and heat. Other categories are those of technological threats (such as those posed by nuclear power), and the "sick building syndrome". All these types of factors causing stress will be considered in turn.

As we will see, the amount of stress we experience when exposed to stressors such as noise or heat depends on a number of factors. However, as Cohen (1986) pointed out, feelings of control are of central importance. In general terms, any stressor is likely to have more severe effects on us when we feel unable to control it.

Stressful life events

Some of the best-known work on stressful life events was reported by Holmes and Rahe (1967). They found that patients tended to have experienced several stressful life events in the months preceding their illness. This led them to develop the *Social Readjustment Rating Scale*, on which people indicate which out of 43 life events have happened to them over a period of time (generally six months or twelve months). These life events are assigned a value in terms of their likely impact. The panel on the opposite page shows the top six and the bottom six items from the questionnaire, with the value in life change units shown in brackets.

You may be surprised to see holidays and Christmas regarded as sources of stress. However, Holmes and Rahe (1967) argued that any change (whether desirable or undesirable) can be stressful. Thus, for example, they included marital reconciliation (45 life change units), gain of a new family member (39), and outstanding personal achievement (28) among the 43 life events.

There have been numerous studies using the Social Readjustment Scale. Those experiencing events totalling more than 300 life change units

Stressful life-events

Ranking of some stressful life events. Life change units are given in brackets.

Top six

1. Death of spouse (100)
2. Divorce (73)
3. Marital separation (65)
4. Jail term (63)
5. Death of close family member (63)
6. Personal injury or illness (53)

Bottom six

38. Change in sleeping habits (16)
39. Change in number of family get-togethers (15)
40. Change in eating habits (15)
41. Vacation (13)
42. Christmas (12)
43. Minor violations of the law (11)

What are the advantages and disadvantages of the Social Readjustment Scale?

PLUS

- The Social Readjustment Scale has generated a considerable amount of interesting research.
- It is reasonable to assume that life events affect stress-related illnesses.

MINUS

- It is often not clear whether life events have caused some stress- related illness, or whether stress caused the life events; for example, stress may play an important part in producing life events such as marital separation, change in sleeping habits, or change in eating habits.
- The impact of most life events varies from person to person; for example, marital separation may be less stressful to someone who has already established an intimate relationship with someone else.
- Memory failures can reduce the usefulness of the Scale: people are often rather poor at remembering minor life events from several months ago.
- Holmes and Rahe assumed that desirable life events could cause stress-related illnesses; however, most of the evidence does not support this assumption (Martin, 1989).

over a period of one year or so are more at risk for a wide range of physical and mental illnesses. These illnesses include heart attacks, diabetes, TB, asthma, anxiety, and depression. However, it should be emphasised that the correlations between life change units and susceptibility to any particular illness tend to be rather low. Thus, there is only a weak association between life events and illness.

Noise

Many people, especially those living in large cities or near airports, find that noise is a major source of stress in their everyday lives. There is growing awareness of "noise pollution". Research indicates that intense noise increases physiological arousal in several ways: increased heart-rate, increased blood pressure, higher levels of adrenaline and noradrenaline, and so on (Eysenck, 1982). It has also been found that these physiological effects tend to increase in line with the intensity of noise (Eysenck, 1982).

We might assume that it is the intensity of noise that determines how annoying or stressful it is. However, there are several other aspects of noise that influence its effects. Borsky (1969) identified five factors other than intensity which cause noise to be regarded as stressful:

1. It is perceived as unnecessary.
2. The people responsible for the noise are thought to be unconcerned about its effects on others.

Photo courtesy TRIP, photographer D. Rayers.

3. The individual dislikes other features of the environment (e.g. overcrowding).
4. The individual believes that noise is harmful to health.
5. The noise is associated with fear.

Cerderloff et al. (1967) provided clear evidence that the stressfulness of noise does not only depend on its intensity. Some of those living near a Swedish airforce base were sent a souvenir book celebrating the 50th anniversary of the Royal Swedish Airforce. According to the (false) information in the book, all of their neighbours felt that the airforce was of vital importance to the country. This information had the effect of reducing the perceived stressfulness of aircraft noise, and this effect was still present several years later.

If loud noise causes stress, then it should often reduce performance. This prediction has been tested several times, generally using white noise (meaningless noise consisting of all sound frequencies and sounding like hissing). One of the main findings is that people carrying out a fairly complex task in loud noise find it hard to maintain their concentration on the task (Broadbent, 1957). However, what someone *expects* the effects of noise to be helps to determine its actual effects. Noise tends to worsen work performance in those who expect it to, whereas those who expect noise to improve performance tend to benefit from its introduction (Mech, 1953).

Heat

There is much anecdotal evidence that we tend to be more irritable and stressed when the weather is very hot. In the United States, it has been found that group violence in cities is much more common during the hot summer months than at other times of year. There is experimental evidence to support the notion that extreme heat is stressful. In one study (Griffitt & Veitch, 1971), subjects were exposed to a temperature of 93.5°F (34°C). This caused them to feel more aggressive, tired, and sad, and it reduced their vigour and ability to concentrate. In addition, they also felt more negative about other people.

The precise effects of heat on people's moods and behaviour do not only depend on how extreme it is. Some relevant evidence was reported by Baron and Bell (1976). They studied the effects of heat on aggression by seeing how willing participants were to give electric shocks to another person. Temperatures within the range 92–95°F (33–35°C) generally increased the level of aggression. Somewhat surprisingly, extreme heat was associated with a reduced level of aggression towards another person when that person had provided a negative evaluation of the subject. In those conditions, the participants were very stressed. If they gave shocks to the other person, they would have to deal with his angry reactions, and they felt unable to deal with the added stress.

The effects of heat on work performance have also been studied. The maximum temperature at which workers can carry out continuous mental work without their performance being impaired is about 87°F (31°C) over a four-hour period (Wing, 1972). However, temperatures as high as 93°F (34°C) can be coped with if the work period is no longer than one hour.

An important factor in determining whether heat will reduce work performance is the worker's skill level. Mackworth (1961) studied telegraphy workers who had skill levels ranging between poor and good. The adverse effects of heat on performance were much greater among those with poor skill levels. Ramsey (1983) explained this, and other findings, in the following way: "If the work task does not load the operator, the addition of heat creates an arousal effect that will enhance the performance, but if the work task has already created an overload situation, additional heat will tend to degrade the performance."

We have focused largely on the negative effects of heat. However, the effects of heat on stress depend very much on the overall situation in which heat is experienced. Millions of British people regularly spend their summer holidays in hot places. It is unlikely that they would do this if they regarded heat as unpleasant and stressful!

Photo courtesy
TRIP,
photographer
H. Rogers.

Technological threats

There has been growing concern in recent years about a variety of technological threats. These include polluted rivers and seas from industrial waste and sewage, chemicals used in food production, the possibility of nuclear war, and accidents at nuclear power stations. Tallis et al. (1992) devised the Worry Domains Questionnaire, which assesses how much people worry in six domains ranging from relationship to socio-political concerns. People reported more worry about socio-political concerns (e.g. nuclear power) than about any other domain. However, there must be some doubts as to whether most people are actually more worried about such concerns than about themselves and their future personal lives.

Photo courtesy TRIP, photographer N. Ray.

It might be expected that major accidents at nuclear power stations, such as those at Three Mile Island and Chernobyl, would greatly increase worries and stress about nuclear power. Shortly after the accident at Three Mile Island, Baum et al. (1983) compared people living within five miles of the nuclear installation with those living near an undamaged nuclear plant. There was evidence of a low level of stress in those living near Three Mile Island, based on their levels of adrenaline and noradrenaline, and the symptoms they reported. The effects on stress were probably fairly modest because no-one was killed in the incident, and the estimates of radiation-linked deaths were low.

The accident at Chernobyl in 1986 was much more serious than the one at Three Mile Island. England is several hundred miles away from Chernobyl, but Brown and White (1987) found that the accident at Chernobyl increased the percentage of English people worried about nuclear power from 27% to 41%. More strikingly, 800,000 people phoned some agency seeking information about Chernobyl in the few days after the accident. The agencies contacted included the Department of the Environment, Friends of the Earth, and the *Sun* newspaper.

Architecture

In comparison with some of the causes of stress we have already considered, it may seem that architecture is stressful in a very minor way. This is probably true, but there is increasing concern about what has been

"Sick building syndrome" is avoided when the needs of the building's users are considered as carefully as the aesthetic, technical and economic factors.

called "sick building syndrome". The notion of sick building syndrome refers to the fact that some buildings are so poorly designed that they do not cater properly for the needs of those who work and/or live in them.

People are less stressed when inside a building providing natural light, adequate warmth, and air conditioning in hot and humid weather. However, many buildings do not provide all of these features. Several years ago I spent a few months working in the psychology department of a large university in Florida. The building in which the psychology department was housed had been built so that there were no windows on most floors. This was done to cut down on the cost of air conditioning. It was fairly stressful to spend all day in artificial light, knowing that outside the day was sunny with blue skies.

One of the key features of a building in which people work is the extent to which it makes it easy for people to communicate with each other. Szilagyi and Holland (1980) studied professional American workers who moved their offices from one building to another. When the move reduced their physical closeness to other workers, this led to reduced satisfaction, increased role conflict, increased role ambiguity, and a reduction in friendship opportunities. In contrast, when the move increased their closeness to other workers, precisely the opposite pattern of findings was reported.

Although reasonable closeness to other workers is clearly desirable, it is possible to carry this notion too far. Oldham and Brass (1979) looked at a newspaper company of reporters, receptionists, clerks, and so on who moved from ordinary offices into a single, large, open-plan office with no interior walls higher than three feet. This move led to a considerable increase in stress. There was decreased job satisfaction, reduced friendship opportunities, and reduced ability to concentrate. The open-plan office meant that there was an almost total lack of privacy, and this led to dissatisfaction and stress.

How can we make sense of the findings of Szilagyi and Holland (1980) and Oldham and Brass (1979)? It appears that people prefer buildings that are intermediate in terms of the closeness of other workers. They do not like to feel isolated and a long way away from other people. On the other hand, they do not like to feel that other workers can see and hear everything they are doing.

Further reading

Cox, T. (1978). *Stress*. London: Macmillan Press. A good, readable introduction which covers the main issues.

Sarafino, E.P. (1990). *Health psychology: Biopsychosocial interactions.* Chichester: Wiley. The health implications are dealt with at length in this book.

References

Holmes, T., & Rahe, R. (1967). The social readjustment rating scale. *Journal of Psychosomatic Research, 11*, 213–218.

Lazarus, R.S. (1982). Thoughts on the relations between emotion and cognition. *American Psychologist, 37*, 1019–1024.

Selye, H. (1956). *The stress of life*. New York: McGraw-Hill.

Summary

- Stress is associated with four major kinds of effects: emotional; physiological; cognitive; and behavioural.
- According to the transactional model, stress depends on the interaction between an individual and his or her environment.
- According to Selye, prolonged stress produces the general adaptation syndrome, consisting of three stages: alarm reaction; resistance; and exhaustion.
- Stress generally leads to the use of various coping strategies; these strategies can be task-oriented, emotion-oriented, or avoidance-oriented.
- Stress can be measured by means of self-report, physiological, biochemical, and performance measures.
- Stress often depends in part on recent life events, which can be assessed by the Social Readjustment Rating Scale.
- It is often unclear whether stress has caused life events, or life events have caused stress.
- The impact of any life event depends on how it is interpreted by the individual.
- The stressful effects of noise depend partly on its intensity; however, its effects also depend on whether it is perceived as necessary and whether those responsible for the noise appear to care about its effects on others.
- Extreme heat can cause irritability, aggression, and other stress-related effects; however, its effects depend in part on the overall situation (e.g. holidaymakers may regard high temperatures as pleasurable rather than stressful).
- Technological threats (e.g. those posed by pollution or the possibility of nuclear war) can produce small increases in stress; major accidents such as Three Mile Island or Chernobyl cause greater stress.
- Buildings that make people feel isolated or which prevent privacy can cause stress; this is part of the "sick building syndrome".

Key terms

Adrenaline: a hormone found in states of stress; it is released during the alarm reaction stage of the **general adaptation syndrome**.

Cognitive appraisal: assessment of a situation to decide whether it is threatening and whether the individual has the resources to cope with it.

Coping strategies: processes used to handle difficult or dangerous situations.

Cortisol: a hormone found in states of stress; it is released during the alarm reaction stage of the **general adaptation syndrome**.

General adaptation syndrome: the bodily response to stress, consisting of three stages—alarm reaction; resistance; and exhaustion.

Noradrenaline: a hormone found in states of stress; it is released during the alarm reaction stage of the **general adaptation syndrome**.

Parasympathetic nervous system: this is involved in energy-storing processes during the resistance stage of the **general adaptation syndrome**.

Sick building syndrome: poor building design, making a building unsuited to our needs and preferences.

Stress: this is a negative state involving emotional, physiological, cognitive, and behavioural effects.

Sympathetic nervous system: this is involved in preparing the body for fight or flight during the alarm reaction stage of the **general adaptation syndrome**.

Trait anxiety: a personality dimension involving high levels of anxiety and other negative emotions.

Type A Behaviour Pattern: a way of behaving involving impatience, time pressure, competitiveness, and hostility.

Yerkes-Dodson law: according to this law, performance is best when the level of stress or arousal is neither very low nor very high.

Structured essay questions

1. What is stress? How can it be measured?
2. What are some of the main causes of stress? How do they cause stress?
3. What is the psychological approach to understanding stress? What is the physiological approach to understanding stress?
4. Describe some of the ways in which people try to cope with stress. Why are there various ways of coping with stress?

Self-assessment questions

1. The stressed state is associated with:
   a) emotional effects
   b) emotional and physiological effects
   c) emotional, physiological, and cognitive effects
   d) emotional, physiological, cognitive, and behavioural effects

2. The general adaptation syndrome consists of:
   a) alarm reaction, resistance, and exhaustion stages
   b) widespread adaptation
   c) activation of the sympathetic nervous system
   d) activation of the parasympathetic nervous system

3. Stress can be measured by means of:
   a) self-report and physiological measures
   b) self-report, physiological, biochemical, and performance measures
   c) biochemical and performance measures
   d) none of the above

4. Adrenaline, noradrenaline, and cortisol are all:
   a) irrelevant to stress
   b) artificial drugs that can make people feel stressed
   c) hormones that occur in high levels during stress
   d) hormones that occur in low levels during stress

5. According to the Yerkes-Dodson law:
   a) performance is best at intermediate levels of stress
   b) performance is best at high levels of stress
   c) performance is best at low levels of stress
   d) none of the above

6. The Social Readjustment Rating Scale:
   a) measures only undesirable life events
   b) measures only desirable life events
   c) measures both desirable and undesirable life events
   d) does not measure life events

7. Noise causes stress:
   a) only because of its intensity
   b) only when it is intense or it is perceived as unnecessary
   c) when it is intense, is perceived as unnecessary, or the people responsible for the noise are thought to be unconcerned
   d) when it is intense, is perceived as unnecessary, the people responsible for the noise are thought to be unconcerned, or those affected are middle-aged or old

8. Provided that the work period is no longer than one hour, workers can perform as normal up to a temperature of:
   a) 87°F (31°C)
   b) 84°F (29°C)
   c) 90°F (32°C)
   d) 77°F (25°C)

Theories of emotion 5

Definition and measurement of emotion

The study of emotion is of great importance to psychologists. However, it is not very easy to define what it means. According to Drever (1964, p.82), emotion involves "bodily changes of a widespread character—in breathing, pulse, gland secretion, etc.—and, on the mental side, a state of excitement or perturbation, marked by a strong feeling, and usually an impulse towards a definite form of behaviour".

We can go beyond Drever's definition to identify the following components of emotion:

- *Cognitive or thinking:* emotions are usually directed towards people or objects (e.g. we are in an anxious emotional state because the situation is dangerous), and we know the situation is dangerous rather than harmless as a result of thinking.
- *Physiological:* there are generally a number of bodily changes involved in emotion; many of them (such as increased heart-rate, increased blood pressure, increased respiration-rate, sweating) occur because of arousal in the sympathetic division of the autonomic nervous system (see Chapter 3).
- *Experiential:* the feeling that is experienced, which can only be assessed in the human species.
- *Expressive:* facial expression and other aspects of non-verbal behaviour such as bodily posture.
- *Behavioural:* the pattern of behaviour (e.g. fight or flight) produced by an emotional state.

It seems reasonable to assume that all five components of the emotional response would mostly be in agreement with each other. For example, if someone is placed in a dangerous situation, we would expect high levels of physiological arousal, conscious feelings of anxiety, an anxious facial

Personal viewpoint

Sometimes you probably find it hard to tell whether you are experiencing a weak emotion or no emotion at all. How would you decide which it is? There are several different emotions, such as love, joy, fear, and anger. In your experience, does each of these emotions seem to differ in terms of the kinds of physiological activity that accompany it?

expression, and behavioural signs of anxiety (such as flight). In fact, the picture is often more complicated than that. The various components often agree only modestly, and sometimes do not agree at all. For example, think of someone behaving with courage. What we mean by courage is that a person's behaviour does not reflect the anxiety that is apparent in the other components of emotion.

Some of the difficulties involved in measuring emotion can be seen if we consider some of the major measures that are used. The experiential component is often assessed by means of self-report measures. For example, someone might be given a list of adjectives (tense, worried, frightened, etc.), and asked to indicate which of these adjectives describes the way he or she feels at that moment. The main problem with such self-report measures is social desirability bias: because it is regarded as socially undesirable to experience negative emotional states such as anxiety or anger, people may simply pretend that they are not experiencing these emotional states.

There is a similar problem with the use of facial expression as a measure of emotion. Up to a point, we can control our facial muscles so as to create the impression that we are happier or less anxious than we feel. However, Ekman (1985) found that some facial muscle movements (such as the raising and pulling together of the eyebrows when afraid) are very difficult to produce at will.

The physiological or arousal component of emotion has been measured in many ways. The measures used include heart-rate, breathing or respiration-rate, and skin resistance (a measure that is based on sweating of the hand). There are various problems with such measures:

- Even though they are all supposed to measure physiological arousal, the various measures usually do not agree closely with each other.
- There are some differences in physiological measures from one emotion to another; however, it is usually hard to tell which emotion someone is experiencing purely on the basis of physiological measures.
- Physiological arousal often occurs in situations in which the individual experiences little or no arousal; jogging and working on an interesting task are two examples.

In view of the problems with the various measures of emotion, what should psychologists do? The best answer is usually to measure a number of different components of emotion in order to have a full picture. If someone appears anxious in terms of facial expression and physiological arousal but not in terms of self-report, then it is probable that they are actually anxious but are reluctant to admit it.

Cross-cultural differences

An important issue relating to the measurement of emotion is whether there are large cross-cultural differences in the expression of emotions. There are some cross-cultural differences, but the similarities tend to be more apparent. Ekman (1973) found that people in many different countries all have very similar facial expressions for six basic emotions: happiness; anger; disgust; sadness; fear; and surprise. This was true even in tribes that had had little contact with the West or with mass media. The main exception is that there are some cultures, especially in the Far East, in which people are taught not to display certain emotions.

There are other kinds of evidence indicating that there are natural and unlearned links between certain facial expressions and certain emotions. Charlesworth and Kreutzer (1973) found that even individuals blind from birth showed the normal facial expressions when experiencing different emotions.

Theories of emotion

James–Lange theory

The first major theory of emotion was put forward independently in the United States by William James and in Denmark by Carl Lange. For obvious reasons, it later came to be known as the *James–Lange theory*. According to the theory, the following states are involved in emotion:

- An emotional stimulus is presented (e.g. a car coming rapidly towards you as you are crossing the road).
- This produces bodily changes (e.g. arousal in the autonomic nervous system).
- Feedback from the bodily changes leads to the experience of emotion (e.g. fear or anxiety).

These three stages can be seen in the following example taken from James (1890): "I see a bear, I run away, I feel afraid". Stage 1 is seeing the bear, running away is stage 2, and feeling afraid is stage 3.

As Gross (1992) pointed out, there is some support for the theory in a rather unusual study carried out by Laird (1974). Students watched cartoons while controlling their facial expressions so that they were smiling, frowning, or whatever. The key finding was that the facial

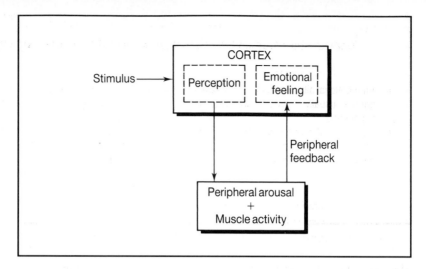

The James-Lange
theory.

CORTEX

Stimulus → Perception | Emotional feeling

Peripheral
feedback

Peripheral arousal
+
Muscle activity

expression had an impact on the students' emotional state. For example, smiling increased happiness, and frowning increased anger. These findings suggest that bodily changes can affect emotional experience as predicted by the James–Lange theory.

More evidence providing some support for the James–Lange theory was reported by Hohmann (1966). He studied 25 paralysed patients who had suffered damage to the spinal cord; this damage greatly restricted their awareness of physiological arousal. For those patients with the least awareness of arousal, there was a great reduction in their emotional experiences of anger, grief, and sexual excitement. In the words of one patient, "Sometimes I act angry when I see some injustice. I yell and cuss and raise hell … but it just doesn't have the heat to it that it used to. It's a kind of mental anger".

According to the James–Lange theory, the emotion we experience (such as anger, anxiety, or happiness) depends on the particular bodily changes that occur. This suggests that each emotion should have its own pattern of bodily changes. There is some support for this view. Smiling is associated with happiness, crying with misery, and running away with fear. Ax (1953) compared the physiological responses to fear and to anger. Fear was created by leading the participants to believe that they might receive an unpleasant electric shock, and anger was created by having a technician make a series of rude and unpleasant remarks to the participants and the experimenter. The physiological responses of fear were similar to those produced by the hormone adrenaline, whereas the responses of anger were like those produced by a combination of adrenaline and noradrenaline.

Some early evidence against the James–Lange theory was reported by Sherrington (1906). Surgical procedures were carried out on dogs so that most of the feedback from the internal organs and from the skeletal muscles no longer reached the brain. According to Sherrington, "anger, joy, disgust, and, when provocation arose, fear, remained as evident as ever following such operation." He claimed that this evidence tended to disprove the James–Lange theory, but there are two reasons for not accepting this conclusion. First, there was still some feedback from the internal organs and the skeletal muscles to the brain. Second, according to the James–Lange theory, it is emotional experience rather than emotional behaviour that would be lost if sensory feedback were abolished.

Cannon–Bard theory

The *Cannon–Bard theory* was put forward as an alternative to the James–Lange theory. When someone is put in an emotional situation, a part of the brain known as the thalamus is activated. This is followed by two separate effects: (1) the appropriate emotional state is experienced; and (2) another part of the brain (the hypothalamus) is activated, producing physiological changes such as arousal in the sympathetic division of the autonomic nervous system.

According to the Cannon–Bard theory, our feelings are not determined at all by the level of physiological arousal. As a result, this theory has no problem with the fact that our experience of emotion can occur before the relevant bodily changes have taken place. However, it does have problems with Hohmann's findings on

The Cannon–Bard theory.

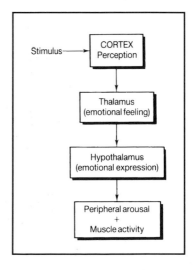

patients with damage to the spinal cord. If perception of the bodily changes in emotion has no effect on emotional experience, it is hard to explain why such patients show much reduced emotionality.

Another major problem for the Cannon–Bard theory is that it is very limited. For example, it is assumed that perception of an emotional situation produces activation of the thalamus. However, many situations are ambiguous (e.g. your teacher asks you to stay behind for a few minutes after school). The Cannon–Bard theory tells us nothing about how the cognitive system decides whether a given situation is emotional.

Cognitive labelling theory

Schachter and Singer (1962) started the modern era in emotion research with their very influential *cognitive labelling theory*. It owes much of its impact to the fact that it was one of the first theories of emotion to focus on cognitive factors. Their main suggestion was that there are two factors, both of which are essential for emotion to be experienced:

- High physiological arousal.
- An emotional interpretation (or label) of that arousal.

According to Schachter and Singer, an emotional state will not be experienced if either of these two crucial factors is missing. A study by Maranon (1924) fits that prediction. Participants were injected with adrenaline, a drug whose effects are like those of a naturally occurring state of arousal. When they were asked how they felt, 71% simply reported their physical symptoms with no emotional experience. Most of the remaining participants reported "as-if" emotions, in which they reported an emotion lacking its normal intensity. Why did almost none of the participants report true emotions? They interpreted (or labelled) their state of arousal as having been produced by the drug, and so failed to attach an emotional label to it.

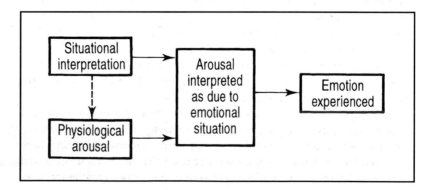

Cognitive labelling theory.

What are the advantages and disadvantages of cognitive labelling theory?

PLUS	MINUS
• Cognitive processes are important in determining *whether* emotion will be experienced, and *which* emotion will be experienced.	• It has proved very hard to repeat the findings of Schachter and Singer (1962); for example, Marshall and Zimbardo (1979) found that large doses of adrenaline reduced (rather than increased) participants' happiness in the euphoria or joy condition. This may be because a high level of unexplained arousal is generally regarded as unpleasant.
• Cognitive labelling theory led several other theorists to develop more cognitive approaches to emotion.	• The situation used by Schachter and Singer is very artificial; in our everyday lives, we rarely experience high levels of arousal that are hard to interpret.
	• The level of arousal generally has some effect on the intensity of emotional states; however, the effect is often much weaker than would be expected according to cognitive labelling theory (Reisenzein, 1983).

Schachter and Singer (1962) carried out an expanded version of Maranon's study. All the participants were told the study was testing the effects of the vitamin compound "Suproxin" on vision. In fact, they were injected with either adrenaline (to produce arousal) or a salt-based solution having no effect on arousal. Some of those given adrenaline were correctly informed about the effects of the drug, but others were misinformed or uninformed (being told simply that the injection was mild and would have no side-effects). After the injection, the participants were put in a situation designed to produce either euphoria (joy) or anger. This was done by putting them in the same room as someone who acted in a joyful way (making paper planes and playing paper basketball) or in an angry way (reacting to a very personal questionnaire).

Which groups were the most emotional? In terms of the theory, it should have been those groups who were given adrenaline (and so were very aroused), but who would not interpret the arousal as having been produced by the drug. Thus, it was predicted that the misinformed and uninformed groups given adrenaline should have been most emotional.

The findings broadly supported the predictions, but many of the effects were rather small.

One of the reasons why the study by Schachter and Singer did not produce strong effects may be because those given the salt-based solution may have become physiologically aroused by being put into an emotional situation. If that were the case, then they would have had the high arousal and emotional label which led to the experience of emotion. Schachter and Wheeler (1962) argued that the way to stop people becoming aroused was to give them a depressant drug that reduces arousal. Participants were given a depressant, or adrenaline, or a substance having no effects, and told that the drug had no side-effects. They then watched a slapstick film called *The Good Humour Man*. As predicted, those given adrenaline (and thus aroused) found the film the funniest, whereas those given the depressant (and thus de-aroused) found it least funny.

Physiological correlates of emotion

The three theories of emotion we have discussed differ from each other in terms of the relevance of physiological activity to emotion. According to the James–Lange theory, each emotion has its own pattern of physiological activity. In contrast, according to cognitive labelling theory, there is a similar state of physiological arousal associated with each emotion. Finally, according to the Cannon–Bard theory, the level of physiological arousal does not determine emotional experience. In view of these differences, it is worth considering the physiological evidence in more detail.

As we have seen, most emotional states involve activity in the sympathetic division of the autonomic nervous system. This produces a general increase in metabolic rate and energy mobilisation; in other words, the body is getting ready for "fight or flight". Among the responses that occur are the following: increased heart-rate and blood pressure; increased breathing rate; constriction of the blood vessels in the skin; pupil dilation; a reduction in stomach activity; reduced salivation or dry mouth; and increased activity of the sweat glands. These responses are partly determined by increased release of adrenaline, which can cause trembling and feelings of cold.

People tend to assume that different emotions are associated with distinctive bodily states. However, as we have seen, the actual physiological differences among emotions are usually rather small. It is possible that the weak emotional states studied in the laboratory are less clearly distinguished physiologically than are the stronger emotions of everyday life.

It is also possible that individuals in different emotional states focus on different aspects of their own physiological activity. For example, someone who is feeling embarrassed may be very aware that he or she is blushing, whereas angry people ignore the fact that they are blushing.

Cognitive appraisal

The most influential modern theory of emotion is rather different from any of the theories we have discussed so far. According to the cognitive appraisal theory of Lazarus (1982), emotion depends mainly on the ways in which we interpret situations. For example, think of being woken up in the middle of the night by a noise outside. If you interpret the noise as a burglar trying to break in, then you will probably experience anxiety. On the other hand, if you decide the noise was caused by a cat knocking over milk bottles, then you probably experience no emotion at all.

According to Lazarus (1982), the *cognitive appraisal*, or interpretation, of situations is divided into three parts. First, there is primary appraisal, in which the situation is evaluated as positive, stressful, or irrelevant to well-being. Second, there is secondary appraisal, in which the individual takes into account his or her resources for coping with the situation. Third, there is re-appraisal, in which the situation and the coping strategies are monitored, with the primary and secondary appraisals being modified if necessary.

The importance of cognitive appraisal to emotion was shown in a number of studies discussed by Lazarus (1966). In one study, participants were shown a film of an accident in which a board caught in a circular saw drives through the mid-section of a worker, who then dies writhing on the floor. Giving participants a suitable cognitive appraisal (such as telling them that those involved in the film were actors) considerably reduced the emotional impact of the film as assessed by physiological measures.

Smith and Lazarus (1993) argued that emotional states can be distinguished on the basis of what happens during primary and secondary appraisal. For example, anger is experienced when a goal is blocked and the individual blames someone else, whereas guilt is experienced when a goal is blocked and the individual blames himself or herself. Smith and Lazarus tested these ideas by using scenarios in which participants were told to identify with the central character. In one scenario, the central character has performed poorly in an important course, and he appraises the situation. When he put the blame on the unhelpful teaching assistants, anger was the main emotion experienced by the participants. In contrast, when he accepted that he had made a lot of mistakes (e.g. doing work at the last minute), then guilt was the main emotion.

Cognitive
appraisal.

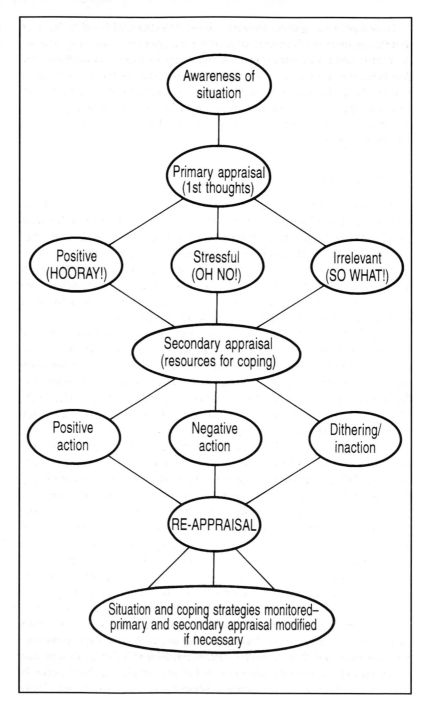

How useful is cognitive appraisal theory? On the positive side, it is true that the experience of emotion depends to a large extent on our appraisals or interpretations of situations. On the negative side, it is unlikely that that is the whole story. According to the James–Lange theory and cognitive labelling theory, emotional experience depends on feedback from bodily changes. What is probably the case is that cognitive appraisal is crucial to the experience of emotion, but feedback from bodily changes also plays a part.

Happiness

Unpleasant emotional states such as fear and anger have been studied more often than pleasant ones. However, we are starting to understand some of the more positive emotions, including happiness. In everyday life, we use the word "happiness" in at least two rather different ways. One way refers to brief feelings of joy ("I was so happy at the party last night"), and the other way is in the sense of long-lasting satisfaction or contentment ("Last year was a happy year for me"). We will consider happiness mostly in the sense of long-term contentment.

Why do you think some people are much happier than others? Part of the answer is that they tend to have deeper relationships with other people, more friends, more interesting jobs, and so on. For example, there is good evidence that married people are on average much happier than those who have never married, divorced, or been widowed (Eysenck, 1990). However, an equally important part of the answer is that happy people tend to have a certain type of personality.

Costa and McCrae (1980) assumed that happy people experience many pleasant emotions, but very few unpleasant ones. They found that those who are high on extraversion (a personality dimension involving being sociable and outgoing) experience much more pleasant emotion than those who are low on extraversion (see Chapter 18). They also found that those who are high on neuroticism (a personality dimension involving being anxious and depressed) experience many more negative emotions than those low on neuroticism. Those individuals high on extraversion and low on neuroticism were happy with their lives, whereas those who were low on extraversion and high on neuroticism were unhappy.

The experiences that we have obviously influence our level of happiness, and this is most true of our close relationships (Eysenck, 1990). However, most experiences have less long-term effect on happiness than might be expected. Brickman et al. (1978) considered individuals who had either won a fortune on the Illinois State Lottery, or who had been severely paralysed as the result of an accident. Winning a fortune produced a large increase in happiness, and being paralysed reduced happiness considerably. However, as the months went by, Brickman et al. found that the happiness levels of the lottery winners were coming down towards the normal level, and those of the accident victims were increasing steadily. It seems that we adjust reasonably well to most of life's experiences, because our expectations increase or decrease as a result of what happens to us.

Learning and early experience

Fear conditioning

Individuals are said to suffer from a phobia when they respond to a relatively harmless situation or object with great fear and avoidance. Snake and spider phobias are relatively common, but some people experience phobias for closed spaces, open spaces, or heights. What makes phobias puzzling is that most people suffering from them realise that the object or situation causing extreme fear is not actually dangerous.

According to Watson and Rayner (1920), fears and phobias can be produced by means of conditioning (see Chapters 2 and 7). A small boy (Little Albert) liked a rat, but Watson and Rayner made him fearful of it by making a loud noise with a steel bar every time he reached for it. The fear that had initially been associated only with the loud noise was now also produced by the rat. This suggested that a process of classical conditioning had taken place.

Watson and Rayner then tried to remove Little Albert's fear of the rat by a process of extinction. The loud noise was no longer presented along with the rat, and Little Albert was given sweets when he saw the rat. As a result, his fear slowly disappeared.

There are at least two problems with the view that all fears and phobias depend on classical conditioning. First, many phobic individuals deny that they have ever had unpleasant experiences associated with the object of their phobia. Second, attempts to repeat the findings of the study on Little Albert have generally failed.

Seligman (1971) pointed out that we tend to develop extreme fears or phobias to certain types of objects (such as snakes and spiders) but not to other, more dangerous, objects such as electricity sockets and cars. Why is this? Seligman said that we need to think in terms of *preparedness*: we are biologically prepared to associate fear with dangers that have faced the human race for thousands of years (such as snakes). However, we are not biologically prepared to link fear with relatively recent inventions such as electricity and cars.

A study fitting this notion of preparedness was reported by Garcia, McGowan, and Green (1972). They found that rats rapidly learned to avoid the taste of a given food if they were made to feel sick afterwards. This makes sense, because it is important for the survival of the species to avoid eating food that is poisonous or dangerous to health.

Learned helplessness

A major way in which learning can affect emotion (especially depression) was proposed by Seligman (1975). He and his associates carried out a series of studies on dogs. The dogs were first of all exposed to electric shocks which they could not avoid. After that, they were put in a box with a barrier in the middle. The dogs were given electric shocks after a warning signal, but they could escape by jumping over the barrier into the other part of the box. However, most of the dogs passively accepted the shocks, and did not learn to escape. In contrast, dogs who had not previously received unavoidable shocks rapidly learned to avoid the shocks by jumping over the barrier as soon as the warning signal was presented.

Seligman (1975) used the term *learned helplessness* to refer to the passive behaviour of the dogs when put in an unpleasant situation which could have been improved. He argued that the learned helplessness shown by the dogs is very similar to the passive helplessness displayed by humans suffering from clinical depression. This idea was developed by Abramson, Seligman, and Teasdale (1978). They argued that people respond to failure (e.g. losing their job) in various ways:

- Attributing the failure to an *internal* cause (themselves) or to an *external* cause (other people; circumstances).
- Attributing the failure to a *stable* cause (likely to continue in future) or to an *unstable* cause (might easily change in future).
- Attributing the failure to a *global* cause (applying to a wide range of situations) or to a *specific* cause (applying only to one situation).

People with learned helplessness tend to attribute failure to internal, stable, and global causes. In other words, they feel personally responsible for failure, they think the factors causing that failure will persist, and they think that those factors will affect most situations in future. In view of these negative and pessimistic thoughts, it is no surprise that sufferers from learned helplessness are depressed.

Evidence supporting this theory of learned helplessness was reported by Metalsky et al. (1987). They asked students to complete the Attributional-Style Questionnaire some time before they sat an examination in introductory psychology. Two days after the results of the examination were given, those students who tended to attribute failure to global and stable causes were more depressed than those who attributed failure to specific and unstable causes.

The evidence indicates that depressed people tend to have the attributional style towards failure predicted by Abramson et al. (1978). However, there are various ways of interpreting that finding. Abramson et al. assumed that the depressive attributional style is a long-lasting part of the make-up of depressed people, and that this style plays a part in making people feel depressed. It is also possible that being depressed makes people adopt a particular attributional style. In that case, individuals who have the depressive attributional style when they are depressed might no longer have it when they stop being depressed. Evidence more in line with the second possibility was reported by Hamilton and Abramson (1983). They gave depressed patients the Attributional-Style Questionnaire when they were very depressed and just before they were discharged from hospital. These patients showed the depressive attributional style on the first occasion but not on the second. These findings cast doubt on the notion that the depressive attributional style is long-lasting and helps to cause depression.

Early experience

Early experience can have large effects on emotional development. For example, Levine (1960) compared anxiety in two groups of adult rats when put into a novel situation. The group that had been handled when very young seemed to be less anxious than the group that had not been handled. Did the handling have this effect because it got the rats used to being stressed, or because of the comfort it provided? Levine found that rats which were given electric shocks when very young also showed less stress in adult life, suggesting that early exposure to stress can reduce later stress. It might seem that handling is not stressful, but just imagine being handled by a creature that is about 50 times larger than you are!

Levine also found that the handling had to take place within the first five days of life for it to be effective. This is what is known as a *critical period*. Finally, Levine looked at the adult rats' physiological reactions to electric shock in the form of steroids in the blood. Steroids are chemicals that occur when a person or animal is stressed. The rats that had been stressed in early life showed more rapid reductions in steroids after shock than did those which had not been stressed when young.

The work of Levine suggests that stimulation of all kinds in infancy provides protection from adult stress, at least in rats. In the case of human babies, it might be thought that more handling, being talked to more often, and so on, would benefit them. What is more likely is that most babies already receive as much stimulation as they need for good development. Only the small minority of babies who receive very little stimulation would gain from extra stimulation.

Further reading

Parkinson, B. (1994). Emotion. In A.M. Colman (Ed.), *Companion Encyclopaedia of Psychology*, (Vol. 1). London: Routledge. There is a good account of theory and research on emotion in this chapter.

References

Ekman, P. (1973). *Darwin and facial expression: A century of research in review*. New York: Academic Press.

James, W. (1890). *The principles of psychology*. New York: Holt.

Lazarus, R.S. (1966). *Psychological stress and the coping process*. New York: McGraw-Hill.

Schachter, S., & Singer, J.E. (1962). Cognitive, social and physiological determinants of an emotional state. *Psychological Review, 69*, 379–399.

Seligman, M.E.P. (1975). *Helplessness: On depression, development and death*. San Francisco: W.H. Freeman.

Summary

- Emotions consist of several components: cognitive; physiological; experiential; expressive; and behavioural. These components are often not in agreement with each other.
- According to the James–Lange theory, emotional stimuli cause bodily changes, and feedback from these changes produces emotional experience.
- It is assumed by the James–Lange theory that each emotion has its own distinctive pattern of bodily activity, but this is not the case.
- According to the Cannon–Bard theory, emotional stimuli activate the thalamus, leading to emotional experience and separately to activation of the hypothalamus and of the autonomic nervous system.
- It is assumed by the Cannon–Bard theory that feelings do not depend on the perception of physiological arousal, but patients with spinal cord damage sometimes report much reduced emotional experience.
- According to Schachter's cognitive labelling theory, emotional experience requires both a state of high physiological arousal and an emotional interpretation (or label) applied to that arousal.
- Changes in physiological arousal have less effect on emotional experience than is predicted by cognitive labelling theory.
- The sympathetic nervous system, which produces arousal and a readiness for fight or flight, is involved in most emotional states.
- According to Lazarus' cognitive appraisal theory, appraisal or interpretation of situations is of central importance in emotion.
- Happiness is greatest among those with a particular type of personality (high on extraversion and low on neuroticism) who have one or more close relationships.
- Fear responses can be learned and extinguished by means of classical conditioning; this may explain how some phobias (extreme fears) develop.
- Learned helplessness develops when nothing can be done to improve a stressful situation; those suffering from learned helplessness tend to attribute failure to internal, stable, and global causes.
- Theorists assume that a depressive attributional style helps to cause depression; however, depression may cause people to adopt a depressive attributional style.
- The work of Levine suggests that infants who receive more stimulation of all kinds in early life will be better protected against adult stress.

Key terms

Behavioural component of emotion: the behavioural pattern associated with each emotional state.

Cognitive appraisal: the interpretation of situations that may or may not lead to the experience of emotion.

Cognitive component of emotion: the **cognitive appraisal** that leads to emotional experience.

Critical period: in Levine's theory, the first few days of life in rats during which handling can reduce anxiety in later life.

Emotion: a complex state, including cognitive, experiential, expressive, behavioural, and physiological components.

Experiential component of emotion: the conscious experience of emotion.

Expressive component of emotion: the non-verbal aspects of emotion (e.g. facial expression).

Happiness: a long-lasting feeling of contentment or satisfaction with life; also short-lived joy.

Learned helplessness: passive behaviour produced by the perception that punishment is unavoidable.

Phobia: extreme fear and avoidance in response to a fairly harmless situation or object (e.g. spiders; snakes).

Physiological component of emotion: the bodily changes involved in emotion.

Preparedness: the notion that we are biologically prepared to associate fear with objects that used to be more dangerous to the human race than they are now (e.g. snakes; spiders).

Structured essay questions

1. What is emotion? How can it be measured?
2. What is involved in emotional development? How important is early experience?
3. Describe briefly two major theories of emotion. What are the strengths of these theories? What are the weaknesses of these theories?

Self-assessment questions

1. Emotions consist of the following components:
   a) physiological and experiential
   b) expressive, physiological, and experiential
   c) expressive, physiological, experiential, and cognitive
   d) expressive, cognitive, physio-logical, behavioural, and experiential

2. According to the James–Lange theory:
   a) feedback from bodily changes produces the experience of emotion
   b) the experience of emotion causes bodily changes
   c) the experience of emotion has nothing to do with bodily changes
   d) none of the above

3. According to the cognitive labelling theory, emotion:
   a) depends only on the interpretation of the situation
   b) depends only on a high level of physiological arousal
   c) involves high physiological arousal and an emotional interpretation of that arousal
   d) involves an emotional interpretation of the situation causing a high level of physiological arousal

4. Most emotional states involve mainly:
   a) decreased activity in the sympathetic nervous system
   b) decreased activity in the parasympathetic nervous system
   c) increased activity in the parasympathetic nervous system
   d) increased activity in the sympathetic nervous system

5. Cognitive appraisal consists of:
   a) thinking about oneself
   b) primary appraisal, secondary appraisal, and re-appraisal
   c) evaluating the situation
   d) evaluating one's coping resources

6. Learned helplessness is likely to occur when failure is attributed to:
   a) internal, stable, and global causes
   b) external, unstable, and specific causes
   c) internal, unstable, and global causes
   d) external, stable, and global causes

7. Levine argued that handling rats when very young:
   a) made them more stressed in adulthood
   b) made them less stressed in adulthood because of the comfort provided
   c) made them less stressed in adulthood because they were used to being stressed
   d) none of the above

Aggression 6

I n this chapter we will consider aggression and violence. Aggression involves hurting others on purpose. It has been defined as "any form of behaviour directed towards the goal of harming or injuring another living being who is motivated to avoid such treatment" (Baron & Richardson, 1993). The hurting must be deliberate, because someone who slips on the ice and crashes into somebody by accident is not behaving aggressively.

Different forms of aggression can be identified. A distinction can be drawn between *person-oriented aggression* and *instrumental aggression*. Person-oriented aggression is designed to hurt someone else, and so causing harm is the main goal. In contrast, instrumental aggression has as its main goal obtaining some desired reward (e.g. an attractive toy), with aggressive behaviour being used to obtain the reward.

A distinction can also be drawn between proactive aggression and reactive aggression. Proactive aggression is aggressive behaviour that is started by an individual in order to achieve some desired outcome (e.g. gaining possession of an attractive toy). Reactive aggression is an individual's reaction to the aggression of someone else.

It is perhaps natural to think of aggressive behaviour in terms of fighting and other physical attacks. This is certainly the case with very young children. However, children by the age of 4 or 5 usually have a good command of language, and make increasing use of teasing and other forms of verbal aggression.

Cultural differences in aggression

It cannot be denied that members of the human race often behave aggressively and violently. For example, there have been about 15,000 wars in the last 5600 years, which works out at almost 2.7 wars per year. However, there are cultural differences in terms of the magnitude of the problem

> **Personal viewpoint**
>
> You have probably had the misfortune to meet some people who seem very aggressive and difficult to handle. What do you think it is that causes some people to be aggressive, whereas other people are gentle and unaggressive? Is it a question of personality, the experiences that people have had, or are the media to blame? What advice would you give someone who wanted to become less aggressive?

posed by aggression and violence. For reasons that are not clear, violence is a particular problem in the United States. The murder rate there is between 4 and 73 times greater than in other industrialised countries.

Some of the best-known evidence about cultural differences in aggression comes in the work of the anthropologist Margaret Mead (1935). She compared three New Guinea tribes living fairly close to each other. In one tribe, the Mundugumor, both men and women were very aggressive and quarrelsome in their behaviour. At times, the Mundugumor had been cannibals who killed outsiders in order to eat them. In a second tribe, the Arapesh, both men and women were non-aggressive and co-operative in their treatment of each other and their children. When they were invaded, the Arapesh would hide in inaccessible parts of their territory rather than fight the invader. In the third tribe, the Tchambuli, the men carved and painted and indulged themselves with elaborate hairdos, whereas the women were relatively aggressive.

Mead found important cultural differences, but it is probable that she exaggerated their extent. For example, even in the Tchambuli tribe it was the men who did most of the fighting in time of war.

There are two important points to make about cultural differences in aggression. First, relatively little is known about the reasons why some cultures tolerate much higher levels of aggression than others. Second, it should not be assumed that what is true of a culture is true of all members of that culture. For example, the American culture is an aggressive and violent one, but millions of Americans are gentle and non-aggressive individuals.

Television is an important cultural influence in many societies. The average 16-year-old in Western societies has seen about 13,000 violent murders on television, and this almost certainly influences aggressive behaviour. Lefkotwitz et al. (1977) measured the amount of television watched by 8-year-old children, and then examined their criminal behaviour at the age of 30. There was a strong association between the amount of television watched and the tendency towards criminality. It could be argued that at least part of this occurred because aggressive children choose to watch more television (and especially violent programmes) than non-aggressive children. However, when Lefkotwitz et al. took account of the children's initial level of aggressiveness, they still found that watching television was related to subsequent criminality.

Theories of aggression

Psychodynamic approach

The views of Sigmund Freud on aggression were much influenced by the wholesale human slaughter of the First World War, in which millions of people were killed. The fact that the human race was capable of such atrocities suggested to him that aggression stems from our biological nature. He argued that everyone has a death instinct (thanatos), which is basically an aggressive instinct. In early life, this death instinct is aimed at self-destruction, but it is then re-directed towards other people. This often takes the form of *displacement*. If aggression cannot be directed towards the source of one's anger (e.g. the boss), then it is displaced on to someone or something else (e.g. kicking the cat).

According to Freud, aggressive energy builds up inside the individual until it demands release. This aggression can be released in very destructive ways. However, it can also be channelled into mastery of the environment (such as mountain-climbing), sport, and so on.

Limited support for Freud's theory comes from the study of violent criminals and murderers. Some of them had appeared to be gentle and very unaggressive for several years preceding the crime. They tend to be over-controlled individuals who perhaps allowed aggressive energy to

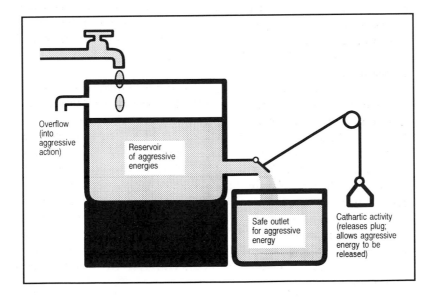

Overflow (into aggressive action)

Reservoir of aggressive energies

Safe outlet for aggressive energy

Cathartic activity (releases plug; allows aggressive energy to be released)

The psychodynamic model of aggression.

build up to an excessive level before turning it into action (Megargee, 1966). However, there is very little evidence that aggressive energy builds up progressively over time in most people. In a nutshell, Freud focused too much on *internal* factors causing aggressive behaviour and not enough on *external* factors. Thus, for example, he minimised the extent to which aggressive behaviour depends on the precise nature of the social situation and on the amount of provocation (e.g. insults) in that situation.

Ethological approach

During the 1930s and 1940s, a new approach to the study of animals was introduced by Niko Tinbergen and Konrad Lorenz. It was known as *ethology* (see also Chapter 3), and involved studying animals under natural conditions rather than in the laboratory. They did not carry out experiments on animals; rather, detailed observations were made of the animals' behaviour.

The ethologists focused on other species, but tried to apply their findings to humans. Lorenz (1966) put forward a theory of aggression resembling Freud's earlier theory. He argued that aggression in all species springs mainly from an inherited *fighting instinct*. Fighting is often closely related to mating, and so the fighting instinct helps to ensure that it is the strongest individuals who pass their genes on the next generation. According to Lorenz, aggressive energy builds up in all species regardless of what happens to the person or animal. Overt aggression depends on the level of aggressive energy and on the presence of aggression-releasing stimuli (e.g. being attacked).

There are also some differences in aggression between the human species and other species. Aggression in other species is well-regulated and can actually be useful. In contrast, Lorenz claimed that human aggression is often very destructive.

Aggression in other species is controlled by *ritualisation* and *appeasement rituals*. Ritualisation is aggression expressed in a stereotyped fashion, so that injury and/or death are rare. For example, when two wolves fight, the loser exposes his jugular vein, which brings the fight to an end. Appeasement rituals (e.g. surrendering) are designed to prevent a fight starting in the first place. Lorenz accepted that humans sometimes control aggression in similar ways to other species. He referred to smiling and begging for forgiveness as human appeasement rituals. However, technology has led to the development of weapons such as rifles and bombs, with the result that the killer and victim are often very far apart. This means that the rituals that are so effective in other species often cannot be used.

What are the advantages and disadvantages of the ethological approach?

PLUS

- The ethologists made detailed observations of animals in their natural environment rather than in the laboratory.
- Aggression in many species is controlled by appeasement rituals.

MINUS

- It is not only humans who kill others of the same species; for example, male lions taking over a group or pride of lions often kill all the cubs.
- Lorenz's assumption that aggression is almost entirely determined by biological factors is wrong: human aggression reveals itself in very different ways from one culture to another.
- The notion that aggression occurs spontaneously rather than in response to specific situations is wrong: only a few cases of over-controlled violent criminals provide support for this.

The ethological approach to aggression is very biological in nature. For example, it is assumed that aggressive energy naturally increases until it is released. There is very little evidence for this assumption. Ethologists assume that aggressive behaviour is inevitable, whereas most psychologists assume that human behaviour is much more flexible than that. Whether or not people behave aggressively is determined by their moral values, details of the social situation, their ability to understand the feelings of others, and so on, rather than by their level of aggressive energy.

Learning theory approach

Think about the situations that make you think and act in an aggressive way. It is likely that you are thinking of occasions when you were frustrated in your attempts to do something. Dollard, Doob, Miller, Mowrer, and Sears (1939) agreed with this view in their *frustration–aggression hypothesis*. According to this hypothesis, frustration always leads to aggression, and aggression is always caused by frustration.

A diagram of the Dollard et al. frustration–aggression hypothesis.

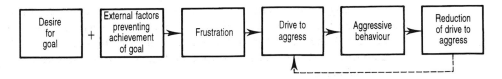

Theories that make bold assumptions usually turn out to be wrong, and the frustration–aggression hypothesis is no exception. Frustration can lead to constructive attempts to remove its source or to resignation as well as to aggression. Frustration produces aggression mainly among those who have learned to respond aggressively to frustration. In addition, aggressive behaviour does not always stem from frustration. In Zimbardo's Stanford prison experiment (see Chapter 15), the mock prisoners did less and less to frustrate the wishes of the mock warders, but the mock warders became increasingly aggressive. In war, soldiers behave aggressively towards the enemy because they are under orders to do so rather than because they are frustrated.

A revised version of the frustration–aggression hypothesis was offered by Berkowitz (1989). He argued that an aversive or unpleasant event causes negative feelings. These negative feelings activate tendencies towards aggression and towards flight. However, what we decide to do depends on various thought processes (e.g. our interpretation of the situation). For example, suppose that someone knocks into you as you are walking along the pavement. This may cause negative feelings and a tendency towards aggression. However, if you realise that it was a blind person who knocked into you, aggressive tendencies are replaced by guilt. According to this theory, a frustrating situation is an example (but not the only one) of an aversive event, and behaving aggressively is only one of several possible ways of responding to frustration. That position is more reasonable than the original frustration–aggression hypothesis, and is more in line with the experimental evidence.

What are the advantages and disadvantages of the learning theory approach?

PLUS

- The frustration–aggression hypothesis was an improvement on the psychodynamic and ethological approaches in that it considered one of the main external conditions (i.e. frustration) causing aggression.
- Some of the ideas in the frustration–aggression hypothesis have been developed and improved by Berkowitz.

MINUS

- Frustration does not always lead to aggression, nor is aggression always caused by frustration.

Animal versus human aggression

According to most of the theories of aggression that we have considered, there are important similarities between human and animal aggression. This is particularly clear in the case of the ethologists, who basically assumed that most of what they had discovered about aggression in animals also applied to human aggression. In addition, the psychodynamic notion of aggressive energy and the frustration–aggression hypothesis can both be seen as applying to other species.

One important similarity in aggression across different species is at the physiological level. Aggressive behaviour motivated by anger involves activity in the sympathetic nervous system (Zillmann, 1989). This is the "fight-or-flight" system which causes increased heart-rate, sweating, and increased levels of adrenaline. In terms of brain systems, it seems that the *limbic system* is very much involved in aggression (Gross, 1992).

Several species (including apes and monkeys) establish *dominance hierarchies*, in which there is general agreement on the status of animals within the group. The existence of dominance hierarchies has the advantage that aggression is rare between animals far apart on the hierarchy, because the lower-status animal has very little chance of winning the fight. Strayer (1991) found that 3- and 4-year-old children formed dominance hierarchies. He also reported that these hierarchies seemed to deter low-status children from aggression towards high-status children.

There are also important differences in aggression between animals and humans. Most aggression in animals is triggered by a small number of situations, such as having their territory invaded, losing their food supply, or being attacked. In contrast, there are almost limitless situations that can cause aggression in people. Threats to an individual's self-esteem (e.g. being snubbed; being laughed at) can cause as much aggression as physical threats. In a nutshell, people respond aggressively to psychological as well as physical threats, whereas other species respond mainly to physical threats.

Humans also differ from other species in their aggressive behaviour. Most aggressive behaviour in other species takes the form of physical attacks on other animals. Human aggression can take many different forms, including subtle non-verbal behaviour (e.g. raised eyebrows), sarcastic remarks, deliberately ignoring someone, or playing unpleasant practical jokes on someone. Our possession of language greatly increases the ways in which we can be aggressive. As we saw earlier in the chapter, even young children make much use of teasing as well as physically attacking other children.

Child-rearing styles

Modelling

Albert Bandura is a social learning theorist who disagreed with Freud
and Lorenz. He claimed that most behaviour (including aggressive
behaviour) is learned. *Observational learning* or *modelling* is of particular importance here, with children being very likely to imitate the
behaviour of other people. As Bandura (1983), made clear, the main
goal of social learning theorists is to explain the details of human
behaviour: "The specific forms that aggressive behaviour takes, the
frequency with which it is expressed, the situations in which it is
displayed, and the specific targets selected for attack are largely determined by social learning factors."

A classic study showing the importance of modelling was reported
by Bandura, Ross, and Ross (1963). Young children were shown one of
two films. One film showed a female adult model behaving in an aggressive way towards an inflated clown known as a Bobo doll, punching it
and sitting on it. The other film showed the same adult model acting in
a non-aggressive way towards the Bobo doll. Afterwards, those children
who had seen the model behave aggressively were much more likely to
attack the Bobo doll than were those who had watched the non-aggressive model.

Adult models and
children attacking
the Bobo doll. ©
Albert Bandura.
Reprinted by
permission.

Bandura's research on modelling has been very influential. However, it is likely that he exaggerated the extent to which children imitate the behaviour of models. He found that children are very likely to imitate aggressive behaviour towards a doll, but they are much less likely to imitate aggressive behaviour towards another child. The Bobo doll is of interest to young children, because it has a weighted base and so bounces back up when it is knocked over. It has been found that its novelty value is important: children unfamiliar with the doll were five times more likely to imitate aggressive behaviour against it than were children who had played with it before (Cumberbatch, 1989).

Punishment

One of the most controversial issues relating to child-rearing styles concerns the effectiveness of punishment in producing well-behaved, non-aggressive children. Some of the best evidence was obtained by Patterson (1982). He studied what happened in the homes of very aggressive boys aged between 3 and 13, as well as what happened in the homes of non-aggressive boys. Punishment and aggression by the parents were much more common in the homes of the aggressive boys. The parents of aggressive boys punished their children more often than the parents of non-aggressive boys punished their children, even when the children were well-behaved.

There are two main factors producing the findings reported by Patterson. First, boys whose parents punish them a lot are likely to model their parents' aggressive behaviour in the way assumed by social learning theorists. Second, parents who have a badly behaved and aggressive boy are more likely to punish him than are the parents of a non-aggressive boy.

It should not be assumed from Patterson's research that punishment is always an ineffective way of controlling aggression. As Bower and Hilgard (1981) pointed out, punishment is most likely to be effective when there is only a short interval between an aggressive action and punishment, and when the person punished understands clearly *why* punishment has been given.

There is also evidence that the threat of punishment is more effective in reducing aggression when someone is mildly rather than strongly provoked. Baron (1973) allowed male students to give electric shocks to another man who had provoked them either mildly or strongly. Before they did so, they were told that there was a low, moderate, or high probability that this other person would later have the chance to get his own back by giving shocks to them. Those who had been mildly provoked gave much weaker shocks when they thought that there was a high probability of retaliation than when there was a low probability. In contrast, those who had been strongly provoked gave fairly powerful shocks regardless of the chances of being shocked themselves.

Monitoring

Parents differ considerably in terms of the extent to which they monitor or pay attention to what their children are doing. The amount of parental monitoring seems to be important in determining the child's level of aggression. Patterson and Stouthamer-Loeber (1984) found that aggressive and delinquent adolescent behaviour (e.g. harassing teachers; fighting with other children) was commonly associated with a lack of parental monitoring. In their own words, "parents of delinquents are indifferent trackers of their sons's whereabouts, the companions they keep, and the type of activities in which they engage."

Reducing aggression

There is evidence from crime figures that mugging, rape, and other violent crimes are more common now than they were a few years ago. It is thus more important than ever to find ways in which aggressive behaviour can be controlled and reduced. Psychologists have suggested a number of possible solutions, and we will consider them in turn.

Catharsis

According to Sigmund Freud's psychodynamic theory, aggressive energy builds up inside people until it is released in behaviour. It follows from this theory that it is better for people to find relatively harmless ways of acting aggressively (e.g. playing sport) rather than allow their aggressive energy to increase to the level at which they become violent. This view is sometimes known as the *catharsis* ("letting off steam") *hypothesis*.

Most of the evidence fails to support the catharsis hypothesis. Indeed, the findings of many studies are exactly the opposite of what would be expected on that hypothesis. Walters and Brown (1963) allowed some children to hit, kick, and punch an inflatable doll to reduce their aggression, whereas other children were not allowed to do so. After that, those who had attacked the doll were much more likely than the other children to behave in an aggressive fashion towards their classmates.

Another failure of catharsis to occur was reported by Mallick and McCandless (1966). Two groups of 9-year-old boys were asked to build a house of bricks in order to win a prize. One group was prevented from doing this by a disruptive boy who was working with the experimenter, whereas the other group was not. Then some of the boys shot at animated targets of people and animals, which might be expected to produce catharsis. Finally, all of the boys had the chance to give electric shocks to the disruptive boy (no shocks were actually given). Shooting at targets had no effect on aggressive behaviour in terms of shocks given.

Removing rewards

One of the reasons why people behave aggressively is because it can be rewarding or reinforcing. For example, one boy may attack another boy who is playing with a video game, in order that he can start playing the game immediately instead of waiting his turn. Among adults, a mugger may steal the wallet from the person who has been mugged. It follows that it should be possible to reduce aggressive behaviour by arranging matters so that such behaviour is no longer rewarded.

Aggression can be reduced by removing rewards. One way in which this can be done is by use of the *time-out technique*. Children who behave aggressively are prevented from continuing with such behaviour (e.g. by being sent to their rooms). This technique has been found to work reasonably well, especially when helpful non-aggressive behaviour is rewarded (Parke & Slaby, 1983).

Another way of removing rewards is the *incompatible-response technique*. The basis of this technique is the assumption that children often behave aggressively in order to gain the reward of receiving attention from an adult. In the incompatible-response technique, children's aggressive behaviour is ignored (to remove attentional reward), but their helpful behaviour is rewarded. This technique has been found to produce substantial reductions in aggression (Slaby & Crowley, 1977).

Modelling

As we saw earlier in the chapter, aggressive behaviour can be increased by exposing individuals to other people behaving in an aggressive fashion. If there is a general tendency to imitate or model the actions of others, then exposure to non-aggressive models should reduce aggressive behaviour. This was found by Baron and Kepner (1970). Participants watched someone in the role of a teacher behave in an aggressive or a non-aggressive way towards a learner. When it was their turn to play the role of teacher, participants imitated the aggressive or non-aggressive behaviour of the model they had observed.

Stronger evidence of the value of observing a non-aggressive model comes in work by Baron (1971). He was interested in what would happen if participants observed an aggressive and a non-aggressive model. What happened was that most of the participants imitated the non-aggressive rather than the aggressive model.

Fostering empathy

Aggressive children tend to focus on the wrongs (real or imagined) that another person has done to them, whereas non-aggressive children focus more on the feelings and thoughts of the other person. The term empathy is used to refer to the ability to understand the feelings of others. As would be expected, those children who experience the most empathy tend to be the least aggressive in their behaviour (Miller & Eisenberg, 1988).

Zahavi and Asher (1978) tried to use increased empathy as a way of controlling the aggressive behaviour of unruly pre-school boys. The boys were told that aggression often hurts other people, that it causes resentment, and that it makes other people unhappy. This training produced a substantial reduction in aggressive behaviour and a large increase in desirable behaviour.

Anything that makes clear the plight of the victim can increase empathy and reduce aggression. For example, Baron (1978) used a situation in which adults thought they were giving electric shocks to someone. When they heard expressions of pain and anguish from the victim, they were less aggressive than when the victim didn't make any sound.

Human violence

There are numerous reasons for the existence of criminal violence. Many of these reasons revolve around disadvantaged living conditions, including poverty, unemployment, divorce, and so on. However, much of the research into violence has focused on certain kinds of personality, especially *anti-social personality disorder* and *psychopathy*.

Individuals with anti-social personality disorder are aggressive, and their behaviour is often irresponsible and unlawful, showing a disregard of social conventions. There are far more men than women with anti-social personality disorder, possibly four or five times as many. Individuals with psychopathy have very poor behaviour control, they lack empathy, and they show little or no remorse after hurting other people.

There are convincing links between these personality disorders and criminality. About 40%–50% of prisoners in American prisons have anti-social personality disorder, and a further 25%–30% have psychopathy.

There are two important implications of the notion that aggressive and violent behaviour depends in part on relatively unchanging personality characteristics based on heredity. First, there should be evidence that biological factors play a role in violence. Second, adults who behave in an aggressive and criminal fashion should tend to have been aggressive as children. Evidence on biological factors was reported by Brunner et al.

1993). They studied a large Dutch family in which the male members of the family were very aggressive. Two were arsonists (people who deliberately cause fires), one tried to run his boss over, one made his sisters undress at knife point, and one raped his sister and attacked a man with a pitchfork. It was discovered that these men suffered from a mutant gene which played a part in causing their aggressive actions.

Aggression from childhood continuing into adulthood was considered by Stattin and Magnusson (1989) in a study of over 1000 people aged between 10 and 26 years. Over a half of the boys who were judged to be very aggressive went on to commit crimes (many of them serious) in adult life.

In sum, the evidence indicates that aggressive and violent behaviour is more likely to occur in individuals with certain kinds of personality (e.g. anti-social personality disorder). However, criminal violence is most common in individuals with those kinds of personality who also have disadvantaged lives.

Further reading

Shaffer, D.R. (1993). *Developmental psychology: Childhood and adolescence* (3rd edn.). Pacific Grove, CA: Brooks/Cole. This book gives a clear account of research on aggression.
Cole, M. & Cole, S.R. (1993). *The development of children* (2nd edn.). New York: Scientific American Books. Chapter 10 is also of interest.

References

Baron, R.A. (1977). *Human aggression*. New York: Plenum.
Dollard, J., Doob, L.W., Miller, N.E., Mowrer, O.H., & Sears, R.R. (1939). *Frustration and aggression*. New Haven, CT: Harvard University Press.
Lorenz, K.Z. (1966). *On aggression*. London: Methuen.
Mead, M. (1935). *Sex and temperament in three primitive societies*. New York: Dell.

Summary

- Mead identified important cultural differences in aggression in three tribes in New Guinea; however, there are considerable individual differences in aggression within any society.
- According to psychodynamic theory, aggression occurs because aggressive energy stemming from the death instinct (thanatos) demands release; there is very little support for this theory.
- The ethologists' approach is similar to psychodynamic theory, in that the emphasis is on the inevitable build-up of aggressive energy; social and cognitive factors affecting aggression are ignored.
- The frustration–aggression hypothesis is an example of the learning theory approach; according to this approach, frustration always leads to aggression, and aggression is always caused by frustration.
- The evidence indicates that frustration does not always lead to aggression, nor is aggression always caused by frustration.
- Animal and human aggression involve the limbic system and the sympathetic nervous system.
- Human aggression differs from aggression in other species in that it is triggered by psychological as well as physical threats; in addition, human aggressive behaviour takes more forms than animal aggressive behaviour.
- Children tend to imitate aspects of their parents' behaviour, and so parents act as models.
- Parents who punish a lot tend to have more aggressive children than those who use little punishment.
- Punishment can be effective when it is given very shortly after an aggressive action.
- According to psychodynamic theory, being aggressive in a harmless way (e.g. in sport) should cause catharsis and reduce subsequent aggression; typically, it does not.
- Removing rewards (e.g. time-out technique), modelling, and fostering empathy are three ways in which children's aggressive behaviour can be reduced.
- Human violence depends on many factors; however, those with anti-social personality disorder or psychopathy are particularly likely to be aggressive and violent in their behaviour.

Key terms

Aggression: behaviour intended to harm or injure another living being.

Anti-social personality disorder: a type of personality involving aggressive behaviour and irresponsible and unlawful actions.

Appeasement rituals: actions (e.g. surrendering) designed to prevent aggression in others.

Catharsis hypothesis: Freud's view that violent behaviour can be prevented if individuals behave aggressively in harmless ways, such as by playing sport.

Displacement: a term used by Freud to describe aggression that is directed towards someone other than the source of one's anger.

Dominance hierarchies: social groups in some species (e.g. apes), in which the status or dominance of individual members is fixed.

Empathy: the ability to understand well the feelings of other people.

Ethology: an approach in which the focus is on studying species in their natural surroundings.

Fighting instinct: according to Lorenz, the inborn tendency for members of a species to fight and to be aggressive.

Frustration–aggression hypothesis: the notion that frustration always produces aggression, and that aggression is always the result of frustration.

Incompatible-response technique: a way of reducing aggressive behaviour in which it is not rewarded by having attention paid to it.

Instrumental aggression: harming someone else as the means to some desired goal, rather than as the goal itself; see **person-oriented aggression**.

Limbic system: a part of the brain involved in aggression.

Modelling: see **observational learning**.

Observational learning: a form of learning based on imitating or copying the behaviour of others; also known as **modelling**.

Person-oriented aggression: this has harming someone else as its main goal; see **instrumental aggression**.

Psychopathy: a mental disorder involving poor control over one's behaviour, a lack of empathy, and few feelings of remorse or guilt.

Ritualisation: aggression expressed in a stereotyped way so as to reduce the possibility of injury.

Time-out technique: a way of reducing aggressive behaviour by removing the individual from the situation in which he or she has been aggressive.

Structured essay questions

1. What is aggression? What are some of the main factors causing aggression?
2. Describe two theories of aggression. What are the strengths and weaknesses of each theory?
3. What can be done to produce non-aggressive children? If they behave aggressively, what techniques can be used to improve their behaviour?

Self-assessment questions

1. Instrumental aggression is aggression that:
   a) involves using a weapon
   -b) has obtaining some desired reward as its main goal
   c) has causing harm as its main goal
   d) is a reaction to the aggression of someone else

2. According to the ethologists, aggression occurs mainly because of:
   a) aggression by others
   b) the need to obtain some desired reward
   c) an inherited fighting instinct
   d) none of the above

3. According to the frustration–aggression hypothesis:
   a) aggression can cause frustration
   b) frustration can cause aggression
   c) life's problems cause frustration and aggression
   d) frustration always leads to aggression, and aggression is always caused by frustration

4. Punishment is most likely to reduce aggression in children when:
   a) there is a short interval between an aggressive action and punishment, and the child understands why punishment has been given
   b) there is a long interval between an aggressive action and punishment, and the child understands why punishment has been given
   c) there is a short interval between an aggressive action and punishment, and the child does not understand why punishment has been given
   d) there is a long interval between an aggressive action and punishment, and the child does not understand why punishment has been given

5. The notion that it is better to find harmless ways of acting aggressively rather than allowing aggressive energy to build up is known as:
   a) the frustration–aggression hypothesis
   b) the catharsis hypothesis
   c) social learning theory
   d) none of the above

6. In the time-out technique, children who behave aggressively:
   a) are rewarded
   b) are ignored
   c) are prevented from continuing with such behaviour
   d) spend time in prison

7. The great majority of prisoners in American prisons suffer from:
   a) psychopathy
   b) anti-social personality disorder
   c) remorse
   d) psychopathy or anti-social personality disorder

Behaviourist approach

part 2

Learning and human behaviour 7

Compared to other species, we are extremely good at learning. In view of its obvious importance, the study of learning has been of central concern to psychologists. One of the main issues is to identify the different forms of learning of which we are capable. It has proved very hard to reach agreement on this issue, but some of the major forms of learning are discussed in this chapter.

Behaviourism was a school of psychology that was started in the United States by John Watson (1913). Watson and the other behaviourists argued that psychology should just be the study of behaviour, because behaviour is objective and observable. They assumed that learning can be understood in terms of conditioning principles. They were very impressed by the work of Pavlov on dogs (discussed later), and felt that this work gave clues about the nature of human learning.

It is now thought that there is much more to human learning than was suggested by the work of Pavlov. For example, much of human learning is based on imitation of the behaviour of others in social situations, and this form of learning was ignored by the behaviourists. With this brief overview of the rise and fall of behaviourism behind us, let us turn without more ado to a more detailed consideration of conditioning and other forms of learning.

John Watson. Photograph reproduced by the permission of the Archives of the History of Psychology.

Classical conditioning

Imagine that you have to go to the dentist. As you lie down on the reclining chair and see the range of instruments around you, you may feel frightened. Why are you frightened before the dentist has caused you any pain? The sights and sounds of the dentist's surgery lead you to expect or predict that you are shortly going to experience pain. In other words, you have formed an *association* between the neutral stimuli of the surgery and the painful stimuli involved in drilling; such associations are of central importance in classical conditioning.

Basic findings

The best-known example of classical conditioning comes from the work of Ivan Pavlov (1849–1936) on dogs. Dogs (and other animals) salivate when food is put in their mouths. In technical terms, what we have here is an unlearned or *unconditioned reflex* involving a connection between the *unconditioned stimulus* of the food in the mouth and the *unconditioned response* of salivation. Pavlov found he could train a dog to salivate to other stimuli. In some of his studies, he presented a tone (the training stimulus) just before food on a number of occasions, so that the tone signalled that food would be arriving soon. Finally, he presented the same tone (the test stimulus) on its own without any food following, and found that the dog salivated to the tone. In technical terms, the dog had learned a *conditioned reflex*, in which the *conditioned stimulus* (the tone) was associated with the unconditioned stimulus (sight of food), and the *conditioned response* was salivation.

Pavlov discovered various features about classical conditioning. One of these was *generalisation*. The conditioned response of salivation was greatest when the tone presented on its own was the same as the tone that had previously been presented just prior to food. However, a smaller amount of salivation was obtained when a different tone was used. Generalisation refers to the fact that the strength of the conditioned response (e.g. salivation) depends on the similarity between the test stimulus and the previous training stimulus.

Pavlov also demonstrated the phenomenon of *discrimination*. Suppose that a given tone is paired several times with the sight of food. The dog will learn to salivate to the tone. Then another tone is presented on its own. It produces a smaller amount of salivation than the first tone through generalisation. Next the first tone is paired with food several more times, but the second tone is never paired with food. Salivation to the first tone

Personal viewpoint

Human beings spend most of their time learning about the world, about themselves, and about other people. Some of them spend a lot of time trying to learn enough to pass examinations. These are examples of complex learning, but we also engage in much simpler forms of learning (e.g. learning to salivate when a meal is put on the table). How many different kinds of learning do you think there are? What factors determine how well we learn?

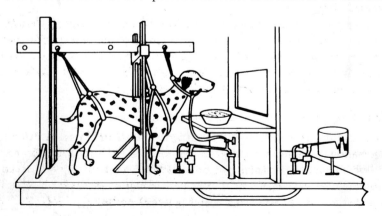

Pavlov's experimental apparatus.

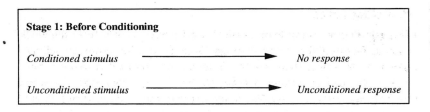

Stage 1: Before Conditioning

Conditioned stimulus ——————————————▶ *No response*

Unconditioned stimulus ——————————————▶ *Unconditioned response*

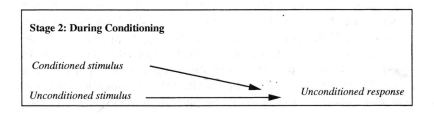

Stage 2: During Conditioning

Conditioned stimulus

Unconditioned stimulus ——————————————▶ *Unconditioned response*

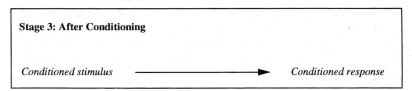

Stage 3: After Conditioning

Conditioned stimulus ——————————————▶ *Conditioned response*

The three stages of classical conditioning.

increases, whereas that to the second tone decreases. In other words, the dog has discriminated clearly between the two tones.

Another key feature of classical conditioning is *experimental extinction*. When Pavlov presented the tone on its own several times, he found that there was less and less salivation. In other words, the repeated presentation of the conditioned stimulus in the absence of the unconditioned stimulus removes the conditioned response. This finding is known as experimental extinction.

Extinction does not mean that the dog or other animal has lost the relevant conditioned reflex. Animals brought back into the experimental situation after extinction produce some salivation in response to the tone. This is known as *spontaneous recovery*. It shows that the salivary response to the tone was inhibited rather than lost during extinction.

Explanations of classical conditioning

What is going on in the classical conditioning situation? It is crucial for an association to be formed between the conditioned and unconditioned stimuli. For that to happen, it is important for the two stimuli to occur close together in time. Conditioning is usually greatest when the conditioned stimulus precedes the unconditioned stimulus by a short interval of time (about half a second is ideal) and stays on while the unconditioned stimulus is presented. If the unconditioned stimulus is presented shortly before the conditioned stimulus, however, there is little or no conditioning. This situation is known as *backward conditioning*.

What is important is that the conditioned stimulus (i.e. tone) allows the dog to *predict* that the unconditioned stimulus (i.e. food) is about to be presented. The tone provides a clear indication that food is about to arrive, and so it produces an effect (i.e. salivation) which is similar to that produced by the food itself. Experimental extinction or the disappearance of salivation occurs when the tone no longer predicts the arrival of food. This explains why backward conditioning is so ineffective. If the conditioned stimulus is only presented after the unconditioned stimulus, then it cannot predict its arrival.

Kamin (1969) provided evidence that conditioning depends on expectation. The animals in the experimental group received light paired with electric shock, and learned to react with fear and avoidance when the light came on. The animals in the contrast group had no training. Then both groups received a series of trials with a light–tone combination followed by shock. Finally, both groups of animals received only the tone. The contrast group responded with fear to the tone on its own, but the experimental group did not.

What is going on here? The experimental animals learned that light predicted shock, and so they ignored the fact that tone also predicted shock. The contrast animals learned that tone predicted shock, because they had not previously learned something different. The term *blocking* is used to refer to what happened with the experimental animals: a conditioned stimulus does not lead to conditioning if another conditioned stimulus is already being used to predict the onset of the unconditioned stimulus.

Evaluation of classical conditioning

Classical conditioning is an important form of learning. Phobias (strong fears of certain objects or situations) can be produced in humans through classical conditioning. For example, as we have already seen, Watson and Rayner (1920) studied a little boy called Albert who had a pet rat. They used classical conditioning to make him frightened of this rat by pairing the sight of the rat with a loud noise (see Chapters 2 and 5).

Most human learning is not based on classical conditioning, however. In classical conditioning, a *passive* animal is presented with various conditioned and unconditioned stimuli. In real life, on the other hand, learning generally involves the animal or human interacting *actively* with the environment.

Classical conditioning is more complex than used to be believed. It used to be thought that classical conditioning occurs only after many training trials, and that the unconditioned stimulus must follow the conditioned stimulus very closely. A dramatic exception was discovered by Garcia et al. (1966). Indeed, it was such an exception to what generally happens that many psychologists initially refused to believe the findings, and Garcia had great difficulty in publishing his findings.

Garcia et al. studied taste aversion. Rats were given saccharin-flavoured water followed by a drug that caused intestinal illness several hours later. This produced *one-trial learning*, with the rats only needing to be sick once in order to avoid drinking the water thereafter. Why was conditioning so rapid in this case? Animals are biologically prepared to learn to behave in ways that will ensure the survival of their species, and it is obviously important for animals to learn to avoid poisoned food.

The early behaviourists assumed that the strong associations needed for classical conditioning could be formed between almost any conditioned stimulus and any unconditioned stimulus. This notion has been disproved, because some associations are much easier to form than others. In one study, rats learned to associate saccharin-flavoured water with illness produced by X-rays, but they did not learn to associate light and sound with illness. Rats naturally learn to associate taste with illness, but are not equipped biologically to associate external stimuli like light and sound with illness.

Instrumental conditioning

In everyday life, people are often persuaded to behave in certain ways by the offer of some reward. For example, students deliver the morning papers because they are paid, and amateur athletes take part in competitions because of the praise they receive for performing well. These are merely two examples of what is known in psychology as *instrumental conditioning*. Much of instrumental conditioning is based on the *law of reinforcement*: the probability of a response occurring increases if that response is followed by a reward or positive reinforcer such as food or praise.

Basic findings

The best-known example of instrumental conditioning is provided by the work of B.F. Skinner (1904–1990). He placed a hungry rat in a small box (often called a Skinner box) containing a lever. When the rat pressed the lever, a food pellet appeared. The rat slowly learned that food could be obtained by lever pressing, and so pressed the lever more and more often.

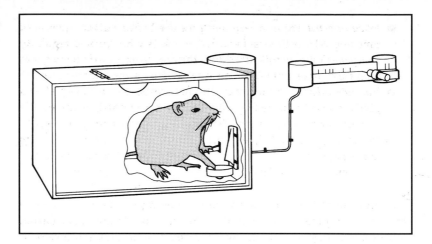

The Skinner box for rats.

This is a clear example of the law of reinforcement. Not surprisingly, the effects of a reward are greater if it follows shortly after the response has been produced than if it is delayed.

The probability of a response has been found to decrease if it is not followed by a positive reinforcer. This phenomenon is known as *experimental extinction*. As with classical conditioning, there is usually some *spontaneous recovery* after extinction has occurred.

There are two major types of positive reinforcers or rewards: *primary reinforcers* and *secondary reinforcers*. Primary reinforcers are stimuli that are needed to live (e.g. food, water, sleep, air). Secondary reinforcers are rewarding because we have learned to associate them with primary reinforcers. Secondary reinforcers include money, praise, and attention.

Schedules of reinforcement. It seems sensible that we tend to keep doing things that are rewarding and stop doing things that are not rewarding. However, Skinner found some complexities in instrumental conditioning. We have so far looked at *continuous reinforcement*, in which the reinforcer or reward is given after every response. However, it is very rare in everyday life for our actions to be continuously reinforced. Consider what happens with *partial reinforcement*, in which only some of the responses are rewarded. There are four main schedules of partial reinforcement:

- *Fixed ratio:* every *n*th (e.g. fifth, tenth) response is rewarded; workers who receive extra money for achieving certain targets are on this schedule.
- *Variable ratio:* on average, every *n*th response is rewarded, but the actual gap between two rewards may be very small or fairly large; this schedule is found in fishing and gambling.

- *Fixed interval:* the first response produced after a given interval of time (e.g. 60 seconds) is rewarded; workers who are paid regularly every week are on this schedule—they receive reward after a given interval of time, but do not need to produce a specific response.
- *Variable interval:* on average, the first response produced after a given interval of time (e.g. 60 seconds) is rewarded; however, the actual interval is sometimes shorter than this and sometimes longer; as Gross (1992) noted, self-employed workers whose customers make payments at irregular times are rewarded at variable intervals, but they do not need to produce a specific response.

It might seem that continuous reinforcement (with reward available after every response) would lead to better conditioning than partial reinforcement. In fact, the opposite is the case. Continuous reinforcement leads to the lowest rate of responding, with the variable schedules (especially variable ratio) leading to very fast rates of responding. This helps to explain why gamblers find it hard to stop their addiction.

What about extinction? Those schedules of reinforcement associated with the best conditioning also show the most resistance to extinction. Thus, rats who have been trained on the variable ratio schedule will keep responding in extinction (in the absence of reward) longer than rats on any other schedule, whereas rats trained with continuous reinforcement stop responding the soonest. One reason why continuous reinforcement

Schedule	Outcome
Continuous	Moderate rate of response; low response to extinction
Fixed interval	Slow rate of response; low resistance to extinction
Variable interval	Steady rate of response; high resistance to extinction
Fixed ratio	Very high rate of response; low resistance to extinction
Variable ratio	High rate of response; high resistance to extinction

Schedules of reinforcement.

leads to rapid extinction is that there is a very obvious shift from reward being provided on every trial to reward not being provided at all. Animals trained on the variable schedules are used to reward being provided infrequently and irregularly, and so it takes much longer for them to realise that they are no longer going to be rewarded for their responses.

Shaping.   One of the features of instrumental conditioning is that the required response has to be made before it can be reinforced. How can we condition an animal to produce a complex response that it would not produce naturally? The answer is by means of *shaping*, in which the animal's behaviour moves slowly towards the desired response through successive approximations. Suppose we wanted to teach pigeons to play table tennis. To begin with, they would be rewarded for making any contact with the table-tennis ball. Over time, their actions would need to become more and more like those involved in playing table tennis for them to be rewarded. In this way, Skinner actually persuaded pigeons to play a basic form of table tennis!

Latent learning.   There are clear links between learning and per-formance. The easiest way of knowing that someone has learned some-thing is by observing appropriate changes in their behaviour. However, it is possible for learning to occur without any obvious effects on performance if positive reinforcement is not provided; this is known as *latent learning*.

Several studies of latent learning have focused on rats running in mazes (see diagram below). Rats who explore a maze but who receive no

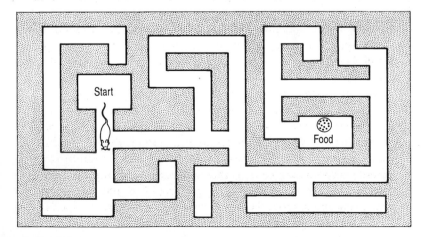

A typical maze.

food reward for doing so appear from their behaviour to have learned very little. However, when food is provided in the goal box at the end or centre of the maze, the rats run rapidly to it, indicating that latent learning has occurred. In one study, Tolman and Honzik (1930) compared maze running in rats who had received no reward over the first 10 days with rats who had been rewarded every day. When the former group started to receive food reward, their performance rapidly improved to the level of the latter group. Thus, latent learning can be as good as learning based on instrumental conditioning.

Negative reinforcement and punishment.   So far we have considered the effects of positive reinforcers or rewards on performance. However, instrumental conditioning can also involve unpleasant or *aversive stimuli* such as electric shocks. Humans and other species learn to behave in ways that reduce their exposure to aversive stimuli just as they learn to increase their exposure to positive reinforcers or rewards.

Punishment.   Instrumental conditioning in which a response is followed by an aversive stimulus is known as *punishment training*. If the aversive stimulus occurs shortly after the response, then it has the effect of reducing the likelihood that the response will be produced in future. However, if there is a substantial delay, then the effects of the aversive stimulus are much reduced.

According to Skinner, punishment can suppress certain responses for a while. However, he claimed that punishment does not produce new learning. Evidence supporting this view was reported by Estes (1944). Two groups of rats learned to press a lever for food, and were then given a series of extinction trials. One group was given a strong electric shock for every lever press during the early stages of extinction, whereas the other group was not. The punishment reduced the rate of responding for a while (suppression), but in the long run the two groups produced the same number of responses. This suggested that the effects of punishment are short-lived.

Most experts do not agree with Skinner and Estes that punishment has only temporary effects on behaviour. One of the features of the study by Estes is that the only way in which the rats could obtain positive reinforcement was by pressing the lever. Punishment has a more lasting effect when it is possible to obtain positive reinforcement with some response other than the one that has been punished. For example, a child who is punished for putting his or her elbows on the table at mealtime is most likely to stop doing this if he or she is also rewarded for sitting properly.

Avoidance learning.   Nearly all drivers stop at traffic lights because of the possibility of aversive stimuli in the form of an accident or trouble with the police if they do not. This is a situation in which no aversive stimulus is presented if suitable action is taken, and it is an example of *avoidance learning*. Many aversive stimuli strengthen any responses that stop the aversive stimuli being presented; they are known as *negative reinforcers*.

Evaluation of instrumental conditioning

Instrumental conditioning is often very effective. It is possible to control the behaviour of humans and other species by clever use of reinforcement. For example, the training of circus animals is largely based on the principles of instrumental conditioning.

Skinner believed in the notion of equipotentiality, according to which virtually any response can be conditioned in any stimulus situation. However, this is not the case. It would be very hard to train an animal to run away from the sight of food to receive food reinforcement! Other psychologists (e.g. Seligman, 1970) have argued for the notion of *preparedness*. According to this notion, each species finds some kinds of learning much easier than other kinds because of its biological make-up. For example, it is natural for pigeons to peck for food, and Skinner found that it was easy to train pigeons to peck at coloured discs for food.

Many psychologists have argued that instrumental conditioning is the main way in which learning occurs. However, instrumental conditioning usually has more effect on performance than it does on learning. Suppose you were offered a reward of £1 every time you said, "The earth is flat". You might (especially if short of money!) say it hundreds of times, so that the reward would have influenced your performance or behaviour. However, it is very unlikely that it would affect your knowledge or learning so that you really believed that the earth was flat.

According to Skinner, we are motivated to carry out tasks because of the external rewards or reinforcers that will follow their successful completion. However, that is not the whole story. People are often motivated by internal factors such as curiosity or the desire to feel competent. In a nutshell, Skinner exaggerated the importance of external influences on behaviour and tended to ignore internal influences.

Social learning: Imitation

It used to be thought that all learning occurred as a result of classical or instrumental conditioning. However, there is also *social learning*, which is based on observing the behaviour of other people. What generally happens is that one person (known as the model) behaves in a particular fashion, with the observer of that behaviour then imitating it.

Social learning was studied by Rosekrans and Hartup (1967). Some children watched a model who behaved in an aggressive way, and who was rewarded for this behaviour. The children then imitated this aggressive behaviour, showing the power of social learning. Other children also saw the model behave in an aggressive way, but this time the model was punished for being aggressive. These children had learned the aggressive behaviour, but they did not imitate it because of the potential threat of punishment. This is another example of latent learning.

Applications of conditioning procedures

Many of the conditioning procedures discussed in this chapter have been used in the treatment of clinical patients. Since the late 1950s, there has been a rapid growth in *behaviour therapy*, which is defined as therapy based on the laws of conditioning. Some of the forms of behaviour therapy will be dealt with here.

Token economy

One form of therapy based on instrumental conditioning is known as the *token economy*. Token economies have been used with patients living in hospitals or other institutions. The patients are given tokens (e.g. poker chips) for behaving in appropriate ways. These tokens can then be used to obtain various rewards, such as cigarettes.

Ayllon and Azrin (1968) used a token economy with female patients who had been hospitalised for an average of 16 years each. The patients were given tokens for making their beds, combing their hair, and other desirable actions. The tokens were exchanged for pleasant activities such as seeing a film or having an extra visit to the canteen. This token economy was very successful, with the number of chores performed each day by the patients increasing eightfold from five to forty.

The main problem with the token economy is that its useful effects sometimes disappear when patients return to normal life. The token economy works because it is carefully arranged so that good behaviour is rewarded, but bad behaviour is not. The outside world is very different, and patients find it hard to transfer what they have learned in a token economy to the much less structured environment outside the hospital.

Aversion therapy

Another way in which patients can be treated with conditioning is by punishing unwanted behaviour by associating it with an aversive stimulus such as electric shock. This is precisely what is involved in *aversion therapy*, which has been used to treat alcoholism. What is often done is to require the alcoholic to take a drug such as disulfiram or Antabuse. This causes violent vomiting if he or she then drinks alcohol. The fact that drinking is followed almost immediately by vomiting often leads to a dramatic reduction in the alcoholic's drinking.

There are two main problems with aversion therapy. First, while it is often very effective in the therapist's office, it can be much less so in the outside world. For example, many alcoholics dislike taking Antabuse, and may simply stop taking it unless there is constant supervision from the therapist. Second, there are serious ethical issues. There is rightly concern about the pain and discomfort caused by giving strong electric shocks or nausea-inducing drugs to patients, even though the patients have provided informed consent for the treatment.

Programmed learning

Skinner used some of the principles of instrumental conditioning to develop new methods of learning for students. He is particularly associated with *programmed learning*, which typically involves the following features:

- The learning material is presented in a series of small steps; this can be done via special books, teaching machines, or a computer.
- The student is asked questions at each step to ensure that he or she has understood the material.
- The student is provided with almost immediate feedback, indicating whether each answer is correct or incorrect.
- The programmes are either linear or branching. Linear programmes work through the material in a single, unchanging order; branching programmes are more flexible, allowing more able students to proceed more quickly through the material.

The use of small steps in programmed learning means that most students make very few errors as they work their way through the material. Thus, they receive much positive reinforcement (being told they are correct), which should enhance learning according to Skinner. Furthermore, this reinforcement is provided shortly after the students have responded, which should also be beneficial to learning.

Most of the evidence suggests that programmed learning is about as effective as other forms of learning (e.g. lectures), but is generally not superior. Programmed learning is most useful for teaching specific knowledge or skills, and it is less successful when used to teach more general or complex knowledge (Taylor, 1964).

Further reading

Mackintosh, N.J. (1994). Classical and operant conditioning. In A.M. Colman (Ed.), *Companion encylopaedia of psychology* (Vol. 1). London: Routledge. This contains detailed accounts of classical and instrumental conditioning, and interesting comparisons between these two forms of conditioning

Eysenck, M.W. (1994). *Individual differences: Normal and abnormal.* Hove, UK: Lawrence Erlbaum Associates Ltd. Chapter 7 discusses the uses of conditioning techniques in behaviour therapy.

References

Ayllon, T., & Azrin, N.H. (1968). *The token economy: A motivational system for therapy and rehabilitation.* New York: Appleton-Century-Crofts.

Garcia, J., Ervin, F.R., & Koelling, R. (1966). Learning with prolonged delay of reinforcement. *Psychonomic Science, 5,* 121–122.

Kamin, L.J. (1969). Predictability, surprise, attention and conditioning. In R. Campbell & R. Church (Eds.), *Punishment and aversive behaviour.* New York: Appleton-Century-Crofts.

Seligman, M.E.P. (1970). On the generality of the laws of learning. *Psychological Review, 77,* 406–418.

Summary

- The importance of classical conditioning was emphasised by the behaviourists.
- Classical conditioning involves the formation of an association between a conditioned stimulus and an unconditioned stimulus to produce a conditioned response.
- There are several phenomena in classical conditioning, including generalisation, discrimination, experimental extinction, and spontaneous recovery.
- Classical conditioning occurs when the conditioned stimulus predicts the arrival of the unconditioned stimulus; this is usually best achieved by presenting the conditioned stimulus about half a second before the unconditioned stimulus.
- Classical conditioning often plays a part in the development of fears; however, most human learning is active, whereas classical conditioning is a rather passive form of learning.
- The ease of achieving classical conditioning depends on whether the association of conditioned and unconditioned stimuli makes biological sense; this has been shown most clearly with taste aversion, in which one-trial learning has been obtained.
- According to the law of reinforcement, the probability of a response occurring increases if that response is followed by a positive reinforcer or reward.
- Primary reinforcers (e.g. food) are needed to live, whereas secondary reinforcers (e.g. money) are rewarding because we have learned to associate them with primary reinforcers.
- Variable ratio and variable interval schedules of reinforcement lead to the most rapid response rates and most resistance to interference.
- Complex responses can be produced in instrumental conditioning by means of shaping, in which there are successive approximations to the required response.
- Latent learning (learning in the absence of performance) occurs when positive reinforcement is not provided.
- Punishment training occurs when a response is weakened by being followed by an aversive stimulus; avoidance learning occurs when a response is strengthened because its occurrence stops an aversive stimulus from being presented.
- It is easier to produce instrumental conditioning when there is a biological preparedness to produce that response in that situation.
- Instrumental conditioning generally has more effect on performance than on learning.
- Social learning is based on observing the behaviour of others.
- Conditioning principles have been applied in various forms of behaviour therapy, including token economies and aversion therapy, and in programmed learning.

Key terms

Aversion therapy: a form of therapy in which unwanted behaviour is punished by associating it with an aversive stimulus (e.g. electric shock).

Avoidance learning: a form of **instrumental conditioning** in which an appropriate avoidance response prevents presentation of an unpleasant or aversive stimulus.

Backward conditioning: a form of **classical conditioning** in which the **unconditioned stimulus** is presented before the **conditioned stimulus**; it produces very weak conditioning.

Behaviour therapy: forms of clinical therapy based on the laws of **classical conditioning** and **instrumental conditioning**.

Behaviourism: an approach to psychology started in the United States by John Watson, according to which most learning can be accounted for in terms of conditioning principles.

Blocking: the lack of a **conditioned response** to a **conditioned stimulus** if another **conditioned stimulus** already predicts the onset of unconditioned stimulus.

Classical conditioning: a basic form of learning in which simple responses (e.g. salivation) are associated with a new or **conditioned stimulus**.

Conditioned reflex: the new association between a **conditioned stimulus** (e.g. a tone) and an **unconditioned stimulus** (e.g. sight of food) producing a **conditioned response** (e.g. salivation).

Conditioned response: the new response that is produced as a result of **classical conditioning**; see **conditioned reflex**.

Conditioned stimulus: a neutral stimulus (e.g. a tone) which is paired with an **unconditioned stimulus** (e.g. sight of food) to produce **classical conditioning**; see **conditioned reflex**.

Continuous reinforcement: the state of affairs in **instrumental conditioning** in which every response is followed by reward.

Discrimination: learning in which a **conditioned response** is made to some stimuli but not to others in **classical conditioning**.

Experimental extinction: the elimination of the **conditioned response** when the **conditioned stimulus** is not followed by the **conditioned response** on several occasions in **classical conditioning**.

Generalisation: the tendency of a **conditioned response** to occur in a weaker form to stimuli similar to the **conditioned stimulus**.

Instrumental conditioning: a form of learning in which behaviour is controlled by rewards or positive reinforcers, or by unpleasant or aversive stimuli.

Latent learning: learning occurring in the absence of changes in behaviour; this form of learning usually occurs when reward or positive reinforcement is not provided.

Law of reinforcement: the probability of a response occurring increases if followed by a reward or positive reinforcer.

Key terms (continued)

Negative reinforcers: unpleasant or aversive stimuli which strengthen any responses that stop the aversive stimuli being presented.

One-trial learning: a **conditioned reflex** that is formed on the basis of a single pairing of the **conditioned stimulus** and the **unconditioned stimulus**.

Partial reinforcement: the state of affairs in **instrumental conditioning** in which only some responses are followed by reward or reinforcement; see **continuous reinforcement**.

Preparedness: the notion that the biological make-up of the members of a species makes **instrumental conditioning** easier with some stimuli and responses than with others.

Primary reinforcers: rewarding stimuli that are needed for life (e.g. food); see **secondary reinforcers**.

Programmed learning: a form of learning in human students, based on the principles of **instrumental conditioning**.

Punishment training: a form of **instrumental conditioning** in which the probability of an undesired response being made is reduced by following it soon after with an unpleasant or aversive stimulus (e.g. electric shock).

Secondary reinforcers: rewarding stimuli (e.g. money) which are associated with **primary reinforcers**.

Shaping: a form of **instrumental conditioning** in which behaviour is changed slowly in the desired direction by requiring responses to become more and more like those desired in order for reward or reinforcement to be given.

Social learning: learning based on observing the behaviour of others.

Token economy: a form of therapy based on **instrumental conditioning** in which tokens are given to criminals or mental patients; these tokens can then be exchanged for rewards.

Unconditioned reflex: a well-established association between an **unconditioned stimulus** and an **unconditioned response**.

Unconditioned response: the well-established reaction (e.g. salivation) to a given **unconditioned stimulus** (e.g. sight of food) in an **unconditioned reflex**.

Unconditioned stimulus: the stimulus that produces a well-established **unconditioned response** in an **unconditioned reflex**.

Structured essay questions

1. What is classical conditioning? What are some of the main phenomena of classical conditioning?

2. What is instrumental conditioning? What are some of the ways in which it has been applied in the real world?

Self-assessment questions

1. In a conditioned reflex:
   a) a conditioned stimulus is associated with an unconditioned stimulus to produce a conditioned response
   b) two conditioned stimuli are associated to produce a conditioned response
   c) two unconditioned stimuli are associated to produce a conditioned response
   d) a conditioned stimulus is associated with an unconditioned stimulus to produce an unconditioned response

2. Experimental extinction occurs when:
   a) there is repeated presentation of the unconditioned and conditioned stimuli
   b) there is repeated presentation of the unconditioned stimulus in the absence of the conditioned stimulus
   c) there is repeated presentation of the conditioned stimulus in the absence of the unconditioned stimulus
   d) no stimuli are presented

3. One-trial learning is found when:
   a) clever animals are used in the experiment
   b) the learning may help to ensure the survival of the species
   c) there is a short interval between the conditioned and unconditioned stimuli
   d) there is a long interval between the conditioned and unconditioned stimuli

4. Secondary reinforcers are:
   a) stimuli that are needed to live
   b) interesting stimuli
   c) stimuli such as food and water
   d) stimuli that are rewarding because we have learned to associate them with primary reinforcers

5. A variable interval reinforcement schedule involves:
   a) rewarding every nth response
   b) on average, rewarding the first response produced after a given interval of time
   c) on average, rewarding every nth response
   d) rewarding the first response produced after a given interval of time

6. Conditioning in which a response is followed by an aversive stimulus is known as:
   a) latent learning
   b) shaping
   c) partial reinforcement
   d) punishment training

7. Therapy in which patients are given tokens for behaving appropriately which can then be used to obtain rewards is known as:
   a) the token economy
   b) behaviour therapy
   c) partial reinforcement
   d) none of the above

8. Programmed learning involves:
   a) presenting the learning material in large steps, and providing almost immediate feedback
   b) presenting the learning material in large steps, and not providing feedback
   c) presenting the material in small steps, and providing almost immediate feedback
   d) presenting the material in small steps, and not providing feedback

Developmental approach

part 3

Jean Piaget, circa 1978. From J.J. Ducret (1990) *Jean Piaget: Biographie et Parcours Intellectual*, published by Editions Delachaux et Niestlé, Lausanne.

tween "me" and "not-me". This body schema helps the infant in its attempts to explore and make sense of the world.

Equilibration is based on the notion that the individual needs to keep a stable internal state (equilibrium) in a complex and changing environment. When a child tries unsuccessfully to understand its experiences in terms of existing schemas, there an unpleasant state of disequilibrium. This leads to the process of equilibration, in which the child uses the processes of assimilation and accommodation to restore a state of equilibrium. In other words, disequilibrium motivates the child to learn new skills and knowledge so as to return to the desired state of equilibrium.

Stages of development

According to Piaget, children's cognitve development goes through a series of stages, each of which is very different from the others. There are four stages:

1. Sensori-motor stage.   This stage lasts from birth to about 2 years of age. It can be regarded as the stage of intelligence in action, since the infant learns much knowledge by moving around his or her environment. The key achievement of this stage is the concept of *object permanence*. This allows the child to be aware of the existence of objects when they are not in view. In the early part of the sensori-motor stage, the infant has no awareness at all of the continued existence of objects when they disappear from view: it is literally a case of "out of sight, out of mind". The concept of object permanence develops as the child moves actively around his or her environment.

2. Pre-operational stage.   This key stage lasts between the ages of about 2 and 7 years. Thinking during this stage is dominated by perception, and this can lead to error. The reason for this is that things are not always the way they look. Piaget argued that children in the pre-operational stage often pay attention to only part of a given situation; this is called *centration*. The way in which centration produces errors has been shown in studies of *conservation*. Conservation refers to an understanding that certain aspects of an object remain the same in spite of various changes to it.

In his classic studies on conservation of quantity, Piaget gave the child two glasses of the same size and shape containing the same quantity of liquid. When the child agreed there was the same quantity of liquid in both glasses, all the liquid from one of the glasses was poured into a glass that was taller and thinner. Pre-operational children failed to show conservation. They argued either that there was more liquid in the new container ("because it's higher") or that there was more liquid in the original glass ("because it's wider"). In either case, the child centres, or focuses, on only one dimension (height or width).

According to Piaget, pre-operational children lack what is known as *reversibility*. This is the ability to undo mentally, or reverse, some operation that was carried out previously. Reversibility in the study just described involves realising that the effect of pouring the liquid from one container into another could be reversed by pouring it back.

Apart from too much reliance on perception, pre-operational children also show *egocentrism*. Egocentrism involves children assuming that their way of thinking about things is the only way. One of Piaget's tasks to study egocentrism was the three mountains task. Children were presented with a three-dimensional model of an imaginary scene containing three

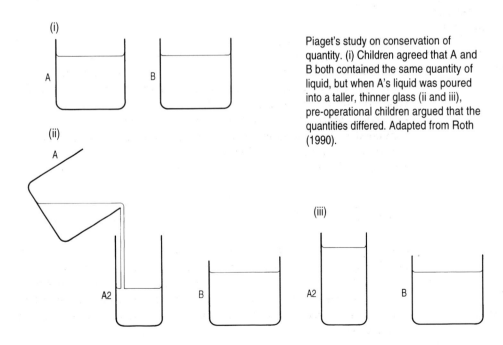

Piaget's study on conservation of quantity. (i) Children agreed that A and B both contained the same quantity of liquid, but when A's liquid was poured into a taller, thinner glass (ii and iii), pre-operational children argued that the quantities differed. Adapted from Roth (1990).

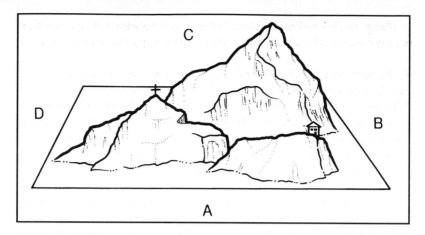

The three mountains task, which was used by Piaget to illustrate egocentrism in children.

mountains. They looked at the scene from one angle (e.g. from position A), and a doll was placed at a different location. Then the children were shown a series of pictures of the three mountains (e.g. from positions B, C or D), and were asked to choose the one showing the scene as it appeared to the doll.

What Piaget found was that 4-year-old children chose the picture that was the same as their own view of the scene. The child's assumption that what the doll can see is exactly the same as what he or she can see is an example of egocentrism. Piaget found that it was only when children reached the age of 7 or 8 that they were able to select the picture showing the scene as it appeared from the doll's position.

3. Concrete operations stage.   This stage lasts between the ages of about 7 and 11. The main advance shown by children in the concrete operations stage over pre-operational children is that thinking becomes much less dependent on perception. Underlying this advance is the development of a number of logico-mathematical operations. These operations include the actions indicated by common symbols such as +, − , ÷, x, > (more than), < (less than), and =. The most important aspect of such operations is reversibility, in which the effects of a perceptual change can be cancelled out by imagining the reverse change.

Piaget stressed that cognitive operations are usually organised into a system or structure (termed a *group* by Piaget). For example, an operation such as "greater than" should be considered together with "less than". A child has not grasped the meaning of "A is greater than B" unless he or she realises that this statement means the same as "B is less than A". The main limitation of children in the concrete operations stage is that their thinking is directed at concrete situations. The ability to escape from the limitations of immediate reality into the realm of abstract ideas is one that is found only in the fourth, and final, stage of cognitive development.

4. Formal operations stage. Children from the age of 11 or 12 enter the stage of formal operations. In this stage, they develop the ability to think in terms of possible (rather than simply actual) states of the world. In other words, individuals in the stage of formal operations can manipulate ideas to a far greater extent than those in the concrete operations stage.

A good example of the difference between the two stages comes from Dworetzky (1981). He asked several individuals to indicate what it would be like if people had tails. Some concrete operations children said that it was a silly question, whereas others indicated where the tail might be on the human body. In contrast, those in the formal operations stage were more willing to consider the possibilities (e.g. that people would get out of lifts quickly; that dogs would know when people were happy).

Evaluation of Piaget

Piaget's theory of cognitive development was an ambitious attempt to explain how children move from being irrational and illogical to being rational and logical. The notion that children learn certain basic operations (e.g. reversibility), and that these operations then allow them to solve a wide range of problems is a valuable one. Certainly no-one before Piaget had provided a detailed account of the ways in which children's thinking changes during childhood.

Piaget argued that all children go through a sequence of four cognitive stages. The great danger with stage theories is that the differences between stages will be over-estimated, whereas the differences within stages will be under-estimated. For example, Piaget assumed that children who show conservation of quantity for one material possess the operation of reversibility, and so should show conservation with other materials. In fact, children generally show conservation of quantity for familiar materials some time before they show it for unfamiliar materials. This indicates that successful performance depends on *specific* learning experiences as well as the *general* cognitive operations emphasised by Piaget.

Another problem with Piaget's work is that he often presented his tasks in confusing ways that made it hard for children to do well. In the conservation task (e.g. pouring a liquid from a broad, short glass into a tall, thin glass), the experimenter deliberately alters the situation. As a result children may assume that he or she intends to change the amount of liquid in some way. This notion was tested by McGarrigle and Donaldson (1974) with number conservation. Six-year-old children were presented with two rows of counters. They all agreed there were equal numbers of counters in each row. In one condition, the experimenter deliberately messed up one of the rows. In the other condition, a "naughty teddy bear" messed up one row in what looked like an accidental way. Only 16% of the children showed conservation when the experimenter moved the counters; in contrast, 62% showed conservation when the counters were moved by naughty teddy.

It has been argued that the three mountains task does not make much sense to young children because it does not relate to their own experience. Donaldson (1984) discussed a study by Hughes using a situation like the three mountains task, but more realistic. There were two walls in the shape of a cross, two policemen dolls, and a boy doll. Children between the ages of 3½ and 5 were given the task of hiding the boy doll so that neither of the policemen could see him. About 90% of the children were able to do this, even though they themselves could still see the boy doll. Thus, even young children are much less egocentric than was assumed by Piaget.

The evidence from studies such as those of McGarrigle and Donaldson and of Hughes indicates that Piaget under-estimated the cognitive skills of pre-operational children. He selected tasks that were rather abstract and lacking in meaning for the child, and which needed careful attention to the precise words used by the experimenter. Such tasks produce much worse performance than tasks that are concrete and meaningful to children.

Piaget provided a detailed *description* of the major cognitive changes in development. However, he did not provide an adequate *explanation* of

An experiment used to show how Piaget had overstated egocentrism in young children.

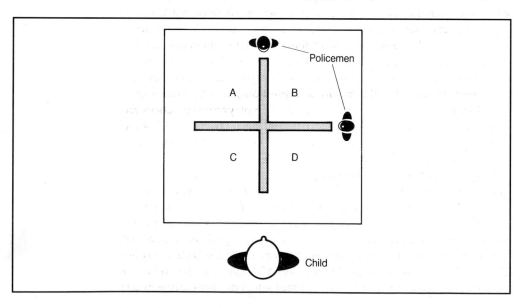

the factors producing these changes. According to Piaget, conflict such as when there is a difference between the child's expectations of what will happen and what actually happens leads to the development of new cognitive structures. However, he did not make it clear how this happens.

Implications for education

The views of Piaget have been influential not only within psychology but also in education. Piaget himself did not focus very much on the usefulness of his theory for educational practice, but many people working in education have done precisely this. As Gross (1992) pointed out, there are three main ways in which Piagetian theory has been applied in education:

1. What can children learn? According to Piaget, what children can learn is determined by their current stage of cognitive development. In other words, it is very much limited to what they are "ready" to learn. This prediction has received little support. Several attempts have been made to teach concrete operations to pre-school children. As the ability to perform concrete operational tasks is normally learned at about the age of 7, it should not be possible, according to Piaget, for much younger children to perform them successfully. However, provision of suitable training to 4-year-olds usually leads to reasonably good performance on such tasks (Brainerd, 1983).

2. How should children be taught? According to Paget, children learn best when they engage in a process of active *self-discovery*. Children apply the processes of assimilation and accommodation to their active involvement with the world around them. Teachers can encourage this by creating a state of disequilibrium, in which the child's existing schemas or cognitive structures are shown to be inadequate. Disequilibrium can be created by asking children difficult questions, and by encouraging them to ask questions. The same ideas apply to playgroup practices and to children playing with toys. According to Piaget, children will obtain the most benefit from playgroups and from toys when they are involved in a process of self-discovery.

Piaget's preferred educational approach can be contrasted with the more traditional approach, in which the teacher provides relatively passive children with knowledge. According to Piaget, this approach (sometimes called tutorial training) is much less effective than self-discovery. Brainerd (1983) reviewed the relevant studies, and concluded that, "although self-discovery training can produce learning, it is generally less effective than tutorial learning." Meadows (1994) arrived at a similar, but broader, conclusion: "Piagetian theory emphasises the individual child as the virtually independent constructor of his own development, an emphasis that under-values the contribution of other people to cognitive development and excludes teaching and cultural influences."

3. What should children be taught?   According to Piaget, cognitive development depends very much on children learning a range of schemas or cognitive structures (e.g. operations). Many of these schemas are based on mathematical or logical principles. It follows that it is useful for children to study mathematics and logic, as well as science subjects which provide illustrations of these principles at work.

The major weakness of Piaget's position is that the cognitive structures he emphasised are of rather limited value for many kinds of learning. For example, it is not clear that learning concrete and formal operations is of much relevance to the learning of foreign languages or of history. Thus, his approach applies only to a small number of the subjects taught at school.

In sum, Piaget's ideas have influenced educational practice in several countries. However, the available evidence indicates that this influence has been of limited value. In some cases (e.g. tutorial training), the more traditional approach appears to be superior to Piaget's alternative approach.

Bruner's developmental theory

Jerome Bruner (1966) proposed a theory of cognitive development that is like the earlier ideas of Piaget in many ways. The central assumption of his theory is that we can represent the world in three ways or modes:

- *Enactive:* based on action.
- *Iconic:* based on mental images.
- *Symbolic:* based on language and other symbols (e.g. mathematical).

The *enactive mode* involves representing the world through actions. In the same way that Piaget emphasised the importance of the baby's own actions and movements during the sensori-motor stage, so Bruner argued that its knowledge of the world initially depends heavily on its behaviour. The development of the enactive mode of representation leads to object permanence, as in Piaget's theory.

The *iconic mode* involves representing the world in the form of mental images. These images generally combine information from a number of different experiences. The iconic mode is of major importance between the ages of 18 months and 7 years.

The *symbolic mode* of representation becomes important at about 6 or 7 years of age. A symbol is something that stands in the place of something else. Words are important symbols which often stand for objects (e.g. the word "cow"), and the full use of the symbolic mode depends on the development of language. Numbers are also important symbols.

An interesting study concerned with the iconic and symbolic modes of representation was reported by Bruner and Kenney (1966). Nine plastic cups of different sizes were arranged in three rows and three columns (see figure below). After children of various ages had studied the display, the cups were moved around. The children were then given one of the following tasks:

1. *Reproduction:* the cups had to be arranged exactly as in the original display; this task required the iconic mode.
2. *Transposition:* the cups that had been in the left column had to be placed in the right column, and vice versa; this task required the symbolic mode.

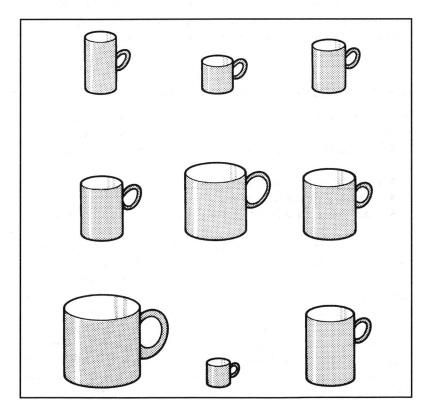

Bruner and Kennedy's (1966) study concerning iconic and symbolic modes of representation.

Of the 5-year-old children, 60% could do the reproduction task, but none could do the transposition task. Of the 7-year-old children, 80% could do the reproduction task and 79% the transposition task. These findings suggest that use of the symbolic mode develops rapidly between the ages of 5 and 7.

Bruner argued that the enactive mode is used first in development, and it is then followed by the iconic mode and the symbolic mode. However, it should not be thought that the earlier modes are no longer used when children start to use the symbolic mode of representation. What actually happens is that older children are able to choose whichever mode of representation is most useful in any given situation.

Development of visual perception

So far in this chapter, we have considered general theories of cognitive development. At a more specific level, it is important to consider the ways in which visual perception develops in children. There is some overlap between the two topics. Older children have developed cognitive processes, structures, and ways of representing the world that are not available to younger children, and this cognitive development is likely to be of use to the development of visual perception. On the other hand, many visual processes (e.g. detection of movement) may be very basic and not depend on cognitive development.

One of the main issues in the development of visual perception is that of the relative importance of innate or inborn factors and of learning in perception. If cognitive development is important to visual perception, then we would expect learning to play a key role. If, however, cognitive development is of little relevance to the development of visual perception, then it is likely that perception depends on innate factors.

One way of studying this issue is to look at humans who have had little or no relevant perceptual experience. If visual perception is innately determined, then their perceptual processing should be adequate. In contrast, if perception depends on learning, then their perceptual processing should be very poor.

You might think that new-born infants (or neonates as they are usually called) would be ideal participants. There are, however, great problems in deciding what (if anything) they are perceiving, because they cannot describe their perceptual experience. However, there is evidence from neonates that some perceptual skills do not require learning. Adams et al. (1986) found that neonates could distinguish grey from colours such as green, yellow, and red. For each of these colours, the neonates preferred colour and grey draughtboards to grey squares of the same brightness. Thus, some degree of colour vision and discrimination is present very shortly after birth.

The issue of whether perception is innate has also been looked at by studying adults who were blind at birth, but who later gained their sight (e.g. through the surgical removal of cataracts). Von Senden (1932) discussed several such individuals, all of whom found visual perception very difficult. Indeed, some of them never moved beyond basic visual skills. This suggests that visual perception is not innate or inborn, but there are strong grounds for doubting such a conclusion. Those concerned had all spent several years developing special skills to compensate for their lack of vision, and these skills may have interfered with the learning of visual skills. In addition, the sudden change from being blind to being sighted often led to emotional and motivational problems, and these slowed down the development of visual perception.

Perception in infants

In view of the problems with studies on neonates and adults who have recovered their sight, many psychologists have focused on perceptual development in infants. It used to be thought that the perceptual experience of infants was, in the words of William James, a "blooming, buzzing confusion". However, it is now generally accepted that infants possess reasonably good perceptual skills. Research carried out by Robert Fantz (1961) helped to change the climate of opinion. He showed head-shaped discs to infants between the ages of 4 days and 5 months (see figure below). Infants of all ages looked most at the realistic face and least at the blank face. On the basis of this, and other findings, Fantz (1966, p.171–172) came to the following conclusion:

Fantz's discs.

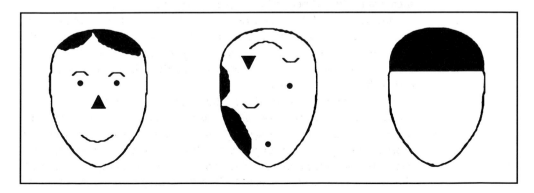

The findings have tended to destroy ... myths—that the world of the neonate is a big booming confusion, that his visual field is a form of blur, that his mind is a blank slate ... The infant sees a patterned and organised world which he explores discriminatingly within the limited means at his command.

Fantz's findings do not really justify this conclusion. He found that the difference in time spent looking at the real and the scrambled faces was fairly small, and other researchers have sometimes been unable to find any difference at all. In addition, infants may look more at the real face not because it is a face, but simply because it is a complex, symmetrical visual stimulus.

The visual cliff.   Eleanor Gibson and Richard Walk (1960) also argued that infants have well-developed perceptual skills. They made a "visual cliff", which was actually a glass-top table. There was a check pattern close to the glass under one half of the table (the "shallow" side), but it was far below the glass under the other half (the "deep" side). Infants between the ages of 6½ and 12 months were placed on the shallow side of the table, and encouraged to crawl over the edge of the visual cliff on to the deep side by being offered toys or by having their mothers call them. Most of the infants did not respond to these incentives, presumably because they possessed at least some of the elements of depth perception.

Work on the visual cliff does not prove that depth perception is innate. The reason is that infants who are several months old might have learned about depth perception from their daily experience. Some evidence suggests that learning is important in the visual cliff situation. Nine-month-old infants had faster heart-rates than normal when placed on

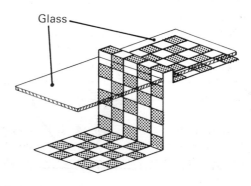

Glass

The visual cliff of
Gibson and Walk
(1960).

the deep side, presumably because they were afraid. In contrast, infants of 2 months actually had slower heart-rates than usual when placed on the deep side, suggesting that they were unafraid because they did not perceive depth. This slowing of heart-rate probably reflected interest on their part.

Other evidence.   Stronger evidence that infants have the basics of depth perception was reported by Bower et al. (1970). They showed two objects to infants under 2 weeks of age. One object was large and approached to within 20 centimetres of the infant's face, whereas the other was small and approached to 8 centimetres. The two objects had the same retinal size (i.e. size at the retina) at their closest point to the infant. In spite of this, the infants were more disturbed by the object that came closer to them. They made use of information about depth to identify which object posed the greater threat.

A key feature of adult perception is the existence of various kinds of constancy (see Chapter 20). We perceive a given object as having the same size and shape almost regardless of its distance from us. This is more of an achievement than might be supposed, because the retinal image of an object is much smaller when it is a long way away than when it is very close. Bower (1964) asked whether infants show size constancy in the following study (illustrated in the diagram overleaf).

The first stage of the study involved teaching the infants to look at a 30-centimetre cube placed about 1 metre from them. He then compared the length of time spent looking at the same cube placed 3 metres from the infant and a 90-centimetre cube placed 3 metres away. The former stimulus had the same real size as the original cube, but a much smaller retinal image. In contrast, the latter stimulus had a much greater real size but the same retinal size as the original cube. Some size constancy was shown by the fact that the infants were almost three times more likely to look at the former than the latter object. However, the infants failed to show total size constancy, because they were more likely to look at the 30-centimetre cube when it was placed 1 metre away rather than 3 metres away.

Bower was studying infants who were 2 or 3 months of age. It is thus possible that they may have learned at least some of the perceptual skills involved in size constancy. However, the exploratory and reaching activities that might lead to the learning of relevant perceptual skills do not usually begin until infants are at least 3 months of age.

Heredity or environment?   The issue of whether visual perception depends mainly on heredity or on environment is an important one. However, it is very difficult to carry out studies on infants that will

Bower's (1964) study to show whether infants show size constancy.

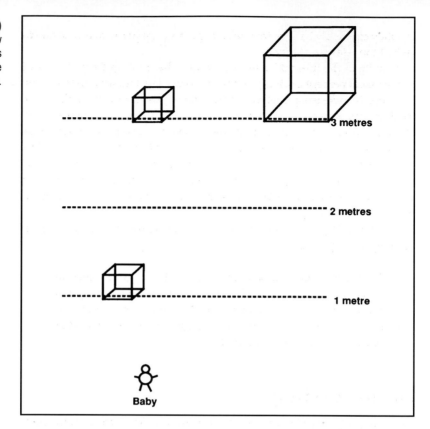

provide clear evidence. Some of the difficulties have already been discussed, but at this point it is worth focusing on the major problems with infant research. Suppose that we test infants of 1 or 2 months of age on some aspect of visual perception. If the infants show the perceptual ability being tested, then it is tempting to conclude that that ability is innate. However, we generally cannot be sure that the infants' learning experiences during their short lives have had no effect on developing that perceptual ability.

Suppose that we test the same infants on another task, and find that they do not show the perceptual ability assessed by the task. It is tempting to conclude that the ability in question depends on environmental factors and a lengthy learning period. However, there is another possibility. The infants may possess the particular perceptual ability, but fail to show it because they do not understand what is required of them. Experienced researchers learn how to make perceptual tasks meaningful for infants, but they can rarely be sure that infants' poor visual performance is due to lack of the relevant ability.

In spite of the difficulties in interpreting the findings from studies of infant visual perception, it is possible to draw a few tentative conclusions.

There is increasing evidence that infants possess more of the basic mechanisms of perception than was previously thought. However, they obviously do not make as much sense of their perceptual environment as adults. They are very good at locating objects within the visual field, but they are not able to process visual information in the systematic and precise way that adults can. For example, if infants are shown a complex visual object, they tend to fixate on just part of it rather than exploring all of its main features.

Salter (1990, p.262) came to the following reasonable conclusion regarding infant perception:

> Early perceptual competence is matched by cognitive incompetence, and much of the re-organisation of perceptual representation is dependent upon the development and construction of cognitive structures that give access to a world of objects, people, language, and events.

Further reading

Meadows, S. (1994). Cognitive development. In A.M. Colman (Ed.), *Companion encyclopaedia of psychology*. London: Routledge. Meadows provides a good account of various theories of cognitive development, including that of Piaget.

References

Brainerd, C.J. (1983). Modifiability of cognitive development. In S. Meadows (Ed.), *Development of thinking*. London: Methuen.

Bruner, J.S. (1966). On the conservation of liquids. In J.S. Bruner, R.R. Olver, & P.M. Greenfield (Eds.), *Studies in cognitive growth*. New York: Wiley.

Donaldson, M. (1984). *Children's minds*. London: Fontana.

Gibson, E.J., & Walk, P.D. (1960). The visual cliff. *Scientific American, 202,* 64–71.

Piaget, J. (1970). Piaget's theory. In P.H. Mussen (Ed.), *Manual of child psychology*. London: Wiley.

Summary

- Piaget argued that adaptation to the environment requires accommodation and assimilation.
- Piaget used the term schema to refer to organised knowledge used to guide action, and equilibration to refer to the need to maintain a stable internal state in a changing environment.
- Piaget identified four stages of development: (1) sensori-motor (intelligence in action); (2) pre-operational (thinking dominated by perception); (3) concrete operations (cognitive systems can be applied to the real world); (4) formal operations (cognitive systems can also be applied to possible worlds).
- Piaget exaggerated the importance of general cognitive operations and minimised the importance of specific learning experiences; he under-estimated children's cognitive skills; and he described rather than explained the stages of cognitive development.
- Piaget's approach has influenced educational practice via his notion of "readiness" to learn, the claimed value of active self-discovery, and his emphasis on the acquisition of logical and mathematical principles; this approach greatly under-estimates the value of tutorial training.
- Bruner put forward three modes of thinking: enactive (action-based); iconic (imagery-based); and symbolic (largely language-based).
- Neonates possess basic visual processes.
- Fantz found that infants looked more at realistic faces than at other stimuli, suggesting they have reasonably good visual perception.
- Studies by Gibson and Walk with the visual cliff, and by Bower suggest that infants have the basics of depth perception.
- There are problems with deciding whether visual perception is innate or acquired; however, basic perceptual processes may be innate, whereas complex interpretive processes need to be learned.

Key terms

Accommodation: in Piaget's theory, changes in an individual's cognitive organisation to deal with the environment.

Assimilation: in Piaget's theory, dealing with new environmental situations by using existing cognitive organisation.

Centration: in Piaget's theory, the tendency to attend to only part of a situation; it is found between the ages of 2 and 7.

Conservation: an understanding that certain aspects of an object remain the same in spite of changes to it; it depends on **reversibility**.

Egocentrism: the young child's assumption that its way of thinking about things is shared by everyone else.

Enactive mode: in Bruner's theory, the young child's tendency to represent the world through actions.

Equilibration: using the processes of **accommodation** and **assimilation** to restore a state of equilibrium.

Group: the organisation of various cognitive operations (e.g. **reversibility**) into a system or structure.

Iconic mode: in Bruner's theory, the child's representation of the world in mental images.

Object permanence: the belief that objects still exist even when they cannot be seen; attained by children during the first two years of life.

Reversibility: the ability to undo mentally, or reverse, some operation that has been carried out; see **conservation**.

Schema: in Piaget's theory, organised knowledge which is used to guide action.

Self-discovery: an approach to teaching children, in which the emphasis is on their active involvement in the learning process; an approach favoured by Piaget.

Symbolic mode: in Bruner's theory, the older child's representation of the world in terms of language.

Structured essay questions

1. Describe Piaget's stage theory of cognitive development. How adequate is this theory?
2. Discuss studies of visual perception designed to discover whether it is due more to innate factors or to learning. What do the various findings suggest?
3. What are the strengths of stage theories of cognitive development? What are the weaknesses of such theories?
4. What influence has Piaget had on educational practice? How useful has this influence been?

Self-assessment questions

1. In Piaget's theory, the process of the individual adjusting to the outside world by altering his or her cognitive organisation is known as:
    a) schematic processing
    b) equilibration
    c) assimilation
    d) accommodation

2. During the pre-operational stage, children:
    a) are unaware of the existence of objects when they are not in view
    b) show reversibility and various logico-mathematical operations
    c) show centration and egocentrism
    d) are too little influenced by perception

3. During the stage of formal operations, children:
    a) develop the ability to think in terms of possible states of the world
    b) think only in terms of actual states of the world
    c) develop no new abilities that are not found during the concrete operations stage
    d) none of the above

4. According to Piaget, children learn best when there is:
    a) self-discovery training
    b) tutorial learning
    c) formal teaching by teachers
    d) passive reception of information

5. According to Bruner, the order in which children learn different ways of representing the world is as follows:
    a) iconic, then enactive, then symbolic
    b) enactive, then iconic, then symbolic
    c) enactive, then symbolic, then iconic
    d) iconic, then symbolic, then enactive

6. The visual cliff is used to study:
    a) children's ability to move
    b) children's fears
    c) depth perception
    d) courage

7. Infants in size constancy experiments:
    a) show complete size constancy
    b) show some size constancy
    c) show no size constancy at all
    d) cannot do the task

Language development 9

As this chapter is concerned with language development, it is useful to start by defining the term "language". According to Sternberg (1995), it can be defined as "an organised means of combining words in order to communicate." Parrots say certain words, but they are not using language. What they say is not organised, nor does it involve combining words to pass on a message to others.

Perhaps the most remarkable achievement of young children is the breathtaking speed with which they acquire language. By the time they are 2 years old, most children use language to communicate hundreds of messages. By the age of 5, children who may not even have started to go to school have mastered most of the grammatical rules of their native language. What is especially impressive is that very few parents are able to tell their children about the rules of grammar, because they are not consciously aware of these rules. Thus, young children simply "pick up" the complex rules of grammar without the benefit of any formal teaching.

There have been various attempts to explain how children learn language. Some of the major theories are discussed here, after we have identified the major stages in language development. Finally, the issue of whether language is unique to the human species is addressed in the context of attempts to teach language to chimpanzees.

Stages of language development

The first point that needs to be made about language development is that we need to distinguish between *receptive language* (language comprehension) and *productive language* (language expression or speaking). Young children of 1 year and above (and adults as well) have better receptive language than productive language. It is possible to under-estimate the language skills of children by assuming that their speech reflects all the knowledge of language they have learned.

As Shaffer (1993) pointed out, children learning language need to learn at least four kinds of knowledge:

> **Personal viewpoint**
>
> Language is of great importance to the human species. Normal life is impossible for those who do not have a good ability to use and to understand language. Mastering language is very complicated, but nearly all young children do so with apparent ease. How do you think they manage to do this? Attempts have been made to teach language to chimpanzees. Do you think any of these attempts have been successful?

1. *Phonology:* the sound system of a language.
2. *Semantics:* the meaning conveyed by words and by sentences.
3. *Syntax:* the set of grammatical rules indicating how words may and may not be combined to make sentences.
4. *Pragmatics:* the principles determining how language should be modified to fit the context (e.g. it may be necessary to speak slowly and distinctly when speaking to a foreigner).

Children learn about language in the order listed. That is, they first of all learn to make sounds, followed by developing an understanding of what those sounds mean. After that, they learn grammatical rules and how to change what they say to fit the situation.

One-word stage

Up until the age of about 18 months, young children are limited to single-word utterances. Nelson (1973) studied the first 50 words used by infants, and put them into six categories. The largest category was classes of objects (e.g. cat; dog; car). The next largest category was specific objects (e.g. Mummy; Daddy). The other four categories used by young children were (in descending order of frequency): action words such as "go" and "come"; modifiers (e.g. "mine"; "small"); social words (e.g. "please"; "no"); and function words (e.g. "for"; "where").

Almost two-thirds of the words used by young children refer to objects or people. Why is this so? Children use language to refer to things that are of interest to them, which are mainly the people and objects that surround them.

Young children often make mistakes with word meanings. Some words are initially used to cover more objects than they should. This is known as *over-extension*. It can be embarrassing, as when a child refers to every man as "Daddy". The opposite mistake, in which the meaning given to a word covers too few objects, is known as *under-extension*. For example, the child may think that the word "cereal" refers only to the brand of cereal he or she has for breakfast.

McNeill (1970) and others have referred to the one-word stage as the *holophrastic period*. What is meant by this is that young children are trying to convey much more meaning than their utterance would suggest. For example, an infant who says "ball" while pointing to a ball may mean that he or she would like to play with the ball. McNeill claimed that infants only produce one-word utterances because they have a limited attention span and and a small vocabulary.

It is difficult to test McNeill's notion of a holophrastic period. In its favour is the fact that young children often suggest by their actions or by their tone of voice that they are trying to communicate more than just one word. On the other hand, young children have very limited cognitive development. This must restrict their ability to have complex ideas.

Telegraphic period

The second stage of language development is known as the *telegraphic period*. It begins at, or shortly after, 18 months of age. Its name arises because the speech of children in this stage is rather like a telegram. Telegrams tend to cost so much per word, and so senders of telegrams try to make them as short as they can. In order to do this, content words such as nouns and verbs are included, but function words such as "a", "the", "and", pronouns, and prepositions are left out. The same is true of the speech of young children. However, they leave out even more than is left out of a telegram. For example, they omit plurals and tenses.

Even though young children are largely limited to two-word utterances, they are still able to communicate numerous meanings. One reason for this is that a given two-word utterance may mean different things in different situations. For example, "Daddy chair" may mean "I want to sit in Daddy's chair", "Daddy is sitting in his chair", or "Daddy, sit in your chair."

Telegraphic speech is based on rules. One kind of rule was explored by Braine (1963). He carried out a distributional analysis, in which he considered the frequency with which different words occurred in children's speech, and their usual position in their speech. This analysis suggested that early speech consists of two main classes of words: *pivot* words and *open* words. Pivot words always occur in the same place within an utterance, there are few of them, and they are used very often. In contrast, open words appear in different places in different utterances, there are many of them, and each open word is used fairly rarely. Most telegraphic sentences consist of a pivot word plus an open word. Braine recorded these examples of a pivot word followed by an open word from one child: all broke; all clean; all done; all dressed; all gone; all messy.

The speech of many children does seem to be based on the distinction between pivot and open words. However, this distinction does not account for the utterances of all young children, especially those speaking languages other than English.

Another, more important, way in which telegraphic speech is based on rules was identified by Roger Brown (1973). He argued that young children possess a basic order rule: a sentence consists of agent + action + object + location (e.g. "Daddy eats lunch at home"). Their two-word utterances follow the basic order rule. For example, an utterance containing an agent and an action will be in the order agent–action (e.g. "Daddy walk") rather than the reverse order ("walk Daddy"). In similar fashion, action and object will be spoken in the order action–object (e.g. "drink Coke").

One of the most important aspects of telegraphic speech is that it is very similar regardless of the language to which the child has been exposed. For example, children all over the world construct two-word utterances that obey the basic order rule.

Subsequent developments

Children's language develops a lot between 2½ years and 5 years of age. The most obvious change is in the mean length of utterance, which is usually measured in terms of the number of morphemes (meaningful units) produced. Another important change is based on the learning of what are known as *grammatical morphemes*. These include prepositions, prefixes, and suffixes (e.g. "in"; "on"; plural -s, "a"; "the"). What is striking is that all children learn the various grammatical morphemes in the same order (de Villiers & de Villiers, 1973). They start with simple ones (e.g. including "in" and "on" in sentences) and then move on to more complex ones (e.g. reducing "That is" to "That's" or "They are" to "They're"). The grammatical morphemes that are learned are basically rules which can be applied to most situations.

It could be argued that children are simply imitating other people rather than learning rules. However, there is much evidence to show that children are really learning rules. Some of the evidence comes from cases in which children make grammatical errors. A child will say, "The dog runned away", which is a sentence that parents and other adults are unlikely to produce. Presumably the child is applying the rule that the past tense of a verb is usually formed by adding -ed to the present tense. The tendency to use a rule in situations in which it does not apply is known as *over-regularisation*.

Those who believe that children learn language by imitation might argue that over-regularisation occurs because children imitate what other children say. However, the issue was settled by Berko (1958). Children were shown two pictures of an imaginary animal or bird and told, "This is a wug. This is another wug. Now there are two …" Berko found that even young children produced the regular plural form "wugs", even though they had never heard the word before.

Between the ages of 2½ and 5, children start to use more complex sentences containing a number of different ideas. When my daughter Fleur was 2 years old, we were crossing

This is a wug

Now there is another one.
There are two of them.
There are two _____

the Channel when I pointed out what I thought was a boat to her. Her (entirely accurate) reply was, "Daddy, that's not a boat, it's a yacht."

Finally, children at this stage develop a good grasp of pragmatics, or the need to make what they say fit the situation. Shatz and Gelman (1973) analysed the speech of 4-year-old children when talking about a new toy to a 2-year-old or to an adult. The children used complex sentences and were polite when talking to the adult. In contrast, they used short sentences when talking to the young child, and focused on holding its attention (e.g. "Look at this!").

Nativist theories of child language

Language acquisition device

One way of explaining how it is that young children learn the complexities of language so rapidly and with such apparent ease is to adopt a nativist approach. Those who have put forward *nativist theories* of child language argue that infants are born with knowledge of the structure of human languages. For example, Chomsky (1965) argued that humans possess a *language acquisition device*, which consists of innate knowledge of grammatical structure.

In developing the notion of a language acquisition device, Chomsky drew a distinction between the surface structure and the deep structure of a sentence. The surface structure is based on the actual phrases used in a sentence, whereas the deep structure reflects its meaning. For example, the sentence, "Visiting relatives can be boring", has only one surface structure. However, it can mean either that it is sometimes tedious to visit relatives or that relatives who come on a visit can be boring. The two meanings of this, and other sentences, are distinguished in the deep structure.

The distinction between surface and deep structure is also important in two sentences such as "The man wrote the book," and "The book was written by the man." The meaning of these two sentences is very similar, which is clear in the deep structure, but not in the surface structure.

Chomsky introduced the notion of a *transformational grammar*. This allows us to transform the meaning, or deep structure, of a sentence into the actual words in the sentence (surface structure). According to Chomsky, this transformational grammar is innate and forms a key part of the language acquisition device.

Chomsky assumed that all humans have the same language acquisition device. This view finds some support in the existence of various *linguistic*

occur because it is natural to pay attention first to the person responsible for carrying out an action, rather than to the person or object towards whom the action is directed.

Environmental approaches to language

Skinner's approach

According to the behaviourist B.F. Skinner (1957), language is learned in the same way as other responses. Only those utterances that are rewarded or reinforced become stronger. In other words, language learning involves instrumental conditioning (see Chapter 7). Language develops through a process of shaping, in which the child is rewarded for making successive approximations to accurate speech. This often takes the form of imitation. A child tries to repeat what his or her parent has just said, and is rewarded or reinforced if it is fairly similar.

Problems with Skinner's approach. Detailed analysis of the language behaviour of young children provides evidence against a reinforcement theory of language acquisition. Brown et al. (1969) observed the interactions between middle-class American parents and their young children. Parents rewarded or reinforced the speech of their children on the basis of its accuracy or truth rather than the grammar used. According to Skinner, this training should have produced adults whose speech is very truthful but ungrammatical. In fact, of course, the speech of most adults is grammatical but not always very truthful.

As we saw earlier in the chapter, most children develop an excellent command of language very rapidly. Many experts (e.g. Chomsky, 1959) doubt whether such rapid language acquisition would be possible on the basis of imitation and reinforcement. It can take some time to learn a single response via reinforcement, and yet children learn thousands of words and a good understanding of grammar.

It seems to follow from Skinner's approach that in their speech children should tend to imitate or copy what they have heard other people say. In fact, the telegraphic speech of children under the age of 2 does not usually closely resemble the utterances of other people. As children's language develops, it tends to become more and more creative. Children will often produce sentences that they have never heard before.

Finally, and most importantly, Skinner focuses on the learning of specific responses (e.g. pressing a lever; saying a word) by means of reinforcement. However, much of the knowledge of language possessed by children is not in the form of specific responses at all. They know a lot about grammatical rules, but it makes no sense to argue that a grammatical rule is a response that can be rewarded. Skinner's instrumental conditioning principles may be of some relevance in understanding how children learn individual words. However, they are of little or no value in understanding how they acquire a knowledge of grammar.

Social context

Skinner focused on certain experiences (e.g. imitation; reinforcement) that children have during the course of language development. As we have seen, his approach is seriously deficient. However, other psychologists have argued that children's experiences are important, but that Skinner did not identify the key experiences. For example, Bruner (1975) emphasised the importance of social interaction between the mother and her child. According to him, a mother with her child will often talk about events and objects with which the child is involved. The child can use its knowledge of what it is doing to help in the task of understanding language.

Harris et al. (1985) studied mothers and young children between the ages of 7 months and 16 months. They were particularly interested in the reasons why mothers changed the topic of conversation. They found that this generally happened when the child looked in a different direction or when it moved. In other words, mothers tried to fit what they said to their child's focus of attention.

Important evidence that language development depends on a close association between the mother's speech and the child's current activity was reported by Harris et al. (1986). They found on average that 78% of what mothers said to their 16-month-old children related to the objects to which the children were attending. This figure was much lower (49%) in a group of children whose language development was poor at the age of 2.

Mothers clearly play a major role in their children's language development. However, children are sometimes influenced too much by the ways in which their mothers use language. For example, a small boy called James initially used the word "Mummy" when he was trying to give a toy to his mother, but he did not use it in other situations (Harris et al., 1988). It turned out that his mother most often used the word "Mummy" when she wanted him to give her a toy. However, James rapidly learned to use the word "Mummy" in more flexible ways, and children generally only use words in too narrow a fashion for a short period of time.

Motherese and expansions. Several researchers have looked in detail at the ways in which mothers talk to their young children. They tend

The earliest form of interpersonal expression. A 6-week-old girl smiles at her mother's face, then responds to gentle baby-talk with cooing vocalisation and a conspicuous hand movement. In the third picture, the mother is imitating the preceding vocalisation of her baby. From: Olsen D.R. (1980). *The social foundation of language and thought*. New York: W.W. Norton.

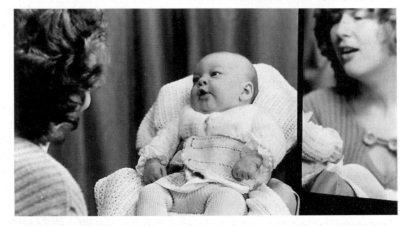

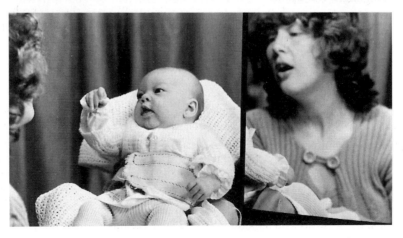

to use very short, simple sentences; this is often called *motherese*. The length and complexity of what the mother says to her child gradually increase as the child's own use of language develops (Shatz, 1983). Perhaps even more importantly, the mother tends to use sentences that are a little bit longer and more complicated than the sentences produced by her child (Bohannon & Warren-Leubecker, 1989).

Mothers, fathers, and other adults also help children's language development by means of *expansions*. Expansions consist of fuller and more grammatical versions of what the child has just said. For example, a child might say, "Cat out", with its mother responding, "The cat wants to go out."

The language development of children is greatly helped by conversations with adults involving motherese, expansions, and so on. However, it is not certain that this kind of help is needed for normal language development. As Shaffer (1993) pointed out, there are several cultures (e.g. the Kaluli of New Guinea) in which adults talk to children as if they were adults. In spite of this, children in these cultures seem to develop language at about the normal rate (Gordon, 1990).

Animal language

It might seem that we are unlikely to learn much about human language by studying language in other species. However, this is not accurate so far as the issue of deciding whether chimpanzees can learn language is concerned. Some theorists (e.g. Chomsky) argue that language is unique to the human species, whereas others (e.g. Skinner) dispute this. According to Chomsky, as the human species is the only one with a language acquisition device, there is no way in which other species could develop language. The opposite prediction follows from Skinner's (1957) reinforcement approach to language. According to Skinner, there is nothing special about language, and thus there is no reason why language could not be learned by other species.

Gardner and Gardner

The attempt to teach language to chimpanzees started in earnest in 1966. Allen and Beatrice Gardner began to teach American Sign Language to a 1-year-old female chimpanzee. After four years of training, Washoe knew 132 signs, and could arrange them in novel ways. For example, when she saw a swan she signed, "water bird". There was also evidence that she had grasped some of the elements of grammar. For example, she signed "tickle me" much more often than "me tickle", and "baby mine" more frequently than "mine baby". In view of what Washoe was able to do, the Gardners concluded that she had learned language.

Key terms

Critical-period hypothesis: the notion that language learning is easier before puberty than it is afterwards.

Expansions: utterances of parents and other adults which consist of fuller and more accurate versions of what a child has just said.

Grammatical morphemes: prepositions, prefixes, suffixes, and so on, which help to indicate the grammatical structure of utterances.

Holophrastic period: the earliest stage of children's speech, during which one word is used to express a lot of meaning.

Language: "an organised means of combining words in order to communicate" (Sternberg, 1995).

Language acquisition device: innate knowledge of grammatical structure, which is used to help language learning.

Linguistic universals: features (e.g. nouns; verbs) that are common to nearly all languages.

Motherese: the short, simple sentences used by mothers when talking to their young children.

Nativist theories: theories that emphasise innate factors.

Open words: words used in different places within the speech of children; used in the **telegraphic period**.

Over-extension: use of a word to cover more objects than it should be applied to.

Over-regularisation: tendency of children to use a rule in situations to which it does not apply.

Phonology: the sound system of a language.

Pivot words: words always used in the same place within children's speech; used during the **telegraphic period**.

Pragmatics: the principles involved in deciding how to use language to fit the situation.

Productive language: language expression or speaking.

Receptive language: comprehension or understanding of language.

Semantics: the meaning conveyed by words and sentences.

Syntax: the set of grammatical rules indicating the ways in which words can be combined to form sentences.

Telegraphic period: the second stage of language development, during which children's speech is like a telegram (much information contained in two or three words).

Transformational grammar: in Chomsky's theory, what allows the meaning of a sentence to be turned into the words actually used in the sentence.

Under-extension: the use of a word to cover fewer objects than it should be applied to.

Structured essay questions

1. Describe the early stages of language development. What are the main changes that occur?
2. Describe some of the work on animal language. Does it indicate that other species can learn language?
3. How did Skinner account for language development? Does the evidence support his account?
4. What is a language acquisition device? Does it account for language development?

Self-assessment questions

1. Language can be defined as:
   a) involving only combining words in an organised way
   b) involving combining words in an organised way in order to communicate
   c) involving only the attempt to communicate
   d) being able to say many words

2. The stage at which young children produce two-word utterances is known as:
   a) the holophrastic period
   b) the grammatical period
   c) the telegraphic period
   d) none of the above

3. The tendency to use rules in situations in which they do not apply is known as:
   a) being ungrammatical
   b) imitation
   c) under-regularisation
   d) over-regularisation

4. The language acquisition device:
   a) consists of innate knowledge of grammatical structure
   b) is acquired during the first few years of life
   c) consists of innate knowledge of grammatical structure and vocabulary
   d) is only acquired during adolescence

5. According to the critical-period hypothesis:
   a) language can best be learned at a very early age
   b) language learning is easier before puberty than after
   c) language learning is equally easy at all ages
   d) language learning is easier after puberty than before

6. According to Skinner, language develops through:
   a) shaping, imitation, and classical conditioning
   b) shaping and imitation only
   c) shaping, imitation, and instrumental conditioning
   d) classical and instrumental conditioning

7. Mothers talking to their children tend to:
   a) use sentences that are a little longer and more complicated than the sentences of their children
   b) use sentences that are a little longer but less complicated than the sentences of their children
   c) use sentences that are a little shorter and less complicated than the sentences of their children
   d) use sentences that are a little shorter and more complicated than the sentences of their children

8. With training, chimpanzees can learn to produce:
   a) all aspects of language
   b) dozens of words, but mostly in very short utterances
   c) dozens of words, often in long utterances
   d) dozens of words, mostly in spontaneous utterances

Moral development 10

This chapter deals with the changes in morality that occur as children grow up into adults. What do we mean by "morality"? According to one definition, morality implies "a set of principles or ideals that help the individual to distinguish right from wrong and to act on this distinction" (Shaffer, 1993).

Why is morality important? One key reason is that society cannot work properly unless there is general agreement on what is right and what is wrong. There will always be some moral issues (e.g. animal experiments; nuclear weapons) on which people in a given society will have very different views, and which will lead to campaigns, marches, and other forms of protest. However, if there were controversy about all major moral issues, then society would become chaotic.

As Shaffer (1993) pointed out, there are three main moral components. First, there is the *cognitive component*. This is concerned with the ways in which we think about moral issues, and decide what is right and wrong. Second, there is the *emotional component*. This is concerned with the feelings associated with moral thoughts and behaviour; these feelings include pride, guilt, and shame. Third, there is the *behavioural component*. This is concerned with the ways in which we behave, and includes the extent to which we lie, steal, cheat, and behave honourably.

There are two major reasons for distinguishing among these three moral components. The first reason is that there is often a difference between two components. We may know at the cognitive level that it is wrong to cheat, but we still go ahead and cheat at the behavioural level. Alternatively, some people lead blameless lives (behavioural component), but still feel guilty and ashamed

Photo courtesy TRIP, photographer R. Turner.

(emotional component). The second reason is that theories of moral development generally focus mainly on only one moral component. As we will see, Piaget and Kohlberg emphasised the cognitive component, Freud emphasised the emotional component, and the social learning theorists concentrated on the behavioural component.

Psychodynamic theory

Sigmund Freud argued in his psychodynamic theory that the human mind is divided into three parts: the *ego*, the *id*, and the *superego*. The ego is concerned with conscious thinking; the id deals with basic motivational forces (e.g. the sexual instinct); and the superego is concerned with moral issues. More specifically, the superego consists of the conscience and the ego-ideal. Our conscience makes us feel ashamed or guilty when we have behaved badly, whereas our ego-ideal makes us feel proud of ourselves when we have behaved well in the face of temptation.

According to Freud, the superego develops around the age of 5 or 6. Boys develop sexual desires for their mother, and this leads to an intense rivalry with their father. This state of affairs is known as the *Oedipus complex*, and makes boys fearful because they are much weaker than their father. The situation is resolved when boys identify with their father. By so doing, they adopt their father's moral standards, and so form a superego.

A somewhat similar process is supposed to occur in girls at about the same age. They develop an *Electra complex* based on their desires for their father. This complex is resolved by identifying with their mother and adopting her moral standards. According to Freud, girls do not identify with their mother as strongly as boys identify with their father. As a consequence, girls develop weaker superegos than boys. However, Freud did admit that, "the majority of men are far behind the masculine ideal [in terms of strength of superego]."

As we have seen, Freud argued that a child's superego is based in large measure on the moral values of its same-sexed parent. In some ways, the conscience represents the punishing parent and the ego-ideal represents the rewarding parent. Freud claimed that fear of the same-sexed parent was of crucial importance in producing the superego. It follows that parents who are aggressive and punishing should have children who have strong superegos. In fact, the opposite seems to be the case. Parents who make the most use of spanking and other forms of punishment tend to have children who behave badly and who experience little guilt or shame (Hoffman, 1988).

Freud's notion that girls have weaker superegos than boys has been disproved in several studies. Hoffman (1975) discussed various experiments in which the tendency of children, when on their own, to do what they had been told not to do was assessed. There was no difference between boys and girls in most of the studies. In those few studies in which there was a sex difference, it was the girls (rather than the boys) who were better at resisting temptation.

There are three other major problems with the psychodynamic theory of moral development. First, Freud exaggerated the importance of the same-sexed parent in the development of children's morality. The other-sexed parent and other children also generally play an important role (Shaffer, 1993). Second, Freud focused too much on emotional factors in morality and not enough on the thought processes that help to determine whether we behave well or badly. Later theorists such as Piaget and Kohlberg argued that such thought processes were the key to moral development. Third, Freud argued that children make dramatic progress in moral development at the age of 5 or 6, far more than they will make in later childhood or adulthood. In fact, there is substantial moral development in late childhood and adolescence. For example, Colby et al. (1983) found that there were large changes in moral reasoning between the ages of 10 and 16.

Piaget's cognitive–developmental theory

According to Jean Piaget's theory of cognitive development (see Chapter 8), children's thinking goes through a series of stages. The early stages focus on what the child can see and hear, whereas the later stages involve the ability to think in an abstract way about possible events that may never happen. In a similar way, Piaget argued that children's moral reasoning also proceeds through a number of different stages.

Piaget developed his ideas about moral reasoning by playing marbles with children of different ages. He was interested in seeing how well they understood the rules of the game, how important they thought it was to obey those rules, and so on. His observations led him to propose the following series of stages in his cognitive–developmental theory of moral development:

1. *Premoral period* (0–5 years): children in this stage have very little understanding of rules or other aspects of morality.
2. *Stage of moral realism or heteronomous morality* (5–10 years): children at this stage are rather rigid in their thinking—they believe that rules must be obeyed no matter what the circumstances are (e.g. it's wrong to tell a lie even if it will spare someone's feelings). Children at this stage think that rules are made by important other people (e.g. parents), and that how bad an action is stems from its consequences rather than from the intentions of the person carrying out the action. Piaget told children at this stage about a boy called John who opens a door and by so doing breaks 15 cups on the other side of the door. Even though John had no idea there were any cups there, he was still regarded by the children as being naughty.

   There are two other key features of the moral reasoning of children at the stage of moral realism. First, they believe in what is known as *expiatory punishment*: the naughtier the behaviour, the greater should be the punishment, but there is no idea that the punishment should fit the crime. For example, a child who drops a freshly baked cake on the floor should be spanked rather than having to help to bake another cake. Second, children between the ages of 5 and 10 are strongly in favour of the notion of fairness. This lead them to believe in *immanent justice*, which is the idea that naughty behaviour will always be punished in some way.
3. *Stage of moral relativism or autonomous morality* (10 years upwards): children at this stage think in a more flexible way about moral issues. They understand that moral rules evolve from human relationships, and that people differ in their standards of morality. They also understand that most rules of morality can be broken in some situations. For example, if a violent man with a gun demands to be told where your mother is, it is perfectly acceptable to tell a lie and say that you do not know where she is.

   There are other major differences between this stage of moral development and the previous one. First, the child now thinks that the wrongness of an action depends far more on the individual's intentions than on the consequences of his or her behaviour. Second, children in this stage believe in *reciprocal punishment* rather than expiatory punishment. In other words, the punishment should fit the crime. Third, children in this stage have learned that people often behave wrongly but manage to avoid punishment. Thus, they no longer believe in immanent justice.

Piaget's cognitive–developmental account of the various stages of moral development has now been discussed in some detail. Why does moral reasoning change in these ways? According to Piaget, there are two main factors involved:

1. Young children are egocentric in their thinking; that is, they see the world only from their own point of view. At about the age of 7, they become less egocentric. Their growing awareness of the fact that other people have a different point of view allows them to develop more mature moral reasoning.
2. Older children develop flexible ideas of morality because they have considerable exposure to the different views of other children of the same age. This exposure leads them to question their own values. In contrast, most younger children have rather rigid ideas of morality. What counts as good or bad behaviour is determined very much by the reactions of their parents.

Experimental evidence

There is much evidence that children in most Western societies go through Piaget's stages of moral development (Shaffer, 1993). Younger children attach more importance to the consequences of an action than older children when deciding how naughty it is. However, they attach less importance to the intentions of the actor (Shaffer, 1993).

In spite of these successes for Piaget's theory, it has become clear that young children think about moral issues in more complex and mature ways than Piaget believed. This was shown in a study by Nelson (1980). She used drawings and detailed descriptions of situations so that the 3-year-old children in her study could understand clearly what was happening in various stories. Her key finding was that even young children take much account of the actor's intentions, regarding his or her behaviour as much better when the intentions were good than when they were bad. This is several years earlier than Piaget had assumed.

According to Piaget, children at the stage of moral realism follow the rules of parents and other authority figures in an accepting and rather

What are the advantages and disadvantages of Piaget's theory?

PLUS	MINUS
• Piaget was right to assume that there are close links between cognitive development in general and moral development in particular. • Most children in Western societies show roughly the shift from moral realism to moral relativism predicted by Piaget.	• Young children have more complex and mature ideas about morality than was assumed by Piaget. • Piaget's assumption that 10- and 11-year-old children have reached an adult level of moral reasoning is incorrect (see next section on Kohlberg). • Piaget focused on children's views on moral issues, and so was concerned with their knowledge of how they ought to behave; however, their *thinking* may be rather different from their actual *behaviour* when faced with a moral dilemma.

uncritical way. However, this only applies to certain rules. Most children between the ages of 6 and 10 accept their parents' rules about honesty and stealing. However, they are much less willing to allow their parents to make and enforce rules about who they may have as their friends or what they should do in their free time.

Kohlberg's cognitive-developmental theory

Lawrence Kohlberg (1963) agreed with Piaget that we need to focus on children's cognitive structures to understand how they think about moral issues. However, the cognitive–developmental theory he proposed differs from that of Piaget in that he argued that moral reasoning often continues to develop through adolescence and early adulthood.

Kohlberg's main experimental approach was to present his participants with a series of moral dilemmas. Each dilemma forced them to decide whether it is better to uphold a law or other moral principle or to reject the moral principle in favour of some basic human need. In order to make clear what Kohlberg did, here is one of the moral dilemmas he used:

> In Europe, a woman was dying from cancer. One drug might save her, a form of radium that a druggist in the same town had recently discovered. The druggist was charging 2000

dollars, ten times what the drug cost him to make. The sick woman's husband, Heinz, went to everyone he knew to borrow the money, but he could only get together about half of what it cost. He told the druggist that his wife was dying and asked him to sell it cheaper or let him pay later. But the druggist said "No". The husband got desperate and broke into the man's store to steal the drug for his wife.

The moral principle or law here is that stealing is wrong. However, it was the good motive of wanting to help his sick wife that led Heinz to steal the drug. It is precisely because there are powerful arguments for and against stealing the drug that there is a moral dilemma.

Kohlberg followed Piaget in assuming that all children follow the same sequence of stages in their moral development. However, Kohlberg's three levels of moral development (with two stages at each level) do not correspond closely to those put forward by Piaget:

Level 1: pre-conventional morality. At this level, what is regarded as right and wrong is determined by the rewards or punishments that are likely to follow, rather than by thinking about moral issues. Stage 1 of this level is based on a *punishment-and-obedience orientation*. Stealing is wrong because it involves disobeying authority, and because it leads to punishment. Stage 2 of this level is based on the notion that the right way to behave is the way that is rewarded. There is more attention to the needs of other people than in Stage 1, but mainly on the basis that if you help other people then they will help you.

Level 2: conventional morality. The greatest difference between Level 1 and Level 2 is that the views and needs of other people are much more important at Level 2 than at Level 1. At this level, people are very concerned to have the approval of others for their actions, and to avoid being blamed by them for behaving wrongly. At Stage 3, the emphasis is on having good intentions, and on behaving in ways that conform to most people's views of good behaviour. At Stage 4, children believe that it is important to do one's duty, and to obey the laws or rules of those in authority.

Level 3: post-conventional or principled morality. Those at the highest level of post-conventional or principled morality recognise that the laws or rules of authority figures should sometimes be broken. Abstract notions about justice and the need to treat other people with the respect they deserve can over-ride the need

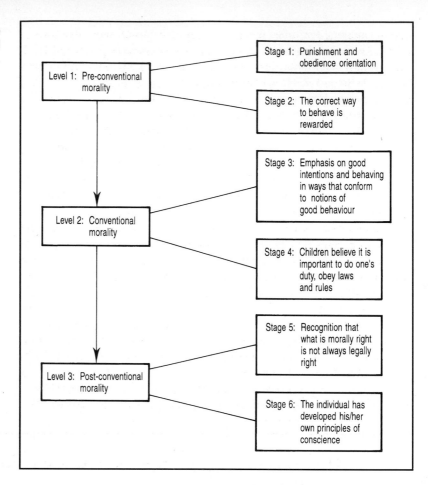

Kohlberg's three levels of moral development.

Level 1: Pre-conventional morality

Stage 1: Punishment and obedience orientation

Stage 2: The correct way to behave is rewarded

Level 2: Conventional morality

Stage 3: Emphasis on good intentions and behaving in ways that conform to notions of good behaviour

Stage 4: Children believe it is important to do one's duty, obey laws and rules

Level 3: Post-conventional morality

Stage 5: Recognition that what is morally right is not always legally right

Stage 6: The individual has developed his/her own principles of conscience

to obey laws and rules. At Stage 5, there is a growing recognition that what is morally right may not be the same as what is legally right. Finally, at Stage 6, the individual has developed his or her own principles of conscience. A key feature of this stage is that the individual takes into account the likely views of everyone who will be affected by a moral decision; Kohlberg (1981) described this as a kind of "moral musical chairs". In practice, it is very rare for anyone to operate most of the time at Stage 6.

Experimental evidence

Kohlberg's main theoretical assumption is that all children follow the same sequence of stages. The best way of testing this is by carrying out a longitudinal (long-term) study to see how children's moral reasoning changes over time. This was done by Colby et al. (1983), who did a 20-year study of 58 American males. There was a substantial drop in Stage 1 and Stage 2 moral reasoning between the ages of 10 and 16, with a large increase in Stage 3 and Stage 4 moral reasoning occurring at the same time. Most impressively for Kohlberg's theory, all the participants progressed through moral stages in exactly the theoretically expected sequence.

Another key aspect of Kohlberg's theory is the notion that certain kinds of general cognitive development must occur before an individual can advance a stage in his or her moral reasoning. For example, those whose moral reasoning is at Stage 5 make use of abstract principles (e.g. of justice), and so they must presumably be good at abstract thinking. Tomlinson-Keasey and Keasey (1974) found that those girls of 11 and 12 and women who showed Stage 5 moral reasoning were good at abstract thinking on general tests of cognitive development. However, some of them could think abstractly but did not show Stage 5 moral reasoning. These findings suggest that the ability to think abstractly is a necessary (but not sufficient) requirement for someone to attain Stage 5 or post-conventional morality.

Most of Kohlberg's work was concerned with people's moral reasoning when given artificial moral dilemmas to consider. However, their responses to those dilemmas may not predict how they would behave in real-life situations. It has been found (e.g. Santrock, 1975) that young children show very little consistency between their level of moral reasoning and their tendency to cheat when provided with the opportunity.

What are the advantages and disadvantages of Kohlberg's theory?

PLUS	MINUS
• Moral development follows the invariant sequence of stages proposed by Kohlberg. • Progressing through the stages of moral development requires that certain kinds of cognitive development have already taken place.	• The stage of moral reasoning that an individual has reached does not always predict how he or she will behave in real-life situations. • Kohlberg assumed that moral decisions are based on cool reasoning; in fact, such decisions are often based on intuition and influenced by powerful emotions. • Kohlberg assumed that justice is the most important principle in moral development; however, he somewhat neglected other principles such as sympathy and courage.

However, there is more evidence among adults that the stage of moral reasoning can predict behaviour. For example, Kohlberg (1975) compared cheating behaviour among students at different levels of moral reasoning. As many as 70% of students at the preconventional level cheated, compared to only 15% of those at the postconventional level, with students at the conventional level being intermediate (55%).

Gilligan's theory

Carol Gilligan (1977) argued that there are important problems with Kohlberg's theory of moral development. In particular, she accused him of sexist bias, and of ignoring the fact that men and women have rather different moral values. The evidence for these claims is discussed next.

Kohlberg proposed his stages of moral development on the basis of interviews with male participants, which suggests that bias may have been introduced. In several studies, Kohlberg reported that most women were at Stage 3 of moral development, whereas men were at Stage 4. Gilligan argued that this does not mean that women have inferior moral values to men. It is rather the case that women are more concerned than men about other people and about interpersonal relationships. Such concerns (rather than moral inferiority) lead women to be assigned to Stage 3 of moral development.

Gilligan (1982) followed up her attack on Kohlberg by putting forward her own theory of moral development. She argued that boys develop the *morality of justice*, in which they focus on the use of laws and moral principles to ensure that justice is served. In contrast, girls develop the *morality of care*, in which their main focus is on human well-being and on compassion for others. According to Gilligan, one of the major problems with Kohlberg's approach is that he regarded the morality of justice as superior to the morality of care.

Gilligan argued that there are three stages that girls and women go through in the morality of care. First, there is the stage of *self-interest*, in which moral decisions are made on purely selfish grounds. Second, there is the stage of *self-sacrifice*, in which the interests of others are put above those of the woman herself. Third, there is the stage based on the *principle of non-violence*, in which an attempt is made to be fair to everyone concerned in a moral decision. Gilligan found evidence for all of these stages in a study on women deciding whether or not to have an abortion.

Experimental evidence

There is relatively little evidence supporting Gilligan's position. It is true that Kohlberg sometimes found that women were at a lower stage than

What are the advantages and disadvantages of Gilligan's theory?

PLUS	MINUS
• Gilligan was right to argue that morality is multi-dimensional, and includes compassion and concern for others as well as respect for laws and justice.	• It has proved difficult to find any major differences in moral reasoning between men and women.

men on his stages of moral reasoning. However, it has more commonly been found that there are no differences between men and women in their stage of moral reasoning (Walker, 1989).

Convincing evidence that men and women are actually very similar in their moral reasoning has been found in studies in which people discuss moral dilemmas they have experienced. Contrary to what would be expected on Gilligan's theory, men as well as women focus on interpersonal responsibility and the well-being of others at least as much as they consider laws and justice (Walker et al., 1987). There may be some small sex differences in moral reasoning, but they are outweighed by the similarities.

Social learning theory

Social learning theorists such as Bandura (1973) have put forward a rather different theory of moral development to any of those considered so far. According to Bandura, children's behaviour changes over time because of observational learning, in which they learn to imitate the behaviour of various models (e.g. parents). Children's moral behaviour is also influenced by the patterns of reward and punishment they receive for behaving well and badly.

According to the theories of Freud, Piaget, and Kohlberg, each individual is at a given stage of moral development, and this determines the way he or she thinks about most moral issues. Thus, there is a high level of consistency about their moral decisions in different situations. In contrast, it is assumed by social learning theorists that an individual's behaviour in any situation is determined by the rewards and punishments he or she has received in similar situations in the past. As a result, they may show great inconsistency of behaviour in different situations.

The largest study ever carried out on children's morality considered the issue of consistency. Hartshorne and May (1928) looked at stealing, cheating, and lying in 12,000 children between the ages of 8 and 16. They

As children grow up and start going to school, they are increasingly influenced by their peers (other children of the same age). According to Piaget, interactions with peers force children to question their moral values, and this leads to moral development. Social learning theorists agree that peers play an increasingly important role in children's moral development. The reason is that their behaviour is strongly affected by the rewards and punishments given by other children.

In view of the role played by parents and peers in moral development, it is important to consider in more detail what is involved. Most of the relevant research has concerned different parenting styles, and so this will be our central focus. Hoffman (1970) identified three major styles used by parents in the moral development of their children:

1. *Induction:* explaining why a given action is wrong, with special emphasis on its effects on other people.
2. *Power assertion:* using spankings, removal of privileges, and harsh words to exert power over a child.
3. *Love withdrawal:* withholding attention or love when a child behaves badly.

Brody and Shaffer (1982) reviewed studies in which the effects of parenting style on moral development had been assessed. The findings in those studies where there was a definite link between parenting style and moral development were striking. There was a beneficial effect of induction on moral development in 86% of those studies. In contrast, power assertion improved moral development in only 18% of studies, and love

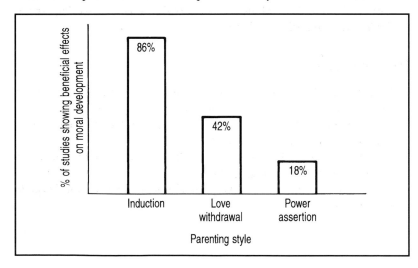

Results of Brody and Shaffer.

withdrawal in 42% of studies. As power assertion had a negative effect on moral development in 82% of studies, it is clearly a very ineffective parenting style. Power assertion produces children who are aggressive and do not care about others (Zahn-Waxler et al., 1979).

One reason why induction is so effective is that it provides the child with useful information that helps the development of moral reasoning. Another reason is that induction encourages children to think about other people. Considering the needs and emotions of others is of vital importance if moral development is to occur.

As Shaffer (1993) pointed out, what the findings tell us is that there is an association between parental use of induction and good moral development. Although the main reason for this association is probably that inductive parenting benefits children's moral development, that may not be the whole story. It is also likely that children who are well-behaved are more likely to be treated in a reasonable, inductive way by their parents. In contrast, children who are badly behaved and aggressive may cause their parents to use power assertion. In other words, parenting style affects children's behaviour, but children's behaviour may also affect parenting style.

Further reading

Shaffer, D.R. (1993). *Developmental psychology: Childhood and adolescence* (3rd edn.). Pacific Grove, CA: Brooks/Cole. There is thorough coverage of the major theories of moral development in Chapter 14.

Gross, R.D. (1992). *Psychology: The science of mind and behaviour*. London: Hodder & Stoughton. Many of the issues discussed in this chapter are dealt with more fully in Chapter 27.

References

Gilligan, C. (1982). *In a different voice: Psychological theory and women's development*. Cambridge, MA: Harvard University Press.

Hoffman, M.L. (1970). Conscience, personality and socialisation techniques. *Human Development, 13*, 90–126.

Kohlberg, L. (1963). Development of children's orientations toward a moral order. *Vita Humana, 6*, 11–36.

Piaget, J. (1932). *The moral judgement of the child*. London: Routledge & Kegan Paul.

Summary

- Morality implies "a set of principles or ideals that help the individual to distinguish right from wrong and to act on this distinction" (Shaffer, 1993).
- Morality can be divided into cognitive, emotional, and behavioural components.
- According to psychodynamic theory, the superego consists of the conscience (punishing parent) and ego-ideal (rewarding parent).
- The superego is formed by identifying with the same-sexed parent.
- The role of the other-sexed parent and of other children in moral development is largely ignored in psychodynamic theory.
- Piaget argued that moral development proceeds through three stages: premoral period; moral realism; and moral relativism.
- According to Piaget, moral reasoning develops along with cognitive development in general, and is influenced by the child's increased exposure to the opinions and beliefs of others.
- Moral development continues later into adolescence than Piaget assumed.
- Piaget focused on children's ways of thinking about moral issues; however, there are important differences between thinking and behaviour.
- Kohlberg argued that moral development always proceeds in order through three levels: pre-conventional morality; conventional morality; and post-conventional or principled morality.
- The evidence supports Kohlberg's three levels of morality, and his view that the development of moral reasoning depends on more general cognitive development.
- Kohlberg focused on the cognitive component of morality, and paid too little attention to the emotional and behavioural components.
- Gilligan argued that males develop a morality of justice, whereas females develop a morality of care.
- Males and females typically focus on both justice and the well-being of others in their moral decision-making.
- According to social learning theory, behaviour (including moral behaviour) depends on reward, punishment, and observational learning.
- Social learning theorists have not explained why it is that most people go through the same stages of moral development.
- Children's moral development is helped by an inductive parenting style, but power assertion has negative effects.

Key terms

Behavioural component of morality: behaviour or actions that are related to morality; these actions include lying, stealing, and accepting responsibility.

Cognitive component of morality: thinking about moral issues and deciding what is right and wrong.

Conventional morality: the second level of moral development in Kohlberg's theory; at this level, moral reasoning focuses on having the approval of others and avoiding being blamed by them.

Ego: in Freud's theory, the part of the mind concerned with conscious thinking.

Electra complex: in Freud's theory, the notion that young girls desire their father.

Emotional component of morality: the feelings produced by thoughts and behaviour related to morality; these feelings include shame, guilt, and pride.

Expiatory punishment: the view that the amount of punishment should match the badness of behaviour, but without the idea that the form of punishment should fit the crime; see **reciprocal punishment**.

Id: in Freud's theory, the part of the mind dealing with basic sexual and other motivational forces.

Immanent justice: the view that bad behaviour will always be punished in some way.

Induction: a parenting style in which children are taught to behave morally by emphasising the effects of wrong actions on others.

Love withdrawal: a parenting style in which children are taught to behave morally by their parents withholding love and attention for wrong actions.

Morality of care: a focus on human well-being and on compassion for others to produce a moral world; see **morality of justice**.

Morality of justice: a focus on the use of laws and moral principles.

Observational learning: learning to imitate others by observing their behaviour.

Oedipus complex: in Freud's theory, the notion that young boys desire their mother sexually and so experience rivalry with their fathers.

Post-conventional morality: the third level of moral development in Kohlberg's theory; at this level, moral reasoning focuses on justice and the need to treat others with respect.

Power assertion: a parenting style in which children are taught to behave morally by being punished for wrong actions.

Pre-conventional morality: the first level of moral development in Kohlberg's theory; at this level, moral reasoning focuses on rewards and punishments for good and bad actions.

Reciprocal punishment: the view that the form of punishment should fit the crime; see **expiatory punishment.**

Superego: in Freud's theory, the part of the mind concerned with moral issues; the superego makes us feel guilty if we behave badly and proud if we behave well.

Structured essay questions

1. Describe the psychodynamic theory of moral development. How adequate is this theory?

2. What are the main stages of moral reasoning in Piaget's theory. What are the strengths of this theory? What are its weaknesses?

3. Describe the levels of moral development proposed by Kohlberg. How useful is this theory?

4. What are the main features of the social learning approach to morality? What problems are there with this approach?

Self-assessment questions

1. The main components of morality are:
   a) the cognitive and emotional components
   b) the emotional and behavioural components
   c) the internal and external components
   d) the cognitive, emotional, and behavioural components

2. In the Oedipus complex:
   a) boys develop sexual desires for their mother and intense rivalry with their father
   b) girls develop sexual desires for their father and intense rivalry with their mother
   c) boys identify with their father
   d) girls identify with their mother

3. During Piaget's stage of moral realism, children:
   a) believe in reciprocal punishment and immanent justice
   b) believe in reciprocal punishment but not in immanent justice
   c) believe in expiatory punishment and immanent justice
   d) believe in expiatory punishment but not in immanent justice

4. In Kohlberg's theory, children have a punishment-and-obedience orientation during:
   a) the level of conventional morality
   b) stage 1 of the pre-conventional morality level
   c) stage 2 of the pre-conventional morality level

   d) the level of post-conventional or principled morality

5. According to Gilligan:
   a) boys develop a morality of justice, whereas girls develop a morality of care
   b) boys develop a morality of care, whereas girls develop a morality of justice
   c) boys and girls both develop a morality of justice
   d) boys and girls both develop a morality of care

6. According to social learning theory:
   a) moral behaviour depends on rewards and punishments, and is consistent in different situations
   b) moral behaviour does not depend on rewards and punishments, and is consistent in different situations
   c) moral behaviour depends on rewards and punishments, and is inconsistent in different situations
   d) moral behaviour does not depend on rewards and punishments, and is inconsistent in different situations

7. The most effective of Hoffman's parenting styles for children's moral development is:
   a) power assertion
   b) power assertion plus love withdrawal
   c) love withdrawal
   d) induction

Sex and gender

11

When a baby is born, a key question everyone asks is, "Is it a boy or a girl?". As the baby develops, the ways in which it is treated by its parents and other people are influenced by its sex. In the fullness of time, the growing child's thoughts about itself and its place in the world are likely to depend on whether it is male or female. This chapter is concerned with some of these issues. Before proceeding, however, it is important to define some of the key terms we will be using:

- *Sexual identity:* this is determined by the biological factors that have made us male or female; it can usually be assessed from the genital organs.
- *Gender identity:* this is a child's or adult's awareness of being male or female; it is socially rather than biologically determined, and emerges during the early years of childhood.
- *Sex role:* the expectations of society concerning the appropriate behaviour and attitudes of males and females; these expectations are in the form of *sex-role stereotypes.*
- *Sex-typed behaviour:* the forms of behaviour deemed appropriate for members of each sex within a particular culture.

Observed sex differences

Some sex-role stereotypes about appropriate ways for males and females to behave are in decline. For example, few people accept any more that men should go out to work and have little to do with looking after the home and the children, whereas women should stay at home and concern themselves only with home and children. However, many sex-role stereotypes still exist. Before discussing these stereotypes in detail, we should consider the actual behaviour of boys and girls. Do they really differ, or are sex differences a figment of the imagination?

A full review of the relevant research was reported by Eleanor Maccoby and Carol Jacklin (1974). According to them, there are only four differences between boys and girls for which there is strong evidence:

whereas crewing a fire engine and being a pilot were seen as men's jobs. Then the children were asked what job they wanted to have in adult life. They preferred the kinds of jobs that they had seen members of their own sex carrying out on television.

Cultural differences

We have focused so far on gender development in Western societies. In those societies, boys are generally encouraged to develop an *instrumental role*, in which they are assertive, competitive, and independent in their behaviour. In contrast, girls are encouraged to develop an *expressive role*, in which they are co-operative, supportive, and sensitive in their dealings with other people. These are sex-role stereotypes, of course, and we have already seen that there are rather small sex differences in behaviour.

There have been great changes in most Western societies in recent years. Thirty or forty years ago many fewer women than men went to university, but now the number of female university students exceeds the number of male students in several countries. The same is true of employment. In many countries, there has been a large increase in the number of women in the workforce, combined with a reduction in male employment. In spite of these changes, and the rise of feminism, many of the old sex-role stereotypes have changed very little. For example, American students during the 1980s still believed in an instrumental role for men and an expressive role for women (White et al., 1989).

What about other cultures? Socialisation pressures in 110 non-industrialised countries were explored by Barry et al. (1957). They considered five characteristics: nurturance (being supportive); responsibility; obedience; achievement; and self-reliance. There was more pressure on girls than on boys to be nurturant in 75% of the non-industrialised societies, with none showing the opposite pattern. Responsibility was regarded as more important in girls than in boys in 55% of the societies, with 10% showing the opposite pattern. Obedience was stressed for girls more than for boys in 32% of societies, with 3% showing the opposite. There was more pressure on boys than on girls to acquire the other two characteristics: achievement was emphasised more for boys in 79% of societies (3% showed the opposite); and self-reliance was regarded as more important in boys in 77% of societies, with no societies regarding it as more important in girls.

These findings indicate that the sex-role stereotypes of females being expressive and males being instrumental are very widespread. However, there are few societies in which boys are not expected to become nurturant and girls self-reliant. Simply because a society argues that nurturance is more important for girls than for boys does not mean that it does not matter for boys.

There are major similarities in sex-role stereotyping across most cultures. However, it would be a mistake to ignore cultural differences altogether. Margaret Mead (1935) studied three tribes in New Guinea, and found important differences among them (see Chapter 6). In the Mundugumor tribe, both men and women adopted the aggressive, instrumental style of behaviour that is supposed to be more characteristic of males. In the Arapesh tribe, both sexes adopted the caring, expressive style commonly associated with females. Most dramatically, the females in the Tchambuli tribe behaved in an assertive and independent fashion, whereas the males were nurturant and dependent.

Explanations of sex-role stereotypes

The fact that instrumental behaviour is associated with males and expressive behaviour with females probably owes its origins to physical differences. In primitive societies, the greater strength and speed of males make them better able to fight and to kill animals for food. In contrast, females bear children and breast-feed them, and so it is important for females to be caring and nurturant. Of course, matters are very different in industrialised societies. However, the sex-role stereotypes tend to remain.

It could be argued that cross-cultural similarities in sex differences are based on biology. However, as Willerman (1979) pointed out, "one should not expect too much of the genetic differences between males and females. The two sexes have forty-five/forty-six of their chromosomes in common, and the one that differs (the Y) contains the smallest proportion of genetic material."

Sex hormones may be of more importance. Males produce more of the sex hormone testosterone, whereas females produce more estrogens and progesterone. Money and Ehrhardt (1972) discussed cases of females who were exposed to male sex hormones prior to birth. Even though their parents treated them as girls, they tended to be tomboys. They played with boys, and they fought with them, and they avoided more traditional feminine activities. However, many of these girls were given the hormone cortisone to prevent them from becoming too masculine anatomically. One of the effects of cortisone is to increase activity level, and this may have made their behaviour more tomboyish.

Evidence that social factors can over-ride biology was reported by Money and Tucker (1975). They studied male identical twins, one of whom had his penis very severely damaged during circumcision. He had an operation at the age of 21 months to make him anatomically a girl. His parents treated him like a girl, and this affected his behaviour. He asked for toys such as dolls and a doll's house, whereas his brother asked for a garage. He was neater and more delicate in his behaviour than his identical twin.

In sum, most societies expect boys to become assertive and self-reliant and girls to become nurturant and co-operative. It can be argued that these differences make much more sense in primitive societies than in developed ones. Biological factors (especially sex hormones) play a part in determining sex differences; however, as we will shortly see, social factors are of great significance.

Theories of gender development

Psychodynamic theory

One of the best-known (but controversial) theories put forward by Sigmund Freud was his theory of psychosexual development. According to this theory, even infants possess a sex instinct and sexual energy (which he called *libido*). However, it is important to note that Freud used the term "sex" to refer to a very wide range of motives and behaviour having little or nothing to do with sexual intercourse.

In order to understand how psychodynamic theory accounts for gender development, it is necessary to focus on the phallic stage of development. This occurs between the ages of about 3 and 6, and is the first stage of development at which libido or sexual energy is focused on the genitals. According to Freud, boys during the phallic stage develop an *Oedipus complex*. This involves sexual desires for their mother combined with intense jealousy of their father, who is regarded as their rival. As boys are much weaker than their father, they are frightened of the possible reactions of their father to this rivalry. This leads to a castration complex, in which they fear their father will castrate them. The normal resolution of the problems of the Oedipus complex is *identification*, in which the boy starts to copy his father and tries to be like him. The process of identification plays a major role in the development of sex-typed behaviour.

The position of girls during the phallic stage is rather different to that of boys. When girls reach the age of about 3, they realise that they don't have a penis. They blame their mother for this lack, and this causes them to love their father more than their mother. According to Freud, this process goes so far that girls want to have their father's baby. This state of affairs is known as the *Electra complex*. Freud found it hard to explain how the Electra complex is resolved. He suggested that the Electra complex may disappear when girls realise that it is unrealistic to have a child with their father. Girls develop sex-typed behaviour because they are rewarded by their father, who is the central focus of their affection.

Freud was correct in his assumption that the father plays an important role in the development of sex-typed behaviour. For example, boys whose fathers are missing during the phallic stage show less sex-typed behaviour than boys whose fathers are present throughout (Stevenson & Black, 1988).

In nearly all other respects, Freud was wrong. Indeed, his account of gender development tells us more about his powers of imagination than it does about what actually happens. There is no real evidence that boys fear castration or that girls think they have been castrated. As Freud argued that the identification process depends on fear, it might be expected that a boy's identification with his father would be greatest if his father was a threatening figure. In fact, however, boys tend to identify much more with warm and supportive fathers than with overbearing and threatening ones (Mussen & Rutherford, 1963). The psychodynamic theory of gender development should be regarded as an historical curiosity rather than as a useful theoretical contribution.

Social learning theory

Albert Bandura (1977) and Walter Mischel (1970) have proposed a social learning theory of sex differences and the development of sex roles. According to this theory, two factors are of importance:

1. *Observational learning:* children learn sex-typed behaviour by observing the actions of various models of the same sex, including other children, parents, and teachers.
2. *Direct tuition:* this is based on reinforcement or reward; sex-appropriate behaviour is rewarded, whereas sex-inappropriate behaviour is punished.

Sex-typed behaviour is learned in part through direct tuition. Fagot and Leinbach (1989) carried out a long-term study on children. They found that parents encourage sex-typed behaviour and discourage sex-inappropriate behaviour in their children even before the age of 2. For example, girls are rewarded for playing with dolls, and discouraged from climbing trees. Those parents who make most use of direct tuition tend to have children who behave in the most sex-typed way.

Direct tuition is also used by other children. Fagot (1985) studied the behaviour of children aged between 21 and 25 months. She found that boys made fun of other boys who played with dolls or with a girl, and girls did not like it when one of them started playing with a boy.

What are the advantages and disadvantages of social learning theory?

PLUS	MINUS
• Much sex-typed behaviour in children occurs because it has been rewarded, whereas sex-inappropriate behaviour has been discouraged. • Observational learning is of some importance, but probably mainly from the age of 6 upwards.	• Young children do not consistently imitate same-sex models. • Social learning theory seems to regard young children as passive individuals who are taught how to behave by being rewarded and punished; in reality, children make an active contribution to their own development.

There is less convincing evidence that observational learning works in the way assumed by social learning theorists. Masters et al. (1979) studied 4- and 5-year-old children. When boys saw another boy playing with a toy that was described as a "girl's toy", they generally refused to play with it. However, they were willing to play with a "boy's toy" that had been played with by a girl. These findings suggest that young children are less concerned to imitate a same-sex model than to behave in a sex-typed way.

Masters et al. (1979) studied fairly young children. Ruble et al. (1981) obtained rather different findings when they studied 6- and 7-year-old children. These older children paid more attention to same-sex models than to opposite-sex models. They also avoided playing with toys that had been played with by someone of the opposite sex.

Cognitive–developmental theory

Lawrence Kohlberg (1966) put forward the cognitive–developmental theory of the development of sex-typed behaviour. In some ways, his theory is very different from social learning theory. According to social learning theory, children develop a gender identity as a result of attending to same-sex models. According to cognitive–developmental theory, the causality goes in the opposite direction: children attend to same-sex models because they have developed a consistent gender identity. It follows from this theory that children find it rewarding to behave in line with their consistent gender identity. This contrasts with social learning theory, according to which rewarding behaviour is behaviour that other people regard as being appropriate.

The notion of gender identity is of great importance within cognitive–developmental theory. According to Kohlberg, children go through three stages in the development of gender identity:

1. *Basic gender identity* (age 2 to 5 years): boys know they are boys, and girls know they are girls, but they believe that it would be possible to change sex (e.g. by wearing clothes appropriate to the opposite sex).
2. *Gender stability* (5 and 6 years): there is an awareness that sex is stable over time (e.g. boys will become men), but less awareness that sex remains stable across different situations, such as wearing clothes normally worn by members of the opposite sex.
3. *Gender consistency* (6 or 7 years upwards): children at this stage realise that sex remains the same over time and across situations.

There is evidence that children do, indeed, progress through the three stages proposed by Kohlberg. In a cross-cultural study, Munroe et al. (1984) found that children in several different cultures have the same sequence of stages on the road to full gender identity.

One of the predictions of cognitive–developmental theory is that children who have reached the stage of gender consistency will pay more attention to the behaviour of same-sex models than children at earlier stages of gender identity. This finding was reported by Slaby and Frey (1975).

Gender-schema theory

Martin and Halverson (1987) put forward gender-schema theory. They argued that children as young as 2 or 3 who have acquired basic gender identity start to form *gender schemas*. These schemas consist of organised beliefs about the sexes, and they help to determine what the child attends to and how he or she interprets the world. The first schema that is formed is an in-group/out-group schema; this consists of organised information about which toys and activities are suitable for boys and which are suitable for girls. Another early schema is an own-sex schema: this contains information about how to behave in sex-typed ways (e.g. how to dress dolls for a girl).

According to the theory, gender schemas are used by children to organise and make sense of their experiences. If they are exposed to information that doesn't fit one of their schemas (e.g. a boy combing the hair of his doll), then it is predicted that the information will tend to be distorted to make it fit the schema. This notion was tested by Martin and Halverson (1983). They showed 5- and 6-year-old children pictures of schema-consistent activities (e.g. a girl playing with a doll) and schema-inconsistent activities (e.g. a girl playing with a toy gun). One week later, the children's memory was tested. Schema-inconsistent activities were often misremembered as schema-consistent (e.g. it had been a boy playing with a toy gun).

As Shaffer (1993) pointed out, another study that supports gender-schema theory was reported by Bradbard et al. (1986). Boys and girls between the ages of 4 and 9 were presented with gender-neutral objects such as burglar alarms and pizza cutters. They were told that some of the objects were "boy" objects, whereas others were described as "girl" objects. There were two key findings. First, children spent much more time playing with objects that they had been told were appropriate to their sex than with sex-inappropriate objects. Second, even a week later the children remembered whether any given object was a "boy" or a "girl" object.

The concept of androgyny

Most boys and girls develop appropriate sex-typed behaviour, and this is often regarded as healthy and desirable. However, Sandra Bem (1975) argued that it is less desirable than is usually thought. Boys learn to inhibit the "feminine" side of their personality, and girls learn to inhibit the "masculine" side of their personality. According to Bem, the healthiest state of affairs is *androgyny*. Individuals (whether male or female) are androgynous if they possess a large number of both masculine and feminine characteristics. Masculine characteristics are those fitting an instrumental role, such as dominance, competitiveness, and assertiveness. Feminine characteristics are those involved in an expressive role, including sensitivity to others and co-operativeness.

A key advantage of androgyny is that it allows people to handle situations in flexible ways, with either the masculine or the feminine side of their personalities as appropriate. Another advantage is that androgynous people are not suppressing part of themselves simply in order to fit in with sex-role stereotypes.

Various measures have been devised to assess androgyny. Spence et al. (1975) produced the *Personal Attributes Questionnaire*, which contains masculine and feminine trait terms. Separate scores are obtained for masculinity and femininity, allowing people to be assigned to four categories:

1. *Androgynous:* high on masculinity; high on femininity.
2. *Masculine sex-typed:* high on masculinity; low on femininity.
3. *Feminine sex-typed:* low on masculinity; high on femininity.
4. *Undifferentiated:* low on masculinity; low on femininity.

How many people are androgynous? Spence and Helmreich (1978) gave the Personal Attributes Questionnaire to a large number of American college students. They found that about 30% of them were androgynous, with most of the others being masculine sex-typed or feminine sex-typed.

There is some support for Bem's assumption that it is better to be androgynous than to be traditionally sex-typed. For example, androgynous children have higher self-esteem and are better liked by other children than are sex-typed children (Boldizar, 1991). However, psychological well-being (e.g. absence of anxiety and depression; high self-esteem) is linked more with masculinity in both males and females than with androgyny or femininity (Taylor & Hall, 1982). This suggests that Western society favours the assertiveness and aggression that are characteristic of masculinity.

Bem's approach is over-simplified. It is not clear that there are coherent sets of "masculine characteristics" and "feminine characteristics". It is also not clear that masculinity and femininity are dimensions that are entirely independent of each other.

Further reading

Gross, R.D. (1992). *Psychology: The science of mind and behaviour*. London: Hodder & Stoughton. Chapter 23 provides much useful information about sex and gender.

Shaffer, D.R. (1993). *Developmental psychology: Childhood and adolescence* (3rd edn.). Pacific Grove, CA: Brooks/Cole. Chapter 13 is particularly good on theories of gender development.

References

Barry, H., Bacon, M., & Child, I.L. (1957). A cross-cultural survey of some sex differences in socialisation. *Journal of Abnormal and Social Psychology, 55*, 327–332.

Bem, S.L. (1974). The measurement of psychological androgyny. *Journal of Consulting and Clinical Psychology, 42*, 155–162.

Kohlberg, L. (1966). A cognitive–developmental analysis of children's sex-role concepts and attitudes. In E.E. Maccoby (Ed.), *The development of sex differences*. Stanford, CA: Stanford University Press.

Maccoby, E.E., & Jacklin, C.N. (1974). *The psychology of sex differences*. Stanford, CA: Stanford University Press.

Money, J., & Erhardt, A.A. (1972). *Man and woman, boy and girl*. Baltimore: Johns Hopkins University Press.

Summary

- Sexual identity is determined by biology, whereas gender identity is socially determined.
- Boys have greater visual and spatial abilities, more arithmetical ability, and are more aggressive; girls have greater verbal ability.
- Exposure to television tends to increase sex-typed behaviour and sex-role stereotypes.
- Nurturance and responsibility in girls are stressed in most societies, compared to achievement and self-reliance in boys.
- Similarities in sex-role stereotyping across cultures may have arisen because of the needs of primitive societies; differences depend on social factors.
- According to psychodynamic theory, identification with the same-sexed parent in childhood plays a major role in the development of sex-typed behaviour.
- The psychodynamic view that identification stems from the resolution of the Oedipus complex (in boys) or Electra complex (in girls) is incorrect.
- According to social learning theorists, sex-role development depends on observational learning, reward, and punishment.
- Young children are less passive than is assumed by social learning theorists.
- According to Kohlberg's cognitive–developmental theory, children attend to same-sex models because they have developed a consistent gender identity.
- There are three stages in the development of gender identity: basic gender identity; gender stability; gender consistency.
- Kohlberg largely ignored the external factors (e.g. reward) producing early sex-typed behaviour.
- According to gender-schema theory, even young children use gender schemas (organised beliefs about the sexes) to interpret the world.
- Gender-schema theory minimises the role of parents and other children in the development of sex-typed behaviour.
- Androgynous people possess masculine and feminine characteristics; psychological well-being is associated more with masculinity than with androgyny.

Key terms

Androgyny: having a mixture of masculine and feminine characteristics.

Direct tuition: learning by having one's actions rewarded or reinforced.

Electra complex: in Freud's theory, the notion that young girls desire their fathers.

Expressive role: co-operative, supportive, and sensitive behaviour.

Gender identity: our awareness of being male or female, which is based on social rather than biological factors; see **sexual identity**.

Gender schemas: organised beliefs about the sexes.

Identification: in Freud's theory, children's imitation of the beliefs and behaviour of the same-sexed parent to resolve the **Oedipus complex** in boys and the **Electra complex** in girls.

Instrumental role: assertive, competitive, and independent behaviour; see **expressive role**.

Libido: sexual energy in Freud's theory.

Observational learning: learning by observing the actions of other people.

Oedipus complex: in Freud's theory, the notion that young boys desire their mothers and regard their fathers as rivals.

Personal Attributes Questionnaire: a test that assesses masculinity and femininity; it is used to identify **androgyny**.

Sex role: society's expectations about the ways in which males and females should behave; these expectations are organised into **sex-role stereotypes**.

Sex-role stereotypes: organised information about the **sex-role** expectations that society has about male and female behaviour.

Sex-typed behaviour: the kinds of behaviour regarded as suitable for males and females within a culture.

Sexual identity: maleness or femaleness based on biological factors; it can usually be assessed from the genitals; see **gender identity**.

Structured essay questions

1 How do the media influence sex-role stereotypes? Does biology influence sex-role stereotypes?
2. In what ways do boys and girls behave similarly? In what ways do boys and girls behave differently?
3. Describe the theories of sex-role development put forward by Kohlberg and by Martin and Halverson. What are the strengths and weaknesses of these theories?
4. What are some of the main cross-cultural differences between boys and girls? What are the similarities?

Self-assessment questions

1. An individual's awareness of being male or female is known as:
a) sexual identity
b) gender identity
c) sex role
d) sex-role stereotype

2. The evidence suggests that:
a) boys have greater verbal ability than girls, but worse visual and spatial abilities
b) boys and girls do not differ in either verbal ability or visual and spatial abilities
c) girls have greater verbal ability than boys, but worse visual and spatial abilities
d) girls have greater verbal ability than boys, and they have greater visual and spatial abilities

3. In most societies:
a) girls are supposed to show nurturance and boys achievement
b) girls are supposed to show achievement and boys nurturance
c) girls are supposed to show nurtance and achievement
d) there are the same expectations for boys and girls

4. According to Freud, sex-typed behaviour in boys depends on:
a) the Oedipus complex
b) the Electra complex
c) them regarding their fathers as rivals
d) identification with their fathers

5. According to social learning theory, the development of sex roles involves:
a) observational learning and direct tuition
b) only observational learning
c) only direct tuition
d) none of the above

6. According to Kohlberg, children believe they could change sex during:
a) the stage of gender stability
b) the stage of gender consistency
c) the stage of basic gender identity
d) all three stages

7. According to Bem, those who are high on masculinity and high on femininity are:
a) androgynous
b) masculine sex-typed
c) feminine sex-typed
d) undifferentiated

Social approach

part **4**

Attachment, separation, and socialisation

12

Infants rapidly learn useful information about other people and about the world in which they live. Perhaps the most important aspect of this early learning occurs in the area of emotional development. There is the development of *attachment*, which has been defined as "a close emotional relationship between two persons, characterised by mutual affection and a desire to maintain proximity [closeness]" (Shaffer, 1993).

In the normal course of events, the main attachment of the infant is to its mother. However, strong attachments can be formed to other people with whom the infant has regular contact (Schaffer & Emerson, 1964). This is generally the father, but is sometimes other relatives.

Attachment

Psychoanalytic approach

Sigmund Freud, the originator of the psychoanalytic approach to psychology, put forward a very simple account of the baby's attachment to its mother. According to Freud (1926), "The reason why the infant in arms wants to perceive the presence of its mother is only because it already knows by experience that she satisfies all its needs without delay." In other words, babies are initially attached to their mothers because their mothers are a source of food as well as a source of comfort and warmth.

The evidence indicates strongly that attachment behaviour in babies does not depend only on the provision of food. Harry Harlow carried out a series of well-known studies on very young monkeys. These monkeys had to choose between two surrogate (or substitute) mothers, one of which was made of wire and the other of which was covered in cloth. Milk was provided by the wire mother for some of the monkeys, whereas it was provided by the cloth mother for the others. The findings were clear-cut. The monkeys spent most of their time

Contact comfort from a surrogate mother. Photograph courtesy of Harlow Primate Laboratory, University of Wisconsin.

clinging to the cloth mother, presumably because of the "contact comfort" she provided. Freud's notion that the first attachment is to a food source was not supported. The monkeys spent little time on the wire mother even when she supplied milk.

It could be argued that Harlow's work on monkeys is not relevant to the study of human attachment. However, Schaffer and Emerson (1964), in the study mentioned earlier, found with about 40% of humans infants that the adult who fed, bathed, and changed the infant was not the person to whom the infant was most attached. Once again, there is not the simple link between food and attachment behaviour assumed by Freud. Infants were most likely to become attached to adults who were responsive to them, and who provided them with much stimulation in the form of touching and playing.

Caregiving hypothesis: Ainsworth

If we are to develop a full understanding of the attachment between mother and child, it is necessary to have good ways of measuring it. Ainsworth and Bell (1970) developed what is known as the "strange situations" test. The infant (normally about 1-year old) is observed during a sequence of eight short episodes. For some of the time, the infant is with its mother, whereas at other times it is with its mother and a stranger, just with a stranger, or entirely on its own. The child's reactions to the stranger, to separation from the mother, and especially to being re-united with its mother are all recorded. These reactions allow the infant's attachment to its mother to be placed in one of three categories:

1. *Secure attachment:* the infant is distressed by the mother's absence, but it rapidly returns to contentment after the mother's return, immediately seeking contact with her. There is a clear difference in reaction to the mother and to the stranger. About 70% of American infants show secure attachment.
2. *Anxious and resistant attachment:* the infant is insecure in the presence of the mother, becomes very distressed when the mother leaves, resists contact with the mother after her return, and is wary of the stranger. About 15% of American infants are anxious and resistant.
3. *Anxious and avoidant attachment:* the infant does not seek contact with the mother, shows little distress when separated from the mother, and avoids contact with the mother upon her return. The infant treats the stranger in a similar way to the mother, often avoiding or ignoring him or her. About 15% of American infants are anxious and avoidant.

Why do some infants have a secure attachment with their mother, whereas others do not? According to Ainsworth's *caregiving hypothesis*, the sensitivity of the mother (or other caregiver) is of crucial importance. Most of the mothers of securely attached infants are very sensitive to their needs, and are emotionally expressive. The mothers of anxious and resistant infants are interested in them, but often misunderstand their behaviour. Of particular importance, these mothers tend to vary in the way they treat their infants. As a result, the infant cannot rely on the mother's emotional support.

Finally, there are the mothers of anxious and avoidant infants. Many of these mothers are relatively uninterested in their infants, often reject them, and tend to be self-centred and rigid in their behaviour. However, some mothers of anxious and avoidant infants behave rather differently. These mothers act in a rather suffocating way, always interacting with their infants even when they don't want any interaction. What these two types of mothers have in common is that they are not very sensitive to the needs of their infants.

Cultural differences

So far we have discussed findings obtained mainly from the middle-class American culture. However, there are interesting cross-cultural differences in the type of attachment shown by children. This issue was explored by Sagi et al. (1991; see figure overleaf). They used the strange situations test with infants in the United States, Israel, Japan, and Germany. Their findings for the American infants were similar to those mentioned previously: 71% of them showed secure attachment, 12% showed anxious and resistant attachment, and 17% were anxious and avoidant.

The Israeli infants behaved rather differently from the American ones. Secure attachment was shown by 62% of them, 33% were anxious and resistant, and only 5% were anxious and avoidant. These infants were living in a kibbutz or collective farm, and were looked after by strangers much of the time. However, they had a close relationship with their mothers, and so tended not to be anxious and avoidant.

Japanese infants are treated very differently from Israeli infants. Japanese mothers practically never leave their infants alone with a stranger. In spite of the differences in child-rearing practices in Japan and Israel, the Japanese infants showed similar attachment styles to the Israeli ones. Two-thirds of them (68%) had a secure attachment, 32% were anxious and resistant, and none was anxious and avoidant. The complete absence of anxious and avoidant attachment may have occurred because the infants were faced with the totally new situation of being on their own with a stranger.

others because they wanted to see how other participants were coping with the threat of shock.

Cutrona (1986) looked at affiliation in a natural setting. College students were asked to keep a daily record of their social interactions and stressful experiences for 14 days. The main finding was that they were very likely to seek out other people when they were feeling stressed.

Separation

So far we have looked at the factors involved in determining the nature of the attachment that an infant forms with its mother or other caregiver. In the real world, unfortunately, there are often circumstances (divorce; death of a parent) that can disrupt the infant's attachments, or even prevent them from being formed in the first place. In this section of the chapter, we will discuss the effects on the infant of being separated from one or more of the most important adults in its life.

Maternal deprivation hypothesis: Bowlby

John Bowlby was a child psychoanalyst who was particularly interested in the relationship between mother and child. In 1951, he argued that "an infant and young child should experience a warm, intimate and continuous relationship with his mother (or permanent mother-figure) in which both find satisfaction and enjoyment." No-one would disagree with that. However, Bowlby went on to propose the more controversial *maternal deprivation hypothesis*. According to this hypothesis, a breaking of the maternal bond with the child during the early years of life is likely to have serious consequences for its intellectual, social, and emotional development. He also claimed that many of these negative effects of maternal deprivation were permanent or irreversible.

Bowlby was influenced in the development of his ideas by the work of the ethologists, who studied animals in their natural surroundings. One of the ethologists (Konrad Lorenz, see photograph opposite) kept some goose eggs beside him. When the goslings had hatched, they followed him around rather than their mother. Lorenz used the term *imprinting* to refer to the learned response of following the first moving object they see, which is found in some species of birds. He argued that imprinting can only occur during a short critical period very early in the bird's life. When imprinting has occurred, it is irreversible in the sense that the bird will continue to follow the object on which it is imprinted.

Bowlby argued that something like imprinting occurs in infants. According to his notion of *monotropy*, they are born with a strong tendency to become attached to one particular individual. This individual will

usually (but not always) be the infant's mother. He also argued that there is a *critical period* during which the infant's attachment to the mother or other caregiver must take place. This critical period ends at some point between 1 year and 3 years of age. After that time, it is no longer possible to establish a powerful attachment to the mother or other individual.

Experimental evidence. Bowlby's maternal deprivation hypothesis was based in part on the work of Spitz (1945) and Goldfarb (1947). Spitz went to South America, and visited several very poor orphanages and other institutions. Most of the children in these orphanages received little attention or warmth from the staff, as a result of which they became apathetic. Many of the children suffered from *anaclitic depression*, a state involving resigned helplessness and loss of appetite.

Goldfarb compared two groups of infants from a poor and inadequately staffed orphanage. One group consisted of those infants who spent only the first few months of their lives in the orphanage before being fostered. The other group consisted of infants who spent three years at the orphanage before fostering. These two groups were tested at various times up to the age of 12. Those children who had spent longest in the orphanage did less well than the others on intelligence tests at all ages, they were less socially mature, they were more often loners, and they were more likely to be aggressive.

The findings of Spitz and Goldfarb provide less support for the maternal-deprivation hypothesis than Bowlby assumed. The institutions they studied were very deficient in several ways, with the children suffering peers (other adolescents of the same age). They were less likely than other children to have a special friend or to regard other adolescents as sources of emotional support.

In sum, the long-term effects of maternal deprivation depend to a great extent on what happens after the period of deprivation has ended. The love and involvement provided by adoptive parents can do much to allow deprived children to develop close relationships and to become well-adjusted. However, if deprived children are returned to their own families when they are not really wanted, the outlook is much less favourable.

A few researchers have looked at the effects of very extreme privation and isolation on children. In general, it is surprising how resilient these children appear to be. Koluchova (1976) studied identical twins who had spent most of the first seven years of their lives locked in a cellar. They had been treated very badly, and were often beaten. They were barely able to talk, and relied mainly on gestures rather than speech. The twins were fostered at about the age of 9. By the time they were 14, their behaviour was essentially normal. By the age of 20, they seemed to be of above average intelligence, and had excellent relationships with the members of their foster family.

Social learning theory

It is possible to consider attachment and separation from the point of view of social learning theory. According to the social learning theorist Bandura, observational learning is very important in children's development. *Observational learning* involves learning by observing the ways in which models behave. If infants and young children see their parents behaving in caring and loving ways towards them and towards each other, this makes it easier for them to behave in similar ways to other people. Children who are separated from their parents, and who do not observe strong attachment behaviour in others, find it much harder to develop attachments themselves.

Evidence that observational learning can be effective in improving the ways in which children relate to other people was reported by O'Connor (1972). Children who avoided playing with other children were shown a film of children being sociable and playing happily together. Every child who saw the film played more with other children afterwards, and this effect seemed to last for a long time.

Photo courtesy TRIP, photographer H. Rogers.

As Mischel (1973) pointed out, observational learning can be very specific in its effects. For example, a young child may observe obvious signs of attachment between her parents in the living room but not in the kitchen. This may lead her to learn that attachment behaviour is appropriate in only certain places. In order for observational learning of attachment behaviour to be effective, such behaviour needs to be observed in several different places with different people.

Effects of divorce

One of the major sources of disruption to children's attachments in Western society is divorce. Approximately one-third of marriages in the United Kingdom end in divorce, and the figure is even higher in the United States. There are various stages normally associated with divorce. First, there are marital conflicts which are distressing to children. Second, there is the actual separation, followed by divorce. Third, there are the various adjustments that have to be made by the parents and children. These often include moving house, having less money available, and reacting to new relationships as the parents find new partners and perhaps re-marry.

More than half of children whose parents divorce lose contact with the non-custodial parent (nearly always the father) within two years. The effects are generally more serious than losing a father through death. As Richards (1987) pointed out, children of divorced parents usually feel that the parents chose to divorce, in spite of the fact that the children themselves were opposed to it. This creates feelings of anger and being ignored which are rarely found when the father dies.

There is another important difference between divorce and death of the father. Death usually leads to the relatives on both sides of the family becoming more actively involved in the care of the children. In contrast, divorce often leads to the children losing contact with many of their relatives as well as the absent father.

The different effects of death and divorce can be seen in children's performance at school. On average, divorce reduces the standard of children's schoolwork far more than does a death in the family.

Some of the effects of divorce were studied in detail by Hetherington et al. (1979). They looked at 4-year-old children over a two-year period. They called the first year after divorce the *crisis phase*. During that time, the mothers (who were looking after the children) became stricter than before, and were less affectionate. In return, the children behaved in more aggressive and unchanging ways, and this was especially the case with boys. During this first year, the non-custodial fathers tended to become less strict and often gave treats to their children.

Summary

- Freud argued that babies are initially attached to their mothers because their mothers are a source of food; this is only part of a complex state of affairs.
- It has been found with the "strange situations" test that American infants' attachment to their mother can be described as secure attachment (70%), anxious and resistant attachment (15%), or anxious and avoidant attachment (15%).
- According to Ainsworth's caregiving hypothesis, the attachment of an infant to its mother or caregiver depends mainly on the sensitivity of the caregiver.
- There are cross-cultural differences in the type of attachment shown by children; these probably depend on differences in mothering styles.
- According to Kagan's temperament hypothesis, the attachment of an infant to its mother depends mainly on the infant's temperament.
- According to Bowlby, infants who experience maternal deprivation are likely to suffer severe and irreversible problems with their intellectual, social, and emotional development.
- According to Bowlby's theory of monotropy, babies are born with a strong tendency to become attached to one particular individual.
- Most of the evidence on Bowlby's theories indicates that the adverse effects of maternal deprivation are usually reversible, that it is family discord rather than separation that is the major problem, and that infants often form a number of strong attachments.
- Observational learning can increase attachment behaviour.
- Divorce is usually followed by a crisis phase, lasting for a year or so, and then an adjustment phase.
- Day care can have negative effects if the child is under one year old, if there is poor day-care provision, if the mother would prefer not to go out to work, if it is a single-parent family, or if the daytime caregiver keeps changing.

Key terms

Adjustment phase: the period after the **crisis phase**, during which the parent looking after the children becomes more patient and understanding, and routine and order return to their lives.

Affectionless psychopathy: a disorder found among juvenile delinquents, and involving a lack of guilt and remorse.

Affiliation: social contact and interaction with other people.

Anaclitic depression: a condition experienced by some children who are poorly cared for; it involves loss of appetite and feelings of helplessness.

Anxious and avoidant attachment: an insecure attachment of an infant to its mother, combined with avoidance of contact with her when she returns after an absence.

Anxious and resistant attachment: an insecure attachment of an infant to its mother, combined with resistance of contact with her when she returns after an absence.

Attachment: a close emotional bond between two people.

Caregiving hypothesis: the notion put forward by Ainsworth that **secure attachment** of an infant to its mother is most likely if the mother is very sensitive to her child's needs.

Crisis phase: the period of one to two years after divorce, during which the parent looking after the children becomes stricter and less affectionate.

Critical period: according to the **maternal deprivation hypothesis**, the period during the early years of a child's life during which a strong attachment must occur if its later attachment behaviour is to be satisfactory.

Deprivation: the state of a child who has formed a close attachment to someone, but is later separated from that person; see **privation**.

Imprinting: the tendency among the young of some species of birds to follow the first moving object they see, and to continue to follow it thereafter.

Maternal deprivation hypothesis: the theory of Bowlby, according to which breaking the bond between child and mother during the first few years of the child's life is likely to have serious effects on its development.

Monotropy: the notion that babies are born with a strong tendency to become attached to one particular person, usually the mother.

Observational learning: learning that is based on observing models behaving in various ways.

Privation: the state of a child who has never formed a close attachment with anyone else; see **deprivation**.

Secure attachment: a strong and contented attachment of an infant to its mother.

Temperament hypothesis: the view of Kagan, according to which the child's attachment to its mother depends on the child's temperament or personality.

Structured essay questions

1. What is the maternal deprivation hypothesis? Does the evidence support it?
2. Describe the various forms of attachment that a baby may have with its mother. How does the form of attachment depend on the mother's behaviour?
3. Describe the effects of divorce on children's attachment behaviour. How do these effects differ from those of parental death?

Self-assessment questions

1. According to Freud, infants are initially attached to their mothers because:
   a) their mothers provide comfort
   b) their mothers love them
   c) their mothers are a source of food
   d) their mothers are warm

2. According to Ainsworth, most American infants exhibit the following type of attachment to their mothers:
   a) secure attachment
   b) anxious and resistant attachment
   c) anxious and avoidant attachment
   d) none of the above

3. Very few Japanese infants exhibit the following type of attachment to their mothers:
   a) secure attachment
   b) secure and avoidant attachment
   c) anxious and resistant attachment
   d) anxious and avoidant attachment

4. According to Bowlby's maternal deprivation hypothesis, a breaking of the maternal bond:
   a) usually has few negative effects
   b) often leads to negative effects which are permanent or irreversible
   c) often leads to negative effects which can be reversed
   d) is rarely serious

5. According to Rutter:
   a) deprivation is more serious than privation
   b) privation is more serious than deprivation
   c) deprivation and privation are equally serious
   d) neither deprivation nor privation has serious effects

6. According to Hetherington et al., divorce usually leads to:
   a) a crisis phase lasting for several years
   b) a rapid adjustment to the new circumstances
   c) a crisis phase followed by an adjustment phase
   d) an adjustment phase followed by a crisis phase

7. Infants generally do better in day care if:
   a) they are under 12 months of age, and their mothers would prefer to stay at home
   b) they are over 12 months of age, and their mothers would prefer to stay at home
   c) they are over 12 months of age, and their mothers want to go out to work
   d) they are under 12 months of age, and their mothers want to go out to work

Prejudice 13

Most people regard *prejudice* and *discrimination* as meaning the same thing. In fact, there is an important distinction between them. Prejudice is an attitude, whereas discrimination refers to behaviour or action. Thus, if someone disliked some minority group but did not allow this dislike to affect their behaviour, then that person would show prejudice but not discrimination.

It is now time to define these terms more precisely. According to Baron and Byrne (1991, p.183), prejudice "is an attitude (usually negative) toward the members of some group, based solely on their membership in that group". In contrast, discrimination involves negative actions (e.g. aggression) directed at the members of some group.

Discrimination against other groups can take various forms. Allport (1954) argued that there are five different stages of discrimination. In certain situations (e.g. Nazi Germany), the level of discrimination increases rapidly from the early stages to the later ones. Here are Allport's five stages:

1. *Anti-locution:* there are verbal attacks directed against some other group.
2. *Avoidance:* the other group is systematically avoided; sometimes this involves steps to make it easy to identify members of that group (e.g. the Star of David worn by Jews in Nazi Germany).
3. *Discrimination:* the other group is deliberately treated worse than other groups in terms of civil rights, job opportunities, membership of clubs, and so on.
4. *Physical attack:* members of the other group are attacked, and their property is destroyed.
5. *Extermination:* there are deliberate attempts to kill all members of the other group (e.g. the gas chambers built by the Nazis to murder the Jews).

It may seem natural to assume that people's attitudes and behaviour are usually consistent, in which case prejudice and discrimination would occur together. In fact, inconsistency is very common. LaPiere (1934) took a Chinese couple to 250 hotels and restaurants in the United States. They

Personal viewpoint

You probably know some people who are prejudiced against one or more minority groups. Why do you think it is that these people are prejudiced: is it because of their personality, the experiences they have had, the influence of other people, or what? It is very desirable that society takes steps to reduce and eliminate prejudice. How do you think this might be achieved?

were only refused service on one occasion, suggesting a very low level of discrimination against Chinese people. However, LaPiere then wrote to all the hotels and restaurants, asking them whether they would accept Chinese people. Only half replied, with 90% of those replying saying they would not. This indicates there was considerable anti-Chinese prejudice at that time. Presumably the social pressures to accept Chinese people are much greater in a face-to-face situation than when writing a letter.

There are also social pressures at work when prejudice is measured. Prejudice is generally assessed by means of self-report questionnaires. They are affected by social desirability bias, the tendency to give socially approved answers. Evidence of such bias was reported by Jones et al. (1972). Whites in the United States expressed positive and non-prejudiced attitudes towards blacks on a questionnaire. They were then connected to a *bogus pipeline*. This is a machine with flashing lights, which the experimenter claims can monitor the participant's physiological responses and reveal his or her true opinions. The participants were asked about their attitudes towards blacks while connected to this bogus pipeline. They expressed much more negative attitudes towards blacks than they had on the questionnaire

Stereotypes

Prejudiced people regard all the members of a disliked minority group as being similar to each other. This focus on group membership rather than on an individual's particular qualities is known as *stereotyping*. Stereotyping has been defined as the tendency "to place a person in categories according to some easily and quickly identifiable characteristic such as age, sex, ethnic membership, nationality or occupation, and then to attribute to him qualities believed to be typical of members of that category" (Taguiri, 1969).

A classic study on stereotyping was carried out by Katz and Braly (1933). They asked students to indicate which characteristics were typical of each of a series of groups (e.g. Germans; Negroes; English). There was fairly good agreement that the Germans were efficient and nationalistic, whereas the Negroes were seen as happy-go-lucky and superstitious. Later studies suggested that stereotypes were still common, but they were less likely to be negative.

The most obvious problem with this approach is that the task itself forced the participants to produce stereotypes. A better method was used by McCauley and Stitt (1978), who focused on stereotypes of Germans. They asked their participants a series of questions such as, "What percentage of people in the world generally are efficient?" and "What percentage of Germans are efficient?" The average answer to the former question was 50%, whereas it was 63% to the latter question. This suggests that it is nonsense to suppose that most people think all German people are efficient. Instead, the general feeling is that Germans are somewhat more efficient than other nationalities, which is a much less extreme form of stereotyping.

Over-simplified views

It is often assumed that stereotypes should be frowned on for two main reasons: (1) they can lead to prejudice; and (2) they represent very over-simplified views of the world. It is true that negative stereotypes of other groups can be dangerous. However, it is certainly not true that all stereotypes lead to prejudice. Stereotypes are over-simplified, but they help us to make sense of a very complex world. Even the least prejudiced person probably makes use of stereotypes every day. As Brown (1986) pointed out, most people have stereotypes about night people and day people (people who go to bed early and get up early). We think of night people as being unconventional and rebellious, whereas day people are self-controlled and responsible.

Negative group stereotypes

It may be inevitable that we will form stereotypes of many different groups of people. However, it is generally agreed that some of the negative group stereotypes that were common in the past are now unacceptable. Two obvious examples are sex- and race-based stereotypes. Sexism and racism have caused great damage over the years in terms of both prejudice and discrimination. It is a slow and difficult business to eliminate sexism and racism. However, a reasonable amount of progress has been made. Laws based on the notion of equal opportunities have been introduced in several countries, and have had the effect of preventing some of the discrimination that used to exist. However, it is by no means clear that equal opportunities' laws have removed all forms of discrimination. Discrimination has lessened, but that there is still much underlying prejudice in people's attitudes.

Explanations of stereotyping and prejudice

There are several causes of prejudice. However, there are only three main categories to which most of these causes belong. First, prejudice may depend on the personality of the individual. In other words, some well as the F-Scale. Those who scored high on the F-Scale tended to be more prejudiced than low scorers. They were more racist and anti-Semitic, and also higher in *ethnocentrism* (believing their own ethnic group to be superior to all others). As predicted by the theory, they had been treated more harshly than non-authoritarian individuals during childhood.

In a famous series of experiments, Milgram (1973) found that most people are very obedient to authority. They will give very strong electric shocks to another person when ordered to do so by an authority figure (see Chapter 15). As those with an authoritarian personality are supposed to be submissive to authority, it follows that they should be very likely to give powerful electric shocks. As predicted, high scorers on the F-Scale gave more intense shocks than low scorers (Milgram, 1973).

In spite of the successes of Adorno's theory of the authoritarian personality, critics have argued that prejudice depends much more on cultural norms than on personality. Consider, for example, a study by Pettigrew (1958). He looked at prejudice in South Africa and in the United States. The levels of authoritarianism were equal in the two countries, but there was much more prejudice towards black people in South Africa than in the United States. These findings indicate the importance of cultural norms.

Major historical events can cause a considerable general increase in prejudice. A good example is the impact of the attack on the US fleet in Pearl Harbor on Americans' attitudes to the Japanese. There was a large and immediate increase in prejudice against Japanese people among those with and without authoritarian personalities. Such widespread prejudice cannot be explained by Adorno et al.'s theory, which emphasises individual differences in the tendency to be prejudiced.

 Cognitive approach

There is a fairly close link between prejudice and stereotypes. People who tend to regard all the members of some other group as possessing the same stereotyped characteristics tend to be prejudiced against that group. How do stereotypes lead to prejudice? Perhaps information consistent with our stereotypes is attended to and stored away in memory, whereas information inconsistent with our stereotypes is ignored and/or forgotten.

This cognitive approach was tested by Bodenhausen (1988). He made use of the fact that many Americans have a prejudice against people of Spanish origin. In his first study, American participants were asked to imagine that they were jurors in a court case. The defendant was described to some of them as Carlos Ramirez, a Spanish-sounding name; to others, he was described as Robert Johnson; the participants then read the evidence.

After they had read the evidence, the participants had to decide how likely it was that the defendant was guilty. Those who knew him as Carlos Ramirez rated the defendant as more guilty than those who knew him as Robert Johnson. This suggests that stereotypes lead to biased processing of information.

In his second study, Bodenhausen wanted to find out more about the processes involved. He argued that stereotypes might lead participants to *attend* only to information fitting their stereotype, or it might lead them to *distort* the information to make it support their stereotype. In order to prevent selective attention to stereotype-fitting information, Bodenhausen asked the participants to rate each item of evidence immediately in terms of whether it favoured or did not favour the defendant. There was now no suggestion of Carlos Ramirez being rated as more guilty than Robert Johnson. Thus, stereotypes make us attend to information fitting the stereotype, and to disregard all other information.

Social identity theory

One of the most influential theories of prejudice was proposed by Henri Tajfel (1978, 1981). According to his *social identity theory*, we have a need to understand and to evaluate ourselves. This is achieved to a large extent by a process of self-categorisation, in which we think of ourselves as belonging to a number of categories. Of particular importance here are the various groups to which we belong. According to Tajfel, everyone has a number of *social identities*, based on the different groups with which we identify. These groups can include racial group, nationality, work group, gender, social group, and so on.

The other main ingredient in social identity theory is the need for self-enhancement. People try to increase their self-esteem by regarding the groups with which they identify as being superior to all other groups. This can lead to prejudice and discrimination. In a nutshell, the key assumption of social identity theory is that how good we feel about ourselves depends on how positively we view the groups with which we identify.

tend to become prejudiced against the members of the other group. According to *realistic conflict theory,* such conflicts of interest cause prejudice.

This theoretical approach grew from the well-known Robber's Cave experiment (Sherif et al., 1961). Twenty-two boys spent two weeks at a summer camp in the United States. They were put into two groups (the Eagles and the Rattlers). These groups were told that whichever group did better in various sporting events and other competitions would receive a trophy, knives, and medals. As a result of this competition, a fight broke out between the members of the two groups, and the Rattlers' flag was burned. Prejudice was shown by the fact that each group regarded its own members as friendly and courageous, whereas the members of the other group were thought to be smart-alecks and liars. Prejudice was much reduced when the experimenters replaced the competitive situation with a co-operative one in which the success of each group required the co-operation of the other one.

Similar findings have been reported with various groups (e.g. managers in human relations workshops), and many different cultures (Vivian & Brown, 1994). However, the notion that competition always leads to prejudice and inter-group conflict was rejected by Tyerman and Spencer (1983). They argued that competition only has dramatic effects when those involved do not already have long-term friendships. Tyerman and Spencer observed scouts who already knew each other well as they competed in groups against each other at their annual camp. Competition did not produce any of the negative effects observed by Sherif et al. However, the boys in the Sherif et al. study did not know each other before the summer camp. This probably affected Sherif et al.'s findings.

Relative deprivation

Runciman (1966) argued that we can become prejudiced when there is a gap between what we have done and what we expected to be able to do. He used the term *relative deprivation* to refer to such gaps. When deciding if we are relatively deprived, we often consider our situation or that of groups to which we belong against that of other people or groups. Runciman drew a distinction between two forms of relative deprivation:

1. *Egotistic deprivation,* which stems from comparisons with other individuals regarded as similar to oneself.
2. *Fraternalistic deprivation,* which is produced by comparisons between groups rather than individuals. The notion that one's own group is being unfairly treated by comparison with some other group often reflects group norms or expectations of what is fair and just.

We can see the value of the distinction between egotistic and fraternalistic deprivation by considering the leaders of minority groups protesting about the discrimination shown against the group. Such leaders are usually successful individuals who are not egotistically deprived. However, they have a strong sense of fraternalistic or group deprivation. For example, trade union leaders in the United Kingdom who fight on behalf of their poorly paid members are usually well-paid and successful individuals. In similar fashion, the most militant blacks in the United States during the 1960s and 1970s tended to be well-educated and of fairly high socio-economic status (Abeles, 1976).

Some of the most convincing support for relative deprivation theory was reported by Vanneman and Pettigrew (1972). Those town dwellers in the United States who had the most extreme racist attitudes tended to report being the most fraternally deprived.

Runciman's relative deprivation theory, and especially the notion of fraternalistic deprivation, helps us to understand prejudice. It is based on group norms, and explains the fact that prejudice is often found in most members of a given group. In addition, the notion of egotistic deprivation helps to explain why the level of prejudice and hostility is greater in some individuals than in others. However, for the theory to be convincing, we would need to know in more detail the processes involved in producing fraternalistic deprivation.

Reducing prejudice and discrimination

Common goals

It has often been argued that prejudice and discrimination can be reduced if members of two groups in conflict agree to pursue some common goal. This was seen in the study by Sherif et al. (1961) which has already been discussed. To reduce the conflict between the Rattlers and the Eagles, it was decided that the camp's drinking water should be turned off, with the two groups needing to combine forces to restore the supply. Several other situations were set up in which co-operation on a common goal was essential; these included rescuing a truck that had got stuck, and pitching tents. As a result of pursuing these common goals, the two groups showed much friendlier attitudes towards each other. In fact, the boys chose as their friends more members of the other group than of their own group.

Aronson and Osherow (1980) tried to reduce prejudice in schools by means of co-operation on common goals. The schools in Austin, Texas had recently been desegregated, and there were concerns about the racial conflict that resulted from having black and white children in the same classes. One class of black and white children was divided into small groups for a learning task (e.g. the life of Abraham Lincoln). Within a group, each child was made responsible for learning a different part of the information (e.g. Lincoln's early life; his attitudes to slavery). Each member of the group then taught what he or she had learned to the other group members. After that, all the children received a mark based on their overall knowledge of the topic. This approach was called the *jigsaw classroom*. This was because all the children had an important contribution to make, just as all the pieces in a jigsaw puzzle are needed in order to complete it.

The findings with the jigsaw classroom were promising. The children showed higher self-esteem, better school performance, more liking for their classmates, and some reduction in prejudice. However, most of the effects were rather small. There are two likely reasons for this. First, the jigsaw classroom was only used for 45 minutes a day, three days a week, for a six-week period. Second, the groups did not always work in a co-operative fashion. There was a certain amount of group hostility if one of its members was very slow at learning, because this reduced the marks of all the members of the group.

Pursuing common goals in a co-operative fashion can reduce prejudice and discrimination. However, as was pointed out earlier in the chapter, this approach does not always work. If the common goals are not achieved, or if the groups co-operating with each other feel they are losing their own identities, then prejudice and discrimination may increase rather than decrease (Brown & Wade, 1987).

Social contact

According to the *contact hypothesis* (Allport, 1954), increased contact between prejudiced individuals and the groups against which they are prejudiced reduces prejudice. There are various reasons why this should be the case. First, stereotypes are based on the assumption that everyone of a given group is very similiar, and frequent contact with members of that group disproves that stereotype. Second, interacting with members of another group makes it clear that they are more similar in their attitudes and behaviour to the prejudiced individual than he or she had thought.

Some research supports the contact hypothesis. Deutsch and Collins (1951) compared the attitudes of black and white American housewives living close to each other with those of housewives living in segregated housing. Prejudice decreased over time for the housewives living close to each other, presumably because of the numerous social contacts they had with each other. After a while, their level of prejudice became much less than that of the housewives in segregated housing.

Social contact on its own is not enough, however. As we saw in the summer camp study of Sherif et al., social contact between the two groups led to conflict rather than to harmony. This suggests that other factors need to be added to social contact if prejudice is to be reduced. One of the most ambitious attempts to do precisely this was carried out at Wexler Middle School in Waterford in the United States. A considerable amount of money was spent on the school to provide it with excellent facilities. It was decided that the number of black and white students would be about the same, so that it was not regarded as a white school or as a black school. Much was done to make all the students feel equal, with very little streaming on the basis of ability. Co-operation was encouraged by having the students work together to buy special equipment that they could all use.

The results over the first three years were encouraging. There were many black–white friendships, but these friendships rarely extended to visiting each other's homes. There was much less discrimination, with the behaviour of the black and white students towards each other being friendly. However, some stereotyped beliefs were still found. Black and white students agreed that black students were tougher and more assertive than white students, whereas white students were cleverer and worked harder than black students.

Decategorisation.　　The contact hypothesis has been extended to include decategorisation and the use of positive images. Brewer and Miller (1984) were in general agreement with the contact hypothesis. However, in their decategorisation theory, they argued that social contact will mainly reduce prejudice when the boundaries between the conflicting groups become less rigid and blurred. When this happens, members of each group are less likely to think of members of the other group in terms of categories or group membership. Instead, they respond to members of the other group as individuals.

Some research discussed earlier in the chapter may show the value of decategorisation. Aronson and Osherow (1980) broke down racial barriers in children by having them work together in groups in the "jigsaw classroom". In general, teaching methods that focus on co-operative learning and the removal of group barriers are effective in reducing conflicts and prejudice between groups (Slavin, 1983).

Hewstone and Brown (1986) argued that decategorisation often works only in a limited way. Decategorisation and co-operation may work very well in the situation in which they are used, but the reduction in prejudice often does not extend to other members of the other group or to other situations. Because the techniques used focus on treating members of the other group as individuals, there is likely to be a reduction in prejudice towards those individuals rather than towards the group as a whole.

The key issue here is how to ensure that a pleasant, co-operative experience with one or more individuals belonging to a group leads to reduced prejudice towards all members of that group. Wilder (1984) supplied at least part of the answer. Students had a pleasant meeting with a student belonging to a rival college. This led to reduced prejudice towards the rival college when the student was regarded as a typical member of that college, but there was no reduction when he was regarded as atypical. In other words, it is important that individuals be *representative* of the group to which they belong for a general reduction in prejudice to occur.

Positive images.   Another way in which prejudice can be reduced is by presenting positive images of minority groups. In the United Kingdom, the athlete Linford Christie and the newsreader Trevor McDonald present positive images of successful and famous black individuals in high-status roles. Positive images can also be presented by the media. In the past, black actors and actresses tended to have minor roles in films, but more recently actors such as Eddie Murphy and Denzel Washington have starred in a number of films. Thus, there are indications that more positive images of black people are being presented in the media, but there is still a long way to go in that direction. The indications are that presenting more positive images of any discriminated group can reduce prejudice (Cook, 1978).

Conclusions.   Much research has focused on the contact hypothesis. Although there are inconsistent findings, it appears that some of the main factors that are needed for social contact to reduce prejudice are as follows:

- Co-operation on common goals.
- The members of the different groups must be of equal status; when whites in the United States had black slaves, there was no evidence that this contact reduced prejudice.
- The members of the other group with whom there is contact must be regarded as representative of their group; if they are not, then any reduction of prejudice will not generalise to other members of the group.

Experiencing prejudice

One of the reasons why people are prejudiced is because they do not know what it feels like to on the receiving end of prejudice. It follows that prejudice might be reduced by getting people to experience prejudice for themselves. This notion was tested by Weiner and Wright (1973). White American children aged 9 or 10 were put at random into an orange or a green group, and wore coloured armbands to identify their group membership. On the first day, the orange children were told they were cleverer and cleaner than the green children, and they were given privileges that were denied to the orange children. The situation was reversed on the second day. On each day, the group that was discriminated against felt inferior, showed reduced self-confidence, and did less well in their schoolwork.

In order to see whether the experience of these children had made them less prejudiced, they were asked whether they wanted to go on a picnic with some black children. Nearly all (96%) of the children agreed. In contrast, only 62% of control children who had not been exposed to prejudice agreed to go on the picnic. Thus, experiencing prejudice first-hand can subsequently reduce prejudice towards other people.

Further reading

Vivian, J., & Brown, R. (1994). Prejudice and intergroup conflict. In A. M. Colman (Ed.), *Companion encyclopaedia of psychology* (Vol. 2, pp. 831–851). London: Routledge. This chapter provides a good overall view of theory and research on prejudice.

References

Adorno, T.W., Frenkel-Brunswick, E., Levinson, D.J., & Sanford, R.N. (1950). *The authoritarian personality*. New York: Harper & Row.

Aronson, E., Blaney, N., Stephan, C., Sikes, J., & Snapp, M. (1978). *The jigsaw classroom*. Beverly Hills, CA: Sage.

Brewer, M.B., & Miller, N. (1984). Beyond the contact hypothesis: Theoretical perspectives on desegregation. In N. Miller & M.B. Brewer (Eds.), *Groups in contact: The psychology of intergroup relations*. Orlando, FL: Academic Press.

Sherif, M. (1966). *Group conflict and co-operation*. London: Routledge & Kegan Paul.

Tajfel, H. (1978). *Differentiation between social groups: Studies in the social psychology of intergroup relations*. London: Academic Press.

Structured essay questions

1. Define prejudice and discrimination. What are some of the factors causing prejudice and discrimination?
2. What kinds of people are most prejudiced? How may prejudice depend on social identities and on inter-group conflict?
3. Describe each of the following ways of reducing prejudice: pursuing common goals; increased social contact; and decategorisation.

Self-assessment questions

1. Which of the following is true:
   a) discrimination and prejudice mean the same thing
   b) prejudice is an attitude, whereas discrimination refers to behaviour or action
   c) prejudice refers to behaviour or action, whereas discrimination refers to an attitude
   d) prejudice and prejudice both refer to a mixture of attitude and behaviour or action

2. Which of the following is true:
   a) all stereotypes lead to prejudice and are over-simplified
   b) all stereotypes are dangerous
   c) stereotypes often lead to prejudice, but they help us to make sense of a complex world
   d) only prejudiced people form stereotypes

3. Those with an authoritarian personality:
   a) are impressive leaders
   b) are aggressive towards authority figures
   c) tend to believe in unconventional values
   d) have a rigid belief in conventional values and submissive attitudes towards authority figures

4. Social identity theory assumes that people:
   a) have various social identities and a need for self-enhancement
   b) have one social identity and a need for self-enhancement
   c) have various social identities which are difficult to form
   d) have various social identities and no need for self-enhancement

5. According to realistic conflict theory, prejudice results from:
   a) conflicts between individuals
   b) conflicts between parents and children
   c) conflicts between groups competing for the same goal
   d) conflicts within an individual

6. The jigsaw classroom:
   a) involved co-operation on common goals and reduced prejudice
   b) involved co-operation on common goals, but did not reduce prejudice
   c) involved competition and reduced prejudice
   d) involved competition and did not reduce prejudice

7. According to decategorisation theory:
   a) increased contact between groups is enough to reduce prejudice
   b) blurring the boundaries between conflicting groups is enough to reduce prejudice
   c) people must stop belonging to groups if prejudice is to be reduced
   d) increased contact and a blurring of the boundaries between conflicting groups are both needed for reduced prejudice

Pro-social behaviour 14

The central focus of this chapter is on pro-social behaviour, and on the factors that determine whether someone will behave in a pro-social fashion. *Pro-social behaviour* is behaviour that is of benefit to someone else; it includes actions that are co-operative, affectionate, and helpful to others. The clearest examples of pro-social behaviour are often called *altruism*. Altruism is voluntary helping behaviour that is costly to the person who is altruistic; it is based on a desire to help someone else rather than on any possible rewards. It has often been assumed that altruism depends on empathy. *Empathy* is the ability to share the emotions of another person, and to understand that person's point of view.

A form of pro-social behaviour that has been studied in great detail is *bystander intervention*. Those who study bystander intervention want to understand the factors determining whether or not bystanders give help to a victim. This research is discussed later in the chapter.

The extent to which people behave in pro-social ways depends largely on *social norms* or cultural expectations about standards of behaviour. There are several norms that influence our behaviour, and these norms vary somewhat from culture to culture. Some of the major social norms, and the ways in which they affect pro-social behaviour, are dealt with towards the end of the chapter.

Development of empathy

As was mentioned earlier, empathy refers to the ability to understand the feelings of another person. It has often been assumed that empathy is very important if people are to behave in an unselfish and pro-social fashion. It is largely because children develop an ability to understand the feelings of others that they gradually learn to behave in more helpful and co-operative ways.

Eisenberg et al. (1983) proposed a theory of the development of pro-social moral reasoning and behaviour. In this theory, the growth of empathy is regarded as an important factor in making children's

---

Personal viewpoint

You must have met some people who are very helpful and co-operative, and others who are not. What do you think are some of the factors that lead people to behave in a pro-social fashion? It is sometimes argued that people in Western societies are very stressed and less helpful than those living in non-industrialised countries: do you think that is true? Bystanders who see someone who seems to need help often fail to lend them any: why do you think they are reluctant to help?

behaviour more pro-social. More specifically, Eisenberg et al. argued that there are five levels or stages in the development of pro-social reasoning:

Level 1: Self-centred (up to about the age of 7). The child's main concern is for itself.
Level 2: Needs oriented (about 7 to 11). The needs of other people are considered, but little guilt is felt if help is not given.
Level 3: Approval oriented (about 11 to 14). Helping others depends on whether it will be approved of or praised by others.
Level 4: Empathic (about 12 upwards). There is concern to do what is right, sympathy for the person in need, and guilt if help is not given.
Level 5: Strongly internalised (about 16 upwards). Helping behaviour is based on strongly internalised beliefs and values.

Eisenberg-Berg and Hand (1979) studied the development of pro-social thinking by giving children various dilemmas to think about. Here is an example:

> One day a girl named Mary was going to a friend's birthday party. On her way she saw a girl who had fallen down and hurt her leg. The girl asked Mary to go to her house and get her parents so that they could come and take her to a doctor. But if Mary did ... she would be late for the party and miss the ice cream, cake, and all the games. What should Mary do?

Young children tended to be self-centred, deciding that Mary should go to the party and leave the injured girl. Older children were far more likely to decide that it was more important to help the injured girl than to go to the party.

One of the issues raised by this research is whether children's level of pro-social reasoning predicts their actual behaviour. Eisenberg-Berg and Hand (1979) explored this issue. They found that sharing with other children was more frequent among children at Level 2 of pro-social reasoning than among those at Level 1.

Eisenberg et al. (1991) obtained evidence that empathy (which develops during Level 4) is an important factor in producing pro-social thinking. They found that children given the dilemma about Mary and the injured girl were more likely to provide help if they thought about the injured girl's feelings of pain and anxiety.

There is evidence from other research that empathy may influence pro-social behaviour much earlier than is implied by Eisenberg et al.'s theory. Zahn-Waxler et al. (1979) studied young children between the ages of 18 and 30 months. Even at that young age, many of the infants displayed distress when they saw other children in distress. These infants thus gave some evidence of experiencing empathy. The mothers of these infants had a particular way of dealing with their children when they did harm to another child. They emphasised the distress that their child's behaviour had caused to the other child. They said things like, "Don't hit Mary; you've made her cry" or "Put that bat down; you've hurt John."

Altruism

Empathy–altruism hypothesis

We have seen that there may be close links between empathy and pro-social behaviour during children's development. Daniel Batson argued that the same is true of adults. He proposed the *empathy–altruism hypothesis,* according to which altruistic behaviour is mainly motivated by empathy. He argued that there are two main emotional reactions to observing someone in distress (adjectives describing each reaction are in brackets):

- *Empathic concern:* a sympathetic focus on the other person's distress, coupled with the motivation to reduce it; (compassionate; soft-hearted; tender).
- *Personal distress:* a concern with one's own discomfort, and the motivation to reduce it; (worried; disturbed; alarmed).

Batson et al. (1981) set up a situation in which female students observed another student called Elaine receiving mild electric shocks. After a while, the students were asked whether they would take the remaining shocks instead of Elaine. Some of the students were told they were free to leave the experiment if they wanted. The others were told they would have to stay and watch Elaine being shocked if they would not take the shocks themselves. All of the students were given a placebo drug which actually had no effects at all. However, they were given misleading information about the drug, designed to make them interpret their reactions to Elaine as either empathic concern or personal distress.

The students who felt empathic concern were genuinely motivated to help Elaine. Most of them offered to take the remaining shocks regardless of whether they could easily escape from the situation. In contrast, those who felt personal distress offered to take the shocks when escape was hard, but only 30% agreed to take the shocks when escape was easy. These findings suggest that those feeling personal distress were motivated to help by fear of social disapproval if they did not help rather than by any real desire to help Elaine.

Batson et al. argued that the students feeling empathic concern helped Elaine for unselfish reasons. However, it is possible that they wanted to avoid self-criticism or social disapproval. In order to test this, Batson et al. (1988) carried out an altered version of their earlier study. They told some of their female participants that they would only be allowed to help Elaine by taking some of her shocks if they did well on a hard mathematical task. Someone who was motivated to help Elaine only to avoid social disapproval and self-criticism might well offer to help, but then deliberately not perform well on the mathematical task. This can be regarded as taking the easy way out. Many of those feeling personal distress took the easy way out. However, those feeling empathic concern did very well on the mathematical task. Their refusal to take the easy way out indicates that their desire to help was genuine.

Negative-state relief model

Robert Cialdini et al. (1987) put forward the *negative-state relief model*. According to this theory, someone who feels empathy for a victim usually feels sad as a result. The reason that they help the victim is because they want to reduce their own sadness. Thus, empathic concern will not lead to helping behaviour if steps are taken to remove the sadness that is usually found with empathy.

Cialdini et al. (1987) tested these ideas. They used the same situation as Batson et al. Participants were given a placebo drug having no actual effects. However, they experimenters claimed the drug would "fix" the participants' mood and prevent it being altered. The argument was that participants would be less inclined to help the student being given shocks if this would not reduce their feelings of sadness. As predicted, participants feeling empathic concern were less likely to help if they had been given the drug.

Conclusions

Those who behave in an altruistic fashion are often motivated by empathic concern. The main reason why empathic concern leads to helpful behaviour is probably because it involves a focus on the needs of the victim. However, other factors are also involved. Those who feel empathic concern may experience a range of negative emotions including sadness and guilt. These negative emotions are unpleasant, and they add to the motivation to assist the victim.

Most of this research indicates that empathic concern generally leads to altruistic behaviour. However, as Batson et al. (1983) pointed out, genuine concern for others is often "a fragile flower, easily crushed by egotistic [self-centred] concerns." They provided some evidence for this assertion. They found that 86% of participants feeling empathic concern were willing to take Elaine's place when she received mild shocks. However, this was reduced dramatically to 14% when Elaine received painful shocks.

Cultural influences

Some of the strongest evidence that there are large differences in altruism from one culture to another was reported by Beatrice Whiting and John Whiting (1975). They considered the behaviour of young children aged between 3 and 10 in six cultures (United States; India; Okinawa, an island in South West Japan; Philippines; Mexico; and Kenya). At one extreme, they reported that 100% of young children in Kenya were high in altruism. At the other extreme, only 8% of young children in the United States were altruistic. The other cultures were in between. Over 60% of children in Mexico and the Philippines were altruistic, compared to under 30% in Okinawa and India.

Eisenberg and Mussen (1989) reviewed several studies on cross-cultural differences in altruism. They concluded that there are large differences from one culture to another. In their own words, "Most children reared in Mexican villages, Hopi children on reservations in the Southwest [of America], and youngsters on Israeli kibbutzim are more considerate, kind, and co-operative than their 'typical' middle-class American counterparts."

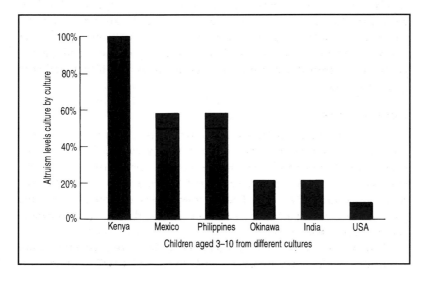

Results of the study by Whiting and Whiting (1975) showing cultural differences in altruism.

What do these findings mean? Two major factors are involved. First, industrialised societies such as most of the United States and Okinawa tend to place much emphasis on competition and personal success, and this is likely to reduce co-operation and altruism. Second, the family structure in non-industrialised cultures such as those of Kenya, Mexico, and the Hopi tends to be very different from that in industrialised cultures. Of particular importance, children in non-industrialised societies are given family responsibilities (e.g. caring for young children), and these responsibilities develop their altruistic behaviour.

Encouraging altruism

The evidence indicates that observational learning from models can be an effective way of increasing altruistic behaviour. In one study (Midlarsky & Bryan, 1972), some children observed a model giving valuable tokens to a charity. Ten days later, these children were more likely than other children to donate sweets to the same charity.

Real-life evidence showing the importance of modelling was reported by Rosenhan (1970). He studied white people who had worked wholeheartedly for the civil rights movement during the 1960s. Most of their parents had argued strongly for the importance of altruism. These parents had set good examples by behaving in a consistently altruistic way, thus providing altruistic models for their children.

Rosenhan also studied white people who had been less involved in the civil rights movement. Their parents had argued in favour of altruism, but were less likely to behave in altruistic ways. Thus, these parents failed to provide models of altruistic behaviour, and this may explain why their children had only been partly involved in the civil rights movement.

Offering rewards for helping is one way of trying to encourage altruism. This may be effective with young children who have not yet developed much empathic concern for others. However, much of the work on older children indicates that rewards or reinforcement can have the opposite effect to that intended. Fabes et al. (1989) promised some children toys if they sorted coloured paper squares for children who were sick in hospital, whereas other children weren't offered any reward. After a while all the children were told they could continue sorting the coloured squares, but they wouldn't receive any reward for doing so. The children who had been rewarded were less likely to continue to be helpful than those who had not been rewarded. This was most true for children whose mothers believed in using rewards to make their children behave well.

Why are rewards so ineffective in producing altruistic behaviour? The main reason is that those who are rewarded for behaving helpfully are motivated by the thought of the reward rather than by the desire to help other people. As a result, removal of the rewards often causes the helpful behaviour to stop.

Bystander intervention

One of the recurring images of our time is that of someone being attacked in the middle of a city, with no-one being willing to help them. This apparent apathy or reluctance to help was shown very clearly in the case of Kitty Genovese. She was stabbed to death as she returned home from work at three o'clock in the morning. Thirty-eight witnesses watched the murder from their apartments, but none of them intervened. Indeed, only one person called the police. Even that action was only taken after he had asked advice from a friend in another part of the city.

Diffusion of responsibility

John Darley and Bibb Latane (1968) were interested in the Kitty Genovese case and in the whole issue of bystander intervention. They wondered why not one out of the numerous witnesses helped her. They argued that a victim may be in a more fortunate position when there is just one bystander rather than several. In such a situation, responsibility for helping the victim falls firmly on to one person rather than being spread among many; in other words, the bystander has a sense of personal responsibility. If there are many observers of a crime, there is a *diffusion of responsibility*. Each person bears only a small portion of the guilt for not helping, and so there is less feeling of personal responsibility.

A related way of considering what is involved here is to think in terms of social norms or culturally determined expectations of behaviour. One of the key norms in many societies is the *norm of social responsibility*: we should help those who need help. Darley and Latane argued that the norm of social responsibility is strongly activated when only one person observes the fate of a victim. However, it is much less likely to influence behaviour when several bystanders are present.

Darley and Latane tested their ideas in a series of studies. Participants were placed in separate rooms, and told to put on headphones. They were to discuss their personal problems, speaking into a microphone and hearing the contributions of others to the discussion over the headphones. They were led to think that there were one, two, three, or six people in the discussion. In fact, all of the apparent "contributions" of other participants were tape-recordings.

Each participant heard that one of the other people in the discussion was prone to seizures, especially when studying hard or taking examinations. Later on, they heard him say, "I–er–I–uh–I've got one of these–er–seizure–er–er–things coming on and–and–and I could really–er–use some help so if somebody would–er–er–help–er–er–help–er–uh–uh–uh [choking sounds] … I'm gonna die–er–er–I'm … gonna die–er–help–er–er seizure–er … [choking sounds, silence]."

Of those participants who thought they were the only person to know that someone was having an epileptic fit, 100% left the room and reported the emergency. In contrast, only 62% of participants responded if they thought there were five other bystanders who knew about the epileptic fit. Participants who thought they were the only bystander responded much faster than those who thought there were five bystanders: 50% of them responded within 45 seconds of the onset of the fit, whereas none of those who believed there were five other bystanders did so.

There were two other interesting findings in the work of Darley and Latane. First, the participants who believed there were five other bystanders denied that this had affected their behaviour. Thus, we are not fully aware of the factors influencing our behaviour. Second, they found that the participants who did not report the emergency were by no means apathetic or uncaring. Most of them asked the experimenter if the victim was all right. Many of them had trembling hands and sweating palms. Indeed, they seemed more emotionally aroused than the subjects who reported the emergency.

Other studies

Interpreting the situation.   In real life, many emergencies have an ambiguous quality about them. Not surprisingly, the chances of a bystander lending assistance to a victim are much greater if the situation is interpreted as a genuine emergency. This was studied by Leonard Bickman. Participants heard a bookcase apparently falling on another subject, followed by a scream. When someone else interpreted the situation as an emergency, the participant offered help much faster than when someone else said there was nothing to worry about.

Victim characteristics.   Bystanders are influenced by the characteristics of the victim. This was shown by Piliavin et al. (1969). They staged a number of incidents in the New York subway, in which a male victim staggered forwards and collapsed on the floor. He either carried a black cane and seemed sober, or he smelled of alcohol and carried a bottle of alcohol. Bystanders were less likely to help when the victim was "drunk" than when he was "ill". Drunks are regarded as responsible for their own plight, and it could be unpleasant to help a smelly drunk who may vomit or become abusive.

Perceived similarity. It seems likely that bystanders will be most likely to help victims they perceive as similar to themselves. This is generally true, but there are some exceptions. Gaertner and Dovidio (1977) used a situation in which white participants heard a victim in the next room apparently being struck by a stack of falling chairs. When it was unclear whether or not there was an emergency (there were no screams from the victim), the white participants helped a white victim faster than a black one. However, when the victim screamed and so it was clear there was an emergency, a black victim was helped as rapidly as a white victim.

How can we explain these findings? Perceived similarity is of importance, as was found in the ambiguous situation. However, the effects of perceived similarity are wiped out by the demands of the situation if it is clear that there really is an emergency.

Knowing how to help. Suppose that a passenger on a plane suddenly collapses, and one of the stewardesses asks for help. It is natural to assume that a doctor will be more likely to offer his or her services than someone who doesn't have any relevant medical skills. There is plenty of evidence to support this assumption. Huston et al. (1981) studied the characteristics of those who helped out in dangerous emergencies. There was a strong tendency for helpers to have training in relevant skills such as life-saving, first aid, or self-defence.

Other activities. Bystanders do not only take account of the emergency itself. They also consider the activity they are involved in when they come upon the emergency. This was studied by Batson et al. (1978). They sent their participants from one building to another to perform a task. On the way, they went past a male student slumped on the stairs, coughing and groaning. Of those participants who had been told that it was important for them to help the experimenter by performing the task, and that they were to hurry, only 10% stopped to help the student. On the other hand, 80% of the participants stopped to help if they were told that helping the experimenter was not very important, and that there was no hurry.

Theoretical ideas

Why do we like some people but dislike others? There are several reasons. However, two major factors are the rewards and costs involved. People can be rewarding because they provide fun, security, reassurance, and so on. They can be costly because they are demanding, disagreeable, time-consuming, and so on. We like people if the rewards are greater than the costs, but we dislike people if the costs are greater than the rewards.

According to *equity theory* (Walter et al., 1978), people in a relationship consider not only their own rewards and costs, but also those of the other person. In a satisfactory relationship, there is fairness or equity on both sides in terms of rewards and costs.

There are other, related notions current in social psychology. It is argued that friendship should be based on equality (Homans, 1974). In other words, two friends should both enjoy about the same rewards and incur about the same costs. There is also what is known as the *reciprocity norm*. According to this norm, people should help those who have helped them in the past, and they should not harm those who have helped. This norm is sometimes expressed as, "Scratch my back, and I'll scratch yours."

The common thread running through equity theory, notions of equality, and the reciprocity norm, is that social interactions are determined by the rewards and costs involved. In similar fashion, it is useful to consider the rewards and costs involved in helping and not helping when trying to predict whether a bystander will help:

- *Costs of helping:* physical harm; delay in carrying out other activities.
- *Costs of not helping:* ignoring personal responsibility; guilt; criticism from others; ignoring perceived similarity.
- *Rewards of helping:* praise from victim; satisfaction from having been useful if relevant skills are possessed.
- *Rewards of not helping:* able to continue with other activities as normal.

Piliavin et al. (1981) made use of ideas about rewards and costs in their *arousal / cost–reward model*. According to this model, there are five steps that bystanders go through before deciding whether or not to assist a victim:

1. Becoming aware of someone's need for help; this depends on attention.
2. Experiencing arousal.
3. Interpreting cues and labelling one's arousal.
4. Working out the rewards and costs of different actions.
5. Making a decision and acting on it.

This model is consistent with most of the research we have discussed. In addition, the model assumes that bystanders observing an emergency are often very aroused emotionally. According to Piliavin et al., high

---

What are the advantages and disadvantages of the arousal/cost–reward model?

PLUS

- It is useful to regard bystander intervention as a decision-making process involving a series of stages.
- Rewards and costs are very important in determining helping behaviour.

MINUS

- The model seems of little relevance to bystanders who immediately and impulsively lend assistance.
- Someone with much experience of similar emergencies (e.g. a doctor responding to someone having a heart attack) may respond smoothly and efficiently without becoming aroused.

---

arousal can make it difficult for bystanders to think clearly what to do. As a result, they may simply not work out the rewards and costs of different actions in a systematic way.

Further reading

Gross, R.D. (1992). *Psychology: The science of mind and behaviour* (2nd edn.). London: Hodder & Stoughton. Chapter 16 has good coverage of bystander intervention, and some discussion of other forms of pro-social behaviour.

Shaffer, D.R. (1993). *Developmental psychology: Childhood and adolescence* (3rd edn.). Pacific Grove, CA: Brooks/Cole. Chapter 14 deals with the development of empathy.

References

Batson, C.D., Dyck, J.L., Brandt, J.R., Batson, J.G., Powell, A.L., McMaster, R.M., & Griffitt, C.A. (1988). Five studies testing two new egotistic alternatives to the empathy–altruism hypothesis. *Journal of Personality and Social Psychology, 55,* 52–77.

Cialdini, R.B., Schaller, M., Houlihan, D., Arps, K., Fultz, J., & Beaman, A.L. (1987). Empathy-based helping: Is it selflessly or selfishly motivated? *Journal of Personality and Social Psychology, 52,* 599–604.

Darley, J., & Latane, B. (1968). Bystander intervention in emergencies: Diffusion of responsibility. *Journal of Personality and Social Psychology, 10,* 202–214.

Whiting, B.B., & Whiting, J.W.M. (1975). *Children of six cultures: A psychocultural analysis.* Cambridge, MA: Harvard University Press.

Summary

- Pro-social behaviour includes co-operative actions that benefit others; altruism is a clear example of pro-social behaviour.
- Pro-social reasoning moves from being self-centred in young children to being focused on the needs of others and the desire to have approval; later increases in pro-social behaviour depend on the development of empathy.
- According to Batson's empathy–altruism hypothesis, altruistic behaviour is mainly motivated by empathy; those who feel empathic concern are more likely to help a victim than those who feel personal distress.
- According to Cialdini's negative-state relief model, altruistic behaviour is often motivated by a desire to reduce the sadness and other negative mood states produced by observing a victim.
- Altruism is more common in non-industrialised cultures than in industrialised ones.
- Children can become more altruistic via modelling procedures, but rewarding altruistic behaviour is usually ineffective.
- Several factors determine whether bystanders will help in an emergency; these include personal responsibility; situation ambiguity; perceived similarity; possession of relevant skills; victim characteristics; the bystanders' competing activities.
- Bystanders consider the costs of helping (including the possibility of physical harm) and the costs of not helping (they may be held responsible; they may feel guilty).
- Bystanders also consider the rewards of helping (praise from the victim and from other people) and the rewards of not helping (they are able to continue with their ordinary activities).
- According to the arousal / cost–reward model of Piliavin et al., bystander intervention involves a five-step process, with the decision about what to do being based on a comparison of the rewards and costs involved.

Key terms

Altruism: a form of **pro-social behaviour** that is costly to the altruistic person, and which is motivated by the desire to help someone else.

Arousal / cost–reward model: the view of Piliavin and others that the decision of bystanders to help a victim depends on their level of arousal, and on the rewards and costs of different possible actions.

Bystander intervention: an area of research concerned with the factors influencing whether bystanders help a victim whom they do not know.

Diffusion of responsibility: the more bystanders that observe a victim, the less the sense of personal responsibility each person has to give help.

Empathic concern: a soft-hearted and tender reaction to the distress of another person; see **personal distress**.

Empathy: the ability to understand another person's point of view, and to share that person's emotions.

Empathy–altruism hypothesis: the view of Batson that **altruism** is motivated by **empathy**.

Equity theory: the notion that people in a relationship want there to be fairness (equity) in the rewards and costs experienced on both sides.

Negative-state relief model: the view of Cialdini and others that someone who feels **empathy** for a victim will help because of the sadness produced by the empathy.

Norm of social responsibility: the expectation in most cultures that help should be given to those who need help.

Personal distress: a disturbed and worried reaction to the distress of another person; see **empathic concern**.

Pro-social behaviour: co-operative, affectionate, or helpful actions designed to be of benefit to someone else; see **altruism**.

Reciprocity norm: the cultural expectation that we should help those who have helped us in the past, and should not harm them.

Social norms: cultural expectations about appropriate and inappropriate ways of behaving.

Structured essay questions

1. When are bystanders likely to help a victim? When are bystanders unlikely to help a victim?
2. How does empathy develop in children? How does empathy lead to altruistic behaviour?
3. What is altruism? How can people be encouraged to become more altruistic?

Self-assessment questions

1. According to Eisenberg et al., children show concern to do what is right, sympathy for the person in need, and guilt if help is not given:
   a) at the self-centred level
   b) at the needs oriented level
   c) at the empathic level
   d) at the approval oriented level

2. According to Batson's empathy–altruism hypothesis, altruistic behaviour:
   a) occurs after there is personal distress
   b) occurs after there is empathic concern
   c) occurs before there is personal distress
   d) occurs before there is empathic concern

3. According to the negative-state relief model:
   a) empathy on its own causes helping behaviour
   b) those who are calm help others
   c) people lend help to reduce their own sadness
   d) none of the above

4. Which of the following is true:
   a) children in non-industrialised societies are given family responsibilities, and this reduces their altruism
   b) children in industrialised societies are given family responsibilities, and this reduces their altruism
   c) children in industrialised societies are given family responsibilities, and this increases their altruism
   d) children in non-industrialised societies are given family responsibilities, and this increases their altruism

5. Which of the following is true:
   a) a bystander is less likely to help a victim if there are several other bystanders; people do not know that the presence of others makes it less likely they will help
   b) a bystander is less likely to help a victim if there are several other bystanders; people know that the presence of others makes it less likely they will help
   c) a bystander is more likely to help a victim if there are several other bystanders; people do not know that the presence of others makes it more likely they will help
   d) a bystander is more likely to help a victim if there are several other bystanders; people know that the presence of others makes it more likely they will help

6. According to the arousal/cost–reward model, help is given when:
   a) a bystander experiences a state of arousal
   b) a bystander experiences arousal, and the rewards for helping are greater than the costs
   c) a bystander decides that the rewards and costs associated with helping are equal
   d) a bystander experiences a state of arousal and does not like it

Social influence and territorial behaviour

15

What we say and the way we behave are influenced by other people. We want to be liked by other people and to fit into society. As a result, we often hide what we really think, and try to behave in ways that will meet with the approval of others. However, the work that has been carried out by social psychologists indicates there is more to social influence. Most of us are much more influenced by other people than we think we are. This is true across a very wide range of situations.

Much social influence depends on what are known as *group norms*. Group norms consist of the rules and expectations about the behaviour of group members. Consider, for example, the norms of a tennis club. It is usually expected that the players will be dressed in white, and that they will accept defeat calmly without shouting or throwing their rackets around.

Social facilitation   acceptance.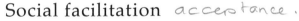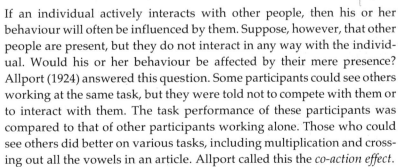

If an individual actively interacts with other people, then his or her behaviour will often be influenced by them. Suppose, however, that other people are present, but they do not interact in any way with the individual. Would his or her behaviour be affected by their mere presence? Allport (1924) answered this question. Some participants could see others working at the same task, but they were told not to compete with them or to interact with them. The task performance of these participants was compared to that of other participants working alone. Those who could see others did better on various tasks, including multiplication and crossing out all the vowels in an article. Allport called this the *co-action effect*.

The effects of others on performance can also be studied in a slightly different way. The focus is on the performance of participants performing a task in front of an audience, who are watching the participant rather than doing the same task as the participant. The presence of an audience improves performance. This is known as the *audience effect*, and it was shown by Travis (1925). Participants learned to track a moving metal

> **Personal viewpoint**
>
> To what extent do we try to behave so as to fit in with the expectations of others? Would you obey the orders of an authority figure if you thought the orders were wrong? In what circumstances are you most likely to conform or to obey authority figures? Why do you think that most people in crowds behave differently from the way they behave when they are on their own?

target, and were then tested alone and in the presence of a handful of spectators who watched quietly. Most of them performed better in front of the audience.

The co-action effect and the audience effect are both examples of what is known as *social facilitation*. Social facilitation is defined as an improvement in an individual's performance which is found when he or she is performing in the presence of others. When the situation is changed, however, we often find *social loafing* rather than social facilitation. Social loafing is defined as the decrease in individual effort that is often found when people work in groups. For example, Latane et al. (1979) asked their participants to cheer or to clap as loudly as they could. They did this on their own, or in groups of two, four, or six people. There was a large drop in the loudness of individual cheering and clapping as the number of people in the group increased.

What determines whether we find social facilitation or social loafing? Social loafing seems to be found mainly when the focus is on the performance of the group rather than on individual members of the group. Williams et al. (1981) asked groups of participants to cheer as loudly as possible; some of them were told that their contribution to the cheering would be identified, whereas others were not told this. Those who thought their individual efforts were being measured did not show social loafing, whereas the other participants did.

Motivation and arousal

As you might imagine, task performance is not always improved by the mere presence of others or by an audience. For example, an actor who is overcome by stage fright and totally forgets his lines cannot be said to benefit from the presence of an audience! Zajonc (1966) tried to explain why the presence of others can either improve or worsen performance. According to him, the presence of others increases the participant's level of motivation and arousal. This high level of arousal increases the tendency to produce dominant or well-learned responses, and reduces the production of non-dominant or new responses.

It follows from Zajonc's theory that the presence of others should improve performance on simple tasks (e.g. crossing out vowels), but should make it worse on complex tasks. There is reasonable support for this prediction. Michaels et al. (1982) argued that pool is an easy task for good players but a difficult one for poor players. Having four people watch a game of pool increased the performance of the good players from 71% good shots to 80%. In contrast, the audience reduced the performance of poor players from 36% good shots to only 25%.

The presence of other people has effects over and above those identified by Zajonc. Other people can be a source of distraction. They can also cause anxiety and embarrassment in the person performing a task, especially if they are people in a position of authority.

Conformity

Conformity can be defined as yielding to group pressures, something that nearly all of us do at least some of the time. Suppose, for example, that you and some of your friends go to see a film. You didn't think the film was much good, but all of your friends thought it was brilliant. You might be tempted to conform by pretending to agree with their verdict on the film rather than being the odd one out. As we will see, conformity to group pressures occurs much more often than most people imagine.

Muzafer Sherif

The first major study of conformity was carried out by Muzafer Sherif in 1936. He made use of what is known as the *autokinetic effect*. If we look at a stationary spot of light in a darkened room, very small movements of the eyes make the light seem to move. In his studies, Sherif first of all tested his participants one at a time. Each participant was asked to say how much the light seemed to move, and in what direction. Then he formed them into groups of three, and again asked each participant to indicate the amount and direction of movement of the light. Participants within a group tended to produce reports that were very close to each other. In other words, they showed conformity, because their reports were affected by what the other members of the group had to say.

What are the advantages and disadvantages of Sherif's approach?

PLUS	MINUS
• He proved the existence of group pressures to conform.	• He used a very artificial situation.
	• There was no correct answer in his situation; it would have been much more impressive to show that people ignore what they know to be the right answer.

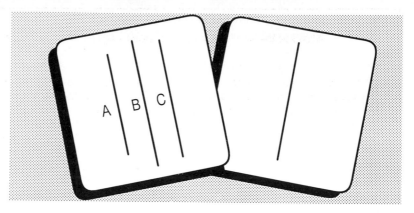

Cards like those
used in Asch's
(1951)
experiment.

Solomon Asch

Solomon Asch (1951) improved on the work of Sherif. He set up a situation
in which about seven people all sat looking at a display like the one shown
in the figure. They were given the task of saying out loud which out of
three lines was the same length as a given stimulus line. All but one of the
participants were "stooges" (they had been told by the experimenter to
give the same wrong answer on some trials). The one real participant was
the last (or the last but one) to offer his or her opinion on each trial.

What do you think the real participants did when faced with this
conflict between what the other members of the group said and what they
knew to be the right answer? On average, one-third of the participants
conformed all the time, and about three-quarters of them conformed at
least once. Thus, only about one-quarter totally refused to conform.

When does conformity break down? Asch found that his results were
quite different when just one of the stooges gave the right answer, rather
than the wrong answer being given by the majority. In those conditions,
conformity occurred only about 5% of the time. It is likely that the
comforting feeling of not being isolated made it easier for the participants
to avoid conforming.

Cultural factors.   One of the possible limitations of Asch's work is
that it was carried out in the United States in the late 1940s and early 1950s.
It is often assumed that Americans are more conformist than other people,
and it may be that people were more willing to conform in the days before
it became fashionable to "do your own thing". Thus, it is possible that the
levels of conformity obtained by Asch reflected the particular culture
prevailing in the United States at that time.

Perrin and Spencer (1980) tried to repeat Asch's study in the late 1970s,
but found very little evidence of conformity. They argued that the Asch

effect was "a child of its time". However, the low level of conformity may have occurred because they used engineering students who had been given training in the importance of accurate measurement.

Perrin and Spencer (1981) carried out two more studies on cultural factors in conformity. In one study, the participants were young men on probation, and the stooges primed to give the wrong answers were probation officers. The level of conformity in this study was about the same as in the Asch studies. In the other study, the participants and the stooges were both young unemployed men with Afro-Caribbean backgrounds. Once again, conformity levels were comparable to those reported by Asch.

Over the years, the Asch task has been used in several different countries. The findings varied somewhat from country to country. However, reasonable levels of conformity have been found in the great majority of countries, and so the findings of Perrin and Spencer (1980) are very unusual. In other words, conformity is found in nearly every culture that has so far been assessed.

Moscovici's social influence theory

Moscovici (1980) argued that Asch had put too much emphasis on the notion that the majority in a group have a large influence on the minority. He argued that it is also possible for the minority to influence the majority. He drew a distinction between compliance and conversion. *Compliance* is involved when a majority influences a minority, and is based on the power of the majority. *Conversion* is how a minority can influence a majority. It involves convincing the majority that the minority's views are correct. For conversion to occur, it is very important for the minority to argue consistently for its point of view.

In one study, Moscovici and Faucheux (1972) tried to show that a minority of two could influence the other members of a group. The members of the group were shown an object coloured blue. When the minority argued consistently that the colour was actually green, they were able to persuade the rest of the group that it was green rather than blue.

Kinds of conformity

Kelman (1958) argued that there are three main reasons why someone behaves in a conforming way: *compliance*; *identification*; and *internalisation*. Compliance involves conforming with the majority in spite of not really agreeing with them. People comply in order to gain social approval or to avoid being rejected by the rest of the group. As the conformity is only superficial, compliance stops when there are no group pressures to conform.

Identification occurs when someone conforms to the demands of a given role in society. The conformity generally extends over several different aspects of behaviour. For example, stewards and stewardesses on planes try to be cheerful, polite, and helpful to the passengers at all times regardless of how they may actually be feeling. They behave in this way because they are conforming to what is expected of them.

Internalisation occurs when someone conforms because they are really in agreement with the views of those who are seeking to influence them. For example, the parents of a small girl may believe that it is very important for her to spend a lot of time with other children. If friends of theirs start sending their daughters to the Brownies, they will probably conform to the suggestion that they might also send their daughter. Conformity based on internalisation is like pushing on an open door, in the sense that the individual is being persuaded to do something he or she really wants to do. As a result, conformity behaviour based on internalisation continues even when there is no external pressure to conform.

✳ Self-fulfilling prophecy

A self-fulfilling prophecy is a prediction that comes true simply because people believe in it (see Chapter 19). An interesting example of a self-fulfilling prophecy was reported by Curtis and Miller (1986). They gave some participants false information that another person liked them. As a result, they behaved in a more likeable way the next time they met that person, and so were actually liked more. In contrast, those participants who were told that they were disliked behaved in an unfriendly way and so were disliked.

Rosenthal (1966) reported several studies in which he looked at the self-fulfilling prophecy. In one study, students were asked to observe flatworms, counting the number of body contractions and head movements. The flatworms were actually handed out at random. However, some of the students were told they had been given an active flatworm, whereas others were told they had been an inactive one. The students reported that the allegedly active flatworms produced almost twice as many body contractions and head movements as the inactive ones. Thus, the expectations of the students about the behaviour of the flatworms produced a self-fulfilling prophecy, perhaps by influencing the ways in which the flatworms were handled.

Rosenthal and Jacobson

The self-fulfilling prophecy became of more interest when Rosenthal and Jacobson (1968) tried to see whether it applies to children at school. They gave an intelligence test to the children at a school in an American city. They told the teachers that this test might be able to predict those children who would show very rapid intellectual development. Some children were selected at random, but the teachers were told that these children were "spurters". These spurters were expected to show great intellectual development over the following year.

What Rosenthal and Jacobson found was that some of these spurters showed large gains in intelligence one year after the start of the study. The teachers' expectations affected the ways they interacted with the spurters, and the extra interest from the teachers improved the children's intellectual growth.

What are the advantages and disadvantages of Rosenthal and Jacobson's approach?

PLUS

- It is an exciting notion that children's intellectual growth can be increased so easily by means of a self-fulfilling prophecy.
- There is good evidence that telling teachers that a child is gifted leads them to devote more time and attention to that child.

MINUS

- Most of the spurters studied by Rosenthal and Jacobson showed no gain in intelligence at all.
- There have been several other studies based on the Rosenthal and Jacobson study; few of them repeated the findings of the original study.

Obedience to authority

It is true of nearly all societies that certain people are given power and authority over others. In our society, for example, parents, teachers, and managers are invested with varying degrees of authority. Most of the time, this does not cause any problems. If the doctor tells us to take some tablets three times a day, we accept that he or she is the expert. As a result, we simply do as we are told without thinking any more about it. However, an issue that has been of interest to psychologists for many years is to work out how far most people are willing to go in their obedience to authority. What happens if you are asked by a person in authority to do something that you think is wrong? The best-known research on this issue was carried out by Stanley Milgram (1974).

Stanley Milgram

In Milgram's studies at Yale University, pairs of participants were given the roles of a teacher and a learner for a simple learning test. The "teacher" was asked to give electric shocks to the "learner" every time the wrong answer was given, and to increase the shock intensity each time. At 180 volts, the learner yelled "I can't stand the pain", and by 270 volts the response had become an agonised scream. If the teacher was unwilling to give the shocks, the experimenter urged him or her to continue. (See page 4 for some photographs of the experiment.)

Do you think you would be willing to give the maximum (and potentially deadly) 450-volt shock in this study? Milgram found that everyone he asked denied that they personally would do any such thing, and psychiatrists predicted that only one person in a thousand would go on to the 450-volt stage. In fact, about 50% of Milgram's participants gave the maximum shock—which is 500 times as many people as the expert psychiatrists had predicted!

One of the most striking cases of total obedience was that of Pasqual Gino, a 43-year-old water inspector of Italian descent. Towards the end of the experiment, he found himself thinking, "Good God, he's dead. Well, here we go, we'll finish him. And I just continued all the way through to 450 volts."

Milgram found that there were two main ways in which obedience to authority could be reduced: (1) increasing the obviousness of the learner's plight; or (2) reducing the authority or influence of the experimenter. The first way was studied by comparing obedience in four situations (the percentage of participants who were totally obedient is given in brackets):

Some of the
conditions in
Milgram's study

Condition	Subjects who obeyed to the end (%)
No sound from the victim throughout	100.0
Victim pounds on wall at 300V	65.0
Victim in same room	40.0
Study conducted in downtown office block	48.0
"Teacher" forces victim's hand onto electrode plate	30.0
Researcher gives directions by telephone	20.5
No orders from researcher: teacher has free choice of shock level	2.5
Researcher apparently just a member of the public	20.0

- *Remote feedback:* the victim could not be heard or seen (66%).
- *Voice feedback:* the victim could be heard but not seen (62%).
- *Proximity:* the victim was only one metre away from the participant (40%)
- *Touch-proximity:* this was like the proximity condition, except that the participant had to force the learner's hand onto the shockplate (30%).

Milgram reduced the authority of the experimenter by carrying out the experiment in a run-down office building rather than at Yale University. He found that the percentage of obedient participants went down from 65% at Yale University to 48% in the run-down office building. The influence of the experimenter was reduced by having him give his orders by telephone rather than having him sitting a few feet away from the participant. This reduced obedience from 65% to 20.5%.

Ethical issues in Milgram's work. The Milgram work caused a lot of controversy. There are various ethical issues involved. As you probably guessed, the learner did not actually receive any shocks, so that was not a problem. However, many of the participants were put into a very distressed state. As one person reported, "I observed a mature and in-itially poised businessman enter the laboratory smiling and confident. Within 20 minutes he was reduced to a twitching, stuttering wreck, who was rapidly approaching a point of nervous collapse." It is now accepted that it is not ethical to put participants into such a state, and this line of research has been abandoned. However, 84% of those who took part in Milgram's studies said they were glad to have done so, and only 1% expressed negative feelings.

Human nature. The other major controversy in Milgram's work concerned what the findings seem to tell us about human nature. They suggest that about half of the human race is cruel and sadistic. Evidence against this comes from the behaviour of the obedient participants. It would have been disturbing if they had looked relaxed and happy while giving severe electric shocks. In fact, however, most of them showed obvious tension and unease as they tried to come to grips with the moral conflict between obeying authority and respecting the rights of the learner.

Philip Zimbardo

In the 1960s, there were numerous reports of problems in American prisons. Many of these reports referred to brutal attacks by prison warders on the prisoners in their care. Why did this brutality occur? One possibility is that prison warders tend to have aggressive or sadistic personalities. Another possibility is that the social environment of prisons, including a rigid power structure, is mainly responsible.

Philip Zimbardo (1973) decided to study this issue in what has come to be known as the Stanford prison experiment. In this experiment, emotionally stable members of society agreed to act as "warders" and "prisoners" in a mock prison. Zimbardo was interested in seeing whether the hostility found in many real prisons would also be found in his mock prison. If hostility were found in spite of not using sadistic warders, this would suggest that the social environment of prisons creates hostility.

In the Stanford prison experiment, the prisoners could only eat at specified times. They needed the permission of a warder to do almost everything, including writing letters and going to the toilet. In all, there were 16 prison rules which the warders were asked to enforce.

What went on within the mock prison was so unpleasant and dangerous that the entire experiment had to be stopped after six days instead of the intended fourteen. Violence and rebellion broke out within two days of the start. The prisoners ripped off their clothing, and shouted and cursed at the warders. In return, the guards put down this rebellion violently using fire extinguishers. They also played the prisoners off against one another and harassed them almost constantly. One of the prisoners showed such severe symptoms of emotional disturbance

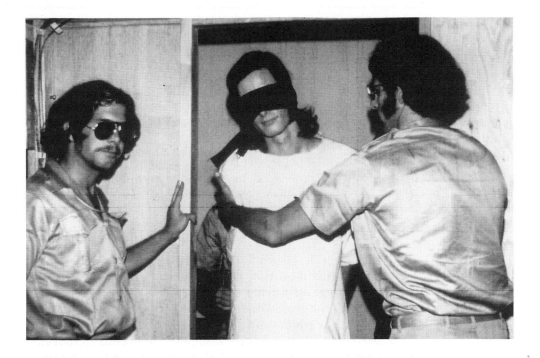

"Guards" and a "prisoner" from the Stanford prison experiment. Photograph © Dr. Zimbardo.

(disorganised thinking, uncontrollable crying and screaming) that he had to be released after only one day. On the fourth day, two more prisoners showed symptoms of severe disturbance and were released.

There were some interesting changes in the behaviour of the warders and prisoners over time. The prisoners became more and more subdued and submissive, often slouching and keeping their eyes fixed on the ground. At the same time, the use of force, harassment, and aggression by the warders increased steadily from day to day. It seemed that the warders began to enjoy the power to control other people, and the passive reaction of the prisoners encouraged them to exert more and more power.

What is the main message of the Stanford prison experiment? According to Zimbardo, the experiment showed the great importance of the power structure within prisons. In his own words, "Power is the most important variable in social psychology and the most neglected."

Ethical issues.   Many critics argued that it was not acceptable ethically for Zimbardo to have exposed his participants to such degradation and hostility. Can one really justify a study in which four participants had to be released because of "extreme depression, disorganised thinking, uncontrollable crying and fits of rage"? Was it reasonable for Zimbardo

PLUS	MINUS
• He showed that giving people power can have a great effect on their behaviour, leading them to behave in ways that they previously thought unacceptable.	• The mock warders may simply have pretended to be aggressive, because that is the way real warders are thought to behave; however, the physical abuse and harassment shown by the warders went beyond what would have been expected from mere play-acting. • There are serious ethical problems with his experiment.

to stand by while the guards forced prisoners to clean toilets with their bare hands, hosed them with fire extinguishers, and made them do push-ups with a guard standing on their back?

Harris Savin had no doubt as to the answers to these questions. In his opinion, the mock prison was a "hell". He compared Zimbardo to used-car salesmen and others "whose roles tempt them to be as obnoxious as the law allows." In reply, Zimbardo pointed out that he had tried to reduce any negative effects on the participants by holding day-long debriefing sessions, in which the moral conflicts posed by the study were discussed. He also pointed out that most of the participants reported that they had learned valuable things about themselves. It is true that the study was of value, but it is not clear that this begins to justify the level of degradation and physical assault that happened.

Hofling

One of the limitations of the Stanford prison experiment is that it was carried out in a mock situation. However, evidence of obedience to authority in a real-life situation was obtained by Hofling (1966). Twenty-two nurses were phoned up by someone who claimed to be Dr Smith. He asked the nurse to check that a drug called Astroten was available. When the nurses did this, they saw on the bottle that the maximum dosage of this drug was supposed to be 10mg. When they reported back to Dr Smith, he told them to give 20mg of the drug to a patient.

There were two good reasons why the nurses should have refused to do as they were instructed. First, the dose was considerably higher than the maximum safe dose. Second, the nurses did not know Dr Smith, and they were only supposed to take instructions from doctors they knew.

However, the nurses' training had led them to obey instructions from doctors: there is a clear power structure with doctors in a more powerful position than nurses. As you have probably guessed, the nurses were more influenced by the power structure than by the two hospital regulations they were meant to obey. All but one of the nurses did as Dr Smith instructed.

The findings of this study are important. They indicate that there is considerable obedience to authority in a naturalistic situation, in which the participants were unaware that an experiment was being carried out.

Crowd behaviour

It is well-known that individuals will often behave differently when they are in a crowd than when they are on their own or with a small group of friends. For example, lynch mobs in the south of the United States murdered about 2000 people (mostly blacks) during the first half of the twentieth century. It seems improbable that those involved in these atrocities would have behaved like that if they had not been part of a highly emotional crowd.

Le Bon (1895) was a French journalist who put forward perhaps the first theory of crowd behaviour. According to him, a man who forms part of a crowd "descends several rungs in the ladder of civilisation, he is a barbarian—that is, a creature acting by instinct … [He can be] induced to commit acts contrary to his most obvious interest and best known habits. An individual in a crowd is a grain of sand amid other grains of sand, which the wind stirs up at will."

Crowds do sometimes behave in senseless ways. However, that is by no means always the case. For example, consider cases of fires in halls and other public buildings, in which several people died as everyone rushed to escape. At first glance, this may seem like senseless and irrational behaviour. However, it would only make sense for each person to walk slowly to one of the exits if they could trust everyone else to do the same. As that trust is usually lacking, the most rational behaviour is probably to behave like everyone else and try to be among those first out of the building.

Crowding and personal space

It seems likely that people often behave aggressively when there is severe over-crowding. Evidence supporting this view was reported by Loo (1979), who studied the behaviour of young children in a day nursery. The overall level of aggressive behaviour went up as the number of children increased. In similar fashion, it has been found that there are more acts of aggression and riots in prisons with a high density of prisoners than in other prisons (McCain et al., 1980).

Research on other species confirms the link between crowding and aggression. Cahoun (1962) carried out a study in which there was a steady increase in the number of rats living in a large enclosure. Even though the rats were well cared for, they grew more and more aggressive as the enclosure became crowded. The level of aggression finally became so high that some of the young rats were killed, and others were simply eaten.

In order to understand why crowding can cause aggression, it is important to consider the notion of *personal space*. This was defined by Sommer (1967) as "an area with invisible boundaries surrounding a person's body into which intruders may not come." Other people have compared personal space to a buffer zone which affords protection against perceived threats.

Felipe and Sommer (1966) observed reactions to invasion of personal space in the grounds of a large mental institution. The experimenter walked around the grounds, and sat about six inches away from any man sitting alone and not involved in any activity. If the man moved his chair, or moved further along the bench, the experimenter moved the same amount to keep the space between them the same as before. The man usually reacted by facing away from the experimenter, placing his elbows by his sides, mumbling, or laughing nervously. Half of the men took flight within nine minutes of the experimenter sitting beside them, and only 8% did not move at all.

Felipe and Sommer (1966) obtained similar findings in an almost empty university library. A female experimenter sat down very close to female college students. Seventy percent of the students left the library within 30 minutes, and only thirteen percent put up with the close proximity of the experimenter and stayed put.

The unease caused by invasion of our personal space helps to explain why overcrowding leads to aggression. However, it is perhaps surprising that people are very unlikely to complain about invasion of their personal space. Felipe and Sommer found that only two of the mental patients and one out of 80 students asked the person invading their space to move away. As Hall (1966) expressed it, "We treat space somewhat as we treat sex. It is there but we don't talk about it."

Hall (1966) argued that personal space can be divided into four zones. These zones apply to most people living in Europe and the United States, but may not be as relevant to those living elsewhere. First, there is the *intimate zone*, which extends up to about 18 inches (45 centimetres). Only lovers, close relatives, and very close friends are normally allowed into this zone (social kissing excepted). Second, there is the *personal zone*,

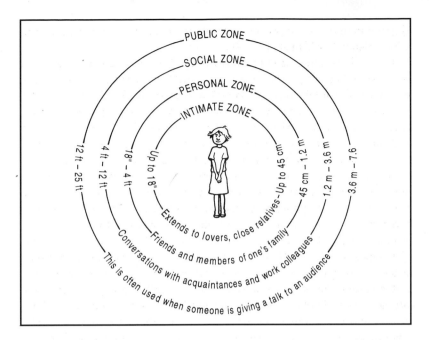

PUBLIC ZONE

SOCIAL ZONE

PERSONAL ZONE

INTIMATE ZONE

12 ft – 25 ft

4 ft – 12 ft

18" – 4 ft

Up to 18"

Extends to lovers, close relatives–Up to 45 cm

Friends and members of one's family

Conversations with acquaintances and work colleagues

This is often used when someone is giving a talk to an audience

45 cm – 1.2 m

1.2 m – 3.6 m

3.6 m – 7.6

Zones of personal space.

which ranges between about 18 inches and 4 feet (1.2 metres). Friends and members of one's family are allowed into this zone. Third, there is the *social zone*, which lies between about 4 and 12 feet (3.6 metres). Conversations with acquaintances and work colleagues usually take place in this zone. Fourth, there is the *public zone*, which extends between about 12 and 25 feet (7.6 metres). This is the zone that is often used when someone is giving a talk to an audience.

The notion that the size of our personal space depends on the precise relationship we have with another person is a valuable one. However, the four zones identified by Hall merge into one another. As a result, it should come as no surprise to find that people sometimes fail to keep within the distances indicated for each zone.

Deindividuation

Another reason for mob behaviour is related to what has been called *deindividuation*. This is the loss of a sense of *personal identity* (our thoughts and feelings about ourselves) that sometimes happens in a large group or crowd. According to Diener (1979), deindividuation can have a number of different effects:

● Poor monitoring of one's own behaviour.
● Reduced concern to have social approval of one's behaviour.

- Reduced restraints against behaving impulsively.
- Greater awareness of one's emotional state.
- Reduced capacity to think rationally.

It is possible that deindividuation was involved in Zimbardo's Stanford prison experiment which was discussed earlier. In that experiment, the participants who acted as prison warders behaved in ways that were quite different from their normal behaviour, suggesting that they had lost their sense of personal identity. Zimbardo (1970) reported a study more directly focused on deindividuation. Female participants were told to give electric shocks to other women in a Milgram-type study. Deindividuation was produced in half the participants by having them wear laboratory coats and hoods that covered their faces. In addition, the experimenter addressed them as a group rather than as individuals. The intensity of electric shocks given by these deindividuated participants was twice that of participants who wore their own clothes, and were treated as individuals.

Jones and Downing (1979) were not convinced that it was really deindividuation which produced the findings of Zimbardo (1970). They pointed out that the clothing worn by the deindividuated participants resembled that worn by the Ku Klux Klan. They found that deindividuated participants who were dressed as nurses actually gave fewer electric shocks than did those who wore their own clothes. Thus, deindividuation generally affects our behaviour, but the consequences can sometimes be desirable rather than undesirable.

Territorial behaviour

Territoriality

It is common in other species for members to have an area or territory that they will defend from any invaders. This territory has typically been selected because it provides a good supply of food. It has been argued that humans show similar *territoriality*, or a need to have and maintain a given area. Territoriality in humans sometimes revolves around access to food, especially in tribal societies, but in Western societies this is rare.

According to Altman (1975), humans make use of three different kinds of territories:

- *Primary territories:* these areas are private, and are restricted to a very small number of people (e.g. one's own bedroom).
- *Secondary territories:* these areas are accessible to many people, but are not accessible to everyone (e.g. bridge club; school).

● *Public territories:* as the term implies, any member of the public is allowed to use these areas (e.g. commons; parks).

Fisher and Byrne (1971) argued that people use various strategies to mark out an area for themselves in secondary territories and public territories. They found that students sitting alone in a library used books, coats, and sweaters to form barriers against intruders. There was an interesting sex difference. Female students tended to erect barriers between themselves and adjacent seats. In contrast, male students tended to erect barriers between themselves and the seat across the table.

Why was there this sex difference? People generally sit face-to-face in competitive situations, and side-by-side in co-operative ones. As men used to be taught to be more competitive than women, it is possible that men view strangers who sit opposite them as a potential threat or challenge. On the other hand, women used to be taught to be more friendly and co-operative than men, and so might view a stranger sitting next to them as an unwanted demand for attention and friendship.

Privacy

Privacy was defined by Lee (1976) as "a condition of optimal access by others to the self (or group)." The basic idea is that everyone has a preferred level of interaction and involvement with other people. If the actual level falls below the preferred level, then people feel lonely or isolated. On the other hand, if the actual level exceeds the preferred level, people feel stressed, and may become resentful. There are large individual differences in privacy. Extraverted individuals who are high in sociability have a much higher preferred level of involvement with others than do introverted individuals who are low in sociability (see Chapter 18).

Privacy is maintained in several different ways. In primary territories, this is often achieved by keeping doors closed and locked, or by erecting a fence around one's property. As Hayes (1984) pointed out, many people whose houses have been burgled are more upset about the invasion of their primary territory than they are about the goods they have lost.

In secondary territories, such as a classroom, students may preserve their desired level of privacy by sitting in the same seat each time with friends on either side of them. In a restaurant, privacy can be maintained by selecting a table that is some way away from any other table. Some people find it disturbing if people at other tables can overhear their conversation during the meal.

Some of the strategies used to preserve privacy in public territories can be seen on crowded beaches. People tend to arrange their belongings (e.g. clothes, picnic basket, chairs) in such a way as to create an area that is theirs rather than anyone else's. In addition, they often sit so as to reduce the possibility of eye contact with others sitting nearby on the beach. Similar strategies were reported by Felipe and Sommer (1966) in their study in which the experimenter sat very close to students in a library. Some of the students tried to create their own territory by using clothes and/or books, whereas others turned their bodies away from the experimenter or wrapped their arms around their work.

In sum, it is clear that most people attach much importance to privacy. This is indicated by the discomfort and protective moves that are made by those whose privacy is invaded.

Defensible space

Crime depends on a number of factors, including unemployment, poverty, and drug use. However, Newman (1972) argued that crime also depends on the physical layout of building developments. He emphasised the notion of *defensible space*, which is space within a building development that is designed in such a way as to minimise crime. In order to produce defensible space, the following four factors are important:

- Each area or space should belong to someone, because unassigned spaces tend to be neglected by everyone.
- All areas within the development should be overlooked, so that those living there can see what is happening and so deter criminals.
- There needs to be easy access between the housing development and the outside world, ideally along wide and brightly lit streets.
- The houses or flats within a housing development should look well-protected and secure; this deters casual burglars from stealing property.

The level of crime tends to be lower in developments with defensible space than in those without it. However, it is probable that general social conditions are easily the most important causes of crime. Crime levels in the United Kingdom doubled during the 1980s, and it is hard to believe that this was due to a large decrease in defensible space. It is much more likely that it was due to the large increase in unemployment and relative deprivation.

Further reading

Hayes, N. (1993). *Principles of social psychology*. Hove, UK: Lawrence Erlbaum Associates Ltd. Chapter 3 contains much information about the various kinds of social influence.

References

Asch, S.E. (1951). Effects of group pressure upon the modification and distortion of judgements. In H. Guetzkow (Ed.), *Groups, leadership, and men*. Pittsburgh: Carnegie.

Hall, E.T. (1966). *The hidden dimension*. New York: Doubleday.

Milgram, S. (1974). *Obedience to authority: An experimental view*. New York: Harper & Row.

Rosenthal, R., & Jacobson, L. (1968). *Pygmalion in the classroom: Teacher expectations and pupils' intellectual development*. New York: Holt, Rinehart, & Winston.

Zajonc, R.B. (1965). Social facilitation. *Science, 149*, 269–274.

Summary

- Our behaviour is much influenced by other people; some of this influence depends on group norms.
- Social facilitation occurs when someone performs a task better in the presence of other people; it is shown in the co-action effect and in the audience effect.
- The presence of others often produces motivation or arousal; this improves performance of easy tasks, but can worsen performance of complex tasks.
- As well as motivational effects, the presence of others can cause the individual to become anxious or embarrassed.
- Conformity occurs when people yield to group norms and pressures.
- Sherif demonstrated conformity with the autokinetic effect, in which a stationary light seems to move.
- Asch showed conformity in an unambiguous situation; only three people needed to give the same wrong answer to produce the maximum conformity effect.
- The Asch conformity effect has generally been found over several decades and in several different countries.
- Conformity can involve: (1) compliance; (2) identification; (3) internalisation.
- Rosenthal and Jacobson claimed that children's intellectual growth can be increased by means of a self-fulfilling prophecy if teachers expect them to show rapid development; this claim has received limited support.
- Milgram found high levels of obedience to authority; the level was lower if the plight of the learner was made more obvious or if the influence of the experimenter was reduced.
- Zimbardo's Stanford prison experiment indicated the importance of power structures: stable individuals given the role of prison warders became aggressive and enjoyed controlling other people.
- Hofling found much obedience to authority in a real-life situation.
- Overcrowding can produce aggression in humans and other species; one reason for this is invasion of personal space.
- People in crowds sometimes show deindividuation.
- Humans show territoriality; there are primary, secondary, and public territories.
- Privacy is "a condition of optimal access by others to the self (or group)"; it is maintained by various strategies.
- Crime can be reduced if housing developments consist of defensible space.

Key terms

Audience effect: the improvement in performance produced by the presence of an audience.

Autokinetic effect: the illusion that a stationary light in a dark room is moving about.

Co-action effect: the improvement in performance produced by the presence of others working at the same task.

Compliance: conformity to gain social approval or to avoid being rejected; it involves the influence of the majority on a minority.

Conformity: behaving in line with group pressures.

Conversion: a minority within a group convincing the majority of its point of view by means of consistent arguments.

Defensible space: space within a building development which is intended to avoid crime.

Deindividuation: loss of a sense of personal identity which can happen in a large group or crowd.

Group norms: the expectations and rules applying to the behaviour of members of a group.

Identification: conformity to the demands of a given role in society, such as a work role.

Internalisation: conformity in which people are really in agreement with those trying to influence them.

Intimate zone: that part of the **personal space** extending up to about 18 inches (45 centimetres) from the body.

Personal identity: the main thoughts and feelings we have about ourselves.

Personal space: the area around people into which they do not want most people to come; it can be divided into the **intimate zone**, **personal zone**, **social zone**, and **public zone**.

Personal zone: that part of the **personal space** extending between about 18 inches (45 centimetres) and 4 feet (1.20 metres) from the body.

Primary territories: private areas restricted to very few people (e.g. one's bedroom).

Privacy: an individual's preferred level of interaction and involvement with other people.

Public territories: areas that are accessible to nearly everyone (e.g. parks).

Public zone: that part of the **personal space** extending between about 12 (3.6 metres) and 25 feet (7.6 metres) from the body.

Secondary territories: areas that are accessible to many people, but not to everyone (e.g. bridge club).

Self-fulfilling prophecy: a prediction that comes true simply because people believe in it.

Social facilitation: improved performance in the presence of others; see **co-action effect** and **audience effect**.

Social loafing: the decrease in individual effort occurring when people work in a group.

Social zone: that part of the **personal space** extending between about 4 feet (1.2 metres) and 12 feet (3.60 metres) from the body.

Territoriality: the need to have, and to keep, an area that will be defended if necessary.

Structured essay questions

1. Describe some studies showing how the presence of others can lead to improved performance. When are these effects not found?
2. What is conformity? What evidence suggests that most people tend to conform?
3. Discuss some of the evidence on obedience to authority. How concerned should we be about the findings?
4. What are personal space and territoriality? How do the needs for personal space and territoriality influence human behaviour?

Self-assessment questions

1. Social facilitation can be seen in:
    a) the audience effect only
    b) the co-action effect only
    c) the audience and co-action effects
    d) none of the above

2. Asch's conformity effect:
    a) has generally been found in different countries and at different times
    b) was "a child of its time"
    c) has only been found in a few countries
    d) has become much stronger in recent years

3. Which of the following is true:
    a) conversion is involved when a majority influences a minority, whereas compliance is involved when a minority influences a majority
    b) compliance is involved when a majority influences a minority, whereas conversion is involved when a minority influences a majority
    c) conversion is involved when a minority influences another minority
    d) compliance is involved when a majority influences a minority, or when a minority influences a majority

4. When people conform to the demands of a given role in society, it is known as:
    a) internalisation
    b) compliance
    c) conversion
    d) identification

5. Milgram's research on obedience to authority:
    a) produced less obedience than most people predicted
    b) produced the level of obedience that most people predicted
    c) produced more obedience than most people predicted
    d) produced complete obedience by nearly all participants

6. In the Stanford prison experiment, the warders:
    a) behaved well towards the prisoners
    b) became less aggressive over time
    c) were very aggressive all the way through the experiment
    d) became more aggressive over time

7. The area between about 18 inches (45 centimetres) and 4 feet (1.2 metres) from us is known as:
    a) the intimate zone
    b) the personal zone
    c) the social zone
    d) the public zone

8. Bridge clubs and schools are:
    a) secondary territories
    b) primary territories
    c) public territories
    d) tertiary territories

Social perception 16

We are social beings who spend most of our time interacting with others within the family, at work, and in various leisure and social activities. Almost every time we meet someone, we form an impression of that person. We may find him or her friendly or unfriendly, aggressive or timid, clever or unintelligent. We generally form impressions of others very rapidly, and often we do not really know why our immediate impressions are positive or negative. As a result, psychologists rarely rely on introspective evidence when trying to understand the processes underlying impression formation and social perception generally. Instead, they have devised various experiments to shed light on the mysteries of social perception.

Most of the research on impression formation and social perception has been done by social psychologists. However, there has recently been more influence from cognitive psychology. Cognitive psychologists are interested in the information we have stored in long-term memory. Much of this information is in the form of concepts and schemas (organised "packets" of knowledge). As we will see, the impressions we form of other people depend in part on the concepts and schemas we possess. For example, suppose that someone has the inaccurate information stored in long-term memory that all Scottish people are mean. That person is likely to observe the financial dealings of any Scottish people he or she meets with particular attention, looking for evidence of their meanness.

The impact of cognitive psychology is discussed towards the end of the chapter. Before that, we will consider more traditional work on social perception.

Implicit personality theory

An important study on impression formation was reported by Solomon Asch (1946). He argued that people forming impressions of others make use of an *implicit personality theory* based on the assumption that a person who has one particular personality trait will tend to have a number of

We like some of the people we meet, and we dislike others. We often have so much information about other people that it is hard to know which information has been crucial in determining our emotional reactions to them. What kinds of information do you think influence your reactions to other people? Are you more affected by their personality or by their personal appearance? Can you think of ways in which the media influence your social perception?

other, related traits. This tendency is much greater for some aspects of personality (central traits) than for others (peripheral traits).

In his test of implicit personality theory, Asch gave his participants a list of seven adjectives which were said to describe someone called Jim. All of them were given the following six adjectives: intelligent, skilful, industrious, determined, practical, and cautious. The seventh adjective was warm, cold, polite, or blunt. Then the participants wrote descriptions of Jim, and indicated whether the adjectives generous, wise, happy, good-natured or reliable applied to him.

The findings were clear. The adjectives warm and cold were central traits, because they had marked effects on how all the other information about Jim was interpreted. For example, when Jim was warm, 91% of the participants thought he was generous and 94% thought he was good-natured. In contrast, when Jim was cold, only 8% of the participants thought he was generous, and 17% thought he was good-natured. Thus, people believe that those who are warm have a wide range of other desirable characteristics, whereas those who are cold have numerous other undesirable characteristics. However, the adjectives polite and blunt were peripheral traits, because they had little impact on impression formation.

Evidence that the warm–cold variable can affect behaviour as well as impression formation was reported by Kelley (1950). A visiting lecturer was described beforehand as either warm or cold. Many more of the students who had been told that he was warm stayed behind after the lecture to talk to him. The same students also rated him in much more positive terms than did the students who had been informed that the lecturer was cold.

Asch's work was put into a broader theoretical context by Rosenberg et al. (1968). They argued that most of our impressions of others relate to two dimensions:

1. *Social:* the good end of this dimension has adjectives such as sociable, popular, and warm, and the bad end includes unsociable, cold, and irritable.
2. *Intellectual:* this dimension ranges from skilful and persistent (good end) to stupid and foolish.

According to Rosenberg et al., we decide whether someone is good or bad on the social dimension, and good or bad on the intellectual dimension. These decisions strongly influence any later judgements about that person.

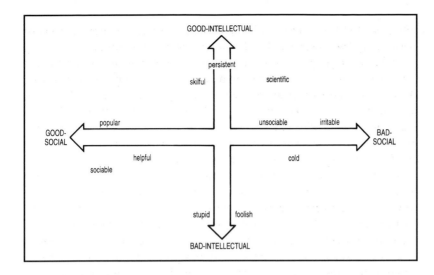

Primacy and recency effects

Suppose you were provided with some favourable and some unfavourable information about someone else. Would it make any difference which information was presented first? Many people argue that first impressions are very important, and this idea was tested by Solomon Asch (1946). Some participants were told that someone was "intelligent, industrious, impulsive, critical, stubborn, and envious." Thus, they were given positive information followed by negative information. Other participants were given the same adjectives, but in reverse order. Those who heard the positive traits first formed a much more favourable impression of the person than did those who heard the negative traits first. For example,

---

What are the advantages and disadvantages of Asch's approach?

PLUS	MINUS
• There is strong support for implicit personality theory, and for the notion that some traits are of more central importance than others.	• The work of Rosenberg et al. confirmed that Asch was right to focus on the social dimension, but he paid too little attention to the intellectual dimension. • Asking people to form impressions of imagined others on the basis of lists of adjectives is very artificial, and may involve different processes to those used in everyday life.

90% of those in the first group predicted that the person would be generous, compared to only 10% in the second group. These findings show what is known as a *primacy effect*; that is, initial information has more impact than later information on impression formation.

Luchins (1959) confirmed the existence of a primacy effect in impression formation using a slightly more naturalistic approach than the one adopted by Asch. Participants read a two-paragraph description of a boy called Jim. Jim behaved in a sociable way in one of the paragraphs, but in a reserved and unsociable way in the other paragraph. The impressions that the participants formed of Jim were influenced much more by the first paragraph they read than by the second one. Those who read the sociable paragraph first found Jim likeable, and thought he would be good-looking. In contrast, those who read the unsociable paragraph first tended to feel that he would be physically unattractive and that they would not like him. Finally, those who had received the sociable description first were more likely to predict that Jim would behave in a sociable way in a range of situations.

There is a considerable amount of evidence for a primacy effect in impression formation, but there is also some support for a *recency effect*. A recency effect occurs when our impression of someone is much affected by the most recent information we have received about him or her. Recency effects are most likely to be found when there is a large gap in time between initially receiving information about someone and then receiving additional information about him or her. Under those circumstances, it is likely that much of the original information has been forgotten, and so can no longer influence judgements about the other person.

Personal constructs

It was assumed in most of the research we have discussed so far that different people tend to form the same impression of any given individual. This assumption was disputed by George Kelly (1955). He argued that everyone has their own particular way of interpreting the behaviour of other people. According to Kelly, each of us possesses a set of *personal constructs* which we use to make sense of the world about us (see Chapter 18). Each of these personal constructs is bipolar, meaning that it has two opposite ends. For example, someone who was brought up by parents who attached great importance to politeness might have polite–rude as one of his or her major personal constructs. As a result, he or she would pay much attention to how polite or rude other people are in their behaviour. In contrast, the polite–rude construct might be less important to someone brought up by liberal-minded parents.

One way of measuring an individual's personal constructs is to use Kelly's repertory grid technique. First of all, the individual thinks of the names of those people who are most important to him or her. Then these people are considered three at a time, with the individual thinking of ways in which two of them are similar and different from the third person. The dimensions used define the individual's personal constructs. People often use about seven major personal constructs when forming impressions of other people.

A completed construct repertory grid. Roth (1990). © The Open University.

	Self	Mother	Father	Brother	Sister	Spouse	Ex-flame	Best friend	Ex-friend	Rejecting person	Pitied person	Threatening person	Attractive person	Accepted teacher	Rejected teacher	Boss	Successful person	Happy person	Ethical person	Neighbour	Constructs
	1	2	3	4	5	6	7	8	9	10	11	12	13	14	15	16	17	18	19	20	
1		⊗	⊗	○	X			X		X			X	X			X	X	X	X	1 kind – cruel
2						X	○	X	⊗		⊗			X	X	X					2 frightening – gentle
3			X	X	X		X						X	X		X	⊗	⊗	○		3 carefree – conscientious
4		X		X		⊗	○	⊗					X	X			X	X	X	X	4 understanding – unsympathetic
5	○		X	X	X	⊗		⊗		X			X	X		X	X	X			5 confident – anxious
6	X	⊗	X			X	⊗	○		X		X				X	X			X	6 simple – intellectual

Matching scores

1–2 4	2–3 8	3–4 13	4–5 13	5–6 8
1–3 12	2–4 5	3–5 18	4–6 7	
1–4 17	2–5 8	3–6 8		
1–5 12	2–6 8			
1–6 10				

What are the advantages and disadvantages of Kelly's approach?

PLUS
- Kelly's personal construct theory takes full account of individual differences in the dimensions used in impression formation.
- The repertory grid technique provides a useful way of measuring personal constructs.

MINUS
- The repertory grid technique focuses only on personal constructs of which the individual has conscious awareness.

need to decide rapidly whether to approach another person or an object, or to run away. In such circumstances, it is better to act on the basis of the best available strategy, as happens with the scanning strategy.

Prototypes

The concepts used by Bruner et al. were very clear and precise. However, most concepts are rather vague or "fuzzy". For example, McCloskey and Glucksberg (1978) asked 30 people whether a "stroke" was a disease: 16 said it was, and 14 said it was not. The same finding was obtained when the same people were asked whether a "pumpkin" was a fruit. Surprisingly, a month later eleven of the participants had changed their minds about a stroke being a disease, and eight had changed their minds about a pumpkin being a fruit.

Why are so many concepts fuzzy in nature? According to Mervis and Rosch (1981), each concept is organised around a *prototype* or set of characteristic features held by most members of the concept. An object is (or is not) accepted as a member of a given concept or category on the basis of the number of characteristic features of that concept which it has. A pumpkin has some (but by no means all) of the characteristic features of a fruit, and so many people are not sure whether or not it is a fruit.

We can see how prototype theory works by considering the concept "bird". Some of the characteristic features of this concept are having wings, the ability to fly, having feathers, and being relatively small. Birds having most of the characteristic features (e.g. robins) are regarded as "better" or more typical birds than those (e.g. ostriches) that do not.

Prototype theorists disagree among themselves about the nature of the underlying prototypes. Some theorists (e.g. Mervis & Rosch, 1981) argue that the prototype is rather abstract and is represented by characteristic features. Others (e.g. Hintzman & Ludlum, 1980) argue that prototypes are more concrete, and consist of the best member of the concept. For example, the prototype of the furniture category might be "chair". It is unclear which of these approaches is better.

Some abstract concepts (e.g. a rule; a belief) do not seem to have prototypes. It may be that the range of possible rules and beliefs is too wide for the entire category to be represented by a set of characteristic features.

Self-concept

The most important concept is the *self-concept*, which consists of the complex set of ideas we have about ourselves (see Chapter 19). Our self-concept influences our perception of others as well as of ourselves.

Carl Rogers was a clinical psychologist who argued that the concept of the self is of great importance (see Chapter 18). According to him, our self-concept is based on our conscious experiences of ourselves and of our position in society. What is of special importance is the relationship between the self-concept and the *ideal self*—that is, between the way we actually are and the way we would most like to be. Some individuals show incongruence, which is a major discrepancy between the self-concept and the ideal self. Some of those with incongruence seek therapy. A major goal of the client-centred therapy provided by Rogers is to increase the individual's self-esteem, and so reduce the discrepancy between his or her self-concept and ideal self.

Higgins (1990) has developed a theory based on some of Rogers' ideas. He argued that the self is compared against "ideal" self-guides (the individual's hopes and aspirations) and "ought" self-guides (beliefs about duties and obligations). There are self-discrepancies when the self is seen to fall short of either guide. For example, a student failing an examination may experience actual–ideal discrepancy through failure to realise educational goals and actual–ought discrepancy through failure to study hard.

Higgins has found that the emotion experienced by an individual depends on the nature of the self-discrepancy. Actual–ideal discrepancies produce dejection and depression. In contrast, actual–ought discrepancies produce agitation. Both kinds of self-discrepancy have negative effects on the perception of the self and on the social perception of other people.

Schemas

We have many expectations in our everyday lives. For example, we expect that people will form an orderly queue at a bus stop, and we expect a waiter or waitress to bring us a menu in a restaurant. Where do these expectations come from? According to many psychologists, schemas are involved. For example, we may have a restaurant schema, which contains information about the normal sequence of events in a restaurant. Schemas provide us with expectations which may or may not be confirmed by reality.

Evidence that we have a restaurant schema was reported by Bower et al. (1979). They first of all asked their participants to produce a list of the things they expected to happen in a restaurant. There was good agreement on many of the expectations (e.g. they expected to be shown to a table, to be handed a menu, and to order the food and drink). Having found out what information was stored in the restaurant schema, Bower et al. then presented a story about a meal in a restaurant. This was followed by a recognition-memory test for the story. Some of the items on the memory test had not appeared in the story, but were part of the information stored also four times as likely to show bravery or heroism. In contrast, girls were six times more likely to show passivity and dependence, and ten times more likely to be victimised and humiliated by the opposite sex.

A more subtle way in which the media influence our stereotypes is by ignoring certain groups in society. The negative stereotypes that many people have of the aged probably owe something to the fact that old people are almost invisible in the media. For example, Gerbner et al. (1980) found that only 2.3% of fictional characters on television were over 65 years of age, in spite of the fact that 11% of the population falls into that age group. When they asked schoolchildren the age at which men and women become elderly or old, those who watched television infrequently said 57 years on average. In contrast, those who watched a lot of television, and were used to seeing mostly young people, said that old age began at the age of 51.

We tend to use our schematic information (e.g. the French are great cooks) to judge individuals or groups. This often leads to distortions in our judgements and in our memory of what we think we know about other people.

A study by Gahagan (1984) shows how schema-based stereotyping can produce distortions in memory. Participants read a description of some of the events in a woman's life. A week later, some of them were told the woman had started a heterosexual relationship after the events described, whereas other participants were told she had started a homosexual relationship. A third group of participants was not given any additional information about the woman's sexual relationships. The three groups were then asked to recall the original description. Only those who were told that the woman had started a homosexual relationship tended to forget the information that she had dated boys during adolescence. Presumably schematic knowledge of the characteristics of lesbians caused this information to be forgotten.

A phenomenon related to stereotyping is *confirmation bias*. This is the tendency to confirm our existing beliefs rather than to look for information that might disprove those beliefs. Thus, if we think that someone is dishonest, we will tend to ignore any information indicating that he or she is basically an honest person. The fact that first impressions usually have more impact than information made available later (the primacy effect) probably reflects confirmation bias.

Stereotyping and confirmation bias both produce distorted impressions of other people. Why, then, do we continue to use them? Stereotyping and confirmation bias help to simplify the complexities of life and so save us time. If we wanted to be very accurate in our judgements of everyone we met, it would take up most of our time to sift through all of the available information about them.

What are the advantages and disadvantages of schema theory?

PLUS	MINUS
• Top-down processing is important, and schema theory has shown how such processing can influence perception and memory.	• It is very hard to know what information is contained in any given schema, and this makes it difficult to test schema theory.
• Most information in long-term memory is well-organised, and is arranged in packets of information resembling schemas.	• Schema theory suggests that perception and memory are often distorted and inaccurate; the distortions predicted by schema theory do occur, but they are less common than would be expected on the theory.

Self-schema

A number of theorists, including Markus (1977), have argued that our knowledge about ourselves is organised in the form of a *self-schema* resembling the self-concept described earlier in the chapter. The self-schema contains the various kinds of information we have about ourselves, and is stored in long-term memory. It is claimed to influence nearly all self-relevant attentional and memory processes. For example, Rogers et al. (1977) found that long-term memory for adjectives was much higher when they had been processed for their self-relevance than when they had not. This may have occurred because the self-schema provided a useful way of organising the adjectives.

Some of the most interesting ideas about self-schemas have emerged from the study of clinical patients. For example, Beck and Clark (1988) argued that anxious patients have schemas containing assumptions and beliefs about danger to themselves and about their reduced ability to cope. Patients with generalised anxiety feel surrounded by physical and psychological threats, and there is an increased sense of vulnerability. Depressed patients have a generally negative self-schema, in which they view themselves as inadequate, deprived, and worthless. According to Beck and Clark, individuals possessing negative self-schemas are vulnerable to emotional disorders of various kinds.

Further reading

Hayes, N. (1993). *Principles of social psychology*. Hove, UK: Lawrence Erlbaum Associates Ltd. There is a readable account of social perception in Chapter 4.

References

Asch, S.E. (1946). Forming impressions of personality. *Journal of Abnormal and Social Psychology, 41*, 258–290.

Kelley, H.H. (1967). Attribution theory in social psychology. In D. Levine (Ed.), *Nebraska symposium on motivation, Vol. 15*. Lincoln: Nebraska University Press.

Kelly, G. (1955). *The psychology of personal constructs*. New York: Norton.

Markus, H. (1977). Self-schemata and processing information about the self. *Journal of Personality and Social Psychology, 35*, 63–78.

Walster, E., Aronson, E., Abrahams, D., & Rottman, L. (1966). The importance of physical attractiveness in dating behaviour. *Journal of Personality and Social Psychology, 4*, 508–516.

Summary

- It is assumed within implicit personality theory that a person having one particular personality trait will have other related traits, and that some personality traits are much more central than others.
- Impression formation is strongly influenced by first impressions (primacy effect), but it is also affected by the most recent information we have received about another person (recency effect).
- According to Kelly's personal construct theory, everyone has their own set of personal constructs which they use to make sense of the behaviour of others.
- Personal constructs can be assessed by the repertory grid technique.
- Our impressions of others are influenced to some extent by factors such as physical attractiveness, dress, and disability.
- According to attribution theory, we decide whether to make a dispositional or a situational attribution of someone else's behaviour on the basis of consensus (do others behave in the same way?), consistency (does he or she usually behave in that way?), and distinctiveness (does he or she behave in that way in other situations?).
- The strategies used in concept formation include conservative focusing, focus gambling, and successive scanning.
- Concepts are organised around prototypes or sets of characteristic features; an object is (or is not) accepted as a member of a given concept on the basis of the number of characteristic features it possesses.
- Our feelings about ourselves depend on our self-concept; incongruence between the self-concept and the ideal self can cause anxiety and depression.
- Schemas play an important role in perception and memory, leading us to draw inferences or fill in gaps in the information available.
- Schemas in the form of stereotypes produce distortions in our perception of, and memory for, other people.
- It is hard to test schema theory, because we usually do not know what information is contained in any given schema.

Key terms

Attribution theory: a theory concerned with the ways in which we explain the behaviour of others; see **dispositional attribution** and **situational attribution**.

Bottom-up processing: processing based directly on the person or object in front of us; see **top-down processsing**.

Confirmation bias: the tendency to attend to information that confirms our beliefs rather than to information that might disprove them.

Discounting rule: the notion that we ignore any evidence suggesting that someone's personality may have caused their behaviour if there is strong evidence that the situation was involved in causing that behaviour; see **situational attribution**.

Dispositional attribution: within **attribution theory**, the decision that someone's behaviour is due to their personality; see **situational attribution**.

Fundamental attribution error: the tendency to think that other people's actions are due to their personality rather than to the situation; see **dispositional attribution**.

Ideal self: the self that we would most like to have; see **self-concept**.

Implicit personality theory: the tendency to assume that someone who has a given personality trait will also have other, related traits.

Inferences: as applied to language understanding, the filling-in of gaps in the information heard or read.

Matching hypothesis: the notion that we are attracted to those who are about as physically attractive as we are.

Mental concept: responding to several different objects or individuals in the same way on the basis of some common feature they all have; see **prototypes**.

Personal constructs: the various concepts used by people to make sense of their world.

Primacy effect: the finding that first impressions are more important than later ones in determining our opinion of others; see **recency effect**.

Prototypes: a set of characteristic features found in most members of a given **mental concept**.

Recency effect: the finding that the most recent information we have received about someone can have a large effect on our impression about that person; see **primacy effect**.

Schemas: organised packets of knowledge in long-term memory.

Self-concept: the set of thoughts and feelings about the self.

Self-schema: stored knowledge about the self, which is used to guide attention and memory processes; it is like the **self-concept**.

Situational attribution: within attribution theory, the decision that someone's behaviour is due to the situation they are in; see **dispositional attribution**.

Stereotyping: categorising people on the basis of superficial features (e.g. skin colour; sex).

Top-down processing: processing based on our expectations and on our knowledge; see **bottom-up processing**.

Structured essay questions

1. What are the primacy and recency effects in impression formation? How does physical attractiveness influence impression formation?
2. What are mental concepts? Describe work on concept learning.
3. What is attribution theory? What kinds of information are used when making attributions?
4. What are schemas? How do they influence our social perception?

Self-assessment questions

1. According to implicit personality theory:
   a) we assume that someone who has one particular personality trait will tend to have other, related traits
   b) we assume that people will have a mixture of good and bad personality traits
   c) we find it hard to understand someone else's personality
   d) personality does not really exist

2. The primacy and recency effects mean:
   a) that only first impressions are important
   b) that only the most recent information we have about someone else is important in impression formation
   c) that first impressions and the most recent information we have about someone else are both important in impression formation
   d) none of the above

3. According to the matching hypothesis, we tend to be attracted:
   a) to those with great physical attractiveness
   b) to others regardless of their level of physical attractiveness
   c) to those with an interesting personality
   d) to those who are about as physically attractive as we are

4. According to the fundamental attribution error, we tend:
   a) to regard other people's behaviour as being due to the situation
   b) to regard other people's behaviour as being due to their personality
   c) to regard other people's behaviour as due to the situation *and* their personality
   d) none of the above

5. In Bruner's work on concept learning, he found that:
   a) participants rarely used any strategy
   b) focusing and scanning strategies were equally effective
   c) scanning was generally more successful than focusing
   d) focusing was generally more successful than scanning

6. Rogers' client-centred therapy is designed to:
   a) increase the discrepancy between the client's self-concept and ideal self, and to increase his or her self-esteem
   b) decrease the discrepancy between the client's self-concept and ideal self, and to increase his or her self-esteem
   c) increase the discrepancy between the client's self-concept and ideal self, and to decrease his or her self-esteem
   d) decrease the discrepancy between the client's self-concept and ideal self, and to decrease his or her self-esteem

7. According to Bransford et al. (1972):
   a) schema-relevant inferences are stored in memory in the same way as the information actually presented
   b) schema-relevant inferences are not stored in memory
   c) schema-relevant inferences are stored in memory in a different way from the information actually presented
   d) schema-relevant inferences are not usually made or stored in memory

Individual differences approach

Intelligence 17

What is intelligence?

Intelligence means different things to different people. However, it is generally agreed that those who are good at abstract reasoning, problem-solving, and decision-making are more intelligent than those who are poor at these mental activities. The ability to think or reason with fairly novel information is of particular importance to intelligence. Many people of low intelligence can display remarkable abilities if they are dealing with very familiar information. Consider *idiots savants*. They are mentally handicapped individuals who can do things such as working out the answer to 465×399 in their heads or rapidly working out the day of the week on which 22 March 1975 fell. Idiots savants have often spent hundreds or thousands of hours in developing ways of performing such feats, and have no other special skills.

The greatest issue about the definition of intelligence concerns how many different abilities should be included. Are "street-wise" individuals, who are very skilful at finding ways of furthering their own ends, always very intelligent? Should someone who is sensitive to the needs and attitudes of others be said to possess social intelligence? Psychologists used to define intelligence narrowly as thinking, reasoning, and problem-solving ability. However, psychologists now accept that the notion of intelligence is broader than that, and should include skills (e.g. street-wisdom; social intelligence) that are valued by the culture or society in which one lives.

It may never be possible to decide on a definition of intelligence that everyone finds acceptable. However, most psychologists would have little quarrel with Sternberg's (1985, p.45) definition: "Mental activity directed toward purposive adaptation to, and selection and shaping of, real-world environments relevant to one's life".

Intelligence testing

Numerous intelligence tests have been produced over the years. In 1905, the French psychologists Binet and Simon produced the first proper intelligence test. It measured comprehension, memory, and various other psychological processes. Among the better-known tests that followed are the Stanford-Binet test produced at Stanford University in the United States; the Wechsler Intelligence Scale for Children; and the British Ability Scales.

These, and other, tests are designed to measure several different aspects of intelligence. They often contain mathematical items, and many contain vocabulary tests in which individuals are asked to define the meanings of various words. They often include problems based on analogies (e.g. "Hat is to head as shoe is to ..."), and tests of spatial ability (e.g. "If I start walking northwards, then turn left, and then turn left again, what direction will I be facing?").

Calculating IQ

All of the major intelligence tests are *standardised tests*. This means that the test has been given to large, representative samples of the age groups covered by the test. As a result, the meaning of an individual's score on the test can be assessed by comparing it against the scores of those on whom the test was standardised.

The best-known measure that is obtained from intelligence tests is IQ or *intelligence quotient*. This is based on performance on all of the sub-tests contained in an intelligence test, and is thus an overall measure of intellectual ability.

In the past, the most popular method to work out the IQ was to use the following formula: mental age divided by chronological age × 100. Chronological age is simply the actual age of the child taking the test, and mental age is the age at which the average child performs at the same level as the child taking the test. Thus, for example, if a child does as well as the average 7-year-old on the test, then his or her mental age is 7 years. An average child will have a mental age that is the same as his or her chronological age, and thus an IQ of 100. Bright children will have a mental age that is greater than their chronological age, and thus their IQs will be above 100. The opposite will be true of dull children, who have IQs below 100.

There are problems with this method of working out IQ. A child of 4 needs a mental age one year ahead of his or her actual age to have an IQ of 125. However, the same child at the age of 12 needs a mental age three years ahead of chronological age to keep the same IQ. An IQ of 125 only means the same throughout childhood if we are willing to assume that intellectual development proceeds in a steady fashion from year to year. This is probably a mistaken assumption.

What is now the most common way of assessing an individual's IQ is to compare his or her performance against that of other children of the same age. Most intelligence tests are devised so that the overall scores are normally distributed. The normal distribution is a bell-shaped curve in which there are as many scores above the mean as below it. Most scores are close to the mean, and there are fewer and fewer scores as you move away from the mean in either direction. The spread of scores in a normal distribution is usually indicated by the *standard deviation*. In a normal distribution, 68% of the scores fall within one standard deviation of the mean or average, 95% fall within two standard deviations, and 99.73% are within three standard deviations. An individual's IQ can be expressed as a *standard score*, which is based on the number of standard deviations above or below the mean of his or her age group that an individual's score falls.

Intelligence tests are typically designed to have a mean IQ of 100 and a standard deviation of about 16. Therefore, an IQ of 116 represents a standard score of +1.0, and means that the individual is more intelligent than 84% of the population. That is the case, because 50% fall below the mean, and a further 34% between the mean and one standard deviation above it.

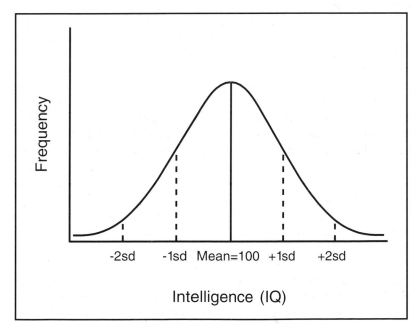

The normal distribution of intelligence (IQ). sd = standard deviation.

Uses of intelligence tests

Intelligence tests have been used in various ways. For example, they have been used to predict school or college performance. Intelligence-test scores generally correlate about +0.5 with such performance. This indicates that those with higher IQs tend to have rather better academic performance than those with lower IQs. However, the correlation is well below +1.0, which would indicate a perfect relationship between IQ and academic performance. In general, the findings indicate that IQ has some relevance to the real world, especially when you consider that academic success at school does not depend solely on intelligence. It also depends on motivation, personality characteristics, and parental encouragement.

Another use of intelligence tests is in connection with careers advice or vocational guidance. People who are successful in a given occupation (e.g. teacher) tend to possess certain characteristics. These characteristics include high IQ, more specific abilities, a certain type of personality, and interests. As might be expected, having a high IQ is much more important for some jobs than for others.

A related use of intelligence tests is in personnel selection. Companies looking for additional staff often make use of a battery of tests, including tests of intelligence and personality. Some people have argued that a general measure of intelligence (such as the IQ) is of most use in personnel selection, whereas others claim that the focus should be on the specific abilities required by the job in question. There is clear evidence that general and specific measures of intelligence are both useful. The relevance of IQ was shown by Schippmann and Prien (1989). They found that IQ correlated +0.35 with rate of managerial progression among nearly 300 managers, indicating that the more intelligent managers tended to enjoy more career success. However, the correlation is fairly low, and means that many other factors are important for career success.

Limitations of IQ testing

If intelligence tests are to be of value, they need to possess *reliability* and *validity*. Reliability means that a test provides consistent findings. We need to be confident that someone who obtains a given score on an intelligence test today will obtain a very similar score next week, next month, or next year. Validity means that a test is measuring what it claims to be measuring.

All the main intelligence tests have good reliability. An individual's IQ rarely differs by more than a few points when he or she does an intelligence test on two occasions. Validity is more difficult to assess. However, the fact that IQ predicts academic success to some extent indicates that intelligence tests have reasonable validity.

In spite of their good reliability and moderate validity, many people doubt the usefulness of intelligence tests. Some of the main reasons for their doubts are as follows:

- IQ is a very general measure of intelligence; it obscures the fact that intelligence also involves more specific abilities (e.g. spatial; numerical; verbal).
- Most intelligence tests are devised by white, middle-class psychologists from Western societies; thus, intelligence tests may be biased against those from other cultures.
- Intelligence tests are rather narrow, and do not measure factors such as social intelligence and creativity.

Heredity and environment

Individual differences in intelligence may depend on heredity, or on environment, or on a mixture of heredity and environment. The issue of the roles played by heredity and environment in determining intelligence has been looked at by many psychologists, and is sometimes known as the *nature/nurture issue*. However, many people argue that the issue is meaningless. For example, Donald Hebb argued that asking whether intelligence is determined more by heredity or by environment is like asking whether the area of a field is determined more by its length or by its width: both are absolutely essential.

Even if the nature/nurture issue is not meaningless, there is the problem that there is no very good way of measuring intelligence. It is worth bearing this in mind as we discuss the relevant evidence.

Twin Studies

Some of the most important work on intelligence has made use of twins. Identical twins (technically known as *monozygotic twins*) have the same heredity, inheriting the same genes. Fraternal twins (known as *dizygotic twins*) are no more similar in their heredity than ordinary brothers and sisters. If heredity is an important determinant of intelligence, then we would expect to discover that identical twins are more alike than fraternal twins in intelligence.

The degree of similarity in intelligence shown by pairs of twins is usually reported in the form of correlations. A correlation of +1.00 would mean that both twins in a pair obtain exactly the same IQ, whereas a correlation of 0.00 would mean that there was no relationship at all between the IQs of twins. Bouchard and McGue (1981) summarised over 100 studies. The average correlation for identical twins was +0.86, compared to +0.60 for fraternal twins. These figures mean that identical twins have very similar IQs, and fraternal twins are fairly similar in IQ.

This difference might be due to the greater genetic similarity of identical twins. However, it might also be due to the greater environmental similarity for identical twins than for fraternal twins. Identical twins spend more time together than do fraternal twins, and they are also more likely to have the same friends. Loehlin and Nichols (1976) found that the parents of identical twins were much more likely than those of fraternal twins to have tried to treat them exactly the same. Of more importance, those identical twins whose parents had tried to treat them exactly the same were more alike in IQ than identical twins who had not been treated the same.

More evidence from twin studies comes from the rather small number of identical twins who were separated in early life and then reared apart. Such twins are very important, because they would appear to have very similar heredity but dissimilar environment. If heredity is of major importance, such twins should have very similar measured intelligence. If environment is of primary importance, there should be little or no similarity in intelligence. One of the few studies to include such twins was that of Burt (1955), whose data are suspect (he either made up most of his data or was careless in the way he presented them). If we exclude his study, then other studies produced an average correlation for identical twins brought up apart of +0.72. This indicates fairly high similarity of IQ between identical twins brought up apart.

If heredity were all-important, then the correlation for identical twins brought up apart should be close to +1.00. The fact that it is a long way below that indicates that environmental factors have a large impact on the measured intelligence of these twin pairs.

There are also problems with the way in which the studies were carried out. In one of the studies, two-thirds of the pairs were brought up in branches of the same family, and the children went to the same school. Many of the twin pairs in the various studies spent the first few years of their lives together before being separated. In addition, there is what is known as selective placement: adoption agencies have a policy of trying to place infants in homes with similar educational and social backgrounds to those of their parents. All in all, it is clear that much of the general similarity in IQ within identical twin pairs brought up apart is due to the fact that they experienced similar environments. It is also clear that studying such twin pairs does not provide an easy way of assessing the relative contributions of heredity and environment to intelligence.

Adoption studies

Another way of studying the heredity–environment issue is to consider adopted children who are brought up by foster parents. The IQs of these children can be compared against those of their biological parents as well as against those of their foster parents. Those who believe in the importance of heredity would expect there to be a closer link with the biological parents than with the foster parents.

Gross (1992) discussed the relevant evidence. On average, the IQs of adopted children correlate about +0.5 with those of their biological mothers, compared with only +0.2 with those of their foster mothers. This evidence is consistent with that from twin studies in suggesting some involvement of heredity in the determination of intelligence. However, there is the problem of selective placement. Some of the correlation between adopted children and their biological mothers may occur because they are living in rather similar environments. It should be noted that this argument does not explain why the correlation between adopted children and their foster mothers is so low.

It is easier to see what is happening if a slightly different approach is used. In essence, families adopting a child are only studied if they also have at least one child of their own. If heredity is important, then it would be expected that the mother's IQ should correlate more highly with that of her own child than with that of her adopted child. In fact, Scarr and Weinberg (1977) and Horn et al. (1979) found that the two correlations were very similar. This suggests that environmental influences are very important.

Environmental factors

Much research has considered the effects of various environmental factors on intelligence. It has been found that extreme environmental conditions have a large effect on intelligence. Wheeler (1942) studied the members of an isolated community in Tennessee in the United States. This community slowly became more integrated into society as schools and roads were built. The intelligence of the members of this community increased by 10 IQ points while these environmental changes were occurring. In contrast, canal-boat children in England who received very little schooling showed a steady decrease in IQ as their years of isolation from society increased (Gordon, 1923).

Evidence of the powerful effects that environment can have on intelligence was provided by Schiff et al. (1978). They looked at 32 French children, born to lower working-class parents, who were adopted by high socio-economic status parents. The IQs of these children were compared against those of their own brothers and sisters who remained with their working-class parents. The adopted children had an average IQ of 111, which was much higher than the average IQ of 95 of the children who remained with their own parents.

Much of the evidence on environmental factors in intelligence has concerned black and white groups in the United States. Whites tend to have a higher average IQ than blacks, but about 20% of blacks have an IQ that is higher than that of the average white person. When whites and blacks are matched in terms of environmental factors such as family income, type of job, and socio-economic status, then there is a large reduction in the difference between the mean IQs of whites and blacks.

Striking evidence that environmental factors (e.g. discrimination) prevent American blacks from realising their intellectual potential was obtained by Scarr and Weinberg (1976). They studied 99 black children who were adopted by white, middle-class parents. The mean IQ of these black children, who had the advantage of a privileged environment, was 110, which is about 25 IQ points higher than the mean of all American blacks. It is probable that the environmental advantages enjoyed by the black children was the main factor responsible for their high mean IQ.

Intervention programmes

If intelligence is affected by the environment, then it should be possible to increase the intelligence of disadvantaged groups by means of intervention programmes. Probably the largest such intervention programme was Operation Headstart, which began in the United States in 1965. Operation Headstart basically involved a one-year pre-school programme designed to facilitate the educational development of disadvantaged children.

The initial evidence was that Operation Headstart had been a failure. Any gains in IQ did not seem to last. There was very little evidence of improved educational performance among the children taking part in Operation Headstart compared to those who did not. However, it turned out that pessimism about the programme was premature. Over their first eight years of schooling, participants in Operation Headstart showed increasingly better performance than non-participants on measures of mathematics, language, and reading (Collins, 1983). Participants were also less likely to drop out, to repeat a year, or to be put into special remedial classes. There were some gains in IQ among the children involved in the Headstart programme, but these gains disappeared within a few years.

In the years since Operation Headstart, various other education programmes have been carried out in the United States. The most common finding is that the greatest beneficial effects on school performance are found when the parents are actively involved in the programme, and so provide a stimulating environment for their children. So far as the nature/nurture issue is concerned, these findings indicate that the environment can have powerful effects on effective intelligence.

Conclusions

Psychologists interested in intelligence have devoted much research to the nature/nurture issue. There is strong evidence that heredity and environment both play important roles in determining individual differences in intelligence, but it is not clear that any more definite conclusions are possible. One of the reasons for this is that we have no experimental control over either heredity or environment. It is not possible ethically to manipulate heredity by a programme of breeding, nor is it possible to achieve much control over the environment in which children develop.

The relative importance of heredity and environment is not fixed and unchanging. The environments experienced by children within Western societies are more similar than those experienced by children in some other societies. For example, nearly all children in the United Kingdom receive at least eleven or twelve years of schooling, whereas large percentages of children in some other societies receive no schooling at all. The relevance of this to the nature/nurture issue is as follows: the more similar the environments are for individuals within a society, the greater will be the apparent impact of heredity in determining individual differences in intelligence. Indeed, if everyone were exposed to exactly the same environment, then all individual differences in intelligence would be due to heredity!

Factor theories

So far in this chapter, we have focused on IQ, which is a very general measure of intelligence. However, more specific abilities also need to be taken into account. For example, some people with average IQ have highly developed abilities in language, mathematics, memory, or some other aspect of intelligence. Theorists such as Spearman, Burt, and Guilford studied these more specific abilities in the first half of this century. They made use of a statistical technique known as *factor analysis*, which is discussed next.

The first step in factor analysis is to give a series of tests to a large number of individuals, and to obtain scores for each individual on each test. The inter-correlations between the tests are then calculated. If two tests correlate highly with each other, this means that those who perform well on one test tend to perform well on the other test. The key assumption is that when two tests correlate highly with each other, they are measuring the same aspect of intelligence. In contrast, if two tests do not correlate, then it is assumed that they measure different aspects of intelligence. The pattern of inter-correlations is used to identify the main aspects of intelligence (or *factors* as they are generally known). Psychologists who try to identify the factors involved in intelligence are known as factor theorists.

There are differences among factor theorists in terms of the number of factors identified. Thurstone argued that there are seven factors or primary mental abilities (spatial ability; numerical ability; memory; verbal fluency; perceptual speed; inductive reasoning; and verbal meaning), whereas Guilford proposed 150 factors. In fact, most of the available evidence is consistent with a hierarchical model of intelligence with three levels:

A three-level hierarchical model of intelligence (based on Carroll, 1986).

- At the top level, there is the general factor of intelligence; this is basically what is measured by IQ.
- At the intermediate level, there are various fairly general group factors, some of which are like those put forward by Thurstone.
- At the lowest level, there are very specific factors associated with only one test or a small number of tests.

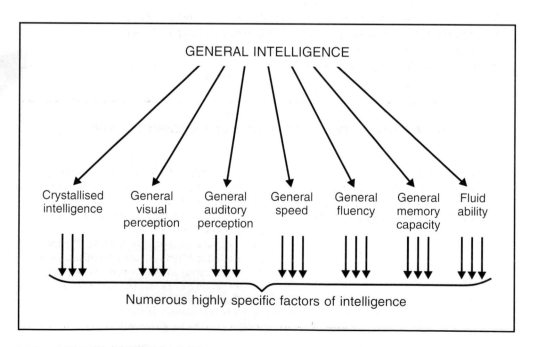

GENERAL INTELLIGENCE

Crystallised intelligence | General visual perception | General auditory perception | General speed | General fluency | General memory capacity | Fluid ability

Numerous highly specific factors of intelligence

An influential version of this hierarchical model was proposed by Carroll (1986). He re-analysed findings from numerous studies, and concluded that the general factor of intelligence is at the top of the hierarchy. Below that are seven factors: crystallised intelligence (previously acquired knowledge); general visual perception; general auditory perception; general speed; general idea production or fluency; general memory capacity; and fluid ability. Finally, there are numerous highly specific factors at the bottom of the hierarchy, but there is little agreement about their nature.

Multiple intelligences

Howard Gardner (1985) argued that there are several independent intelligences. In total, he identified seven intelligences:

- *Logical–mathematical intelligence:* this is of special value in handling abstract problems of a logical or mathematical nature.
- *Spatial intelligence:* this is used when deciding how to go from one place to another, how to arrange suitcases in the boot of a car, and so on.
- *Musical intelligence:* this is used for playing an instrument, singing, and appreciating music.
- *Bodily–kinaesthetic intelligence:* this is used in the fine control of bodily movements (e.g. dancing).
- *Linguistic intelligence:* this is used in reading, writing, and speaking.
- *Intrapersonal knowledge:* this form of intelligence is concerned with sensitivity to one's own abilities and emotional states.
- *Interpersonal intelligence:* this includes communication with, and understanding of, others.

What are the advantages and disadvantages of Gardner's approach?

PLUS	MINUS
• There is reasonable evidence for the seven intelligences proposed by Gardner. • Gardner is right to argue that intelligence tests fail to consider all aspects of intelligence.	• Musical and bodily–kinaesthetic intelligences are less important in everyday life than are the other intelligences: you can be tone-deaf and poorly co-ordinated and still lead a very successful life. • Those who score highly on some intelligences tend to score highly on the other intelligences as well; this suggests that the seven intelligences are not really independent of each other as Gardner argued.

Gardner's theory of multiple intelligences has major implications for intelligence testing. Most standard tests contain items that are relevant to the linguistic, logical-mathematical, and spatial intelligences. However, such tests are not designed to assess the musical, bodily-kinaesthetic, intrapersonal, and interpersonal intelligences. If one accepts Gardner's position, then nearly all existing tests of intelligence are very inadequate.

Further reading

Eysenck, M.W. (1994). *Individual differences: Normal and abnormal.* Hove, UK: Lawrence Erlbaum Associates Ltd. Chapter 2 of this book gives a comprehensive account of intelligence and intelligence testing.
Sternberg, R.J. (1985). *Beyond IQ: A triarchic theory of human intelligence.* Cambridge: Cambridge University Press. There are many interesting ideas about intelligence in this book.

References

Bouchard, T.J., & McGue, M. (1981). Familial studies of intelligence: A review. *Science, 212,* 1055–1059.
Carroll, J.B. (1986). Factor analytic investigations of cognitive abilities. In S.E. Newstead, S.H. Irvine, & P.L. Dann (Eds.), *Human assessment: Cognition and motivation.* Nyhoff: Dordrecht.
Gardner, H. (1983). *Frames of mind: The theory of multiple intelligences.* New York: Basic Books.
Scarr, S., & Weinberg, R.A. (1976). IQ test performance of black children adopted by white families. *American Psychologist, 31,* 726–739.

Summary

- Intelligence is concerned with thinking and reasoning, and with the ability to interact successfully with environments relevant to one's life.
- Intelligence tests provide a measure of IQ (intelligence quotient); this is based on comparing an individual's test performance against that of others of the same age.
- IQ is a general measure of intelligence, but there are also various more specific abilities (e.g. spatial; mathematical; verbal) involved in intelligence.
- Intelligence tests have been used to predict school performance; they are also used by occupational psychologists in vocational guidance and personnel selection.
- Intelligence tests possess good reliability and moderate validity.
- Intelligence testing may be biased against those who are not white, middle-class members of Western society.
- The controversy about the roles of heredity and environment in intelligence is known as the nature/nurture issue.
- The evidence from identical and fraternal twins indicates that heredity plays a part in determining intelligence, and the same conclusion follows from adoption studies.
- Studies on very favourable and unfavourable environments indicate that the environment can have a large impact on intelligence.
- Intervention programmes have had some success in raising the school performance and intelligence of disadvantaged children.
- Factor analysis points to a hierarchical model of intelligence having three levels: a general factor; several group factors; specific factors.
- Gardner proposed that there are seven independent intelligences: logical–mathematical; spatial; musical; bodily–kinaesthetic; linguistic; intrapersonal; interpersonal; most of these intelligences are not assessed by conventional intelligence tests.
- Gardner's seven intelligences are less independent of each other than he argued; some of them (e.g. bodily–kinaesthetic intelligence; musical intelligence) are fairly unimportant in everyday life.

Human personality 18

We all notice in our everyday lives that people differ from each other. Some people are usually cheerful and friendly, others tend to be unfriendly and depressed, and still others are aggressive and hostile. This chapter is concerned with attempts to understand these individual differences in personality.

What do we mean by personality? According to Child (1968, p.83), personality consists of the "more or less stable, internal factors that make one person's behaviour consistent from one time to another, and different from the behaviour other people would manifest in comparable situations". There are really four key words in that definition:

- *Stable:* personality remains relatively constant or unchanging over time.
- *Internal:* personality lies within us, but the ways in which we behave are determined in part by our personality.
- *Consistent:* if personality remains constant over time, and if personality determines behaviour, then we would expect that people would behave in fairly consistent ways.
- *Different:* when we talk of personality, we assume that there are considerable individual differences, which lead different people to behave differently in similar situations.

Temperament is another term that is similar in meaning to personality. It refers to an individual's typical moods and activity level, and it is usually assumed that temperament is determined mainly by heredity. Of the theories dealt with in this chapter, the one by H.J. Eysenck can be regarded as a temperament theory as well as a personality theory.

Psychodynamic theory of personality development

According to Sigmund Freud, the experiences that children have during the first five years of life are very important. Their personalities are developing during that period, and adult personality depends very much on the experiences of early childhood. Freud's psychodynamic approach to personality development was contained in his theory of psychosexual development. According to the theory, children pass through five stages of psychosexual development, as follows: oral stage; anal stage; phallic stage; latency stage; and genital stage. Sometimes children have problems with one of the stages. This leads to *fixation*, in which basic energy remains attached to that stage during adulthood. When an adult has great problems, he or she shows *regression*, with their behaviour becoming more like the behaviour they showed when they were children. Adults normally regress to a psychosexual stage at which they fixated as children.

The oral stage lasts up to the age of 18 months. Young children in the oral stage enjoy various activities involving their mouths, lips, and tongues. Children may experience problems at this stage, for example, because of rapid weaning. These problems can produce adults with an oral personality. Those with oral receptive characters are very dependent on other people, whereas those with oral aggressive characters are aggressive.

The anal stage lasts between 18 months and 36 months, and involves the anal area as the major source of satisfaction. It is during this stage that toilet training occurs. Children who have problems at the anal stage may develop an anal retentive character, making them mean and stubborn, and liking things to be arranged neatly. Another possibility is that they will become very generous and giving.

The phallic stage lasts between the ages of 3 and 6. During this stage, the penis or clitoris becomes the major source of satisfaction. Those who have problems at this stage develop what is known as a phallic character. Men with a phallic character are vain and self-assured. Women with a phallic character fight hard for superiority over men.

The latency stage follows the phallic stage, and lasts until puberty. During this stage, boys and girls tend to ignore each other. The final stage is the genital stage. In this stage, the main source of pleasure is in the genitals, which is similar to the phallic stage. However, there is the key difference that the focus in the genital stage is on sexual pleasure with another person. Children who have avoided problems during the earlier stages develop a genital character. Adults with a genital character are mature, and are able to love and be loved.

What are the advantages and disadvantages of Freud's approach?

PLUS

- Adult personality depends in part on the experiences of early childhood.
- The various personality types suggested by Freud do seem to exist.

MINUS

- Freud exaggerated the importance of early childhood; personality also depends on heredity and on the experiences of adolescence and adulthood.
- It has not been shown that adult personality depends on the specific experiences of, for example, toilet training, in the way that Freud argued.

Experimental evidence

It is very hard to test Freud's theory of psychosexual development. He argued that the experiences of early life determine adult personality, but we cannot usually obtain much information about an adult's early childhood. For example, Freud argued that adults with an anal personality experienced problems during toilet training. However, it is only in rare cases that detailed information about toilet training is available many years after it happened.

At a more modest level, there is some support for the various personality types proposed by Freud. For example, Freud argued that adults with an anal retentive character are stubborn, mean, and like neatness. It has been found (e.g. Pollak, 1979) that these three personal features do tend to be found together in the same person. In a similar way, Kline and Storey (1977) found that some people possess all of the features of the oral receptive character, with others showing all the features of the oral aggressive character.

Behaviourist and social learning theories

According to behaviourists such as Watson and Skinner, individual differences in behaviour are due to the fact that everyone has a unique history of conditioning. Thus, for example, some people enjoy playing tennis because it has been linked with rewards or positive reinforcers such as praise and satisfaction from playing well and winning matches. Other people dislike tennis because they have found it to be a hard game at which most other people perform better than them.

The founder of behaviourism, John Watson, believed strongly that the way in which people behave depends far more on the experiences they have had than on their heredity. According to Watson (1924), "Give me a dozen healthy infants ... and my own specialised world to bring them up in, and I'll guarantee to take any one at random and train him to become any type of specialist I might select—doctor, lawyer, ... and yes, even beggarman and thief, regardless of his talents ... tendencies, abilities ... and race of his ancestors."

The rewards and punishments that we have experienced during our lives do influence how we behave. However, the behaviourist approach is far too limited. As we will see later in the chapter, there is strong evidence that personality depends on heredity as well as on learning experiences. Additional evidence that what we are born with is important comes from studies on infants. Thomas et al. (1970) observed infants and had interviews with parents. They found that some infants were "easy", in the sense that they coped well with new situations and were generally in a good mood. Other infants were "difficult", being slow to adapt to new situations and often being in bad moods. As the infants grew up, they tended to remain easy or difficult. Easy and difficult children seemed to differ in terms of heredity (and so in terms of temperament) rather than in their conditioning histories.

It is worth noting that very few people think that an individual's behaviour depends only on the situation. As Rorer and Widiger (1983) pointed out, "If one really believes that situations determined behaviour, then there is no reason to test or interview prospective employees for jobs such as police officer; it is only necessary to structure the job situation properly. Picking a mate would simply be a matter of finding someone whose physical characteristics appeal to you. In a properly managed class all students would work to their abilities. Do you know anyone who believes these things? Obviously not."

Bandura's social learning theory

Albert Bandura initially supported the basic behaviourist approach. As time went by, however, he began to disagree with the behaviourist view that behaviour can be understood by considering only *external* factors in the environment such as rewards and punishments. Instead, he argued that we also need to look at *internal* factors, such as exactly what it is that someone learns from his or her dealings with the environment. Bandura (1977) used the term *reciprocal determinism* to refer to the fact that the individual (with his or her own cognitive processes and knowledge) has an effect on the environment, and that the environment has an effect on the individual.

According to Bandura's social learning theory, an individual's level of self-efficacy plays a major role in influencing his or her behaviour. *Self-efficacy* refers to people's assessment of their ability to cope well with a given situation. In the words of Bandura (1977), self-efficacy judgements are concerned "not with the skills one has but with judgements of what one can do with the skills one possesses." These self-efficacy judgements "are a major determinant of people's choice of activities, how much effort they will expend, and how long they will sustain effort in dealing with stressful situations."

It should be noted that self-efficacy judgements refer to specific situations. Thus, someone who has high self-efficacy for an examination may have low self-efficacy for becoming a popular member of a group. People's sense of self-efficacy in any given situation depends on four factors:

1. Their previous experiences of success and/or failure in that situation
2. Observing others cope successfully or unsuccessfully with that situation
3. Being persuaded by others that one has the skills needed to succeed in that situation
4. High levels of arousal can reduce feelings of self-efficacy

Evidence that self-efficacy influences behaviour was obtained by Weinberg et al. (1979). They gave their participants false information about

---

What are the advantages and disadvantes of Bandura's social learning theory?

PLUS

- Bandura was correct to argue that human behaviour depends on internal factors (e.g. self-efficacy) as well as on external factors (e.g. rewards).
- Feelings of self-efficacy have been found to predict behaviour in many situations.

MINUS

- Bandura focused on individual differences in behaviour in specific situations, whereas personality theorists try to understand people's behaviour across many different situations; in other words, he has not really put forward a theory of personality.
- Self-efficacy judgements are based on people's conscious awareness of their own internal processes; if this awareness is limited, it reduces the value of self-efficacy judgements.

their performance on tasks of physical endurance. Those who had their self-efficacy beliefs raised in that way put in more effort and performed better. Those who had their self-efficacy beliefs lowered reduced their effort and performed poorly.

Humanism

One of the main ways in which we come to understand others' personality is by listening to them tell us about their own experiences and their emotional reactions to those experiences. Psychologists have sometimes studied personality in a similar way by using a technique known as *phenomenology*. In this technique, individuals simply describe their experience, without trying to make sense of it.

The humanistic approach makes use of phenomenology to understand personality. In the words of Cartwright (1979), humanistic psychology "is concerned with topics that are meaningful to human beings, focusing especially upon subjective experience and the unique, unpredictable events in individual human lives". A topic of particular importance to the humanistic psychologists is the self; this is basically the way in which we see ourselves. According to humanistic psychologists, the self is best studied by asking people to provide reports of their conscious experiences, because this provides the most direct evidence of how the self functions.

The humanistic approach was developed by psychologists such as Carl Rogers and Abraham Maslow, and became important during the 1950s and 1960s. It differs greatly from most other approaches in a number of ways. First, it is in some ways anti-scientific, in that humanistic psychologists deny the value of carefully observing behaviour under laboratory conditions. Second, humanistic psychologists assume that our behaviour is determined very largely by internal factors, especially by the self-concept (our feelings and thoughts about ourselves). In contrast, behaviourists such as Skinner argue strongly that behaviour is determined mainly by outside forces such as rewards and punishments. Third, humanistic psychologists do not believe that physiological and biological factors are of any real significance in human behaviour. This contrasts with the views of many other psychologists, including the trait theorists discussed later in this chapter.

Maslow

Maslow (1954) argued that most theories of human motivation had focused on basic physiological needs, or on our needs to reduce and avoid pain. According to him, motivation is actually much broader than that.

He put forward a *hierarchy of needs*. Physiological needs (such as those for food and water) are at the bottom of the hierarchy. Next come security and safety needs (such as curiosity and the need for understanding) and aesthetic (artistic) needs. Finally, at the top of the hierarchy, there is the need for *self-actualisation* (fully realising what we are capable of achieving). Maslow assumed that the higher needs will emerge only when the lower needs are more or less satisfied.

All the needs towards the bottom of the hierarchy were regarded as deficiency motivation needs. This is because they are designed to reduce inadequacies or deficiencies. In contrast, needs towards the top of the hierarchy (such as self-actualisation) represent growth motivation, and are designed to produce personal growth. Self-actualisation was described in the following way by Maslow (1954): "A musician must make music, an artist must paint, a poet must write, if he is to be ultimately at peace with himself. What a man can be, he must be. This need we may call self-actualisation". Self-actualised individuals have an acceptance of

Maslow's hierarchy of needs.

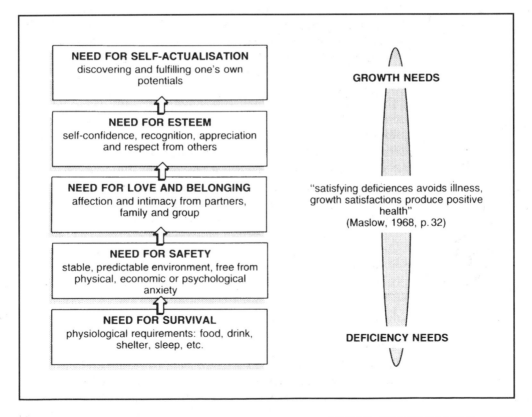

themselves, spontaneity, the need for privacy, resistance to cultural influences, deep interpersonal relations, creativeness, and a philosophical sense of humour. Abraham Lincoln and Albert Einstein were identified as famous examples of people who were self-actualised.

Maslow (1962) studied self-actualisation by focusing on *peak experiences*. In such experiences, the world is accepted for what it is, and there are feelings of joy, wonder, and awe. Peak experiences often happen during sex or when listening to music—and sometimes when doing both at the same time! Maslow assumed that self-actualised individuals would report more peak experiences than other people. Self-actualisation has also been measured by questionnaires such as the Index of Self-actualisation.

Rogers

According to Rogers (1951), the concept of "self" is of great importance. An individual's self-concept is mainly conscious. It consists of our thoughts and feelings about ourselves, both as individuals and in relation to others. There are two "selves" within the theory:

- *Self-concept:* the self as it is currently experienced.
- *Ideal self:* the self-concept that an individual would most like to have.
- Happy people have a much smaller gap between the self-concept and the ideal self than unhappy people.

The self-concept and the ideal self can be measured by using the *Q-sort method*:

- An individual is presented with a pile of cards, each of which contains a personal statement (e.g. "I am a friendly person"; "I am tense most of the time").
- The individual decides which statements best describe himself or herself, which statements are the next best, right down to those statements that are the least descriptive.
- The same procedure is then used with respect to the ideal self.
- The gap between the self-concept and the ideal self is worked out.

According to Rogers, human motivation is largely devoted to the task of actualising (i.e. making real) our needs and potential. The *need for positive regard* (the need to be liked and respected by other people), and the *need for positive self-regard* (the need to like and respect oneself) are of special importance. Problems can arise when there is *incongruence* (a gap) between an individual's self-concept and his or her actual experiences, for example, when a child who believes herself to be unaggressive finds herself behaving aggressively. One reaction to such incongruence is distortion (e.g. the child decides she was merely behaving assertively rather than aggressively). A more extreme reaction is denial of the existence of the experience. Distortion and denial both fail to resolve the incongruence, and make the individual more vulnerable to threat, anxiety, and maladjustment.

Client-centred therapy. On the basis of his theoretical ideas, Rogers put forward a form of treatment known as *client-centred therapy*. It was assumed that incongruence plays a major role in the development of mental illness, and that therapy should be designed to reduce the clients' level of incongruence.

According to Rogers, the best way to reduce a client's incongruence is to be as supportive as possible. This allows the client to relax, and to be open to experience. It follows that good therapists are:

- Always positive in their attitude towards the client no matter what he or she says.
- Genuine.
- Empathic (understanding the client's feelings).

There is some evidence supporting the view that these features are valuable in therapists (Truax & Mitchell, 1971). However, much of the recent evidence indicates that being unconditional in positive regard, genuine, and empathic are less important than was claimed by Rogers (Beutler et al., 1986). Rogers emphasised the role of the therapist, but the attitude of the patient is more important than Rogers assumed. Patients who at the first interview discuss their feelings and problems about important personal relationships in an emotional way succeed much better in therapy than patients who discuss their problems as if they were someone else's (Fiske et al., 1964).

Kelly's personal construct theory

George Kelly (1905–1966) put forward a theory that is similar to the humanistic theories of Maslow and Rogers. He agreed with them that we need to know how other people experience the world if we are to understand their personality. Focusing on an individual's experience of the world provides a way of working out his or her self-concept.

According to Kelly, people have a great need to be able to predict what is going to happen in the future. This is similar to the case with scientists. A scientist forms hypotheses about the world in the hope that these hypotheses will increase his or her ability to predict events. If these hypotheses are wrong, then the scientist changes them to provide a better account of the world. In similar fashion, individuals change their ways of thinking about other people and situations until they feel confident in their ability to predict the future. As Kelly (1955, p.4) expressed it, "Let us ... , instead of occupying ourselves with man-the-biological-organism or man-the-lucky-guy, have a look at man-the-scientist".

According to Kelly, we can understand someone only when we know how he or she construes (interprets the meaning of) the world. This is determined by the system of personal constructs (concepts used to make sense of the world) that the individual has developed over the years. An individual's personality is defined by his or her particular personal construct system.

Role Construct Repertory Test

The *Role Construct Repertory Test* (or Rep Test for short) was devised by Kelly to assess people's constructs. Anyone wanting to use the test has first of all to draw up a Role Title List. This is a list of roles or figures that are thought to be important to all those people who will be given the test. Mother, good friend, or a well-liked teacher are examples of roles that are relevant to most people. The person being tested selects specific individuals to fill each of the chosen roles.

The person carrying out the test then chooses three of the roles, and asks the person being tested to indicate some way in which two of the individuals are alike but different but from the third. For example, the person being tested might say, "My mother and my good friend are both easy-going, whereas a teacher I liked was strict." This would identify:

- Easy-going/strict as a construct.
- Easy-going as the similarity pole of the construct.
- Strict as the contrast pole of the construct.

This exercise is repeated several times with different sets of three individuals being chosen each time. It is hoped to identify the main constructs used by an individual in his or her attempts to make sense of the world. This goal can also be obtained by using a repertory grid, which involves a network of horizontal and vertical lines. The columns represent people and the rows represent personal constructs. Individuals can then be rated in terms of the personal constructs. (See example on p.281.)

Detailed consideration of the results of the Rep Test or repertory grid indicates that personal constructs vary in their significance. *Core constructs* are of great importance to the individual, whereas *peripheral constructs* can be changed with little or no effect on the core constructs.

The Rep Test provides information about an individual's cognitive complexity or simplicity. Those who are high in cognitive complexity have a large number of well-organised personal constructs, whereas those who are low in cognitive complexity do not. Bieri (1955) found that cognitively complex individuals were more accurate than cognitively simple individuals at predicting the behaviour of others. He also found that they were better at identifying differences between themselves and other people.

Clinical applications

People can become emotionally disturbed if they use their constructs to make predictions in ways involving either excessive *tightening* or *loosening*. With tightening, the same predictions are made almost regardless of the particular circumstances. This happens because very little attention is paid to changes in the situation. With loosening, the predictions are very erratic and inconsistent. Schizophrenics, who have loss of contact with reality and distortions of thought, emotion, and behaviour, have been found to display considerable loosening.

The essence of clinical treatment within Kelly's approach is to produce changes in patients' personal construct systems so that they can predict more accurately what is going to happen. Some of the "rules" used to produce beneficial change are as follows:

- The therapist provides an easy-going atmosphere in which new constructs can be "tried on for size" without the patient feeling threatened.
- The therapist agrees to the new constructs the patient is considering.
- The patient tries hard to deal with, and to resolve, new situations.

One of Kelly's favoured methods was *fixed-role therapy*. In this form of therapy, the therapist produces a description of a new person. The patient then tries to behave as if he or she were that person. It is intended that

---

What are the advantages and disadvantages of Kelly's approach?

PLUS	MINUS
• The individual differences in cognitive processing and structure identified by Kelly are probably important in understanding personality.	• People are motivated to make accurate predictions about the world, but there are numerous biological and other motivational and emotional forces which are ignored by Kelly.
• Kelly's notion that clinical treatment should focus on producing cognitive changes is in line with several later developments in therapy; leading therapists such as Albert Ellis and Aaron Beck have developed some of Kelly's ideas.	• The Rep Test and the repertory grid are only able to measure those constructs of which the individual is consciously aware.

playing such a role will produce substantial alterations to the personal construct system. Most patients find it somewhat difficult to pretend to be someone else, and so the therapist plays a key role in making the process work.

Trait theories: Cattell and Eysenck

Many personality theorists have argued that personality consists of a number of *traits*. Traits have been defined as "broad, enduring, relatively stable characteristics used to assess and explain behaviour" (Hirschberg, 1978, p. 45). The inclusion of the word "broad" in that definition is crucial. Smiling, on its own, could not form the basis of a personality trait, because it is too narrow. However, smiling, talkativeness, participation in social events, and so on, could together reflect a personality trait such as "sociability".

Personality traits have most often been measured by means of questionnaires. What usually happens is that a psychologist produces a long list of questions relating to personality (e.g. "Are you generally anxious?"; "Do you have many friends?"; "Do you tend to become angry when you cannot have your own way?"). These questions are then given to hundreds of people.

When the questionnaires are returned, the psychologist looks for questions that tend to be answered in the same way by different people. For example, it might be that nearly everyone who answers "Yes" to the question, "Do you have many friends?" will also answer "Yes" to the question, "Do you like to be involved in numerous social activities?". It is assumed that those questions that generally produce the same answers are measuring the same trait (in this case, it might be sociability). In contrast, those questions that often produce different answers are measuring different traits. *Factor analysis*, a complex statistical procedure, uses this information to work out which questions belong together, and to decide how many factors or traits there are in a test.

Personality questionnaires should possess good *reliability* and *validity*. Reliability involves consistent measurement, with individuals taking a questionnaire twice obtaining similar scores on both occasions. Validity involves a test measuring what it is supposed to measure. Validity can be assessed by seeing whether an individual's personality as indicated by a questionnaire is similar to the ratings of their personality given by friends and relations.

The greatest problem with personality questionnaires is that of *social desirability bias* This is the tendency to respond to questions in a socially desirable, but inaccurate, fashion. Thus, for example, the socially desirable answer to the question, "Do you tend to be moody?", is clearly "No" rather than "Yes". One way of detecting such faking is to use a lie scale. Lie scales consist of items where the socially desirable answer is unlikely to be the true answer (e.g. "Do you ever gossip?"; "Do you always keep your promises?"). If someone answers most of the questions on the lie scale in the socially desirable direction, then it is assumed that they are faking their responses. Of course, this is unfair on the small minority of genuinely saintly people in the population!

Individual differences in personality traits might occur because of heredity. Everyone (except identical twins) differs genetically, and what we inherit genetically might influence our personality. Another possibility is that personality differences come from differences in upbringing. For example, someone who has a very loving and secure childhood may develop a very non-anxious personality, whereas someone who has a difficult and trouble-filled childhood may develop a very anxious personality. In fact, most trait theorists (especially H.J. Eysenck) have argued that heredity is the main factor determining an individual's personality.

Trait theorists assume that behaviour is determined more by personality traits than it is by the situation. However, as Mischel (1968) pointed out, behaviour is often determined more by the situation than by personality. For example, nearly everyone stops their car at a red light and behaves in a respectful fashion during a church service. According to Mischel and other social learning theorists, our behaviour in any given situation is determined by the rewards and punishments we have experienced in similar situations in the past rather than by our personality traits.

There is some truth in the criticisms of social learning theorists. It is now generally agreed that some combination of the trait and social learning approaches is best. According to the interactionist approach (Bowers, 1973), personality traits, the situation, and their interaction are all important determinants of behaviour.

The trait approach differs in various important ways from the humanistic approach. First, trait theorists adopt an entirely scientific approach to the study of human personality, relying on the relatively objective evidence of questionnaire data or behaviour. In contrast, humanistic psychologists tend to be anti-scientific in their approach, relying on phenomenology or subjective experience. Second, trait theorists emphasise the importance of physiology and biology in human personality, whereas humanistic psychologists deny their importance. Third, trait theorists pay little or no attention to the role of cognitive factors in personality, whereas the entire humanistic approach is very cognitive.

Fourth, trait theorists argue that personality normally changes very little over time; in contrast, humanistic psychologists argue that personality in the form of the self-concept can change considerably.

In spite of these differences, there is one important similarity between the trait and humanistic approaches. It is accepted within both approaches that behaviour depends in large measure on internal factors (e.g. the self; traits), and that external factors (e.g. rewards; punishments) are not all-important.

Cattell

Raymond Cattell wanted to identify all of the personality traits possessed by humans. He claimed that the words in the English language provide useful information about personality. The reason is that any important way in which people differ from each other should be represented by some relevant words. He made use of a list of 4500 words that are used for personality description. These words were reduced to 160 trait words by removing unfamiliar words and words of the same meaning. Cattell

Personality factors in Cattell's 16PF test.

Factor	Characteristics	Factor	Characteristics
A	Reserved vs. outgoing	L	Trusting vs. suspicious
B	Less intelligent vs. more intelligent	M	Practical vs. imaginative
C	Affected by feelings vs. emotionally stable	N	Forthright vs. shrewd
E	Humble vs. assertive	O	Placid vs. apprehensive
F	Sober vs. happy-go-lucky	Q1	Conservative vs. experimenting
G	Expedient vs. conscientious	Q2	Group-dependent vs. self-sufficient
H	Shy vs. venturesome	Q3	Casual vs. controlled
I	Tough-minded vs. tender-minded	Q4	Relaxed vs. tense

then added eleven traits from the personality literature, producing a total of 171 trait names which were claimed to cover almost everything of importance in personality.

Cattell then decided to use the information he had obtained to study personality in three different ways:

- *Life (L) data:* observers' ratings of other people's behaviour.
- *Questionnaire (Q) data:* self-report questionnaires.
- *Objective test (T) data:* careful assessment of some aspect of behaviour under controlled conditions (e.g. measuring anxiety by observing how much people sway when standing on tiptoe).

Cattell had hoped that the same personality traits would appear in L, Q, and T data. This was largely true of life and questionnaire data, but objective tests produced rather different traits. This is because objective tests are not a good way of measuring personality. They are unreliable, with people often obtaining different scores when given the same objective test twice. In the questionnaire field, Cattell's main contribution was the *Sixteen Personality Factor (16PF) test* , which was designed to measure 16 aspects of personality.

It is important to note that many of the personality factors in the 16PF are very highly correlated, i.e. they are rather similar to each other. For example, factor C (affected by feelings), factor H (shy), factor O (apprehensive), and factor Q4 (tense) can all be regarded as measuring different aspects of anxiety. The great similarity among different personality factors on the 16PF has led most experts to conclude that the 16PF actually contains far fewer than 16 different personality factors. A very full study

---

What are the advantages and disadvantages of Cattell's approach?

PLUS	MINUS
• He has put considerable effort into the task of providing a complete account of human personality.	• The evidence suggests that far fewer than 16 different personality traits are measured by the 16PF.
• He has done more than anyone else to study personality in several different ways (L, Q, and T data).	• We do not have an adequate account of the role played by heredity, environment, and physiology in producing individual differences in the various personality dimensions.

of the questionnaire was carried out by Howarth and Browne (1971). They used factor analysis, and were able to identify only ten different factors in the 16PF. They concluded (1971, p.117) that "the 16PF does not measure the factors which it purports to measure".

Eysenck

Cattell's main aim was to provide a complete account of all personality traits, even if some of these traits were rather similar to each other. In contrast, H.J. Eysenck argued that it was better to focus on a small number of really important personality traits (sometimes known as *superfactors*). These superfactors were chosen in such a way that they were not at all similar to each other. In technical terms, that was achieved by making sure that none of the factors was correlated or associated with any of the others.

H.J. Eysenck identified three major personality traits or superfactors, all of which are measured by the *Eysenck Personality Questionnaire* (EPQ). These factors are as follows:

- *Extraversion:* those scoring high on extraversion (extraverts) are more sociable and impulsive than those scoring low (introverts).
- *Neuroticism:* those scoring high on neuroticism are more tense and anxious than those scoring low.
- *Psychoticism:* those scoring high tend to be aggressive, hostile, and uncaring.

It was pointed out at the start of the chapter that temperament refers to an individual's typical moods and activity level, and that temperament is believed to be determined mainly by heredity. Eysenck's three factors all relate to individual differences in typical moods. In addition, as we will see shortly, it is assumed that all three factors are determined to a large extent by heredity. Therefore, Eysenck's theory can be regarded as a theory of temperament as well as of personality.

You may well feel that there must be more to personality than these three superfactors. However, many aspects of personality can be under-

- Do you take much notice of what people think?
- Are good manners important?
- Do you prefer reading to meeting people?
- As a child, were you ever cheeky to your parents?
- Are you easily hurt when people find fault with the work you do?

Sample questions from the Eysenck Personality Questionnaire. © H.J. and S.B.G. Eysenck, Hodder & Stoughton Educational (1991).

Further reading

Eysenck, M.W. (1994). *Individual differences: Normal and abnormal*. Hove, UK: Lawrence Erlbaum Associates Ltd. Chapters 3 and 4 deal in detail with the theoretical approaches of Cattell, Eysenck, Kelly, and Rogers.

Pervin, L.A. (1989). *Personality: Theory and research* (5th edn.). Chichester: Wiley. There is thorough coverage of several different personality theories in this book.

References

Bandura, A. (1977). Self-efficacy: Toward a unifying theory of behavioural change. *Psychological Review, 84*, 191–215.

Eysenck, H.J. (1967). *The biological basis of personality*. Springfield, IL: C.C. Thomas.

McCrae, R.R., & Costa, P.T. (1985). Updating Norman's "adequate taxonomy": Intelligence and personality dimensions in natural language and in questionnaires. *Journal of Personality and Social Psychology, 49*, 710–721.

Summary

- According to Freud's theory of psychosexual development, there are five stages: oral stage; anal stage; phallic stage; latency stage; and genital stage.
- According to Freud, adult personality depends very much on the experiences of early childhood, especially problems at any stage of psychosexual development.
- Behaviourists such as Watson and Skinner argued that individual differences in behaviour occur because of different conditioning histories in the form of rewards and punishments; this approach ignores heredity and the impact of the individual on the situation.
- According to Bandura's social learning theory, the individual has effects on the environment, and the environment has effects on the individual.
- According to Bandura, individual differences in behaviour in a given situation can be predicted by people's self-efficacy judgements.
- Humanistic psychologists such as Maslow and Rogers have studied personality through the use of phenomenology.
- In Maslow's hierarchy of needs, deficiency needs (e.g. for food and water) are at the bottom, with growth motivation (e.g. self-actualisation) at the top.
- Maslow ignored non-conscious processes, and rejected the scientific approach to psychology.
- According to Rogers, we have a self-concept and an ideal self, with happy individuals having a smaller gap between the two than unhappy ones.
- Rogers proposed client-centred therapy, in which the therapist tries to reduce the client's incongruence (gap between the client's self-concept and his or her behaviour) by being very supportive.
- Client-centred therapy is effective in treating mild mood disorders; however, it is less successful with more serious disorders, and it is based on an over-optimistic view of human nature.
- According to Kelly, an individual's personality is defined by his or her personal construct system.
- Emotional disturbance can occur if people use their constructs to make the same predictions about the world regardless of circumstances (tightening) or to make erratic and inconsistent predictions (loosening).
- Kelly ignored biological and other motivational forces.
- Cattell and Eysenck study personality traits ("broad, enduring, relatively stable characteristics used to assess and explain behaviour" Hirschberg, 1978); traits are assumed to be determined mainly by heredity.

Summary (continued)

- Trait theorists argue that behaviour is determined by personality traits; however, behaviour is also determined by the situation.
- Cattell used life data (ratings), questionnaire data, and objective test data (controlled assessment of behaviour) to identify 16 personality traits; in fact, his 16PF actually measures far fewer than 16 personality traits.

- Eysenck identified three superfactors (extraversion, neuroticism, and psychoticism), the first two of which have been found repeatedly in personality research.
- Eysenck argued that certain physiological systems were associated with each superfactor; there is little supporting evidence for this, with the possible exception of extraversion.

Key terms

Ascending reticular activating system: a part of the brain producing alertness, and claimed by H.J. Eysenck to be more active in introverts than extraverts.

Client-centred therapy: a form of therapy devised by Rogers, in which a positive, genuine, and understanding therapist tries to reduce the gap between the client's **self-concept** and his or her **ideal self**.

Extraversion: a personality factor based on sociability and impulsiveness.

Eysenck Personality Questionnaire: a test measuring the **traits** of extraversion, neuroticism, and psychoticism.

Factor analysis: a statistical technique used to work out the **traits** contained in a questionnaire or other test.

Fixation: within Freud's theory, the long-term attachment of basic energy to a stage of psychosexual development at which problems were experienced; see **regression**.

Fixed-role therapy: a form of therapy devised by Kelly, in which **personal constructs** are altered through the client pretending to be someone else.

Hierarchy of needs: in Maslow's theory, needs are hierarchically arranged with physiological needs at the bottom and self-actualisation at the top.

Ideal self: the **self-concept** that is most desired by an individual.

Key terms (continued)

Need for positive self-regard: the need to like and respect oneself.

Neuroticism: a personality factor based on negative emotional experience (e.g. anxiety, tension).

Peak experiences: states of euphoria in which there is complete acceptance of the world as it is.

Personal constructs: concepts used by the individual to make sense of the world; some constructs are very important (core constructs), whereas others are less important (peripheral constructs).

Phenomenology: a technique involving the report of direct experience.

Psychotism: a personality factor based on aggresion, hostility, and a lack of caring.

Q-sort method: a test used to assess the gap between the **self-concept** and the **ideal self**.

Reciprocal determinism: the notion that the individual has effects on the environment, and that the environment has effects on the individual.

Regression: within Freud's theory, going back to a less mature way of behaving; see **fixation**.

Reliability: the extent to which the scores on a questionnaire or other test are consistent, with individuals taking the test twice obtaining similar scores on both occasions.

Role Construct Repertory Test (Rep Test): a test devised by Kelly to measure people's **personal constructs**.

Self-actualisation: at the top of Maslow's **hierarchy of needs**, it is the need to make the fullest possible use of our abilities and skills.

Self-concept: an individual's thoughts and feelings about himself or herself; see **ideal self**.

Self-efficacy: within Bandura's theory, an individual's assessment of his or her ability to cope well with a given situation.

Sixteen Personality Factor (16PF) test: a test devised by Cattell.

Social desirability bias: the tendency to describe oneself in a socially desirable, but inaccurate, way; this bias is a problem for personality questionnaires.

Temperament: an individual's typical moods and activity level, usually thought to be determined by heredity.

Traits: long-lasting aspects of a person which influence his or her behaviour.

Validity: the extent to which a questionnaire or other test actually measures what it is claimed to measure.

Visceral brain: a brain system including the hippocampus, amygdala, cingulum, septum, and hypothalamus, claimed by H.J. Eysenck to be more responsive in those high in neuroticism than in those low in neuroticism.

Structured essay questions

1. Describe the humanistic approach. What are its strengths? What are its weaknesses?
2. Describe two trait theories of personality.
   What do they have in common? How do they differ?
3. What is Kelly's personal construct theory? How has it been used in therapy?

Self-assessment questions

1. The third stage in Freud's theory of psychosexual development is:
   a) the latency stage
   b) the anal stage
   c) the genital stage
   d) the phallic stage

2. According to the behaviourists, individual differences in behaviour depend on:
   a) heredity
   b) external factors such as rewards and punishments
   c) internal factors such as personality and knowledge
   d) external factors and internal factors

3. The humanistic approach to psychology focused on:
   a) behaviour
   b) the experiences of early childhood
   c) genetic influences on personality
   d) descriptions of experience

4. Maslow's hierarchy of needs consists of:
   a) physiological needs, security and safety needs, and the need for self-actualisation
   b) physiological needs, security and safety needs, aesthetic needs, and the need for self-actualisation
   c) security and safety needs and the need for self-actualisation
   d) none of the above

5. According to Rogers, people have:
   a) a need for positive regard
   b) a need for positive self-regard
   c) a need for positive regard and a need for positive self-regard
   d) a need for positive regard, a need for positive self-regard, and a need to be famous

6. Kelly's Rep Test:
   a) assesses core constructs and peripheral constructs
   b) assesses core constructs only
   c) assesses peripheral constructs only
   d) none of the above

7. The greatest problem with personality questionnaires is:
   a) poorly worded questions
   b) social desirability bias
   c) a tendency for people to be too modest
   d) a tendency to answer "Yes" to all the questions

8. Cattell found that:
   a) life and questionnaire data produced similar traits, but objective test data produced different traits
   b) life data and objective test data produced similar traits, but questionnaire data produced different traits
   c) objective test data and questionnaire data produced similar traits, but life data produced different traits
   d) life, questionnaire, and objective test data all produced different traits

9. Studies based on Eysenck's theory indicate that:
   a) only extraversion is a major personality trait
   b) only neuroticism is a major personality trait
   c) only psychoticism is a major personality trait
   d) only extraversion and neuroticism are major personality traits

Towards a concept of self 19

It seems natural for people in the United States and Europe to think in terms of a *self-concept*. This self-concept corresponds to the set of ideas that people have of themselves, and is very relevant for cultures in which the focus is on the individual. However, as Ho (1977) pointed out, the emphasis in most Asian cultures is on the group rather than on the individual. As a result, the notion of self loses much of its meaning. For example, the Chinese word *ren* (meaning person) refers to the ways in which an individual's behaviour fits (or does not fit) group standards.

There is a similar state of affairs in Japan. Japanese children are taught very early to think of the effects that their behaviour will have on others. As a result, the Japanese notion of self relates very much to social interaction and social relationships.

In order to set the scene for this chapter, we need to distinguish among a number of similar terms: self-esteem; self-image; self-concept:

- *Self-esteem:* this is the evaluative aspect of the self-concept; it concerns how worthwhile and confident an individual feels about himself or herself.
- *Self-image:* this is the descriptive aspect of the self-concept; it concerns the detailed knowledge that an individual has about himself or herself.
- *Self-concept:* this is all of the thoughts and feelings about the self; it combines self-esteem and self-image.

There are numerous factors influencing the self-concept. However, our relationships with other people are of crucial importance. Charles Cooley (1902) used the term looking-glass self to convey the idea that the self-concept reflects the evaluations of other people. In other words, we tend to see ourselves as others see us. However, other people vary a lot in the impact they have on our self-concept. Those of greatest importance in our lives (e.g. partners; parents; close friends) have a large effect on our self-concept, whereas casual acquaintances have little or no effect.

The idea that the self-concept emerges as a result of our dealings with other people was developed by Mead (1934). He argued that our self-concept is based on our social experience, and that it is controlled by the values and expectations of the culture in which we live. He also argued that the development of the self-concept depends greatly on language, because it is through language that cultural values are often expressed.

An important way in which our self-concept is influenced by other people is by means of *social comparison*: we judge our performance with reference to the performance of others. Ruble et al. (1980) studied the use of social comparison in children aged between 5 and 9. They threw balls into a concealed basketball hoop, and were told how their performance compared to that of other children. Children of 9 judged how good they were at this game by taking account of other children's performance. However, children younger than 9 did not make use of social comparison.

Those who are happy with their self-concept tend to be high in self-esteem, whereas those who dislike their self-concept generally lack self-esteem. Coopersmith (1967) studied some of the factors producing high and low self-esteem in boys aged between 10 and 12. He found that how they were treated by their parents played an important part. The parents of boys having high self-esteem tended to have the following characteristics:

- A general acceptance of their children.
- They set clearly defined limits for their children's behaviour.
- They allowed their children to control their lives and to behave with reasonable freedom within those limits.

Most people try to maintain their self-esteem by means of the *self-serving bias* (Zuckerman, 1979). If you show this bias, you attribute your successes to your own ability or effort, but you attribute your failures to the difficulty of the task or to bad luck. In other words, you accept full responsibility for success, but don't accept responsibility for failure. Individuals who are depressed often show the opposite bias, blaming themselves for failure and attributing success to good luck or some other external factor. As a result, depressed people generally have very low self-esteem and a negative self-concept.

Social roles and self-concept

Nature of social roles

Most adults perform many roles in the course of their daily lives. For example, many women combine the roles of mother, parent, aunt, and teacher or other type of worker. All these roles can be regarded as social roles, which can be defined as "the slots or positions that we occupy in society" (Gahagan, 1984). It is important to consider social roles, because they have substantial effects on our self-concept. The positions or social roles we occupy help to define the kind of person we perceive ourselves to be.

As children grow up, so they occupy more social roles. This was shown in a study by Kuhn (1960). Seven-year-old children and college students were asked to provide 20 answers to the question, "Who am I?". The children produced an average of five different roles, whereas the college students averaged ten roles. The students tended to identify themselves by class, marital status, sex, age, race, religion, occupation, and so on.

People can occupy an almost limitless number of different social roles. However, Linton (1945) suggested that most roles emerge out of five major types of social grouping:

- *Occupational groupings:* these are based on job categories such as journalist and dentist.
- *Status groupings:* these are based on the position held within a work organisation (e.g. managing director; manager).
- *Age and sex groupings:* these include adolescent, girl, and pensioner.
- *Family groupings:* these are based on position within the family structure (e.g. mother; grandmother).
- *Common interest groupings:* these are based on sports, hobbies, or social interests.

Society has certain expectations about those occupying any given social role. According to Krech et al. (1962), "The expectancies making up a role are not restricted to actions; they also include expectancies about motivations, beliefs, feelings, attitudes, and values." Problems in the form of *role conflict* can arise when someone occupies two social roles at the same time. For example, Burchard (1954) interviewed military chaplains who had to combine military and religious roles. Some of the strategies they used were as follows:

- *Rationalisation:* "Someone has to take the gospel to these boys".
- *Repression:* "I don't see any conflict".
- *Withdrawal:* "I don't want to talk about it".
- *Compartmentalisation:* "Some things are important to the military; other things are important to God".

Effects on self-concept

Social roles. We saw earlier that our self-concept has a descriptive dimension (the self-image) and an evaluative dimension (self-esteem). Most of the information about ourselves used to form our self-concept comes from our performance of various social roles. Our self-image is greatly affected by the abilities and skills we demonstrate in our various social, family, and work roles. Our self-esteem depends to a very large extent on how other people react to our behaviour in different social roles. It is much easier for individuals to have high self-esteem if their friends, family, and work colleagues all respond favourably to their role behaviour than if they do not.

The roles forming the self-concept are arranged in a hierarchy (Stryker, 1982). That is to say, people see some of their social roles as much more important than others. Our self-image and self-esteem depend much more on how we perform social roles of central importance to us than on how we perform those of minor significance. For example, losing a tennis match may severely affect the self-esteem of a professional tennis player who has devoted his or her life to the game. However, it may have no effect at all on the self-esteem of someone who only plays the game for fun.

Lieberman (1956) studied the effects of social role on some aspects of the self-concept. At the start of the study, he measured attitudes towards union and management policies held by the workers in a home-appliance factory. One year later, those who had become foremen expressed more positive attitudes towards management policies and officers than they had before. In contrast, those who had become union stewards expressed more positive attitudes towards union policies and officers. Eighteen months later, some of these foremen and union stewards had returned to their original jobs. This led their attitudes to return to what they had been in the first place. These findings indicate that social roles have a large effect on our attitudes.

Personality. Fairly or unfairly, it has often been suggested that certain kinds of jobs produce a particular kind of personality. For example, Waller (1932) argued that teaching creates the "teacher personality": "There is first that certain inflexibility or unbendingness of personality which is thought to mark the person who has taught … One who has taught long enough may wax unenthusiastic on any subject under the sun … the flat, assured tones of voice are bred in the teacher by his dealings in the classroom … It is said, and it would be difficult to deny, that the teacher mind is not creative."

An important issue concerns the relationship between social role and personality. Is the way we perform a social role determined by our personality, or is our personality determined by the social roles we occupy? It is generally assumed that there are effects in both directions (Krech et al., 1962), and the evidence seems to support this.

There are situations in which an individual's behaviour is determined far more by role demands than by his or her personality. A good example is the Stanford Prison Experiment (Zimbardo, 1973; see also Chapter 15).

Emotionally stable individuals played the parts of prison warders and prisoners for six days. The "warders" became more and more aggressive in their treatment of the "prisoners". They enjoyed being in a position of power over the "prisoners", and this led them to harass and humiliate the "prisoners".

There are other situations in which an individual's behaviour depends much more on personality. For example, consider the role of parent. Some parents behave in a gentle and caring fashion to their children, whereas other parents are aggressive and uncaring. It is accepted within society that the role of parent can be carried out in many different ways.

Self-monitoring.   There are important individual differences in the extent to which someone's role behaviour reflects his or her personality. Snyder (1974) argued for the importance of *self-monitoring*. Those high in self-monitoring pay close attention to the expectations of other people, and change their behaviour accordingly. Thus, their role behaviour is determined by social or role expectations rather than by their personality. Those low in self-monitoring act more on the basis of their own person-ality, and are not much influenced by the expectations of others. Their role behaviour is much influenced by internal factors.

Evidence that high self-monitors are much more influenced than low self-monitors by external pressures and role expectations was reported by Snyder and Monson (1975). Participants were placed in groups in which the general view was either that everyone should conform or that every-one should feel free to behave as he or she wanted. The behaviour of high self-monitors was greatly affected by group expectations about role be-haviour, whereas that of low self-monitors was not.

A reasonable view of the relationship between social role and person-ality was suggested by Goffman (1965). According to him, "In order to perform a role effectively, the newcomer has to put on a mask to play the part; when he has acted the part long enough and others have accepted the performance, then this becomes a real part of his personality."

Labelling and self-concept

It is generally accepted that individuals who behave in bizarre ways and show abnormal symptoms should receive a psychiatric diagnosis or label indicating the nature of their abnormality. For example, those who appear very anxious and worried about most aspects of their lives would be labelled as suffering from generalised anxiety disorder.

There may be some dangers in this approach. Someone who is given a psychiatric diagnosis or label may be treated as a mentally ill person. As a result, his or her behaviour may change in ways that make the label more appropriate than it was in the first place. In other words, rather than the symptoms leading to the psychiatric label, it may sometimes be the label that helps to create the symptoms. This view is known as *labelling theory*, and it was originally put forward by Scheff (1966).

Labelling theory was put forward to account for the behaviour of patients with schizophrenia (a very severe condition involving great distortions of thought, emotion, and behaviour). According to Scheff, we should distinguish between major rules of behaviour (e.g. you must not steal; you must not be violent) and less important residual rules (e.g. you must not ignore other people; you must respond emotionally to tragic events). Those who engage in residual rule breaking may be labelled as schizophrenic. This label produces a social role for the person labelled, in which he or she is expected to behave in bizarre and inappropriate ways.

Labelling theory can be applied to a wide range of mental disorders. In every case, the argument is that a psychiatric label creates an abnormal social role, and the person concerned and everyone else then behaves to preserve that social role. The general ideas of labelling theory can be extended to the kinds of labels that are put on normal people in everyday life (e.g. stupid; lazy; incompetent)

To understand labelling theory better, we will consider an imaginary example. Suppose you were told that a stranger you were about to meet had been labelled as a violent psychopath. You would probably behave in a rather wary and careful way with that person. This in turn might cause him or her to respond in a rather peculiar or aggressive way towards you.

Farina et al. (1968) carried out a study similar to our example. Some individuals were told that they were about to interact with someone who thought they were psychiatric patients. This false information led them to behave in a rather odd fashion, and caused them to be rejected by the other person. Thus, the findings were as expected on labelling theory.

Sane or insane?

A famous study of relevance to labelling theory was carried out by David Rosenhan (1973). Eight normal individuals tried to gain admission to a psychiatric hospital. They all complained of hearing indistinct voices which seemed to be saying "empty", "hollow", and "thud". They were all admitted to hospital, and nearly all of them were labelled as suffering from schizophrenia.

After these normal individuals had been admitted to psychiatric wards, all of them said they felt fine and no longer had any symptoms. In spite of this, the label of "schizophrenia" led to them being poorly treated. On numerous occasions, these pseudo-patients went up to a staff member with polite requests for information. These requests were ignored 88% of the time by nurses and attendants, and 71% of the time by psychiatrists. These findings suggest that those who are labelled as schizophrenic are regarded as having very low status within society.

Rosenhan argued that people respond to the label rather than to the individual. According to him, "we cannot distinguish the sane from the insane in psychiatric hospitals." However, it is not clear that the psychiatrists in this study were influenced too much by the schizophrenia label. They can hardly be blamed for not expecting completely normal people to try to gain admission to a psychiatric hospital. Furthermore, most genuine schizophrenics spend long periods of time in hospital before being discharged. In contrast, the pseudo-patients were discharged in an average of under three weeks.

The greatest problem with labelling theory is the assumption that mental illness results only from a labelling process. This is simply wrong when applied to schizophrenia. Paul Meehl, a leading expert, was once interrupted during a talk on schizophrenia by someone arguing that the symptoms of schizophrenia are caused by labelling. Meehl found himself "thinking of a patient I had seen on a ward who kept his finger up his arse 'to keep his thoughts from running out,' while with his other hand he tried to tear out his hair because it really 'belonged to his father.' And here was this man telling me he was doing these things because someone had called him a schizophrenic" (Kimble et al., 1980). Thus, the symptoms of schizophrenia are far too serious to be caused by labelling.

What are the advantages and disadvantages of labelling theory?

PLUS	MINUS
• Patients with a psychiatric or other negative label are often treated much worse than other people.	• Schizophrenia is a serious mental disorder, and its symptoms are affected very little by labelling.
• As Rosenhan discovered, labels can be misused and applied wrongly.	• According to the theory, those who are labelled as schizophrenic should stop their residual rule breaking if they are no longer so labelled; there is no evidence for this.

Self-fulfilling prophecy

When we meet people, we tend to have expectations about their person-alities and the ways in which they are likely to behave. Some of these expectations are based on stereotypes, and influence how we interpret their behaviour (see Chapter 13). Our expectations often influence how we behave towards other people, and this can lead them to behave in such a way that our original expectations are confirmed. This is known as the *self-fulfilling prophecy*.

There are great similarities between the notion of the self-fulfilling prophecy and labelling theory. In both cases, it is assumed that an indi-vidual's behaviour can be influenced by the expectations that others have about him or her. However, there is one important difference. Self-fulfill-ing propecies can apply to all kinds of expectations, whereas labelling theory applies only to expectations in the form of labels. In addition, labelling theory was mainly intended to apply to mental disorders, whereas self-fulfilling prophecies are usually considered in normal indi-viduals.

Let us consider an example of the self-fulfilling prophecy. Suppose you are told that someone you are due to meet is a very warm and friendly person. When you meet that person, this expectation may lead you to behave in a very friendly way towards him or her. This in turn may cause the other person to behave in a very friendly way towards you, thus confirming your original expectation.

Darley and Fazio (1980) have identified a series of steps involved in the self-fulfilling prophecy. According to them, there is the following expectancy–confirmation sequence:

- Someone (A) has an expectancy about someone else (B).
- A acts towards B in line with that expectancy.
- B interprets A's behaviour.
- B responds to A in line with A's original expectancy.
- A interprets B's behaviour as confirming his or her expectancy.

Experimental evidence

A striking example of the self-fulfilling prophecy was discussed by Jahoda (1954). The Ashanti tribe in West Africa believe that a child's personality depends on the day of the week on which it is born, and the names they give their children indicate the day of the week on which they were born. According to the Ashanti, boys born on Monday have a calm and gentle personality, whereas those born on Wednesday have an aggressive per-sonality. As expected on the notion of the self-fulfilling prophecy, boys born on Wednesday are far more likely than those born on Monday to become juvenile delinquents.

Another clear case of self-fulfilling prophecy was reported by Snyder et al. (1977). They asked male students to have "get acquainted" telephone conversations with female students they did not know. Before the conversation, the male students were shown a photograph of a physically attractive or plain female student. They were told that it was a photograph of the student on the other end of the line, but this was not true. The male students were more friendly, open, and sociable when they thought they were talking to a physically attractive member of the opposite sex, than when they believed they were talking to the plain student. More strikingly, the female student appeared more poised, sociable, outgoing, and self-confident when the student with whom she was talking thought she was attractive.

People do not always show the self-fulfilling prophecy. Jones (1986) found three situations in which the expectations and behaviour of one person generally have little or no effect on the behaviour of someone else:

1. When the expectations about the other person differ considerably from that person's own perceptions about himself or herself.
2. When the expectations of the first person are expressed directly rather than indirectly through behaviour.
3. When the expectations are negative and unfavourable.

Those who show the self-fulfilling prophecy make a key error: they fail to notice that their expectations and behaviour are having a significant impact on someone else's behaviour. We tend to believe that other people behave as they do because of their personality rather than because of any influence we are having on them. Striking support for this view was reported by Gilbert and Jones (1986). Their student participants were asked to play the role of interviewers. They were told that the person being interviewed had prepared liberal and conservative answers to their questions. After they had asked each question, the participants pressed a button to indicate whether they wanted the liberal or the conservative answer. Thus, the student participants had total control over the behaviour of those being interviewed. In spite of that, they believed that those giving mainly liberal answers were liberal in their attitudes, whereas those giving conservative answers were basically conservative.

There is much support for the notion of the self-fulfilling prophecy. However, nearly all of the studies focus on short-term changes in behaviour produced by self-fulfilling prophecies. Can self-fulfilling prophecies have long-term effects, including altering someone's self-concept? An

---

What are the advantages and disadvantages of the self-fulfilling prophecy?

PLUS

- The self-fulfilling prophecy is an important phenomenon that has been demonstrated many times.
- People often under-estimate the impact of their behaviour on the behaviour of others.

MINUS

- It is often difficult to know the expectations that one person has about another.
- The self-fulfilling prophecy has short-term effects on behaviour; it may also have long-term effects on behaviour and the self-concept, but there is little clear evidence of this.

---

indication that this may be possible comes from a study by Fazio et al. (1981). Students were asked questions that were designed to persuade them to give extraverted answers (e.g. "What would you do to liven things up at a party?"). This had the effect of increasing their extraversion scores on a questionnaire. We don't know how long this effect lasted, but it is possible that there was a modest shift in part of the students' self-concept.

Further reading

Hayes, N. (1993) *Principles of social psychology*. Hove, UK: Lawrence Erlbaum Associates Ltd. Chapter 1 contains an interesting discussion of the self-concept in different cultures.

Baron, R.A., & Byrne, D. (1991). *Social psychology: Understanding human interaction* (6th edn.). Boston: Allyn & Bacon. Chapter 3 deals with many of the main issues relating to the self-concept.

References

Coopersmith, S. (1967). *The antecedents of self-esteem*. San Francisco: Freeman.

Mead, G.H. (1934). *Mind, self and society*. Chicago: University of Chicago Press.

Rosenhan, D.L. (1973). On being sane in insane places. *Science, 179*, 250–258.

Snyder, M.I., Tanke, E.D., & Berscheid, E. (1977). Social perception and interpersonal behaviour: On the self-fulfilling nature of social stereotypes. *Journal of Personality and Social Psychology, 35*, 656–666.

Summary

- The self-concept corresponds to the set of ideas that people have about themselves; it depends crucially on social interaction and social relationships.

- The self-concept combines self-esteem and self-image.

- Social roles are the "slots or positions that we occupy in society".

- In the course of development, individuals occupy more and more social roles.

- Most social roles emerge out of occupational, status, age, sex, family, and common-interest groupings.

- Social roles, especially those of great importance to us, have an impact on our self-concept.

- It is probable that personality affects our performance of a social role, and that in turn the social role affects our personality.

- According to labelling theory, the psychiatric or other label given to an individual may lead him or her to behave in line with the label.

- Labelling can influence the behaviour of the labelled person and of those around him or her, but it cannot explain the symptoms shown by schizophrenic patients.

- According to the self-fulfilling prophecy, our expectations about another person influence our behaviour; this can lead the other person to behave in such a way that our expectations are confirmed.

- The self-fulfilling prophecy is not found when our expectations about another person differ greatly from their self-perceptions, or when our expectations are expressed directly.

- The self-fulfilling prophecy can produce short-term changes in someone's behaviour; it is less clear whether it can produce long-term changes in self-concept.

Key terms

Labelling theory: the view that applying a psychiatric label to someone may cause that person to be treated as mentally ill.

Role conflict: the problem occurring when someone tries to occupy two **social roles** at the same time.

Self-concept: the total set of thoughts and feelings about the self; it consists of **self-esteem** and **self-image**.

Self-esteem: the part of the **self-concept** concerned with the feelings (positive or negative) that an individual has about himself or herself.

Self-fulfilling prophecy: the notion that our expectations about the ways others will behave may lead them to behave in line with our expectations.

Self-image: the part of the **self-concept** concerned with the knowledge that an individual has about himself or herself.

Self-monitoring: an aspect of personality, with high self-monitors behaving in line with the expectations of others.

Self-serving bias: the tendency to attribute your successes to your own efforts and ability, but to attribute your failures to task difficulty and bad luck; it is used to maintain **self-esteem**.

Social comparison: deciding how well we are doing by comparing ourselves against other people.

Social roles: the various positions that people occupy in society; they can depend on one's job, age, sex, family structure, and leisure interests.

Structured essay questions

1. Define self-esteem. How does self-esteem depend on parental treatment and self-serving bias?
2. What are social roles? How do they relate to the self-concept?
3. What is labelling theory? To what extent does the work of Rosenhan (1973) support the theory?
4. What is the self-fulfilling prophecy? How does it affect people's behaviour and self-concept?

Self-assessment questions

1. Which of the following statements is true?
    a) all children make use of social comparison
    b) no children make use of social comparison
    c) only young children make use of social comparison
    d) only older children make use of social comparison

2. The self-serving bias involves:
    a) attributing success to your own ability or effort, but attributing failure to task difficulty or bad luck
    b) attributing success to task difficulty or good luck, but attributing failure to lack of ability or effort
    c) attributing success and failure to ability or effort
    d) attributing success and failure to task difficulty and luck

3. According to Linton, there are:
    a) three major types of social grouping
    b) four major types of social grouping
    c) five major types of social grouping
    d) six major types of social grouping

4. According to labelling theory:
    a) it is useful to attach labels to people who are mentally ill
    b) those who are mentally ill want to have labels applied to them
    c) attaching a label to those who are mentally ill may help to create some of their symptoms

5. Rosenhan discovered that:
    a) normal individuals could be labelled as schizophrenic
    b) schizophrenics could be labelled as normal
    c) there is nothing wrong with schizophrenics
    d) normal individuals could be treated as schizophrenic for several months

6. The fact that the Ashanti tribe believe that a child's personality depends on the day of the week on which it is born, and that this is what actually happens, is an example of:
    a) stereotyping
    b) self-fulfilling prophecy
    c) labelling
    d) magic

Cognitive approach

Perception 20

This chapter deals with the ways in which we make use of the information presented to our eyes, ears, nose, tongue, and so on. The area of psychology we are concerned with is known as *perception*. This term "refers to the means by which information acquired from the environment via the sense organs is transformed into experiences of objects, events, sounds, tastes, etc." (Roth, 1986, p. 81). Perception can be regarded as involving three aspects:

- There are objects and people out in the environment; these form what is known as the *distal stimulus*.
- There is the stimulus pattern produced at the eye, the ear, and so on; this is known as the *proximal stimulus*.
- There is what we see, hear, taste, smell, and so on; this is our *perceptual experience*.

It is important to distinguish between *sensation* and *perception*. Sensation is basic, unorganised information which depends on the proximal stimulus. Sensations can be thought of as the messages that our brains receive from our senses. In contrast, perception, which is our perceptual experience, is usually organised and three-dimensional. Perception occurs as a result of interpreting or making sense of sensations on the basis of knowledge and past experience. This process of interpretation allows perception to be organised even though sensation is not.

Perception starts at about the point where sensation finishes. However, there is not really a clear boundary between sensation and perception, because the processes involved in sensation and perception often overlap in time.

There is increasing evidence that visual perception is more of an achievement than you might imagine. Different parts of the visual cortex are specialised for processing information about form, motion, and colour (Zeki, 1993). Visual perception involves combining these different kinds of information and making sense of them.

Personal viewpoint

Visual perception is normally very rapid and accurate. However, we do sometimes make mistakes –why do you think this is? When looking at the world, we somehow turn a two-dimensional retinal image into complete three-dimensional perception. What kinds of cues do you think we make use of to see the world as it is rather than the way it appears on the retina?

Perceptual organisation

The information arriving at our senses is generally confusing and disorganised. In the case of vision, there is a mosaic of colours, and the retinal sizes and shapes of objects are often very different from their actual sizes and shapes. In addition, the retinal image is two-dimensional. In spite of these limitations of the retinal image, our perception of the world is well-organised and three-dimensional. Some German psychologists in the early twentieth century argued that trying to understand how disorganised information turns into organised perception is of major importance. They called themselves *Gestaltists*; this is based on the German word "Gestalt" meaning organised whole.

The Gestaltists put forward several laws of perceptual organisation. However, their most basic law was the *law of Pragnanz*. This was expressed as follows by Koffka (1935): "Psychological organisation will always be as 'good' as the prevailing conditions allow. In this definition the term 'good' is undefined." In fact, the Gestaltists regarded a "good" form as the simplest or most uniform of all the possible ways of organising perceptual information.

What the Gestaltists had in mind with their law of Pragnanz can be seen by considering some concrete examples (set out in the figure below). Pattern (a) is more easily seen as three horizontal lines of dots rather than as three vertical lines. It shows the Gestalt law of proximity, according to which visual elements that are close to each other will tend to be grouped together. In pattern (b), vertical columns rather than horizontal rows are seen. This fits the law of similarity, according to which similar visual elements are grouped together. In pattern (c), we tend to see two crossing lines rather than a V-shaped line and an inverted V-shaped line. This fits the law of good continuation, which states that those visual elements producing the fewest interruptions to smoothly curving lines are grouped together. Finally, pattern (d) shows the law of closure: the missing parts of a figure are filled in to complete it. All four laws discussed here are more specific statements of the basic law of Pragnanz.

Gestalt laws of perception.

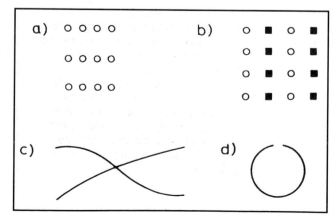

Where do these organisational processes come from? The Gestaltists argued that most perceptual organisation depends on innate factors. In other words, we naturally organise our perceptual experience in line with the law of Pragnanz. The Gestaltists tried to identify some of the brain processes involved, but without any success.

A key assumption of the Gestaltists was that "the whole is more than the sum of its parts". For example, suppose that you hear a tune several times on the radio performed in a particular key. You then hear the same tune performed in a different key. Even though all the notes are different, you would have no problem in recognising the tune. One idea that emerges from this is that the whole may be seen before the parts making up that whole. This may sound like putting the cart before the horse, because we might assume that the parts of an object are processed before the object itself is identified.

This idea was tested by David Navon (1977). He presented his participants with rather strange stimuli, such as a large letter "H" formed out of numerous little letter "S"s. Their task was to identify either the single large letter or the small letters as rapidly as possible. The time taken to identify the small letters was much longer when the large letter was different from them than when it was the same letter, because information about the large letter was available rapidly and disrupted processing of the small letters. However, the time to identify the large letter was not influenced by the nature of the small letters, because information about the whole (i.e. the large letter) was available before information about the parts (i.e. the identity of the small letters).

```
S               S
S               S
S               S
S               S
S               S
SSSSSSSSSSSSS
S               S
S               S
S               S
S               S
S               S
```

What are the advantages and disadvantages of the Gestalt approach?

PLUS	MINUS
• The Gestaltists were right to emphasise the importance of perceptual organisation. • The Gestaltists discovered several major laws of perception.	• The laws tend to be descriptions rather than explanations: they do not tell us why it is that similar visual elements or those close together are grouped. • The Gestaltists may have exaggerated the importance of innate factors; one of the reasons we group similar or close elements is because our experience teaches us that such elements are likely to belong to the same object, but innate factors also seem to be involved.

Visual constancies

Think of a female friend of yours. When you look at her, the information presented to the retina depends on several factors. The further away from you she is, the smaller is your retinal image of her. The angle from which you are looking at her will affect the shape of the retinal image, and the lighting conditions will affect the colour of the retinal image. However, your friend always looks very similar to you in spite of variations in the retinal image. This tendency for perception to remain constant at all times is based on *visual constancies*. Some of the main visual constancies are dealt with in this section.

Shape constancy refers to the fact that the shape of an object seems to remain the same in spite of changes in its orientation. For example, there is a small square table in front of me. The table looks square, even though its retinal image is in the shape of a rectangle.

Colour constancy refers to the fact that the colour of an object looks the same even when the hue or colour is changing. Consider, for example, being at a disco with red lighting. The light reflected from your friends' faces is much redder than usual, but you simply take into account the colour of the lighting and perceive their faces in their usual colour.

Size constancy involves objects looking the same size in spite of changes in the size of the retinal image. The size of the image on the retina increases greatly as someone walks towards us. However, this has little or no effect on our perception of their size.

In general terms, it is clear that perceptual experience is of importance in producing the various visual constancies. Infants show reasonable size, shape, and colour constancy, but complete mastery of the visual constancies takes several months or a few years to develop (Eysenck & Keane, 1995). A detailed account of the processes involved in size constancy is given a little later in the chapter.

Depth perception and size constancy

Depth perception

One of the main achievements of visual perception is the way in which the two-dimensional retinal image is changed into perception of a three-dimensional world. In our everyday lives, cues to depth are often given by movement of ourselves or of objects around us. However, the major focus here will be on cues to depth that are available even if neither the observer nor the objects in the environment are moving. These cues can be divided into monocular and binocular cues. *Monocular cues* are those that require the use of only one eye, although they can also be used easily when someone has both eyes open. Such cues clearly exist, because the world still retains a sense of depth with one eye closed. *Binocular cues* are those involving both eyes being used together.

Monocular cues. There are various monocular cues to depth. They are sometimes called pictorial cues, because they have been used by artists to create the impression of three-dimensional scenes while painting on two-dimensional canvases. One such cue is *linear perspective*. Parallel lines pointing directly away from us seem to get closer together as they recede into the distance (e.g. railway tracks or the edges of a motorway). This convergence of lines can create a powerful impression of depth in a two-dimensional drawing.

A textured gradient formed by a railway track.

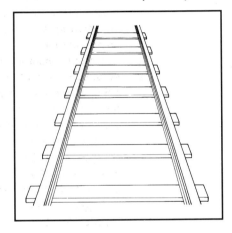

Another cue related to perspective is texture. Most objects (e.g. cobblestoned roads; carpets) possess texture, and textured objects slanting away from us have what Gibson called a *texture gradient*. The texture becomes more dense as you look from the front to the back of a slanting object. If you were unwise enough to stand between the rails of a railway track and look along the track, the distance between the connecting sleepers would seem to reduce.

A further cue is *interposition*, in which a nearer object hides part of a more distant object from view. Some evidence of how powerful interposition can be seen here in Kanizsa's (1976) illusory square. It looks as if there is a white square in front of four black circles, in spite of the fact that most of the contours of the white square are missing.

Kanizsa's illusory square.

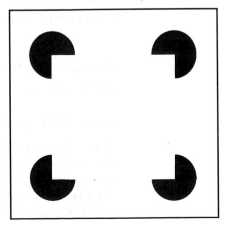

Another cue to depth is given by shading. Flat, two-dimensional surfaces do not cast shadows. As a result, the presence of shading indicates the presence of a three-dimensional object.

The final monocular cue we will discuss is *motion parallax*, which refers to the movement of an object's image over the retina. Suppose that two objects move from left to right across your line of vision at the same speed, but one object is much further away from you than the other. The image cast by the nearer object would move much further across the retina than would the image cast by the more distant object.

Motion parallax is also involved if there are two stationary objects at different distances from the observer, and it is the observer's eyes that move. Some of the properties of motion parallax can be seen through the window of a moving train. Objects that are close to you seem to be moving in the opposite direction to the train, whereas objects further away seem to be moving in the same direction as the train.

Binocular cues. There are three major binocular cues available only to observers using both eyes: convergence; accommodation; and stereopsis. *Convergence* refers to the fact that the eyes turn inwards to focus on an object to a greater extent with a very close object than with one that is further away. *Accommodation* refers to the variation in optical power produced by a thickening of the lens of the eye when focusing on a close object. *Stereopsis* depends on the difference between the images of objects on the retinas of the two eyes. When you look into a stereoscope, two pictures or drawings are presented to you in such a way that each eye receives the information it would receive if the object or objects shown were actually there. The difference in the images presented to the two eyes produces a strong depth effect.

Convergence, accommodation, and stereopsis do not produce depth perception for objects that are at some distance from the observer. So far as convergence and accommodation are concerned, there are doubts as to whether they are of much value under any circumstances (Eysenck & Keane, 1995).

Size constancy

An important aspect of visual perception is known as *size constancy* Familiar objects (e.g. cars; people; buildings) look more or less the same size regardless of their distance away from us. This may not seem surprising, but the retinal image of a person 100 metres away is very much smaller than the retinal image of the same person 10 metres away. How do we show size constancy for familiar and unfamiliar objects? We take account of an object's apparent distance when judging its size. For example, an object may be judged to be very large even though its retinal image is very small if it is a long way away from us.

Size constancy is not always found. Consider what the view looks like from the window of a plane. Cars often look more like toys than like real cars, and people look like ants.

The relationship between size and distance also goes the other way, in that perceived distance is influenced by familiar size. This was shown by Ittelson (1951). He asked participants to look at playing cards through a peep-hole that provided few cues to distance other than familiar size. There were actually three different-sized playing cards (normal size; half-size; and double-size), and they were presented one at a time at a distance of 2.3 metres from the observer. The half-size playing card was judged to be 4.6 metres away, whereas the double-size card was thought to be 1.3 metres away. Thus, familiar size had a large effect on distance judgements.

Distortions based on size constancy. One way of testing the notion that size judgements depend on perceived distance is to consider illusions in which the perceived distance of an object is quite different from its actual distance. A good example of such an illusion is the *Ames room* (below). This is a specially constructed room of a most peculiar shape: the floor slopes and the rear wall is not at right angles to the adjoining walls. In spite of this, the Ames room creates the same retinal image as a normal rectangular room when viewed through a peep-hole at a point in the front wall. The fact that one end of the rear wall is much further from the viewer is disguised by making it much higher. The cues suggesting that the rear wall is at right angles to the viewer are so strong that a person walking backwards and forwards in front of it appears to grow and shrink as he or she moves about!

The Ames room.

The *moon illusion* also shows the ways in which mistakes about perceived distance can affect size judgements. The moon illusion refers to the fact that the moon looks much larger when it is close to the horizon than it does when it is high in the sky. Part of the reason for this is that the moon looks further away from us when it is near the horizon, because there are many depth cues present. Thus, the retinal size of the moon is the same at the horizon and high in the sky, but it looks further away at the horizon. This leads us to conclude that the moon is larger when it is at the horizon.

Kaufman and Rock provided evidence for this explanation of the moon illusion. They asked their participants to look at the moon on the horizon through a small hole, so that they could not use distance cues provided by the horizon. This led to an apparent shrinking of the size of the moon. They also asked participants to look at the moon high in the sky through an artificial horizon drawn on a sheet of clear plastic. This increased the apparent size of the moon.

In sum, the Ames room and the moon illusion are important in that they suggest there is a close link between perceived distance and perceived size. With both illusions, perceived distance is different from actual distance, and this leads to errors in judgements of perceived size.

Factors influencing perception

What we perceive depends mainly on the stimuli presented to us. However, as Gregory (1972) and others have argued, it involves other factors as well. According to Gregory, perception is an active process which depends on what the perceiver brings to the situation in terms of expectations, knowledge, and learning. It also depends on reward, motivation, deprivation, attention, and other factors. These factors are discussed next.

Reward

Schafer and Murphy (1943) considered the effects of reward on perception. They used drawings in which an irregular line had been drawn vertically through a circle so that each half of the circle could be seen as the profile of a face. At the start of the study, each face was presented on its own. One face in each pair was linked with gaining money, whereas

Schafer and Murphy's juxtaposed faces.

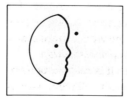  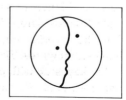

the other face was linked with losing money. When the complete draw-ings were then shown briefly, participants were much more likely to report seeing the previously "rewarded" face than the "punished" one.

The effects of reward on perception were also looked at by Bruner and Goodman (1947). They asked rich and poor children to estimate the sizes of coins. The poor children over-estimated the size of every coin more than did the rich children. This finding may reflect the greater value of money to poor children. However, a simpler explanation is that rich children have more familiarity with coins, and so are more accurate in their size estimates. Ashley et al. (1951) tested these two accounts. They hypnotised adults, and then made them think they were rich or poor. The size estimates of coins were larger when the participants were in the "poor" state. This suggests that the findings of Bruner and Goodman depended on the increased value of coins to poor children.

Deprivation

The effects of deprivation on perception have been looked at by using participants who went without either food or water for several hours. Gil-christ and Nesberg (1952) asked their participants to indicate the amount of light that an object seemed to reflect. The apparent brightness of pictures of food increased as the number of hours without food went up. The same finding was obtained for pictures of liquid for participants deprived of water.

There is a problem with this study by Gilchrist and Nesberg. Partici-pants saw a picture with a given brightness for 15 seconds, the light was then turned off for 10 seconds, and then the picture was presented again. When the picture was presented for the second time, participants had to adjust its brightness to make it the same as before. In other words there was a time delay between seeing the picture on the two occasions. As a result, the effects of deprivation on adjusted brightness may have been due to distortions in memory rather than in perception.

Perceptual defence and sensitisation

One way of studying perception is to present a word very briefly, asking the participant to identify it. If it cannot be identified, it is presented again for slightly longer. What is of interest is to find the fastest presentation time at which the participant can say what the word is. The time needed for identification of sexual or obscene words is greater than that for neutral words. This effect is known as *perceptual defence*. A few people show the opposite effect, identifying sexual or obscene words more easily than neutral words. This effect is known as *perceptual sensitisation*.

The key issue with perceptual defence is whether it is really a percep-tual effect at all. Perhaps people take longer to identify obscene words because they are reluctant to say them out loud. Dixon (1981) discussed one way of getting round this problem. People first of all learned to associate words together (e.g. rape–table; whore–tree). Then the first words in each pair were shown briefly. The participants were told not to say the word itself, but rather the word with which it had been paired. Thus, if "whore" were shown, participants would respond "tree". Studies using this approach have often found evidence for perceptual defence. In other words, identification time depends more on the kind of word presented than on what the participants have to say.

Culture

If visual perception depends on experience and expectations, then we might expect that there would be differences in perception from one culture to another. Evidence of cross-cultural differences in perception was reported by Turnbull (1961). He studied a pygmy who lived in dense forests, and so had limited experience of looking at distant objects. This pygmy was taken to an open plain, and shown a herd of buffalo a long way away. He argued that the buffalo were insects, and refused to believe that they really were buffalo. Presumably he had never learned to use the various depth cues described earlier in the way that people in other cultures do. However, this study is limited because only one person was tested, and it is possible he had never seen buffalo before.

More evidence of cross-cultural differences was reported by Annis and Frost (1973). They considered Canadian Cree Indians. Some of them lived in tepees out in the countryside, and some of them lived in cities. They argued that those who lived in cities would be exposed mainly to vertical and horizontal lines in their everyday lives, whereas those living in tepees would come across lines in all orientations. Both groups were asked to decide whether two lines were parallel. Cree Indians living in tepees were good at this task no matter what angle the lines were presented. In contrast, those living in cities did much better when the lines were horizontal or vertical than when they were at an angle. This suggests the importance of relevant experience to visual perception.

 Allport and Pettigrew (1957) made use of an illusion based on a nearly rectangular "window" fitted with horizontal and vertical bars. When this "window" revolves in a circle, it looks like a rectangular window moving backwards and forwards. Allport and Pettigrew found that people living in cultures without rectangular windows were less likely to experience the illusion. Zulus living in rural areas were less likely than Zulus living in urban areas or than Europeans to see a rectangle moving backwards and forwards.

Most adults in Western societies can easily interpret two-dimensional drawings and pictures as showing three-dimensional scenes. As would be expected, African tribes with no previous experience of such drawings find it very hard to perceive depth in them (Hudson, 1960). However, there are problems with such cross-cultural research. Deregowski et al. (1972) found that members of the Me'en tribe in Ethiopia did not respond to drawings of animals on paper, which was an unfamiliar substance for them. This might suggest that they had poor ability to make sense of two-dimensional representations. However, when the tribespeople were shown animals drawn on cloth (a familiar substance to them), they were generally able to recognise the animals correctly.

In sum, cross-cultural studies of perception suggest that perception is influenced by learning and by the experiences we have had over the years. However, it is sometimes hard to interpret cross-cultural differences in perception. For example, the failure of Me'en tribespeople to respond to animal drawings on paper could have been interpreted as meaning that two-dimensional representations had no meaning for them. As we saw, however, other findings reported by Deregowski et al. indicated that that interpretation would have been quite wrong.

Attention

There are powerful effects of attention on perception. Perception depends on attention, in the sense that we see and hear clearly only those stimuli to which we pay attention. Examples of this will be considered in the fields of hearing and vision.

When you are at a party, there are likely to be several conversations going on around you. However, it is usually possible to follow just one conversation and ignore the others. Evidence that we simply do not perceive the other conversations was obtained by Colin Cherry (1953). He carried out studies in which one auditory message had to be shadowed (i.e. repeated back out loud) at the same time as a second auditory message was played to the other ear. Very little information seemed to be extracted from the second or "non-attended" message. Listeners seldom noticed when that message was spoken in a foreign language or in reversed speech.

Cherry wanted to discover how we are able to select one conversation out of many; he called this the "cocktail party" problem. He found that people make use of various differences between the messages to select one and reject the others. These differences include differences in the sex of the speaker, in voice intensity, and in the location of the speaker. When Cherry presented two different messages in the same voice to both ears at once (thereby eliminating these differences), listeners found it very hard to separate out the two messages on the basis of meaning alone.

We have just seen the importance of selective attention to auditory perception. Selective attention is also important in the case of visual perception. Eriksen (1990) argued that visual attention is rather like a spotlight. Everything within a small area can be seen clearly, but it is much harder to see anything not falling within the beam of the spotlight. According to Eriksen's zoom-lens model, there is an attentional spotlight. However, it has an adjustable beam so that the area covered by the beam can be increased or decreased.

Support for the zoom-lens model was reported by LaBerge (1983). His participants were presented with five-letter words. They could attend either to the central letter or to the whole word depending on the task they were asked to perform.

Perceptual hypotheses

Several theorists (e.g. Bruner, 1957; Gregory, 1972) have argued that perception is influenced by *perceptual hypotheses*. These hypotheses are expectations, informed guesses, and assumptions about presented stimuli and their meaning. Thus, perception involves the combined influences of the presented stimulus and internal hypotheses, expectations, and knowledge. In other words, perception depends on information from the stimulus itself and on stored information and knowledge.

What predictions follow from this view? Perceptual hypotheses and expectations will sometimes be wrong, so it follows that there will be errors in perception. This can be shown by reading the classic phrase within the triangle below. If you did not spot anything odd about it, try reading it again!

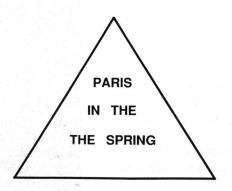

PARIS

IN THE

THE SPRING

The predicted perceptual errors have often been found in laboratory studies. However, perception is normally very accurate in everyday life. If it weren't, we would fall over objects, place our weight on surfaces that could not support it, and so on. How can we explain why it is that perception in the laboratory is much more error-prone than perception in the real world? Many laboratory studies use artificial stimuli, and these stimuli are often presented very briefly. The normal environment presents us with a much richer and more detailed source of information about visual stimuli than is often provided in the laboratory. This additional information tends to prevent errors creeping into perception.

According to hypothesis theorists, the hypotheses formed by observers represent the "best guess" in the light of the available information. However, it can be hard to persuade people to change their hypotheses. Consider, for example, Gregory's "hollow face" illusion (below). In this illusion, observers looking at a hollow mask of a face from a distance of a few feet away report seeing a normal face. Even when they know that it is a hollow face, they still report that it looks like a normal face.

Gregory's "hollow face" illusion. Photograph by Sam Grainger.

Visual perception

A good example of how perception can be influenced by expectations was provided by Bruner et al. (1951). The participants saw playing cards presented very briefly, and had to identify them. When they were shown black hearts, they tended to see them as brown hearts or purple hearts. In other words, what they saw was a mixture of what was presented (black) and what was expected (red).

Sometimes our expectations are determined by the context. For example, Palmer (1975) showed a picture of a scene (e.g. a kitchen), followed by a very brief presentation of a picture of an object. This object could be appropriate to the context (e.g. loaf), or it could be inappropriate (e.g. mailbox or drum). The object was more likely to be identified correctly when it was appropriate to the context.

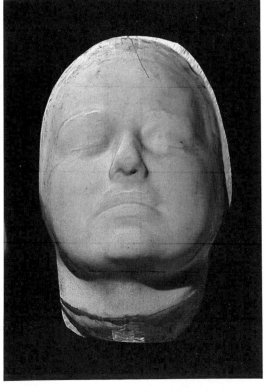

Auditory perception

Knowledge and expectations have also been found to influence auditory perception. Warren and Warren (1970) presented their participants with one of the following sentences (the asterisk refers to an omitted part of the tape):

1. It was found that the *eel was on the axle.
2. It was found that the *eel was on the shoe.
3. It was found that the *eel was on the table.
4. It was found that the *eel was on the orange.

All participants heard the same speech sound "eel", but the way it was heard was influenced by the sentence context. Those who listened to the first sentence heard "wheel", whereas those listening to sentences two, three, and four heard "heel", "meal", and "peel", respectively.

Suppose you listen to someone speaking a foreign language that you don't understand. There seems to be almost continuous speech, with the speaker hardly pausing for breath. In contrast, we hear a series of separate words when listening to someone speaking English. In fact, speech in nearly all languages consists of a continuously changing pattern of sound with relatively few periods of silence. This produces what is known as the *segmentation problem*: how do we identify individual words from continuous sound? It is clear that we make use of the context in which words are heard. Suppose, for example, you heard someone say, "God save the …" You would assume that the word you had not heard clearly was "Queen".

Evidence that context is important was obtained by Lieberman (1963). He spliced words out of spoken sentences and presented them on their own. Only about half of the words could be recognised. In contrast, nearly all of the words were recognised when they were heard in the context of a sentence.

Visual illusions

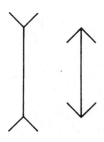

The Muller-Lyer illusion.

Visual perception is usually very accurate. However, nearly everyone makes mistakes when asked to look at what are known as *visual illusions*. These are two-dimensional drawings that most people see inaccurately. In the Muller-Lyer illusion, for example, the vertical line in the figure on the left seems longer than the vertical line in the figure on the right. In fact, they are the same length, as can be proved by using a ruler. Another popular visual illusion is the Ponzo illusion (opposite). When people are asked to compare the lengths of the two horizontal lines A and B, most of them say that the upper line is longer than the bottom one. This is incorrect, because the two lines are the same length.

Gregory (1970) explained these, and other, visual illusions by means of his "misapplied size-constancy" theory. He started with size constancy, which refers to the tendency to see an object as having the same size whether it is looked at from a short or a long distance away. Size constancy applies even though the size of the object in the retinal image becomes smaller and smaller as the object recedes into the distance. We can relate these ideas to the Ponzo illusion. The long lines on each side of the figure look like railway lines or the edges of a road receding in the distance. Thus, the top horizontal line can be seen as further away from us than the bottom horizontal line. As the two lines are the same size in the retinal image, the more distant horizontal line (the top one) must actually be longer than the nearer horizontal line.

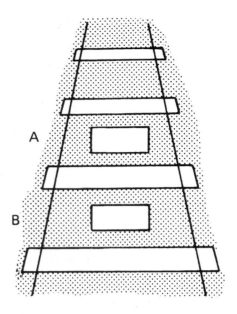

The Ponzo illusion.

The Muller-Lyer illusion can be explained in a similar way. The figure on the left is like the inside corner of a room, and the figure on the right is like the outside corner of a building. Thus, the outgoing fins represent lines approaching us, whereas the ingoing fins stand for receding lines. Thus, the vertical line on the left is in some sense further away from us and so looks longer than the vertical line on the right.

Some evidence supporting this theory was reported by Segall et al. (1963). They argued that the Muller-Lyer illusion would only be perceived by those with experience of a *"carpentered environment"* containing numerous rectangles, straight lines, and regular corners. People in Western societies live in a carpentered environment, but Zulus living in tribal communities do not. Segall et al. found that rural Zulus did not show the Muller-Lyer illusion at all, which seems to fit Gregory's theory. This finding might simply mean that rural Zulus cannot make any sense of two-dimensional drawings, but this is unlikely in view of another of Segall et al.'s findings. They studied the horizontal–vertical illusion, which involves over-estimating vertical extents relative to horizontal ones (see the figure, in which the two lines are of the same length). Rural Zulus showed the horizontal–vertical illusion to a greater extent than Europeans, presumably because of their greater familiarity with large open spaces.

Other researchers have not always been able to demonstrate the importance of living in a carpentered environment in the perception of visual illusions. Gregor and McPherson (1965) compared two groups of

Australian Aborigines. One group lived in a carpentered environment, but the other group lived in the open air in very basic housing. The two groups did not differ on either the Muller-Lyer or the horizontal–vertical illusion. Cross-cultural differences in visual illusions may depend more on training and education than on whether or not a given group lives in a carpentered environment.

Gregory argued that figures such as the Ponzo and the Muller-Lyer are treated in many ways as three-dimensional objects. Why do they seem flat and two-dimensional? According to Gregory, cues to depth are used in a rather automatic way whether or not the figures are seen to be lying on a flat surface. The fact that the Muller-Lyer figures look three-dimensional to most people when presented in the dark as glowing two-dimensional outlines supports this view.

Further reading

Eysenck, M.W. (1993). *Principles of cognitive psychology.* Hove, UK: Lawrence Erlbaum Associates Ltd. Chapter 2 deals at some length with issues relating to perception.

References

Eysenck, M.W., & Keane, M.T. (1995). *Cognitive psychology: A student's handbook* (3rd. edn.). Hove, UK: Lawrence Erlbaum Associates Ltd.

Gregory, R.L. (1970). *The intelligent eye.* New York: McGraw-Hill.

Kaufman, L., & Rock, I. (1962). The moon illusion. *Scientific American, 207,* 120–132.

Warren, R.M., & Warren, R.P. (1970). Auditory illusions and confusions. *Scientific American, 223,* 30–36.

Summary

- Perception involves a distal stimulus, a proximal stimulus, and perceptual experience.
- Sensation is basic, unorganised experience; perception is organised and three-dimensional experience.
- The Gestaltists argued that what we perceive is the simplest or most uniform organisation of perceptual information; this perceptual organisation reflects the innate properties of the perceptual system.
- The visual constancies (size constancy; shape constancy; colour constancy) permit visual perception to remain constant in spite of changes in the retinal image.
- Depth perception depends on a range of monocular cues (e.g. linear perspective; texture; interposition; shading; motion parallax) and binocular cues (convergence; accommodation; stereopsis); of the binocular cues, only stereopsis is of much use.
- Size constancy means that objects look the same size regardless of how far away they are.
- The perception of distance or depth is crucial to size constancy; when there is misleading information available about distance (e.g. Ames room; moon illusion), there are mistaken judgements of size.
- Perception is affected by motivational factors (e.g. reward; deprivation) and by emotional factors (e.g. perceptual defence; perceptual sensitisation); it is important to distinguish between their effects on perceptual responses and their effects on perception itself.
- There are numerous cross-cultural differences in perception, indicating the importance of learning; such differences are often hard to interpret in detail.
- Visual and auditory perception both depend on attentional processes, in which certain stimuli are selected rather than others.
- Hypotheses and expectations influence perception, especially when there is limited information available from the stimulus.
- According to Gregory, many visual illusions can be explained by assuming that the processes used to produce size constancy with three-dimensional objects are misapplied to two-dimensional drawings.

Key terms

Accommodation: a cue to depth associated with a thickening of the lens of the eye when looking at close objects.

Ames room: a special room with a very unusual shape that looks like an ordinary room under some viewing conditions.

Binocular cues: cues to depth that involve the use of both eyes; see **monocular cues**.

Carpentered environment: the type of environment found in Western societies, consisting of numerous rectangles, straight lines, and regular corners.

Convergence: a cue to depth provided by the eyes turning inwards more when looking at a close object than at one further away.

Distal stimulus: objects and people in the outside world; see **proximal stimulus**.

Gestaltists: German psychologists who emphasised the notion that visual perception is highly organised.

Interposition: a cue to depth in which a closer object hides part of an object that is further away.

Law of Pragnanz: the notion that perception will tend to be organised in as simple a way as possible.

Linear perspective: a strong impression of depth in a two-dimensional drawing created by lines converging on the horizon.

Monocular cues: cues to depth that only require the use of one eye; see **binocular cues**.

Moon illusion: the tendency for the moon to look larger when it is near the horizon than when it is high in the sky.

Motion parallax: a cue to depth provided by the movement of an object's image across the retina.

Muller-Lyer illusion: an illusion in which a vertical line with outgoing fins looks longer than a vertical line of the same length with ingoing fins.

Perception: it involves making sense of the information presented to our sense organs; see **sensation**.

Perceptual defence: greater difficulty in perceiving sexual or obscene stimuli than neutral ones; see **perceptual sensitisation**.

Perceptual experience: our conscious experience of the outside world in the various sense modalities (e.g. seeing; hearing).

Perceptual hypotheses: expectations or informed guesses as to what stimuli are being presented, or are about to be presented.

Perceptual sensitisation: easier perception of sexual or obscene stimuli than of neutral ones; see **perceptual defence**.

Proximal stimulus: the stimulus pattern produced at the sense organs (e.g. eye; ear) by some external stimulus; see **distal stimulus**.

Segmentation problem: the issue of hearing separate words when listening to a continuously changing pattern of sound.

Key terms (continued)

Sensation: the basic, unorganised information that our brains receive from our senses; see **perception**.

Stereopsis: a cue to depth based on the fact that objects produce slightly different images on the retinas of the two eyes.

Texture gradient: a cue to depth given by the increased rate of change in texture density as you look from the front to the back of a slanting stimulus.

Visual constancies: aspects of visual perception that remain the same in spite of variations in the **proximal stimulus** at the retina; shape, colour, and size constancy are all found.

Visual illusions: several two-dimensional drawings that are seen inaccurately by nearly everyone; the best-known is the **Muller-Lyer illusion**.

Structured essay questions

1. What are the main monocular cues to depth perception? What are the main binocular cues?
2. What did the Gestaltists say about perceptual organisation? To what extent have studies supported the Gestaltists?
3. Describe some cross-cultural studies of perception. What do they tell us about perception?
4. What are perceptual hypotheses? Describe some studies showing the effects of these hypotheses on perception.

Self-assessment questions

1. The stimulus pattern produced at the eye and the ear is known as:
   a) the distal stimulus
   b) the proximal stimulus
   c) perceptual experience
   d) sensation

2. The law of Pragnanz states that:
   a) visual elements close to each other are grouped together
   b) similar visual elements are grouped together
   c) the missing parts of a figure are filled in to complete it
   d) perception is organised in a simple and uniform fashion

3. The major binocular cues to depth are:
   a) interposition, convergence, and accommodation
   b) convergence, linear perspective, and interposition
   c) convergence, accommodation, and stereopsis
   d) none of the above

4. The moon illusion occurs because:
   a) the moon always looks the same distance away from us
   b) the moon looks further away from us when it is high in the sky
   c) the moon looks further away from us when it is near the horizon
   d) the moon changes size as it moves

5. The finding that a longer presentation time is needed to identify sexual or obscene words than neutral ones is known as:
   a) perceptual sensitisation
   b) perceptual defence

   c) modesty
   d) repression

6. Cherry found that people presented with one auditory message in a male voice and another message in a female voice at the same time:
   a) had no trouble in listening to both messages
   b) were confused, and could not follow either message
   c) could listen to one message very easily, and also follow most of the other message
   d) could listen to one message easily, but extracted very little information from the other message

7. The segmentation problem is based on:
   a) understanding how we identify individual words from continuous sound
   b) understanding why there are so many pauses in most people's speech
   c) understanding why people leave words out of the sentences they say
   d) understanding how we use context to understand speech

8. According to Gregory's misapplied size-constancy theory:
   a) two-dimensional visual illusions look three-dimensional
   b) the cues used to produce size constancy with three-dimensional objects are mistakenly used with two-dimensional visual illusions
   c) visual illusions involve size constancy
   d) visual illusions are not illusions at all

Memory 21

How important is memory to us? Just imagine if we were without it. We would not recognise anyone or anything as familiar. We would not be able to talk, read, or write, because we would remember nothing about language. Experience would have taught us nothing, and we would have the same lack of knowledge as newborn infants.

Every time that we remember something, it is as a result of previous learning. This has led many memory theorists to suggest that memory involves three stages:

- *Encoding*: the processes occurring at the time of learning.
- *Storage*: some of the information presented for learning is stored away in a long-term memory store.
- *Retrieval*: on a memory test, we try to remember or retrieve some of the information stored in long-term memory.

These three stages are closely linked together. In order for information to be retrieved, it must have been stored previously.

Your ability to retrieve or remember stored information can be tested in many ways. You could show that you remember someone you have met before by recognising their face as familiar, or you might remember or recall their name. As you may have found to your cost, it is very possible to recognise someone's face but be unable to put a name to it!

Suppose you were asked to learn a list of words such as the following: CHAIR, CATCH, TABLE, WITCH, MOUTH. Some of the ways in which your memory could be tested are as follows:

- *Free recall*: you would be asked write down as many of the words as you could remember in any order.
- *Cued recall*: you might be given the first few letters of each word, and asked to think of the appropriate list word (e.g. CHA ... ; CAT ...).

Personal viewpoint

In your everyday life, you probably find that your memory for some things is very good, whereas you find it very hard to remember other things. Why do you think this is? More generally, what do you think is the best way to learn information so that you will be able to remember it later? It is very important for eyewitnesses to a crime to remember what happened in detail. However, their memories of the crime are often limited and inaccurate. Why do you think eyewitness testimony tends to be so poor?

- *Recognition*: you might be given the list words as well as other, non-list words (e.g. CHAIR, SHELF, ELBOW, MOUTH, WITCH, FRAME, TABLE, CATCH, PHOTO, WRITE), and asked to select the words that came from the list.

Short-term versus long-term memory

Many psychologists have distinguished between a *short-term memory store* and a *long-term memory store*. Short-term memory is rather fragile and short-lived, and is used when we try to remember a telephone number for a few seconds or when we follow someone else's conversation. Long-term memory is less fragile. It is used when we remember our own telephone number or when we look back at the events of the day.

Richard Atkinson and Richard Shiffrin (1968) used the distinction between short-term and long-term memory stores to develop the *multi-store model* of memory. They argued that information is initially received by sensory registers or modality-specific stores. Each of the senses (e.g. seeing, touch, taste) can be regarded as a separate "modality". Visual stimuli go to a special visual store (the iconic store), auditory stimuli go to a special auditory store (the echoic store), and so on for each of the senses. Information in these stores lasts for short periods of time—up to a second or two. Some of the information from the modality-specific stores is attended to and receives further processing in the short-term store. Any information in the modality-specific stores that is not selected in this way simply decays rapidly.

Short-term memory store

The short-term store has a very limited capacity of not more than about six or seven items, and the information in the store is in a fragile state. These two characteristics of limited capacity and fragility are clearly apparent if you think of remembering a phone number while you dial it. It is very difficult to remember long phone numbers, and the slightest distraction can cause you to forget the number completely.

The capacity of the short-term memory store is approximately seven items. What is an item? According to George Miller (1956), an item is a *chunk*, with each chunk consisting of a familiar unit of information based on previous learning. Thus, for example, IBM is one chunk for those who have heard of the company called International Business Machines, but it is three chunks for those who have not. In general terms, the evidence tends to support Miller's position.

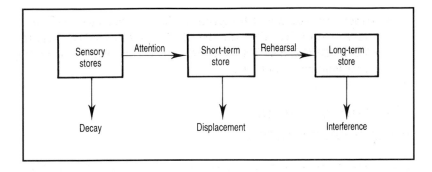

The multi-store model of memory developed by Atkinson and Shiffrin.

Information goes from the short-term store to the long-term store through a process of rehearsal. Suppose you were asked to learn a list of words, then you might try saying them over and over to yourself (i.e. rehearsing them). According to the theory, this would lead to good long-term memory.

Long-term memory store

The long-term store differs from the short-term store in that it has essentially unlimited capacity. According to Atkinson and Shiffrin, nearly all forgetting from long-term memory is due to an inability to find the appropriate memory trace rather than to the disappearance of the trace from the memory system.

Experimental evidence

Attention. According to multi-store theory, it is necessary to attend to an event within the short-term store in order to remember it later. Much of the evidence supports this viewpoint. Moray (1959) presented two auditory messages over headphones to his participants, with one message being presented to each ear. The participants were told to pay attention to one message and to repeat it back out loud as it was being presented; this is known as shadowing. Various words were presented to the other, unattended ear. There was practically no memory for words presented to the unattended ear, even though some of them were presented 35 times each.

We can get some idea what happens to unattended information by considering sleep learning. We do not attend to the external environment in the same way when we are asleep as we do when we are awake. It has often been claimed that sleep learning is an effective way of acquiring knowledge. However, in most of the studies supporting that conclusion there was no attempt to check whether the learners were actually asleep all the time that learning was taking place. There is usually little or no evidence for sleep learning when steps are taken to ensure that the learners are sleeping during the learning period. Bruce et al. (1970) presented information to people who were asleep, and then woke them up almost at once for testing. There was an almost total inability to remember the information presented during sleep.

Short-term vs long-term memory.   Good evidence for the distinction between short-term and long-term memory was obtained by Glanzer and Cunitz (1966). They presented lists of words, and after each list they asked their participants for free recall. They discovered that the last few words in the list were much better remembered than those from the middle of the list, and they called this the *recency effect*. According to Glanzer and Cunitz, words in the recency effect were being recalled from short-term memory, whereas the earlier words in the list were being recalled from long-term memory. What would happen if recall were delayed for 10 or 30 seconds while the participants counted backwards? Because information in short-term memory is much more fragile than information in long-term memory, it was predicted that the delay should eliminate the recency effect (which depends on short-term memory). However, it should have little or no effect on recall from the rest of the list. That is precisely what happened.

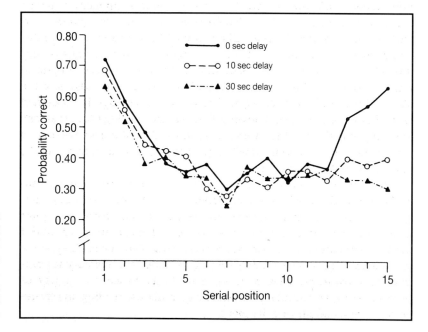

Free recall as a function of serial position and duration of the delay task. (Adapted from Glanzer and Cunitz, 1966.)

Some of the best evidence that there are separate short-term and long-term stores comes from work on brain-damaged patients. The logic of this work is as follows. Suppose there is only one memory system covering both short-term and long-term memory. Patients with brain damage to this system would show poor short-term and long-term memory. Suppose, on the other hand, there are two memory systems, one for short-term memory and one for long-term memory. We might then expect some patients to suffer damage to only one system. That would mean that some patients would have poor short-term memory and normal long-term memory, whereas other patients would have normal short-term memory and poor long-term memory.

Most brain-damaged patients with memory problems suffer from what is known as the *amnesic syndrome*. These patients have normal short-term memory, but their long-term memory is severely disrupted. For example, they will re-read the daily newspaper without realising that they read it a short time ago, or they will fail to recognise someone they met recently.

There are a few brain-damaged patients who show the opposite pattern to amnesic patients. For example, Shallice and Warrington (1974) studied a patient, EF, who had very poor short-term memory but essentially normal long-term memory.

Long-term memory.   Long-term memory contains a huge amount of information. We know what we did yesterday, what happened on our last summer holiday, that 2 + 2 = 4, that Leonardo da Vinci was a painter, and we know how to ride a bicycle. Atkinson and Shiffrin claimed that all this knowledge was contained in the same long-term store, but this is very unlikely. Cohen and Squire (1980) argued that there are two long-term memory systems. One is concerned with *declarative knowledge* and the other with *procedural knowledge*. Declarative knowledge is concerned with "knowing that" (e.g. knowing that we had porridge for breakfast; knowing that Paris is the capital of France). Procedural knowledge is concerned with "knowing how" (e.g. knowing how to ride a bicycle; knowing how to play a piano).

The strongest evidence for the division of long-term memory into declarative and procedural systems comes from the study of brain-damaged patients. Patients with the amnesic syndrome have very poor long-term memory for declarative knowledge. For example, they find it hard to remember that certain words were presented in a list they saw a few minutes ago. However, they show good long-term memory for procedural knowledge. They have normal ability to learn a variety of procedural skills, including dressmaking, billiards, reading mirror-reversed script, and playing the piano.

Levels-of-processing theory

Some psychologists have argued against the whole notion that human memory should be divided up into stores. Among the most influential of these psychologists were Gus Craik and Robert Lockhart. They put forward their *levels-of-processing theory* in 1972. According to this theory:

- Long-term memory depends on the processes that occur at the time of learning.
- If meaning is processed at learning, then long-term memory will be better than if meaning is not processed.
- In their terms, processing of meaning = deep processing; a failure to process meaning = shallow processing.

The basic idea in levels-of-processing theory is that we tend to remember things that are meaningful to us. As you have probably found in your studies, it is important to understand fully the meaning of what you are reading if you are going to be able to remember it later. This idea was tested by Hyde and Jenkins (1973). They gave a list of words to all of their participants. Some participants were given a task to do that involved processing the meaning of the words (e.g. rating the words for pleasantness; rating the frequency of usage). Other participants carried out a task that did not involve processing meaning (e.g. counting the numbers of "e"s and "g"s in each word; deciding whether the words fitted sentence frames). After that, participants were asked to provide free recall of the list words. Those participants who had processed the meaning of the words recalled far more words than those who had not.

Intention to learn

Most people feel that we are more likely to remember something if we deliberately try to learn it. Hyde and Jenkins (1973) looked at this issue. Some of their participants were not told that there would be a test of memory (incidental learning), whereas others were told to try to remember the words for a later test (intentional learning). There was no difference in the memory performance of the incidental and intentional learners. This fits in with levels-of-processing theory. Memory is determined by the nature of the processing that occurs at the time of learning rather than by the presence or absence of intention to learn the material.

Rehearsal

There is an important difference between levels-of-processing theory and the multi-store theory in terms of the role of rehearsal. According to multi-store theory, all rehearsal leads to improved long-term memory. According to levels-of-processing theory, there are two kinds of rehearsal.

One kind of rehearsal involves simply repeating a word over and over again, and is known as maintenance rehearsal. The other kind of rehearsal involves deeper processing of the material that is to be learned, and is known as elaborative rehearsal. It was claimed by Craik and Lockhart that elaborative rehearsal benefits long-term memory, but maintenance rehearsal does not.

The notion that there is a form of rehearsal that does not lead to improved long-term memory is at odds with the multi-store theory. However, it makes some sense. If someone asked you to remember a string of words in a language you didn't know—say, Swedish—you would probably not remember the words a few hours later no matter how many times you had muttered them over to yourself.

The evidence provides some comfort for both multi-store and levels-of-processing theorists. As the multi-store theory predicts, maintenance rehearsal usually leads to improved long-term memory. However, as the levels-of-processing theory predicts, maintenance rehearsal improves memory much less than does elaborative rehearsal.

Memory for sentences

You may have noticed that most of the research has involved lists of words. Does levels-of-processing theory also apply to sentences and connected prose? A prediction that follows from the theory is that there should be better long-term memory for the meaning of sentences than for their wording. Good support for this prediction was obtained by Johnson-Laird and Stevenson (1970). They presented sentences such as "John liked the painting and bought it from the duchess." On a recognition-memory test (i.e. when given a selection of different sentences to choose from) shortly afterwards, participants very often mistakenly claimed that they had heard the following sentence: "The painting pleased John and the duchess sold it to him." In other words, the participants had remembered only the meaning of the original sentence.

With connected prose, other factors come into play. What is remembered from connected prose tends to be information about the central theme or themes of the passage, with the minor details being forgotten. Gomulicki (1956) showed this in an interesting study. One group of participants wrote an abstract or summary of a story that was placed in front of them, and a second group recalled the story from memory. A third group of participants was then given the abstracts and the recalls. They were largely unable to tell the difference. This indicates that story memory is like an abstract, in that people focus on the most important information.

Memory for pictures

We have seen that there is good evidence that long-term memory is generally better when meaning has been processed than when it has not. However, long-term memory also depends on the kinds of stimuli that are being processed. For example, pictures are often much better remembered than words. Standing et al. (1970) presented 2560 pictures to participants over a number of days. In spite of the huge number of pictures presented, the participants were able to recognise about 90% of them on a test of recognition memory.

Why are pictures better remembered than words? According to Paivio (1971), pictures and words can both be processed in terms of their meaning, but pictures have the advantage that they can more easily be processed as images as well. This means that more information is stored about pictures than about words.

Elaboration and distinctiveness

Although depth of processing (or processing of meaning) is important, it became clear to Craik and Lockhart that there are other aspects of processing that influence long-term memory. One such aspect is *elaboration*, which refers to the amount of information that is processed. If one person sees the word "clock" and thinks of the different materials and colours that clocks can be made of, and of specific clocks he or she knows, and of the dictionary definition of "clock", whereas a second person sees the same word but thinks only of its definition, then both people have engaged in deep processing. The first person has processed the word in a much more elaborate or extensive fashion, however, and will thus be more likely to remember the word later.

Evidence for the importance of elaboration was reported by Craik and Tulving (1975). They asked their participants to decide whether words fitted into sentences containing a blank. Some of the sentences were elaborate (e.g. "The great bird swooped down and carried off the struggling ..."), whereas others were not (e.g. "She cooked the ..."). Elaboration was important to memory. The words associated with elaborate sentences were twice as likely to be recalled as those associated with non-elaborate sentences.

It has also been found that memory traces that are high in *distinctiveness* (i.e. unique in some way) are better remembered than those that are not distinctive. A distinctive event, such as a natural disaster, is easy to remember, because it stands out from our everyday memories.

Evidence for the importance of distinctiveness was reported by Eysenck and Eysenck (1980). They presented words having irregular pronunciation (e.g. "comb" in which the "b" is not sounded). They found that the task of simply saying each list word (a shallow task) led to poor recognition memory. Other participants were told to say each word as if it had regular pronunciation (e.g. sounding the "b" in "comb"; making "glove" rhyme with "cove"). This task produced distinctive memory traces, and led to a much higher level of recognition-memory performance.

Conditions of retrieval

According to levels-of-processing theory, deep processing will always lead to better long-term memory than shallow processing. This was disproved by Morris, Bransford, and Franks (1977). They argued that different kinds of processing lead learners to store different kinds of information about a stimulus in memory. Later memory performance depends upon the *relevance* of that information to the kind of memory test that is used. Participants had to process words in terms of their meaning or in terms of their sound. Some of them were tested by a rhyming recognition test. On this test, participants had to select words that rhymed with list words, with the list words themselves not being presented. For example, if the word "whip" was on the rhyming test and the word "ship" had been in the list, participants should have selected it because it rhymed with a list word.

Morris et al. found that recognition memory was much better for words that had been processed in terms of their sound than for those that had been processed for meaning. This disproves the prediction of levels-of-processing theory that deep processing is always better than shallow processing. The reason is that processing the meaning of the list words was of little help when the memory test required the identification of words rhyming with list words. The information acquired from the shallow rhyme task was far more relevant, and so memory performance was higher in this condition.

Proactive and retroactive interference.

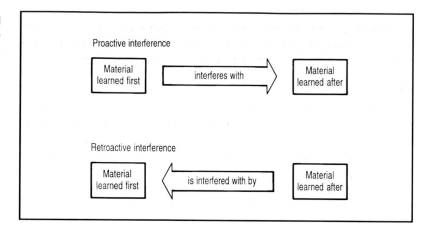

Suppose, for example, that you learn French first and then German. You will then have learned two different foreign words to refer to each English word (e.g. "the boat" is *le bateau* or *das Schiff*). Learning German might interfere with your memory for French via retroactive interference. On the other hand, your knowledge of French might disrupt your memory for German via proactive interference.

The notion that interference is important in forgetting can be traced to the nineteenth century, and to a German psychologist called Hugo Munsterberg. Men had pocket-watches in those days, and Munsterberg kept his watch in one particular pocket. When he started to keep it in a different pocket, he found that he was often fumbling around in confusion when asked for the time.

This story shows the key features of what later became known as *interference theory*. Munsterberg had learned an association between the stimulus, "What time is it?", and the response of removing the watch from his pocket. Later on, the stimulus remained the same, but a different response was now associated with it. As a general rule of thumb, both proactive and retroactive

---

What are the advantages and disadvantages of interference theory?

PLUS
- There is strong evidence that forgetting is sometimes due to proactive and retroactive interference.

MINUS
- Interference theory tells us little about the processes of remembering and forgetting.
- Interference occurs most strongly when the same stimulus is paired with two different responses; this happens rarely in everyday life.

interference are greatest when two different responses have been associated with the same stimulus, intermediate when two similar stimuli are involved, and least when two quite different stimuli are involved.

Repression

One of the best known theories of forgetting was put forward by Sigmund Freud. He argued that much forgetting occurs as a result of *repression*, by which he meant motivated forgetting. For example, those who have suffered sexual abuse when young may be highly motivated to forget or repress the terrible experiences they have had.

Freud claimed that repressed memories are strongly associated with anxiety, guilt, or other negative emotions. It would be unethical to create these emotional states in the laboratory, and so we must rely on studies of repressed memories in the real world. There are numerous reports of repressed memories. For example, Herman and Schatzow (1987) found that 28% of a group of female incest victims reported severe memory deficits from childhood. Such repressed memories were most common among women who had suffered violent abuse.

The main problem is to check the accuracy of these repressed memories, because there is usually no concrete evidence to support them. However, Brewin et al. (1993) argued that repressed memories are likely to be accurate provided that individuals are asked about *specific* personal memories. More general repressed memories or judgements about childhood experiences are often inaccurate.

Eyewitness testimony

When a crime is committed, the criminal often leaves crucial clues behind. Sometimes these clues prove his or her guilt (e.g. fingerprints), but more frequently they are less useful. For example, one or more eyewitnesses may have seen the crime taking place, and their accounts of what happened may form a major part of the prosecution's case. Unfortunately, however, juries are sometimes too inclined to trust eyewitness testimony (evidence). This has led to thousands of innocent people being sent to prison solely on the basis of eyewitness accounts.

Psychologists have investigated the factors that can make eyewitness testimony inaccurate. There are two major kinds of factors:

1. The eyewitness may have failed to attend closely to the crime and/or the criminal.
2. The memory of the eyewitness may have become distorted after the crime has been committed.

It may seem likely that the main reason why eyewitnesses remember inaccurately is because of inattention. However, as we will see, eyewitness memories are fragile and can easily be influenced by later events.

Fragility of memory

Loftus and Palmer (1974) showed participants a film of a multiple car accident. After looking at the film, the participants were asked to describe what had happened in their own words. Then they answered a number of specific questions. Some of the participants were asked, "About how fast were the cars going when they smashed into each other?", whereas for other participants the verb "hit" replaced "smashed into". The estimated speed was influenced by the verb used in the question, averaging 10.5 mph when the verb "smashed" was used versus 8.0 mph when "hit" was used. Thus, the wording of the question influenced the way in which the multiple car accident was remembered.

One week later, all the participants were asked the following question: "Did you see any broken glass?". In spite of the fact that there was actually no broken glass in the incident, 32% of those who had been asked before about speed using the verb "smashed" said they saw broken glass. In contrast, only 14% of those asked using the verb "hit" said they saw broken glass. Thus, our memory for events is rather fragile and can easily be distorted.

Leading questions

Lawyers in most countries are not allowed to ask leading questions which suggest the desired answer (e.g. "When did you stop beating your wife?"). However, detectives and other people who question eyewitnesses shortly after an incident sometimes ask leading questions in their attempts to find out what happened. The effects that this can have on eyewitnesses' memory were shown by Loftus and Zanni (1975). They showed people a short film of a car accident, and then asked them various questions about it. Some of the eyewitnesses were asked the leading question, "Did you see the broken headlight?", which suggests that there was a broken headlight. Other eyewitnesses were asked the neutral question, "Did you see a broken headlight?". Even though there was actually no broken headlight, 17% of those asked the leading question said they had seen it, against only 7% of those asked the neutral question.

Hypnosis

Police forces in several countries make use of hypnosis with eyewitnesses in order to improve their memory. Problems with the use of hypnosis were found by Putnam (1979). He showed his participants a videotape in which a car and a bicycle were involved in an accident. Those who were questioned about the accident under hypnosis made more errors in their answers than did those who responded in the normal state.

Hypnosis makes people less cautious in reporting their memories than they are normally. This lack of caution can lead to the recovery of "lost" memories. However, it also produces many inaccurate memories. For example, hypnotised people will often "recall" events from the future with great confidence!

Confirmation bias

Eyewitness memory can also be distorted through what is known as *confirmation bias*. This bias occurs when what is remembered of an event fits the individual's expectations rather than what really happened. For example, students from two universities in the United States (Princeton and Dartmouth) were shown a film of a football game involving both universities. The students showed a strong tendency to report that their opponents had committed many more fouls than their own team.

Violence

Loftus and Burns (1982) found evidence that the memory of an eyewitness is worse when a crime is violent than when it is not. They showed their participants two filmed versions of a crime. In the violent version, a young boy was shot in the face near the end of the film as the robbers were making their getaway. Inclusion of the violent incident reduced memory for details presented up to two minutes earlier. The memory-reducing effects of violence would probably be even greater in the case of a real-life crime, because the presence of violent criminals might endanger the life of the eyewitness.

Conclusions

There are various reasons why the evidence given by eyewitnesses can be inaccurate. Of particular importance is the fact that an eyewitness's memory for a crime or accident is fragile. It can easily be distorted by questions that convey misleading ideas about what happened.

Further reading

Eysenck, M.W. (1993). *Principles of cognitive psychology*. Hove, UK: Lawrence Erlbaum Associates Ltd. There is a more detailed account of human memory in Chapter 4.

Cohen, G. (1989). *Memory in the real world*. Hove, UK: Lawrence Erlbaum Associates Ltd. Some of the main ways in which everyday memory has been studied are discussed in this book.

References

Atkinson, R.C., & Shiffrin, R.M. (1968). Human memory: A proposed system and its control processes. In K.W. Spence & J.T. Spence (Eds.), *The psychology of learning and motivation* (Vol. 2). London: Academic Press.

Craik, F.I.M., & Lockhart, R.S. (1972). Levels of processing: A framework for memory research. *Journal of Verbal Learning and Verbal Behavior, 11,* 671–684.

Loftus, E.F., & Palmer, J.C. (1974). Reconstruction of automobile destruction: An example of the interaction between language and memory. *Journal of Verbal Learning and Verbal Behavior, 13,* 585–589.

Mandler, G. (1967). Organisation and memory., In K.W. Spence & J.T. Spence (Eds.), *The psychology of learning and motivation: Advances in research and theory* (Vol. 1). London: Academic Press.

Tulving, E. (1974). Cue-dependent forgetting. *American Scientist, 62,* 74–82.

Summary

- Memory involves three stages: encoding; storage; and retrieval.
- Memory tests include free recall, cued recall, and recognition.
- There is an important distinction in the multi-store model between a short-term store and a long-term store.
- Information enters the short-term store through attention, and it goes from the short-term store to the long-term store through rehearsal.
- Instead of a single long-term store, there are separate declarative and procedural memory systems.
- According to levels-of-processing theory, processing of meaning (deep processing) leads to good long-term memory; other factors leading to good long-term memory are elaboration (amount of processing) and distinctiveness (uniqueness of processing).
- Within levels-of-processing theory, maintenance rehearsal does not improve long-term memory, but elaborative rehearsal does improve it.
- The nature of the memory test influences memory performance more than is assumed within levels-of-processing theory.
- Experimenter-imposed organisation and subject-based organisation both lead to good long-term memory.
- Forgetting can be trace-dependent or cue-dependent.
- Proactive interference occurs when previous learning disrupts later learning and memory; retroactive interference occurs when later learning disrupts memory for earlier learning.
- Freud argued that very distressing experiences lead to repression or motivated forgetting.
- Eyewitness testimony is often inaccurate because memories of the event are distorted by information presented later (e.g. leading questions).
- Hypnosis can increase what eyewitnesses can remember; however, it makes them less cautious and more likely to produce inaccurate memories.
- The memory of eyewitnesses is reduced if they observe a violent crime, and their memory can be distorted by confirmation bias (remembering what was expected rather than what actually happened).

Key terms

Amnesic syndrome: a condition in which brain-damaged patients have normal short-term but poor long-term memory.

Categorical clustering: the tendency in **free recall** to produce words on a category-by-category basis.

Chunk: a familiar unit of information.

Confirmation bias: a distortion of memory in which what is remembered is what was expected rather than what actually happened.

Cue-dependent forgetting: forgetting in which the required information is in the **long-term memory store**, but cannot be retrieved without a suitable retrieval cue; see **trace-dependent forgetting**.

Cued recall: a form of memory test in which cues or clues are given to assist remembering; the first few letters of words can be used as cues.

Declarative knowledge: part of long-term memory concerned with general knowledge and personal experiences.

Distinctiveness: the extent to which information is processed in an unusual or unique fashion.

Elaboration: the amount or extent of processing of any given kind.

Encoding: processes involved in learning.

Free recall: a form of memory test in which words from a list are to be remembered in any order.

Levels-of-processing theory: an approach put forward by Craik and Lockhart, according to which meaning must be processed for good long-term memory.

Long-term memory store: a part of the memory system having essentially

unlimited capacity, in which information is stored for long periods of time.

Multi-store model: a theory in which it is assumed that there are separate memory stores; **short- and long-term.**

Proactive interference: disruption occurring when previous learning interferes with later learning and memory; see **retroactive interference**.

Procedural knowledge: part of long-term memory concerned with motor skills (e.g. playing the piano).

Recency effect: good free recall from the end of a list; it is assumed that the words in the recency effect are in the **short-term memory store**.

Recognition: a form of memory test in which decisions have to be made as to whether the items on the test were presented before.

Repression: a term used by Freud to refer to motivated forgetting; it often involves very stressful experiences.

Retrieval: the processes involved in remembering or gaining access to information stored in long-term memory.

Retroactive interference: disruption occurring when later learning disrupts memory for earlier learning; see **proactive interference**.

Short-term memory store: a part of the memory system having very limited capacity, and in which information is fragile and easily forgotten.

Storage: placing information in long-term memory.

Trace-dependent forgetting: the required information has been lost from the **long-term memory store**.

Structured essay questions

1. Describe the short-term and long-term memory stores. What evidence supports that distinction?
2. Describe the levels-of-processing theory. What evidence supports it? What evidence does not support it?

3. Describe the interference theory of forgetting. What factors other than interference cause forgetting?

Self-assessment questions

1. The short-term memory store has a capacity of about:
   a) four letters
   b) four chunks
   c) seven chunks
   d) seven letters

2. The words in the recency effect are:
   a) in the short-term memory store
   b) in the long-term memory store
   c) in both the short-term and long-term memory stores
   d) remembered for a long time

3. According to levels-of-processing theory:
   a) short-term memory is better if meaning is processed at learning
   b) long-term memory is better if meaning is processed at learning
   c) short-term memory is worse if meaning is processed at learning
   d) long-term memory is worse if meaning is processing at learning

4. According to levels-of-processing theory:
   a) maintenance rehearsal and elaborative rehearsal both benefit long-term memory
   b) neither maintenance rehearsal nor elaborative rehearsal benefits long-term memory
   c) maintenance rehearsal benefits long-term memory, but elaborative rehearsal does not
   d) elaborative rehearsal benefits long-term memory, but maintenance rehearsal does not

5. The tendency to recall a categorised word list category by category is known as:
   a) subject-based organisation
   b) categorical clustering
   c) deep processing
   d) organisation in memory

6. Which of the following statements is true?
   a) proactive and retroactive interference are greatest when two different stimuli have been associated with each response
   b) proactive and retroactive interference are greatest when two different stimuli have been associated with different responses
   c) proactive interference is greatest when two different responses have been associated with the same stimulus, but the opposite is the case for retroactive interference
   d) proactive and retroactive interference are greatest when two different responses have been associated with the same stimulus

7. When hypnosis is used with eyewitnesses:
   a) they become less cautious in reporting their memories than they are normally
   b) they become more cautious in reporting their memories than they are normally
   c) they do not become more or less cautious in reporting their memories than they are normally
   d) their memories become much better than usual

Problem-solving and creativity 22

Problems come in many different shapes and sizes. Some problems are fairly trivial and short-term (e.g. how am I going to solve this crossword puzzle?), whereas others are important and long-term (e.g. how am I going to pass my psychology exam?). What, if anything, do all attempts at problem-solving have in common? According to Anderson (1980), problem-solving generally possesses the following three features:

- The individual is goal-directed, in the sense of trying to reach a desired end state.
- Reaching the goal or solution requires various mental processes rather than just one; putting your foot on the brake when you see a red light is goal-directed behaviour, but does not usually involve thinking.
- The mental processes involved do not occur automatically and without thought; this feature needs to be included to eliminate routine sequences of behaviour such as dealing a pack of cards.

The first proper attempt to study problem-solving was by Thorndike (1898). A cat was placed in a puzzle box, from which it could escape only by making an arbitrary response such as clawing at a loop of string. The cat seemed to behave in a rather stupid way, squeezing against the bars, running around the box, jumping on things, and so on. The cat finally made the right response by accident. After that, it gradually became faster at making its escape. According to Thorndike, there is *trial-and-error learning*, with the animal acting in a random way until one response proves successful.

German psychologists known as the *Gestaltists* adopted a very different viewpoint in the early years of the twentieth century. They argued that solving a problem requires *restructuring* or reorganising the problem situation. This restruc-

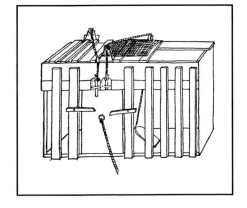

Thorndike's puzzle box.

turing usually involves a flash of *insight* or sudden understanding. Various examples of insight were provided by Wolfgang Kohler (1925), a German psychologist who spent much time during the First World War studying the thinking of apes on the island of Tenerife. In one study, none of the sticks in an ape's cage was long enough for the ape to use it to reach and pull in a banana. The ape spent some time thinking what to do. He then seemed to have a flash of insight. He leapt up and joined two sticks together, using this elongated stick to obtain the banana.

Thorndike regarded problem-solving (at least in animals) as a very slow and difficult business. In contrast, the Gestaltists argued that problem-solving could be very fast and efficient when insight occurred. Who was right? In fact, both theoretical approaches are rather misguided. Thinking and problem-solving usually involve more purpose and direction than Thorndike admitted, and insight happens more rarely than the Gestaltists imagined.

Some of the differences between the two theories can be accounted for by the tasks used by Thorndike and by the Gestaltists. Thorndike's puzzle box did not really allow insight to occur, whereas in Kohler's task there was a meaningful relationship between the animal's responses and their impact on the problem.

Past experience and problem solving

Suppose that you are trying to solve a difficult problem in mathematics. What you probably find yourself doing is thinking back to other, similar problems you have been faced with in the past. This is usually effective, because the experience and knowledge we have gained from the past are of great value in most situations. The useful effects of past experience are known technically as *positive transfer effect*. However, people often possess relevant knowledge, but fail to apply it to a current problem.

Positive transfer effect

One of the clearest examples of positive transfer effect comes from the study of expertise or special skill. Experts in a given area tend to be more naturally gifted than non-experts. However, much of their expertise stems from a vast amount of relevant past experience and knowledge.

Expertise has been studied with respect to the game of chess. The search for the secret of chess-playing expertise was begun by de Groot (1966). He asked grandmasters and expert players to think aloud when choosing their moves. You might imagine that grandmasters would con-

Personal viewpoint

You probably spend much of your time trying to solve problems. Some of the problems are related to your studies, whereas others are to do with your personal life. How useful do you think past experience is when it comes to problem-solving? Creativity is regarded as a very valuable ability, but there is some controversy as to whether it is similar to intelligence. What do you think?

sider more possible moves than the expert players, or that they would think through the possible results of making each of these moves in more detail. However, the two groups did not differ in either respect.

De Groot (1966) then tested the idea that grandmasters may have an advantage because they have more board positions stored in long-term memory. He presented board positions from actual games for five seconds, and then asked chess players to reconstruct them from memory. Grandmasters had a 91% success rate, whereas less expert players were correct only 41% of the time. However, the two groups did not differ in their ability to reconstruct board positions when the pieces were arranged randomly. This indicates that grandmasters do not simply have very good memories. They have a wealth of information about chess positions stored in memory, and they can relate actual board positions to this knowledge.

Studies such as the one by de Groot suggest that grandmasters have somewhere between 10,000 and 100,000 chess patterns stored in long-term memory. However, chess expertise does not consist only of storing lots of chess positions in memory, just as it is not the case that learning all of the words in the dictionary would allow us to write like Shakespeare. Holding and Reynolds (1982) repeated the finding of de Groot that better players do not differ from inferior ones in their ability to reconstruct random board positions. This indicated that the better players had no relevant chess patterns stored in memory. In spite of this, the better players suggested better moves than the inferior ones when asked to decide on the best move to make from these random board positions. Thus, expert players have superior strategic skills as well as more knowledge of chess positions.

Analogical problem-solving

One way in which we use the past to help current problem-solving is by drawing an analogy or comparison between the current problem and some other situation. For example, you may find it easier to understand the game of baseball if you realise that it is analogous or similar to the English game of rounders. We now consider the factors determining when people will make use of analogies.

Gick and Holyoak (1980) used the radiation problem. A doctor wants to destroy a tumour using rays. The problem is that a ray strong enough to destroy the tumour would also destroy the healthy tissue, but a ray that was not strong enough to harm healthy tissue would be too weak to destroy the tumour. Only about 10% of the participants solved the problem without assistance. The answer is to direct several low-intensity rays at the tumour from different directions, so that there is high intensity only at the tumour.

Other participants were given three stories to memorise, one of which was related to the radiation problem (it was about a general capturing a fortress by advancing along several different roads). When the participants were told that one of the three stories might be relevant to solving the radiation problem, 92% of the participants solved it. However, when the hint was not offered, those given the stories to memorise did no better on the radiation problem than those given no stories. Thus, the fact that a relevant analogy is stored in long-term memory does not ensure that it will be used.

The main reason why participants did not immediately link the story about the general capturing the fortress with the radiation problem is because the subject matter is so different in the two cases. Keane (1987) tested this idea. Some participants were given a story that was very close in content to the radiation problem (about a surgeon using rays on a cancer), whereas others received a story having moderate similarity in content (about a general using rays to destroy a missile), and still others were given the story about the general capturing the fortress. Of those given the story about the surgeon, 88% realised its relevance to the radiation problem, compared to only 12% of those given the story about the general capturing the fortress. About half of those given the story about the general using rays to destroy a missile made use of it when solving the radiation problem.

Negative transfer effect

In spite of the fact that past experience is usually helpful, there are several situations in which it actually disrupts problem-solving. The term *negative transfer effect* is used to describe such situations. An example of how past experience can limit our thinking is the well-known nine-dot problem. The task is to join up all the dots with four connected straight lines without lifting your pen from the paper. The problem can only be solved by going outside the square formed by the dots, but very few people do this. It seems that past experience leads us to assume that all of the lines should be within the square.

Functional fixedness.   A classic study on the negative transfer effect was carried out by Duncker (1945). The task was to mount a candle on a vertical screen. Various objects were spread around, including a box full of nails and a book of matches. The solution involved using the box as a platform for the candle, but only a few of the participants found the correct answer. Their past experience led them to regard the box as a container rather than a platform. Their performance was better when the box was empty rather than full of tacks—the latter set-up emphasised the container-like quality of the box.

Duncker's study involved a phenomenon known as *functional fixedness*. This is the tendency to think that objects can only be used for a narrow range of functions on the basis of how they have been used in the past. However, a limitation with Duncker's study is that we really do not know in detail about the participants' relevant past experience. In particular, we do not know the ways in which they had used boxes in the past.

Mental set.   A better approach is to supply the participants with the relevant past experience during the experiment, and then to see what the effects are on later performance. This was done in a famous series of studies by Luchins (1942). He used water-jar problems involving three jars holding different amounts of water. The participant's task was to imagine pouring water from one jar to another in order to finish up with a specified amount of water in one of the jars.

The most striking finding obtained by Luchins can be shown by considering one of his studies in detail. One of the problems was as follows: Jar A can hold 28 quarts of water, Jar B 76 quarts, and Jar C 3 quarts. The task is to end up with exactly 25 quarts in one of the jars. The solution is easy: Jar A is filled, and then Jar C is filled from it, leaving 25 quarts in Jar A. Ninety-five percent of participants who had been given similar problems before solved it. However, the situation was quite different for those participants who had been trained on problems having complex three-jar solutions. Only 36% of them were able to solve the simple problem.

What is going on here? According to Luchins, the participants in his experiments developed a *mental set*, or way of approaching the problems, which led them to think in a rather blinkered way. In his own words, "Einstellung [mental set] … creates a mechanised state of mind, a blind attitude towards problems; one does not look at the problem on its own merits but is led by a mechanical application of a used method".

Levine (1971) increased our understanding of how mental set can disrupt problem-solving. He presented a series of cards, each bearing the letters A and B. One letter was on the left and the other was on the right. On each trial, the participant said "A" or "B", and the experimenter said whether this was correct. For the first few problems, the experimenter explained that the solution involved a position sequence (e.g. the letter on the left should be selected on the first card, the letter on the right on the second card, and so on alternately). According to Levine, these problems led the participants to predict that the solution to all the problems would involve a position sequence.

Suppose that participants are given several problems involving position sequences, and then a very simple problem not involving a position sequence. The number of possible position sequences is very large, and so Levine predicted that the participants would find it hard to solve the simple problem. That is exactly what he found. The simple problem he used was one in which saying "A" was always correct and saying "B" was always incorrect. About 80% of university students failed to solve this problem within 100 trials when it followed a number of position-sequence problems. The reason was that the participants kept on assuming that the answer must be some kind of position sequence.

Evaluation

It is usual for textbooks to emphasise the difficulties that result from making inappropriate use of past experience. It is true, of course, that our thinking is sometimes disrupted in this way. However, the best way of tackling a new problem is usually to make use of our previous experience with similar problems. The fact that adults can solve most problems far more rapidly than children provides striking evidence of the usefulness of past experience, as does the fact that stored knowledge is an important factor in expertise. In other words, although past experience sometimes interferes with problem-solving, it generally has a helpful effect.

The computational approach

Allen Newell and Herb Simon (1972) argued that computers could be programmed to copy the problem-solving behaviour of people. They produced the first systematic computer simulations of human problem-solving with their *General Problem Solver*. They asked people to solve problems, and to think aloud while they were working on the problems. Newell and Simon then used what their participants said as the basis for deciding what general strategy was used most often on each problem. Finally, they specified the problem-solving strategy in enough detail to program it in their General Problem Solver.

Newell and Simon argued that many problems can be represented as a *problem space* consisting of the following:

- *Initial state:* the problem as given to the participant.
- *Goal state:* the solution to the problem.
- *Mental operators:* the moves that are allowed in order to change the state of the problem.

We can consider these notions in the context of a problem known as the Tower of Hanoi. The initial state of the problem consists of three discs piled in order of size on the first of three pegs. The goal state is reached when all of the discs are piled in the same order on the last peg. The rules of the problem specify that only one disc can be moved at a time, and that a larger disc must not be placed on top of a smaller one. These rules limit the possible mental operators on each move. For example, there are only two possible first moves: place the smallest disc on the middle or on the last peg.

How do people select mental operators or moves as they go from the initial state to the goal state? According to Newell and Simon, many problems are so hard that we rely heavily on rules of thumb, or *heuristic methods*. The most important of these heuristic methods is *means–ends analysis*. It consists of the following steps:

- Note the difference between the current state of the problem and the goal state.
- Form a sub-goal that will reduce the difference between the current and goal states.
- Select a mental operator or move leading to the sub-goal.

A reasonable sub-goal during the early stages of the Tower of Hanoi problem is to try to place the largest disc on the last peg. If a situation arises in which the largest disc must be placed on either the middle peg or the last peg, then means–ends analysis will lead to that disc being placed on the last peg.

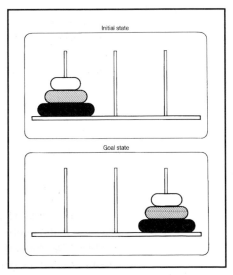

The initial state and goal state in the Tower of Hanoi problem.

Initial state

Goal state

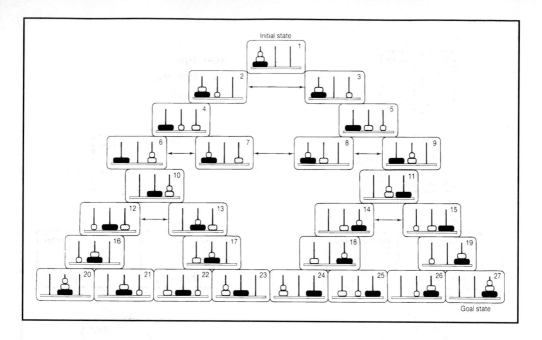

Initial state

Goal state

The Tower of Hanoi problem. If boxes touch each other, or are joined by arrows, this indicates that one is allowed to move from one state to another.

Suppose it is true that people generally make use of means–ends analysis. It follows that they should have difficulties if the problem requires them to make a move that increases the distance between the current state and the goal state. This prediction was tested by Thomas using a modified version of the missionaries and cannibals problem.

In this problem, three missionaries and three cannibals need to be transported across a river in a boat which can only hold two people. The number of cannibals must never exceed the number of missionaries, because then the cannibals would eat the missionaries. (In Thomas's 1974 study, he used hobbits and orcs, with the orcs wanting to eat the hobbits.) A key move involves transferring one cannibal and one missionary back to the starting point, and thus appears to be moving away from the solution (this is the transition between states eight and nine in the figure opposite). It was at this precise point that the participants had their most severe difficulties with the problem.

Newell and Simon assumed that people form a series of sub-goals as they work their way through a problem. This should lead to a number of rapid moves as participants work through the current sub-goal, followed by a pause while they work out the next sub-goal. That was exactly what Thomas found with his modified version of the missionaries and cannibals problem. Participants often made a block of moves with increasing speed, followed by a long pause while the next sub-goal was worked out.

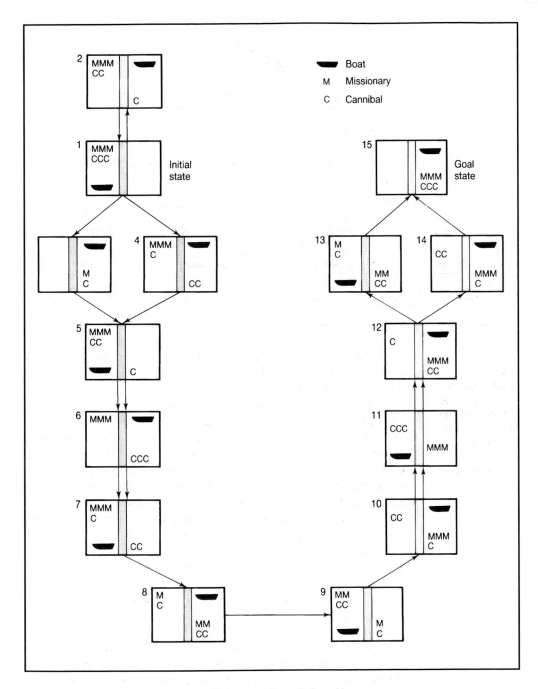

The missionary and cannibals problem.

What are the advantages and disadvantages of the computational approach?

PLUS
- It identified many of the strategies used in problem-solving.
- The use of computer programs to copy human problem-solving led to very precise accounts of how problems are solved.

MINUS
- Newell and Simon focused on well-defined problems in which the initial state, the goal state, and the possible moves are all clear; in real life, we tend to be faced with ill-defined problems (e.g. what to do if you lock your keys in your car).
- People solving well-defined problems usually have little specific knowledge about the problem and so use general strategies such as means–ends analysis; in contrast, we usually make considerable use of specific knowledge and experience when dealing with life's ill-defined problems.

Creativity

According to Guilford (1961), most intelligence tests focus on *convergent thinking*. Convergent thinking is rational or logical thinking in which there is only one right answer. Arithmetic problems such as $4 \times 8 = ?$ or $618 - 479 = ?$ are clear examples of problems that require convergent thinking.

Guilford argued that convergent thinking should be distinguished from *divergent thinking*. Divergent thinking involves non-logical processes, and there may be several relevant answers. We can assess divergent thinking by asking people to think of as many different uses for a brick as possible, or to think of some of the effects of humans having tails. Divergent thinking, or the ability to think of numerous useful ideas in novel situations, is of great relevance to creativity. There have been many definitions of *creativity*, but it clearly involves the ability to produce original and ingenious solutions to problems.

It should not be thought that intelligence as measured by intelligence tests is of no relevance to creativity. As Sternberg (1985) pointed out, intelligence is a necessary but not a sufficient condition for creativity. Creative individuals need to have the good knowledge base found in those with high intelligence in order for their divergent thinking skills to be put to best use.

It is unwise to assume that some people are always convergent thinkers, whereas others are divergent thinkers. Those who are good at divergent thinking are often good at convergent thinking. Whether an individual displays convergent or divergent behaviour depends very much on the precise task demands, so that a given individual may switch rapidly between convergent and divergent thinking.

Getzels and Jackson (1962) compared two groups of adolescent boys. One group was very high in intelligence but relatively low on creativity measures. The other group was high on creativity and lower on intelligence than the first group (but still fairly high on intelligence). The parents of the creative boys valued non-conformity, encouraged intellectual curiosity in their sons, and allowed them to develop their own interests. The two groups had the same level of academic achievement, suggesting that convergent and divergent thinking are both important in education. However, the creative boys were less popular with the teachers than those of high intelligence.

It is very hard to devise good tests of creativity and divergent thinking. Many tests (such as the "uses for a brick" test) that claim to measure divergent thinking or creativity are actually measures of originality rather than creativity. *Originality* is simply the tendency to produce several unusual solutions to a problem, regardless of the quality of those solutions. It is easy to measure originality, but creativity depends more on the quality and usefulness of the proposed solutions rather than simply their number. This is much harder to measure.

Theories of creativity

Graham Wallas (1926) provided one of the first theoretical frameworks for understanding creative thinking. He argued that there are various stages in the creative process:

- *Preparation:* the problem is identified, and initial attempts are made to solve it.
- *Incubation:* the problem is set aside while other tasks are worked on.
- *Illumination:* the solution emerges as a sudden insight.
- *Verification:* the problem-solver checks that the solution really works.

The most interesting idea put forward by Wallas was the importance of allowing incubation to occur. There is some support in the experiences of famous creative people. Ghiselin (1952) reported this quotation from the French mathematician Poincaré: "Having reached Coutances, we entered an omnibus to go some place or other. At the moment when I put my foot on the step the idea came to me, without anything in my former thoughts seeming to have paved the way for it, that the transformations I had used to define the Fuchsian functions were identical with those of non-Euclidian geometry."

Experimental support for the notion of incubation was obtained by Silveira (1971). She used the cheap necklace problem. There are four

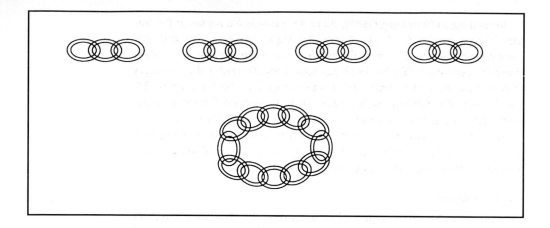

separate pieces of chain, and each of them consists of three links. All of the links within each piece are closed. It costs 2 cents to open a link and 3 cents to close one, and the 12 links must be joined up to form a single circular chain necklace at a cost of no more than 15 cents.

Only 55% of those who worked solidly at this problem solved it within 30 minutes, whereas 64% of those who took a 30-minute break during the task did so. The success rate rose to 85% among those who had a four-hour break. The incubation period reduced the tendency to fixate on wrong methods of approaching the problem. The solution is as follows: open all three links of one chain at a cost of six cents. Then use these three open links to join together the other three pieces of chain at a further cost of nine cents.

Sternberg and Davidson.   The most important aspect of creativity is the insight or sudden understanding that seems to occur just before a creative solution is reached. Sternberg and Davidson (1982) argued that the process of insight is more complex than had been thought previously. They argued that there are at least three different ways in which insight or illumination can occur:

- *Selective encoding:* this involves identifying the crucial information from the total available information.
- *Selective combination:* realising how the relevant pieces of information fit together.
- *Selective comparison:* this involves relating information in the current problem to relevant information from different problems; this is problem-solving by analogy.

According to Sternberg (1985), there are famous examples in the history of science of each of these kinds of insight. Selective encoding was shown by Alexander Fleming. He noticed that bacteria close to a culture that had become mouldy had been destroyed, and this led to the discovery of penicillin. Selective combination was shown by Charles Darwin. He had known the relevant facts about natural selection for many years before he managed to combine them into his theory of evolution. Selective comparison was shown by Kekule. He dreamed of a snake curling back on itself and catching its own tail. When he awoke, he realised that this was an analogy of the molecular structure of benzine.

Conclusions

Creativity is a form of intelligence that is rather different from intelligence as assessed by most intelligence tests. However, a high level of intelligence is needed for most forms of creativity. It is difficult to measure creativity, but originality can be assessed. Originality, or the ability to produce several answers to a problem, is part of what is involved in creativity. However, it is possible to be original without producing useful solutions to a problem. Insight is important in creativity, and it can occur by means of selective encoding, selective combination, or selective comparison.

Further reading

Eysenck, M.W. (1993). *Principles of cognitive psychology.* Hove, UK: Lawrence Erlbaum Associates Ltd. Many of the issues discussed in this chapter are dealt with more fully in Chapter 6.

Sternberg, R.J. (1985). *Beyond IQ: A triarchic theory of human intelligence.* Cambridge: Cambridge University Press. There is an interesting discussion of insight and creativity in this book.

References

De Groot, A.D. (1966). Perception and memory versus thought. In B. Kleinmuntz (Ed.), *Problem-solving.* New York: Wiley.

Getzels, J.W., & Jackson, P.W. (1962). *Creativity and intelligence: Explorations with gifted students.* New York: Wiley.

Luchins, A.S. (1942). Mechanisation in problem-solving: The effect of Einstellung. *Psychological Monographs, 54* (248).

Newell, A., & Simon, H.A. (1972). *Human problem-solving.* Englewood Cliffs: Prentice-Hall.

Summary

- Problem-solving occurs when the individual is goal-directed, a number of processes are needed to reach the goal, and the mental processes involved are cognitive rather than automatic.
- Early research by Thorndike suggested that problem-solving involves trial and error, whereas the Gestaltists emphasised the importance of restructuring and insight.
- There is a positive transfer effect when past experience improves current performance; this is shown by experts, whose high levels of performance depend in part on the relevant knowledge they have stored in long-term memory.
- There is no transfer effect when relevant past experience is not used in current problem-solving; analogies whose content differs greatly from a current problem tend to be ignored.
- There is a negative transfer effect when past experience has a disruptive effect on current problem-solving.
- Negative transfer is involved in functional fixedness, in which our past experience with objects makes it difficult to use them in new ways.
- Negative transfer is also involved in mental set, in which people persist with a previously successful problem-solving strategy even when better strategies could be used.
- According to Newell and Simon's General Problem Solver, many problems have an initial state, a goal state, and possible mental operators to permit moves from one state to the other.
- The most important rule of thumb or heuristic method is means–ends analysis, which involves selecting mental operators that will reduce the difference between the current problem state and the goal state.
- The General Problem Solver is of relevance to well-defined problems rather than to the ill-defined problems of everyday life.
- Creativity involves the ability to produce unusual and ingenious solutions to problems; it is thus more closely associated with divergent thinking than with convergent thinking.
- Intelligence is a necessary, but not sufficient, condition for high levels of creativity.
- Creativity often depends on incubation, or setting the problem aside for a while.
- Creativity depends very much on insight; insight can involve selective encoding, selective combination, or selective comparison.

Key terms

Analogy: as applied to problem-solving, a comparison between the current problem and some other situation.

Convergent thinking: logical thinking in which there is only one correct answer; see **divergent thinking**.

Creativity: the ability to produce original, useful, and ingenious solutions to problems.

Divergent thinking: thinking involving the ability to think of many useful ideas in novel situations or problems where several different answers are possible.

Functional fixedness: a form of **negative transfer effect** in which it is assumed that objects can only be used for purposes or functions for which they have been used in the past.

General Problem Solver: a computer simulation of human problem-solving devised by Newell and Simon.

Gestaltists: German psychologists in the early part of the twentieth century who argued that problem-solving involves **restructuring** and **insight**.

Heuristic methods: rules of thumb used to solve problems.

Incubation: the notion that complex problems can sometimes be solved by setting the problem aside for a while before returning to it.

Insight: a sudden understanding, in which the entire problem is looked at in a different way; see **restructuring**.

Means–ends analysis: an approach to problem-solving based on reducing the difference between the current state of the problem and the solution; it is one of the **heuristic methods**.

Mental set: a fixed or blinkered approach to problems which prevents people from thinking in a flexible way.

Negative transfer effect: the negative effects of past experience on current problem-solving; see **functional fixedness**.

Originality: the tendency to produce a large number of unusual solutions to a problem; these solutions may be useful or useless.

Positive transfer effect: an improved ability to solve a problem because of previous relevant past experience.

Problem space: the possible ways of trying to move from the problem to the solution.

Restructuring: the notion of the **Gestaltists** that problems need re-organising in order to solve them.

Trial-and-error learning: learning in which several random responses are made until the correct one is finally made.

Structured essay questions

1. When does past experience have a positive effect on problem-solving? When does it have a negative effect on problem-solving?
2. What is creativity? How has creativity been studied?

3. What is insight? What effects does it have on problem-solving?
4. Describe the computational approach to problem-solving. How useful has it been?

Self-assessment questions

1. According to Thorndike, animals deal with problems by trial-and-error learning, in which:
   a) they successfully re-organise the problem
   b) they cannot solve the problem at all
   c) they act in a random way until one response proves successful
   d) none of the above

2. The useful effects of past experience and knowledge on current problem-solving are known as:
   a) positive transfer effect
   b) negative transfer effect
   c) memory
   d) good long-term memory

3. The tendency to think that objects can only be used for a narrow range of functions on the basis of how they have been used in the past is known as:
   a) stupidity
   b) functional fixedness
   c) positive transfer effect
   d) none of the above

4. Heuristic methods are:
   a) useful rules of thumb
   b) logical rules
   c) very inaccurate ways of solving problems
   d) very precise ways of solving problems

5. According to Guilford, most intelligence tests use:
   a) divergent thinking rather than convergent thinking
   b) convergent thinking rather than divergent thinking
   c) divergent and convergent thinking
   d) neither divergent nor convergent thinking

6. Which of the following statements is true?
   a) it is easy to measure originality and creativity
   b) it is hard to measure originality and creativity
   c) it is easy to measure originality, but hard to measure creativity
   d) it is easy to measure creativity, but hard to measure originality

Effective learning

Study Skills

Christine Eysenck and Fleur Eysenck

23

This chapter differs in various ways from the other chapters in this book. First, it is designed to help you with your approach to your studies rather than to teach you about psychology. Second, it is written by the author's wife Christine and elder daughter Fleur. Fleur did her GCSEs in the summer of 1995, and we start with her personal viewpoint on study skills based on her experiences in preparing for those examinations.

Fleur's personal viewpoint

My initial response when confronted with a substantial quantity of work is to leave it until the last possible moment, and then to spend a night of what can only be described as hell trying desperately to get it done. There are, of course, a few slightly more methodical (and indeed effective) ways of studying. It is important to remember that on their own, study skills are not a means to an end. Unless they are used in conjunction with a good degree of self-motivation, there is no guarantee of success. They do, however, serve as guidelines for good study habits, enabling students to make the most of their abilities.

Personally, until I was given the benefit of a lesson on study skills at school, I had never considered that studying could be in any way dissected. I had resigned myself to being a bad worker, instead of realising that I was probably only lacking in some aspects of study. On reflection, my greatest trouble seems to have been in the second stage of study [discussed later], and in particular the problem of actually getting started. I seemed to be extraordinarily gifted in the art of finding things to do other than work, my greatest vice being the television. One of the first things that study skills taught me is that working timetables are invaluable, especially during the weeks leading up to examinations. Before my GCSEs, when good management of time was crucial, I found that I came to rely heavily on the study timetable I had made up, and before long I fell into a routine.

Over the last year, I have found that, in my experience, the most important thing study skills have done is to encourage me to form a more systematic approach to work. Although to begin with the idea of sticking to a definite work routine is somewhat unappetising, I discovered that the process became noticeably easier as time went on. Despite sporadic relapses into television addiction, study skills have greatly improved my studying practices. They undoubtedly lifted my exam performance at GCSE level.

Introduction

Good study behaviour is based on a strategic approach involving five key assumptions:

- Good study behaviour is a learned skill; like other areas of skilled performance, it can be learned and improved upon.
- The student really wants to do well, i.e. he or she is well-motivated.
- Study behaviour can be broken down into four major stages; improvement is possible at each of these stages.
- ORGANISATION is a key aspect of good study performance.
- Good study performance involves ACTIVE use of information rather than PASSIVE exposure to it.

Much of the value of thinking about study behaviour, and how to improve it, lies in the fact that you are breaking your performance down into various different skills. Many students think of good study behaviour in very general terms. They will come out with general statements such as, "I'm no good at work", or "I wish I could do better". If you start by identifying what is involved in study performance, then you can make decisions about where you can improve. This makes a good start to the process of improvement.

Have a look at the figure. It shows the way information passes through your processing system broken down into four separate stages. Let us consider the stages one at a time:

Stage 1: You have access to many sources of information; these include teachers, your notes, books, journals, and friends.

Stage 2: When you attend to some of the information available to you in Stage 1, it passes to the brain where it is processed.

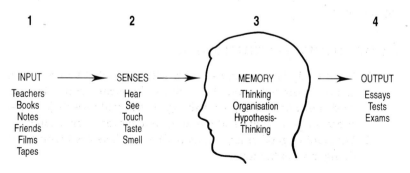

Stage 3: Processing of the information in the brain results in it being organised, stored, and later retrieved.

Stage 4: The information from Stage 3 is used to produce homework, write essays, and to prepare for tests and examinations.

Problems can occur at any of these stages. See if you can identify some areas where you may be having difficulty by answering the following questions:

Stage 1 problems

1. Do you have access to enough information?
2. Do you find that you don't know how to arrange the time spent on any area?
3. Do you find difficulty in knowing what to put into a piece of work and what to leave out?

Stage 2 problems

4. Do you find it difficult to just "get started"?
5. Is there something that seems to stop you from taking in the information?

Stage 3 problems

6. Do you find it difficult to organise your thoughts about a topic?
7. Do you have difficulty in remembering things generally, or especially when it really matters (e.g. for examinations)?

Stage 4 problems

8. Do you find it difficult to revise for examinations?
9. Do your thoughts seem to leave you when you are doing a test or examination?
10. Do you find it hard to write accounts or essays?
11. Does the amount of work seem to overwhelm you?

If the answer is "yes" to any of these questions, then there is scope for improvement.

Good study performance

1. Good study behaviour, like other areas of skilled performance, can be improved upon at any time. The virtue in considering study behaviour lies in identifying its different aspects (input—processing—output), and working on areas for improvement.
2. Developing good study habits is what teachers are involved in doing most of the time.

3. Sometimes we become resigned to a particular level of perform-ance because we feel that excellent performance is beyond us, and is only possible for the most able students. What may really be beyond us is the willingness to commit more than the minimum in terms of energy and time. It is likely that our energy and attentional resources can be put to more efficient use, leading to more effective performance.

4. A major ingredient in good study performance involves the *real* motivation to do well (and not just paying lip service to the idea), and real commitment in terms of our use of time and effort. It is easier to attribute poor performance to factors over which you have no control such as "lack of ability" or "it is a difficult subject" rather than to "inefficient study performance", which involves factors over which you do have control in terms of use of resources.

5. As we turn to the four stages of study performance, bear in mind that what is of major importance is the QUALITY of work rather than the QUANTITY. Good study performance does not have to mean more hard work.

Good study performance: Stages 1 and 2

You can improve your study performance at Stages 1 and 2 in two main ways. First, you can make the most efficient use of your time. Second, you can make sure that incoming information is organised in the best possible way, so that it is more accessible when needed.

Time management

Manage your time effectively by doing the following things:

1. Create a TIMETABLE (see example on facing page) of the time that is available over, say, a whole week. Indicate on it also times that are NOT available. You will probably be surprised at how much time there is, and how much you tend to waste. Now, indicate on your timetable those subjects that are going to be given study time on different days and how much time within each day you are going to spend on any subject.

2. Decide what is, for you, a reasonable span of attention (possibly 30–40 minutes). Set aside a number of periods of time during the week for study. Make a commitment to yourself to use these periods for study.

WEEKLY ACTIVITIES:

	Sleeping	Washing/ Dressing/ Eating	Travelling	Studying at School	P/T Employment	Free time Social life/ private study	Total
Monday							24
Tuesday							24
Wednesday							24
Thursday							24
Friday							24
Saturday							24
Sunday							24
Total							168
Average	56	16	6	25	5	60*	168

* 60 hours' free time a week allows plenty of time for private study and school work.

3. Note that the more of a HABIT studying becomes, the less effort-ful it will be, and the less RESISTANT you will be to making a start.

4. None of us has a limitless amount of CONCENTRATION: incom-ing information tends to slip away unless it is used or acted upon. Studies show that after initially high levels of concentration, the level decreases until the end is in sight. Regular breaks are needed to bring you to a fresh peak of concentration. So, make sure that the time you commit to studying is realistic. The graph below shows what happens when students are instructed to recall a list of 25 words. Notice where the peaks of memory performance are. The top graph on the facing page is similar, but this time concen-tration over time is indicated. The graph below it shows that you can improve your level of concentration by including short (10-minute) rest periods. Also remember to avoid distractions like the television in your study area.

5. During these study times, there will be a great tendency to find other things to do (e.g. watch the end of a television programme; have a drink). This is where the hard bit comes. You must try to be firm and say to yourself that this is time you have committed to studying, and that is what you are going to do. However, you will have time available later for other things. It is difficult to do on the first occasion, but it gets easier.

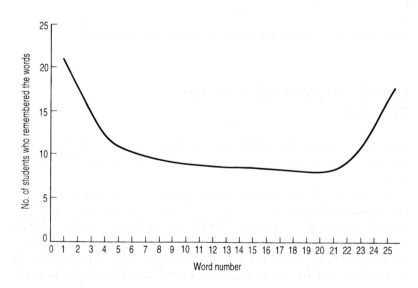

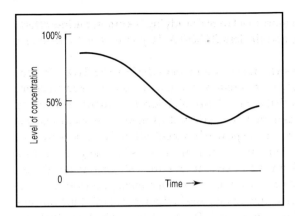

Graph showing decrease in concentration with time (left) and improvement in concentration with inclusion of regular breaks (below)

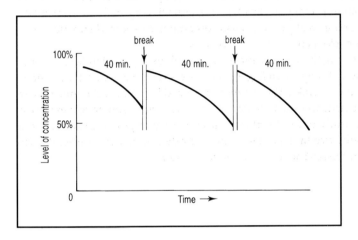

Good study performance: Stage 3

In general terms, incoming information needs to be available for some specific use, such as for assessment, an examination or test, a project, or an essay.

In everyday life, we are exposed to much more information than we need to know. As a result, we tend to select out and forget most of it. For example, it would be very inefficient for your system if you remembered the colours of the front doors of houses on your way to and from school or college. What you may need to know, though, is the sequence of roads that will get you there in an organised way. The point is that your brain reduces or condenses the information to which it is exposed, and it makes use of information that is well organised.

Good study performance involves making use of these features to your advantage. Condense incoming information by trying to select what is RELEVANT from what is IRRELEVANT. Generally, all lessons have a few key ideas which you could consider saying to yourself, writing down in abbreviated form, or simply relaying to someone else. This is the ACTIVE part of the processing of information. In the act of information selection, we are starting the process of imposing a structure on it. By doing something with the information rather than being a PASSIVE recipient of it, we are contributing to the effectiveness of further processing.

Good study performance: Stage 4

Essays and projects: Increasing the active nature of processing

This section is largely to do with the presentation of work for assessment (i.e. essays, accounts, projects) and revision for examinations. These areas SHOW your level of understanding of a topic and how you organise your thoughts about issues.

Breaking down the task. Start by breaking down the stages involved in project preparation or essay writing into smaller units (e.g. finding suitable books, devising a plan) which directly address the title. Then move on to notetaking. A common experience is that it is easier to revise something that has already been written down than to start by only putting pen to paper when you are perfectly satisfied. Like other skills, the more you write, the more confident you become in the use of language.

Patterned notes and essay writing. Organisation in project planning and essay writing may be helped by the use of patterned notes, where factors associated with the title represent major themes that you are going to consider in your account. Many people prefer to look at pictures rather than pages of notes. Studies suggest that it is easier to remember pictures and diagrams than the written word. The model on the facing page shows how you could construct patterned notes.

Remember that the introduction of your essay should include some consideration of what you mean by the title. The conclusion should summarise the main points made in the body of the work.

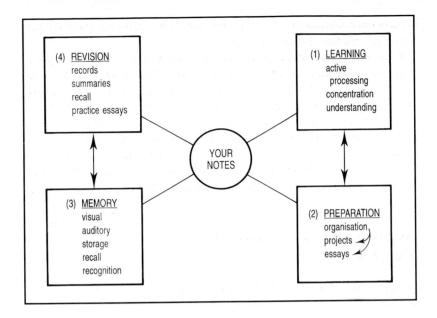

Evaluation. Try to develop the skill of EVALUATION. Think in terms of whether you agree or disagree with what is written or said. Then think of reasons *why* you agree or disagree. You can do this with all kinds of things. Practise by answering questions such as "Do I like the shape of the chair in which I am sitting?". Say why you think as you do. Look for links between ideas, making use of highlighters for the selection of relevant information.

Examination preparation

Here you continue using study skills developed in the body of your course (i.e. the organisation of time and information) to enable active memory-based processing strategies to take place. This time you are starting from a slightly different and better position, in that you already have an overview of an area, and so selection of relevant from irrelevant information should be easier. Here are a few ideas to think about:

(a) Use your notes to list the kinds of issues the examination may be concerned with. For public examinations, use your syllabus to check what may come up.

(b) Generate a study timetable, and include on it time to go over the topics. Get this started as early as possible before an examination or series of examinations, so that you can build into it enough time not only to revise on a single occasion but to REVIEW the topic as often as possible. It is better to spend, say, two sessions of 30 minutes on a topic rather than one session of an hour.

(c) Remember to make sure you know what form an examination will take. Get hold of past papers. Study behaviour is a habit. You are not making the best use of valuable attentional resources if, at examination, you have to start coming to grips with a form of question you are not used to.

(d) Practise working out the skill requirements of questions. For example, some are knowledge-based (e.g. "Describe …"), whereas others are evaluation-based (e.g. "Criticise …"). Practise writing essay plans for potential questions. At examination, students tend to suffer from anxiety and this may make you feel confused and unable to think clearly. The more you can practise the skills required under pressure, the better equipped you will be to produce good answers.

(e) Study MANAGEABLE CHUNKS of information. Don't make the quantity of what you hope to accomplish at any time unrealistically high—especially at examination times. When you are certain of small areas of knowledge, you can build on them.

(f) ORGANISE incoming information by considering topics and writing condensed notes on existing notes. Use highlighters, flow diagrams, and patterned notes. Advantages derive from the fact that these are ACTIVE STRATEGIES which force you to make decisions about incoming information. It is the restructuring of information that is productive.

(g) With oral information from a teacher, try to rephrase or restructure what has been said. Then ask for confirmation or disconfirmation that you have got it correct (e.g. "So what you mean is … ?", "Is this right?"). This means that you have the chance to confirm that you have got it right, or find out the right answer if you have misunderstood.

Finally, the good news about "study skills" is that they are relatively easy to install in our behavioural repertoire. The bad news is that you need MOTIVATION. That's where YOU come in!

Reference

McBride, P. (1994). *Study skills for success*. Cambridge: Hobsons Publishing.

Answers to self-assessment questions

Chapter 1
1 (a)
2 (b)
3 (d)
4 (c)

Chapter 2
1 (c)
2 (a)
3 (d)
4 (a)
5 (b)
6 (d)
7 (c)
8 (d)

Chapter 3
1 (a)
2 (b)
3 (c)
4 (d)
5 (c)
6 (a)
7 (b)
8 (a)
9 (c)

Chapter 4
1 (d)
2 (a)
3 (b)
4 (c)
5 (a)
6 (c)
7 (c)
8 (c)

Chapter 5
1 (d)
2 (a)
3 (c)
4 (d)
5 (b)
6 (a)
7 (c)

Chapter 6
1 (b)
2 (c)
3 (d)
4 (a)
5 (b)
6 (c)
7 (d)

Chapter 7
1 (a)
2 (c)
3 (b)
4 (d)
5 (b)
6 (d)
7 (a)
8 (c)

Chapter 8
1 (d)
2 (c)
3 (a)
4 (a)
5 (b)
6 (c)
7 (b)

Chapter 9
1 (b)
2 (c)
3 (d)
4 (a)
5 (b)
6 (c)
7 (a)
8 (b)

Chapter 10
1 (d)
2 (a)
3 (c)
4 (b)
5 (a)
6 (c)
7 (d)

Chapter 11
1 (b)
2 (c)
3 (a)
4 (d)
5 (a)
6 (c)
7 (a)

Chapter 12
1 (c)
2 (a)
3 (d)
4 (b)
5 (b)
6 (c)
7 (c)

Chapter 13

1 (b)
2 (c)
3 (d)
4 (a)
5 (c)
6 (a)
7 (d)

Chapter 14

1 (c)
2 (b)
3 (c)
4 (d)
5 (a)
6 (b)

Chapter 15

1 (c)
2 (a)
3 (b)
4 (d)
5 (c)
6 (d)
7 (b)
8 (a)

Chapter 16

1 (a)
2 (c)
3 (d)
4 (b)
5 (d)
6 (b)
7 (a)

Chapter 17

1 (c)
2 (c)
3 (d)
4 (a)
5 (b)
6 (c)
7 (c)

Chapter 18

1 (d)
2 (b)
3 (d)
4 (b)
5 (c)
6 (a)
7 (b)
8 (a)
9 (d)

Chapter 19

1 (d)
2 (a)
3 (c)
4 (c)
5 (a)
6 (b)

Chapter 20

1 (b)
2 (d)
3 (c)
4 (c)
5 (b)
6 (d)
7 (a)
8 (b)

Chapter 21

1 (c)
2 (a)
3 (b)
4 (d)
5 (b)
6 (d)
7 (a)

Chapter 22

1 (c)
2 (a)
3 (b)
4 (a)
5 (b)
6 (c)

Index

accommodation, cognitive, 135, 151
accommodation, ocular, 362, 374
affectionless psychopathy, 214, 221
affiliation, 211-12, 221
aggression, 97-111, 185, 267-8
altruism, 241, 243-7, 252, 253
Ames room, 363, 364, 374
amnesic syndrome, 381, 394
anaclitic depression, 213, 221
analogy, 399-400, 411
androgyny, 198-9, 201, 202
animal aggression, 100-1, 103
animal language, 163-5, 167
anti-social personality disorder, 108-9, 111
archive studies, 24, 32
arousal/cost-reward model, 250-1, 252, 253
ascending reticular activating system, 334, 338
assimiliation, 135, 151
attachment, 207-21
attention, 367-7, 379-80
attribution theory, 284-5, 295, 296
audience effect, 255-6, 275
auditory perception, 367-8, 370, 373
authoritarian personality, 227-8, 238, 239
authority, obeying, 262-7, 274
autokinetic effect, 257, 274, 275
autonomic nervous system, 41, 42-3, 56, 63
average, 25-6, 31
aversion therapy, 126, 129
avoidance learning, 124, 128, 129

babies
  attachment & separation, 207-21
  cognitive development, 136

depth perception, 146-7
emotional development, 92-3, 94
language development, 154-5, 167
reflexes, 40
visual perception, 144-50
backward conditioning, 118, 129
Bandura, A.,104, 181, 195, 320-1
behaviour therapy, 125-7, 129
behaviourism, 1, 10, 115, 129
bias
  confirmation, 292, 296, 391, 394
  hindsight, 4-5, 10
  self-serving, 342, 352
  social desirability, 24, 329-30, 339
bottom-up processing, 286, 296
Bowlby, J., 212-16, 220
brain, 43-55, 56, 335
brain scans, 54-5, 57, 58, 59
Bruner, J., 142-4, 150
bystander intervention, 241, 247-51, 252, 253

Cannon-Bard theory, 83-4, 94
caregiving hypothesis, 208-9, 220, 221
carpentered environment, 371-2, 374
case studies, 22, 31, 32
categorical clustering, 386, 394
catharsis hypothesis, 106-7, 110, 111
Cattell, R., 331-3, 337-8
central nervous system, 41, 43-55, 58
cerebral cortex, 46-51, 56, 58
cerebral dominance, 48, 58
children, *see also* babies
  aggression, 104-6, 107, 108-9, 110, 185, 267
  attachment & separation, 207-21
  cognitive development, 135-44, 150

empathy development, 108, 241-3, 246, 252
gender development, 189-98
IQ testing, 302-3
language development, 153-68
moral development, 171-87, 241-3
motor development, 40
personality development, 227, 318-19
psychosexual development, 172-3, 194-5, 318-19
punishing, 105-6, 110, 174, 184
self-concept, 343
self-fulfilling prophecy effects, 261, 274
sex differences, 180-1, 189-92, 201
teaching, 141-2
visual development, 144-50
chimpanzee language, 163-5, 167
Chomsky, N., 157-8, 159, 163, 167
chunk, 378, 394
classical conditioning, 115-19, 128, 129
co-action effect, 255, 275
cocktail party effect, 367-8
cognitive appraisal theory, 62, 77, 87-8, 94, 95
cognitive development, 135-44, 150
cognitive development theory, 173-80, 196-7
cognitive labelling theory, 84-7, 94
computers, problem solving, 402-6
concentration, 420
concepts, 286-9, 295
conditioned reflexes, 116, 129
conditioning, 115-28
confidentiality in research, 30
confirmation bias, 292, 296, 391, 394
conformity, 231, 239, 257-60, 274, 275
consent of research subjects, 29
contact hypothesis, 234-6, 239
convergence, 362, 374
coping strategies, 63-5, 76, 77
correlation studies, 21-2, 27, 31, 32
creativity, 406-9, 410, 411
crime, 108, 272, 391
critical period
    attachment, 213, 221
    emotional development, 92-3, 95
    language development, 158-9, 167, 168

cross-cultural differences, 5-6, 10, 23
    aggression, 97-8, 110
    altruism, 245-6, 252
    attachment, 209-10, 220
    conformity, 258-9
    emotion, 81
    perception, 366-7, 373
    self-concept, 341
    sex-role stereotyping, 192-3
cross-sectional studies, 20-1, 31, 32
crowd behaviour, 267-70, 274
cultural differences, see cross-cultural differences

Darwin, C., 1, 37
data, 13, 25-8, see also results
daycare, 218-19, 220
debriefing research subjects, 29-30, 32
decategorisation theory, 235-6, 238, 239
deception in research, 29
declarative knowledge, 381, 394
defensible space, 272, 274, 275
deindividuation, 269-70, 275
depression, 91-2, 94, 213
deprivation, 214, 221, 365
deprivation theory, 232-3, 238, 239
depth perception, 146-7, 360-4, 373
diffusion of responsibility, 247, 253
disability, 283-4
discounting rule, 285, 296
discrimination, 223-39
divorce, 217, 220
dominance, cerebral, 48, 58
dominance hierarchies, 103, 111

ecological validity, 18, 32
education, 141-2
EEG, 52-3, 57, 58, 335
ego, 172, 187
egocentrism, 137-8, 151, 175
elaboration, 384-5, 394
Electra complex, 172, 187, 194-5, 202
electroencephalogram (EEG), 52-3, 57, 58, 335
emotion, 79-95

empathy, 108, 111, 241-3, 252, 253
empathy-altruism hypothesis, 243-4, 252, 253
environment & intelligence, 307-9, 313
equilibration, 135-6, 151
equity theory, 250, 253
ethics, 28-30, 31, 263-4, 265-6
ethnocentrism, 228, 239
ethology, 38-40, 58, 100-1, 110, 111
evoked potentials, 53-4, 57, 58
evolution, 1
exam preparation, 423-4
experimental designs, 16-18, 31
experimental hypothesis, 14, 31, 32
experimental methods, 13-24, 31, 32
experimental results *see* results
eyewitnesses, 389-91, 393
Eysenck, H.J., 333-5, 337-8
Eysenck Personality Questionnaire (EPQ), 333, 338

F-scale, 227, 239
factor analysis, 309-11, 313, 314, 329
fear conditioning, 90-1, 94
field experiments, 18-19, 31, 32
field observations, 19-20, 32
first impressions, 279-80, 295
fixation, 318, 338
forgetting, 387-9, 393
Freud, S., 2, 7
  aggression, 99-100
  attachment, 207, 220
  gender, 194-5
  morals, 172-3
  personality, 318-19, 337
  repression, 227, 389, 394
frustration-aggression hypothesis, 101-2, 110, 111, 226-7, 238, 239
functional fixedness, 400-1, 410, 411
fundamental attribution error, 285, 296

gender development, 189-98, 201, 202
gender schemas, 197-8, 201, 202
general adaptation syndrome, 63, 77
General Problem Solver, 402-6, 410, 411

Gestaltists, 358-9, 373, 374, 397-8, 411
Gilligan, C., 180-1, 186
graphs, 26-8
Gregory, R.L., 368, 371-2, 373
groups, 226, 230, 238, 239, 255, 275

happiness, 89-90, 94, 95, 324
hearing, 367-8, 370, 373
heat & stress, 71-2, 76
hemispheric specialisation, 48-51, 56-7, 58
heredity *see also* nature vs. nuture
  intelligence, 305-7, 309, 313
  personality traits, 108-9, 334-5, 337
  visual perception, 147-9
heuristic methods, 403, 410, 411
hierarchy of needs, 323, 338
hindsight bias, 4-5, 10
histograms, 26-8
holophrastic period, 154-5, 167, 168
hormones & stress, 61, 63, 66-7, 77
humanism, 322-6, 337
hypnosis, 390-1, 393
hypotheses, 13, 14, 31, 32

"iceberg" theory, 2
id, 172, 187
ideal self, 289, 296, 324-5, 338
idiots savants, 301, 314
implicit personality theory, 277-81, 295, 296
imprinting, 212, 221
incubation, 407-8, 410, 411
induction, 184-5, 187
infants, *see* babies; children
inferences, 290-1, 296
insight, 398, 408-9, 411
instinctive behaviour, 39, 40, 56, 58
instrumental conditioning, 119-27, 128, 129
intelligence, 301-14, 406-7, 409, 410
intelligence quotient (IQ), 302-5, 313, 314
intelligence tests, 302-5, 313, 406, 409
interference theory, 387-9, 393
interposition, 361, 374
interviews, 23-4
introspection, 1, 10
IQ, 302-5, 313, 314